Urban Social Space

MARK LA GORY

The University of Alabama in Birmingham

JOHN PIPKIN

State University of New York at Albany

Wadsworth Publishing Company
Belmont, California
A Division of Wadsworth, Inc.

To Mary Sue and Denice

Sociology Editor: Curt Peoples
Production Editor: Helen Sweetland
Designer: Richard Kharibian
Copy Editor: Robert McNally
Technical Illustrator: Pat Rogondino

Printed in the United States of America

1 2 3 4 5 6 7 8 9 10—85 84 83 82 81

Cover Art: Le Corbusier's Contemporary City, designed in 1922. From *The Urban Pattern*, 3rd ed., by Arthur Gallion and Simon Eisner. © 1975 by Litton Educational Publishing, Inc. Reprinted by permission of D. Van Nostrand Company.

Library of Congress Cataloging in Publication Data

LaGory, Mark.
  Urban social space.
  Bibliography: p.
  Includes index.
  1. Sociology, Urban.   2. City planning—History.
3. Human ecology.   4. Space (Architecture)   5. Social
change.   6. Residential mobility.   I. Pipkin, John,
joint author.   II. Title.
HT153.L26   307.7'6   80-29675
ISBN 0-534-00864-X

Credits

Excerpts on pp. 18, 19 from *The Territorial Imperative* by Robert Ardrey. Copyright © 1966 by Robert Ardrey. Reprinted by permission of Atheneum Publishers.

Excerpts on pp. 31, 42, 43, 45 from *A World of Strangers: Order and Action in Public Space* by Lyn Lofland. © 1973 by Basic Books, Inc., Publishers, New York, N.Y.

Excerpt on p. 37 from P. Hauser, "Statistics and Society." *Journal of the American Statistical Association*, 1963. Reprinted by permission.

Excerpts on pp. 36, 57, 63, 64 from *The City in History* by Lewis Mumford, Harcourt Brace Jovanovich, Inc., 1961. Reprinted by permission of Harcourt Brace Jovanovich, Inc., New York, N.Y., and Martin Secker and Warburg Limited, London, England.

Excerpt on p. 72 from *Urban Society* by Amos H. Hawley, The Ronald Press Company, 1971. Reprinted by permission.

Excerpt on p. 109 from *History of Western Philosophy* by W. T. Jones, Harcourt Brace Jovanovich, Inc., 1952. Reprinted by permission.

Excerpt on p. 115 from Caryl Rivers, "The Specialness of Growing Up in Washington, D.C." © 1972 by The New York Times Company. Reprinted by permission.

Excerpts on pp. 140, 141 from E. G. Moore, *Residential Mobility in the City*, Resource Paper No. 13, Commission on College Geography, Association of American Geographers, 1972. Reprinted by permission.

Excerpt on pp. 161–162 from D. Birch, "Toward a Stage Theory of Urban Growth." *Journal of the American Institute of Planners*, 37, 1971. Reprinted by permission of the American Institute of Planners, Washington, D.C.

Excerpts on pp. 173, 174 from *Urban Economic Problems* by R. F. Muth, Harper & Row, 1975. Reprinted by permission.

Excerpt on p. 177 from *The Urban Villagers* by Herbert J. Gans. Copyright © 1962 by The Free Press of Glencoe, a Division of The Macmillan Company. Reprinted with permission of Macmillan Publishing Company, Inc.

Excerpt on p. 195 from "The Towers of Light," by Suzannah Lessard. © 1978 by The New Yorker Magazine, Inc. Reprinted by permission.

Excerpts on pp. 232, 234 from "Architecture, Interaction, and Social Control: The Case of a Large-Scale Public Housing Project," by William L. Yancey is reprinted from *Environment and Behavior,* Vol. 3, No. 1, March 1971. Reprinted by permission of the publisher, Sage Publications, Inc.

Excerpts on pp. 245, 246 from *The Social Order of the Slum* by Gerald Suttles, 1968. Reprinted by permission of The University of Chicago Press, Chicago, IL.

Excerpt on p. 279 from Gould is reprinted by permission of the National Academy of Sciences, Washington, D.C.

Excerpts on pp. 279, 289 from *The Human Consequences of Urbanization* by Brian J. L. Berry, St. Martin's Press, Inc., 1973. Reprinted by permission.

Excerpt on p. 292 from *I Came to the City* by M. E. Eliot Hurst, Houghton Mifflin Company, 1975. Reprinted by permission.

Contents

Preface

The city and its institutions dominate modern life and in some way or another influence the activities and experiences of each inhabitant of the earth. None of the social, political, or economic problems of the 1980s can be fully addressed without some understanding of their urban components. While an avalanche of social science and policy literature on the city continues to accumulate, this information is far from organized or coherent. There is an urgent need for synthesizing concepts to help social scientists clarify their understanding of the city and allow policy makers to put them to use.

The authors of this book, a sociologist and a geographer, are convinced that spatial structure provides an integrating framework that can produce coherent research and theory about the city. This is not a new idea. Human ecologists and urban geographers have been describing the city in spatial terms for many decades, and urban spatial studies in anthropology, psychology, and economics have flourished recently. Still, workers in these disciplines speak different languages and approach spatial problems differently. To give just one example, modern research in urban sociology and ecology has been inadequately informed by the findings of behavioral geography and environmental psychology on spatial cognition and individual spatial behavior. Work in these fields, conversely, has not been well informed by sociological theory. In this book, we attempt to construct a framework for organizing the scattered literature in urban sociology, human ecology, urban and behavioral geography, economics, and ethology. This was a formidable job, and in the process some traditional themes of urban sociologists and geographers fell by the wayside. It is safe to say, however, that most traditional concerns are covered. The history of the city, urban culture, patterns of human interaction, urban institutions, social stratification, city government, planning and architecture are all given considerable space and discussed in a synthetic rather than topical manner.

The book is organized around three major themes in the literature on urban space. The first of these themes deals with the question of how space is used and arranged in the city. Chapters One to Five provide the reader with an evolving sense of the city form. In these chapters both interactionist and structural perspectives are applied in a comparative format. Major topics include the nature of the space-behavior relationship, the nature of the city as a unique spatial environment, the history of the urban form, and social scientists' descriptions of the city-scape.

The introductory section, then, deals with the static aspects of space without considering the question of how these spatial structures emerge in the community. Section Two discusses the dynamics of neighborhood and community change. In order to fully understand these processes the emergence of spatial arrangements is considered at two levels: the social psychological and the communal. At the micro level, the urban landscape is considered to be the result of innumerable choices made by the individual under certain constraints. This approach views urban space from the perspective of the potential migrant seeking a residence in the city. From the macro level, the social, cultural and economic constraints that encourage population shifts among areas within the city are identified. An attempt is made to integrate information contained within the two approaches to develop a better understanding of why people become segregated in the city.

The final segment of *Urban Social Space* provides a thorough consideration of spatial arrangements as key variables in urban studies. Space is discussed as a reflection of urban social structure as well as a social force which must be dealt with by the urbanite and the city as a whole. With knowledge of the spatial structure of a community one can say a great deal about the community's underlying organization and the role and position of various groups within it. Space, however, does not just mirror the urban society, rather it actually reshapes it. While we have built the urban container, our very thoughts and actions are shaped by it. Given this fact, one means of re-ordering urban society is through the manipulation of space. The concluding chapter of this piece, discusses the possibilities and the problems of this informed view of urban planning.

This book then, gives comprehensive treatment of a variety of what are now scattered fragments in the literature. Its spatial theme is an intriguing one for students. There are several reasons for this subject's attraction. Spatial arrangements are fascinating because space usage provides certain cues and props that the urbanite uses to act efficiently in everyday settings. Spatial structure not only informs the interaction process, but literally shapes the lives of those within the urban container. We build cities, but once created they remake us. This fact is especially intriguing since the container itself is easily reshaped and thus subject to social engineering.

The book is written so that students with little background beyond an introductory level course can read it with relative ease. We believe that some of the ideas here will be useful to the advanced student and the urban researcher, but we have made a concerted effort to make the book self-contained, and generally to appeal to an undergraduate audience. Our own teaching experience with these materials suggests that the book will hold interest and provoke responses in beginning students in urban sociology, urban ecology, and socially oriented urban geography. It is designed for use as either a core text or a supplement in such courses. The book's interdisciplinary flavor, however, combined with a thematic approach, makes it suitable for a wide range of urban courses.

ACKNOWLEDGMENTS

Few books are solely the products of their authors, and this one is no exception. Our teachers Robert Carroll, William Feinberg, Stephen Gale, and Eric Moore must be recognized for their earlier influence. Two colleagues should be singled out for their valued advice and support on this project: Kent Schwirian and Paul Meadows. Additionally, a number of urban scholars reviewed the manuscript at various stages and provided valuable suggestions. These include Rodger A. Bates, Lambuth College; Brian Berry, Harvard University; Ronald Briggs, University of Texas at Dallas; George Carey, Rutgers University; David Cooperman, University of Minnesota; Lester Rowntree, San Jose State University; Leo Schnore, University of Wisconsin; Dale E. Strick, Camden County College; Lloyd Taylor, Phillips University; and Thomas L. Van Valey, Western Michigan University. Our colleagues at SUNY-Albany, Richard Felson, Craig Brown, William Yoels, and Paul Marr, read portions of the manuscript and suggested revisions. Eileen Crary and Kathy Wheeler typed the manuscript for us. Bonnie Fitzwater, Helen Sweetland, and Curt Peoples of the Wadsworth editorial staff helped at various stages of development and production, and Craig La Gory provided valuable design suggestions.

Chapter 1

Introduction: In the Shadow of the City

We live in an urban age, an era in which we are increasingly affected by the culture and social structure peculiar to the city. And even though most of the world's population still lives outside cities, almost no one escapes the city's influence. It has not always been this way. Humans have existed for perhaps three million years, but the city as a distinct form of community did not appear until around 3500 B.C. in Mesopotamia. Large-scale urbanization is even more recent. In 1800 only 3 percent of the world's population was urban; today that figure stands at 39 percent. This world average, though, is deceptive. In industrialized countries 66 percent of the population lives in cities, while in developing nations city dwellers account for around 22 percent of the population. The city has grown so rapidly that the present urban population is substantially larger than the entire population of the earth in 1850. If this rate of growth continues, no less than 90 percent of the world's population will be urban within fifty years (Davis, 1972).

As our world becomes increasingly urban, the problems and promises of cities become ever more important in human affairs. In advanced nations, cities are the primary means of organizing living space. In all nations they are the centers of wealth, innovation, and social change. Indeed, the degree to which a nation is urbanized is one of the clearest indications of its level of development. Before the Industrial Revolution no society achieved even a moderate level of urban growth. Since then, no society has become industrial without becoming highly urbanized. It is, therefore, unsurprising that most contemporary social and economic problems are urban problems.

Although less than half of the earth's population lives in cities, the world is experiencing an urban crisis of immense proportions. The roots of this crisis lie in the sheer complexity of the urban environment. Cities represent large concentrations of differing peoples living on very small amounts of land. Urban populations have remained large and have often grown because cities offer the promise of material goods and opportunities that are simply not available in rural areas. Because of their complexity, however, cities are difficult to manage, and this management problem has produced many unfulfilled dreams for new arrivals to cities.

1

The urban crisis is most severe in the Third World, where economic development has not kept pace with the growing numbers of urban migrants. During the last twenty years, for example, Calcutta has grown by an average of over 100,000 people a year. The majority of the immigrants are unemployable, and hundreds of thousands of people have been forced to live and sleep in the streets—compelling evidence of the severity of urban problems in the Third World. Cities in underdeveloped societies have grown much faster than other places in the modern world during similar stages of development. This fast-paced growth is sometimes described as a condition of *overurbanization* (Davis and Golden, 1954). Unlike the urbanization of past societies, cities have grown without an equivalent growth in urban jobs. Instead, overurbanization results when population pressure on rural land becomes so great that people move to cities even though there is little economic opportunity.

Urban growth in industrialized nations has generally kept pace with economic opportunity and with the availability of material goods. Industrialized nations are not overurbanized, for unlike many cities of the Third World, the elementary requirements of food and shelter are usually met. But the urban problems of industrialized societies are no less real than those of developing nations, and they are even more complex. American urbanization is filled with paradoxes. We are faced with a situation of great urban growth but declining older cities, large pockets of urban poverty that are byproducts of the economic expansion of cities, and rampant urban growth in a society with a distinctly rural bias against cities. In addition, ethnic discrimination, inequality of opportunity, environmental pollution, inadequate waste disposal, eroding tax bases, and political fragmentation are all urban problems. Even inflation and the energy crisis, which are dominant domestic political issues in America in the early 1980s, have distinct urban components. For example, the prices of many goods and services are measurably higher in large cities than in rural areas. And urban transportation, especially the unrestricted use of large automobiles in daily commuting, is central to the energy crisis. Many social scientists and political leaders in the United States consider the urban crisis the central and overriding domestic problem.

Although the city is the first human-controlled environment, we know very little about controlling urban problems because of the enormous complexity of the problems and their potential solutions. To deal with this complexity, the social sciences have divided up the task of urban study, each carving out its own area of study. Sociologists, geographers, economists, political scientists, anthropologists, and historians have all developed their own bodies of theory and observation. This disciplinary specialization has severely curtailed communication among social scientists themselves and between social scientists and policy makers. The mass of urban research is much like a house built without blueprints. Without shared information the end product of uncoordinated construction is an unlivable house. Present knowledge of the city is at such a stage that each discipline "knows" much about the city, but this information has not been coordinated effectively. Only when such knowledge can be pooled and shared among the students of the city will it be truly useful in understanding and resolving problems of the city and city life.

An urgent need has arisen for integrating and organizing concepts that can give meaning to the avalanche of scientific, literary, and popular information on the city. Much has been said about the city and the urbanization process, but the disciplines use different languages and address the same problems in different ways. One integrating concept has proved to be extremely useful in the study of urban society: *spatial structure*. This text attempts to combine spatial understandings of the city from a variety of disciplines.

A SPATIAL APPROACH TO URBAN SOCIETY

Space, someone observed, is what stops everything from being in the same place. It is an elemental aspect of social structure. Without some set of boundaries on activities and populations, human groups could not function. Boundaries simplify interaction by preventing those unlike us from entering our spheres, thereby making clear what kinds of behavior belong within each precinct. Modern society, in particular, provides each individual with a complex and often contradictory set of roles. These roles are easier to perform when each is acted out on a separate stage. Thus the potentially conflicting expectations for the working mother are eased by the physical separation of home and work. The career woman can be a good mother by acting out the parent role at home and a good businesswoman by performing effectively at the office.

Spatial structure is particularly important to the city, for urban society is composed of diverse social groups living close to one another. The city is a compact community. Land is relatively scarce; thus the urban space is necessarily highly organized and segregated. Space is a major social force literally shaping the lives of those within the urban container. We make the city, but once created it remakes us. The buildings we occupy and the neighborhoods we reside in restrict our activities. The buildings and neighborhoods not only limit our social participation but also influence what we think and feel about others who share our city.

This realization is especially intriguing given the fact that the urban container itself is easily manipulable and thus subject to social engineering. It is often easier to control the injustices inherent in the city by manipulating residential space than by remolding the social structures that produced the particular spatial arrangement in the first place. Some have suggested, for example, that the chronic underemployment and undereducation of the ghetto can be resolved by deliberately modifying the spatial arrangement of jobs and schools created by the recent suburbanization of the white middle class.

Many social sciences have participated in the study of urban space, but only two possess a long tradition of explicitly spatial analysis: human ecology, which is a branch of sociology, and urban geography. Both have addressed human-space relationships in the city, though in differing terminology and with little mutual interaction. This book emphasizes the complementarity of the sociological and geographic study of urban social space. The blend of sociological and geographic perspectives can provide students of the city with a renewed appreciation of urban structure and its role in everyday actions and experience. Over twenty years ago C. Wright Mills (1959) suggested the value of the "sociological imagination" in providing a broader understanding of individual experiences. According to Mills, sociology's focus on the relationship between the individual and society stimulated individuals to consider their own experiences in a broader historical and social context. David Harvey further suggests using a geographic perspective to enlarge individual understanding. The "geographic imagination"

> . . . enables the individual to recognize the role of space and place in his own biography, to relate to the spaces he sees around him, and to recognize how transactions between individuals and between organizations are affected by the space that separates them (Harvey, 1970:48).

Space is a scarce resource in cities, yet it is one of the essential qualities of the urban community. At the same time, because space is scarce, it is highly structured. An appreciation of the role of space in our social lives is critical to understand the urban experience. This understanding can only be achieved by artfully blending together the sociological and the geographic imaginations.

SOME ALTERNATIVE
APPROACHES TO URBAN SOCIETY

To appreciate fully the sociospatial view adopted in this book, you need some understanding of the alternative perspectives on urban society in the social sciences. The city is a spatial environment, but it is also a collection of organizations and a cultural context. Thus organizational and cultural views of urban life also contribute to understanding cities. It is artificial to attempt to define urban perspectives too exclusively. Concepts and terminology from all of these approaches will be freely used in subsequent chapters, in addition to spatially oriented ideas from ecology, geography and related fields.

Urban study can generally be divided into several major schools of thought (Sjoberg, 1965). The *urbanization* perspective (Simmel, 1905; Park, 1952; Durkheim, 1947; Wirth, 1938) is concerned with studying the organizational changes wrought by the growth of cities. Most particularly this approach has stressed the basic changes in the social bond that accompany urbanization. According to this view the city can be characterized by role segmentation, the loss of close personal ties, increasing social change, growing ambiguity in the moral order, and a secularization of values. Many sociologists have disputed this pessimistic view of urban life. Most research has failed to show such disorganization in urban communities. Another problem with this approach is that changes in the social bond accompanying the expansion of cities eventually affect the entire society. As a result, many of the organizational attributes identified with the urban order are characteristic of all community forms, both rural and urban, in modern society. In this sense the urbanization perspective is best applied at the level of society rather than community, and an urban social science based solely on this view would have to encompass the study of Western, highly urban societies. It cannot be a truly city-oriented approach.

Several other general approaches take the opposite tack and treat the city as a highly organized system. Two well-developed views of urban organization are the *economic* and the *power* perspectives. The economic view dominates urban economics and regional science. Urban geography (Yeates and Garner, 1976) also contains many economic models of spatial structure, and human ecology itself has been influenced by economic thinking (Hawley, 1950; Duncan, 1959). These approaches focus on the production, exchange, and distribution processes within and between cities. For example, economists such as Alonso (1964b) and Muth (1969) have developed models of the urban land market that provide insight into the processes influencing the internal structure, or neighborhood pattern, of cities. In addition, the study of the economic relationship between cities and their surrounding areas has led to an extensive literature on the economic support of towns by the export or *basic* activity (local production of goods for a nonlocal market) within them. Geographers and regional scientists have placed these external economic relationships in spatial perspective, analyzing the urban networks that provide for the distribution of goods and services. This work is termed *central place theory*.

The sociological version of the economic perspective is sometimes termed the *ecological complex model* (Duncan, 1959). According to this view, changes in cities can be traced to changes in the ecological complex. The ecological complex is composed of four categories of abstract variables: population, organization, environment, and technology. All urban systems and the changes within them can be analyzed in terms of the interaction among these four factors. The ecological complex model has been most useful in studying city growth. It suggests that the size of any community depends on its economic organization as well as its technological capacity and the qualities of its environment.

The power approach concentrates on the political structure of the city (Hunter, 1953; Clark, 1968). Power is unevenly distributed among the population of the city—certain groups are more powerful than others. Some power relations are formally organized, while others are not. Thus the question of who governs the city is important. Of major interest is the ability of various groups to realize their own special interests. Such power can clearly affect the city and its populations.

Cities can be described as cultures as well as types of organizations. They are more than simple economic or political systems—they are a way of life. In short, cities can be viewed in terms of individual perceptions and values (Firey,

1945; Bell, 1958; Gans, 1962a). This *value orientation* school of thought stresses the role cultural values play in the city and the urban experience. The values perspective is especially appropriate to the study of the city, for the modern urban community is characterized by cultural diversity. Urban culture has no single core of values, attitudes, or preferences because the city's inhabitants perform many roles and come from a variety of social and ethnic backgrounds.

None of these perspectives is monopolized by any single social or policy science studying the city. The spatial perspective adopted in this text, however, is somewhat more comprehensive than any alternative view.

HUMAN ECOLOGY AND URBAN GEOGRAPHY: BRINGING THE TWO PERSPECTIVES TOGETHER

Obviously, the organization of space affects the everyday actions and experiences of the urban person. But our understanding of the impact of space on the social fiber has been limited by how space has been studied.

Biology has long held that the relationship of animals to their environment is important. The analysis of this relationship is usually referred to as ecology. In sociology and geography the study of environment and space in human communities has a rather extensive tradition. Sociologists refer to this tradition as *human ecology*, a term first coined by R. E. Park and E. W. Burgess in 1921. For two decades thereafter the sociological study of the city was synonymous with human ecology. Geographers were quick to see the centrality of human ecology, since they had traditionally defined their own discipline as the study of the relationship between humans and the environment. In 1923 H. H. Barrows argued that geography was, or at least should be, human ecology. While there may have been some disagreement over the proper domain for this new "science," both disciplines agreed on its basic subject matter. Human ecology was to clarify the relationships between natural environments and the distribution and activities of people; it was to study human adaptation to the physical environment. Early efforts tended to focus on spatial distributions as adaptations. Writing in 1924, R. D. McKenzie argued that this discipline's fundamental interest was "in the effect of position, in both time and space, upon human institutions and human behavior" (1968:4). In a somewhat similar vein R. E. Park (1952:14) felt spatial study was critical because "most if not all cultural changes in society will be correlated with changes in territorial organization, and every change in territorial distribution . . . affects changes in the existing culture."

Human ecology has strayed from its original interest. The word *ecology* derives from the Greek *oikos*, which means "home" or "place to live." Human ecology originally studied human populations "at home," or in interaction with their environments. The field focused on human-environment relations and emphasized adaptation, the ability of a population to change its structure in order to survive under changing environmental conditions. Clearly this concept views environment as a factor communities and individuals must reckon with. Yet human ecology has failed to develop a clear understanding of environment as a social force. For the most part, the interrelations between environmental context and social factors have been virtually ignored (Michelson, 1976).

In its revised form, ecology has limited its study of environmental forces to social environments (Hawley, 1950). Urban communities adapt to conditions set by the communities that surround them and participate with them in social and economic relations. Neighborhoods within cities, as well, respond demographically and organizationally to changes in the neighborhoods near them.

This limited environmental concept results from an underlying assumption in most social sciences—especially sociology—that cultural evolution allows contemporary humans to remove themselves from environmental influence. In this view, evolution can be characterized as greater and greater control over environmental conditions. Urban environments are to a significant degree man-made. The city itself is an artificially created container in which light, heat, and weather—as well as competing animal and plant forms—are under control. That humans are now a product of their own making rather than the vagaries of the physical environment does not imply that environment is no longer important. In fact, environment should be more significant, for now we can manipulate it. The current problem arises from the social impact of these manipulations, for in designing environments, we essentially know not what we do nor why.

Human ecologists must not limit themselves to what sociologists have traditionally defined as social variables. Urban environment is itself a social product and thus is a social variable capable of influencing as well as reflecting social reality. To be sociological it is not necessary to confine the discussion to social environment in the narrow sense of the human ecologist.

Besides the narrow disciplinary perspective, the development of a satisfactory understanding of the human-environment relationship has been hampered because human ecology has traditionally worked with aggregate-level data (Michelson, 1976); that is, the unit of analysis for ecological investigation has been the population. The city was conceptualized as a series of interdependent *natural areas*, which were unplanned neighborhood units, each having a somewhat unique life because of its physical features (railways, highways, buildings, and geographic configurations). The concept of natural area assumed that people living in areas of the city could be treated as undifferentiated masses responding to pressures exerted by other areas in the city. This concept was practical in that it allowed great masses of data to be presented in a simple and clear fashion. In fact, early ecology was as much a method for data gathering as a theoretical framework for understanding urban dynamics.

The problem with aggregate units such as the natural area is that while aggregation simplifies, it also loses information. Aggregate-level data tell us little about the behavior of individuals in urban settings (Robinson, 1950), forcing the traditional ecologist to ignore social psychological factors that may affect spatial behavior. As Hawley argues:

> Attitudes, sentiments, motivations and the like are eliminated from consideration not because they are unimportant but because the assumptions and point of view of human ecology are not adapted to their treatment (1950:180).

Human ecology's attempt to ignore these micro level concerns is a major reason for its inability to develop a sound understanding of the human-environment relationship. As Chapter 2 points out, humans, unlike other animal forms, perceive territorial stimuli through their culture. Thus spatial behavior in humans can only be understood by incorporating attitude, sentiment, and value factors into the analysis. Sociological human ecology has ignored these variables.

The general objectives of human ecology have been shared by various subdisciplines of geography. When Barrows was arguing for geography as human ecology, most American geographers would have agreed that their central concern was study of the relationship between humans and land. In urban geography during the first quarter of this century, "emphasis tended to focus on specific details of individual towns and cities, the main objective being to identify associations between the absolute locations of places, their character, and the physical environment" (Yeates and Garner, 1976:6). Typical themes were the description and classification of urban forms, the relationship between urban structure and physical environment, and the "areal differentiation" of regions within cities—without, however, the explicitly social focus of human ecology. Since the mid 1950s, geographers have defined their field in more abstract spatial terms. Indeed, many geographers have argued that the essential line of demarcation between geography and other social sciences, including sociology, lies in geography's analytic use of spatial concepts (Bunge, 1962; Haggett, 1965; Cliff et al., 1975). In the study of the city this emphasis has led to generalization and the development of abstract spatial theory (Yeates and Garner, 1976; King and Golledge, 1978). Many geographers, however, have continued to emphasize the importance of studying particular places as well as studying abstract spaces (Tuan, 1974; Buttimer, 1974).

Within modern urban geography one particular strand of work has a close kinship with traditional human and urban ecology, and acknowledges the formative thinking of sociologists such as Park, Burgess, and McKenzie, the so-called Chicago School. This field—social geography—addresses spatial patterns in terms of decision making by individuals and institutions. "Social geographers are concerned with a community's social and geographical structure and the decision-making processes that govern its growth" (Jakle et al., 1976:2). The differences in objectives and methods between urban ecology and social geography are quite minor. Nevertheless, as late as 1979, Schwirian could write, "For many years urban geography and human ecology have developed side by side but each going its own way . . . Only a limited common substantive frame of reference emerged" (1979:212).

Another branch of geography, *behavioral geography* (Cox and Golledge, 1969; Golledge and Rushton, 1976), is concerned with analyzing and measuring spatial attitudes and values and with studying mental maps (cognitive reconstructions of the physical spaces of cities) of urban space. The terminology and philosophical orientation of behavioral geography is foreign to traditional human ecology, with its emphasis on the aggregate. The principal concern of behavioral geography has been cognitive maps of the urban space and their effects on spatial decisions such as migration and everyday travel. Used frequently in this book, the terminology and the orientation of behavioral geography is most closely akin to that of cognitive psychology. Thus the most vigorous investigations of the impact of space cognition and attitudes are being pursued outside traditional human ecology. This fact—and the disciplinary exclusiveness of the sociologists and geographers involved—has obscured the potential complementarity of behavioral geography and the sociological tradition of human ecology.

As we understand spatial behavior in humans, urban social space can only be studied by examining the city at both the macro and the micro levels of analysis. Human ecology and urban geography describe the spatial structure of the city (a macroecology approach), while behavioral geography and environmental psychology describe the urbanite's behavior within spatial structures (a microecology perspective). Our intent in this book is to provide a more complete appreciation of spatial structure and spatial behavior in the historical and contemporary city. This appreciation can only be accomplished by synthesizing micro- and macroecological approaches.

A FRAMEWORK FOR
THE STUDY OF URBAN SPACE

This book grew from the conviction of the authors (one teaching urban sociology, the other, urban geography) that few texts on urban society take full advantage of the wide-ranging literature on the spatial structure of the city. Our intent is to integrate this material with the growing body of research on the use and effects of space in animal ethology, human ecology, social and environmental psychology, urban and behavioral geography, and anthropology. This book is unlike most urban sociology texts, which provide an encyclopedic look at urban organization, environment, culture, and psychology. Instead, it attempts to consolidate extensive materials into an integrated framework that explains the relationship between urban space and the populations and structures contained within it. This is a point-of-view text. Unlike other texts on the city, each chapter is not a self-contained unit dealing with a specific aspect of the city. Rather, each chapter builds toward an integrated understanding of urban space. This enormous task is organized around three major themes.

The first theme concerns the arrangement and use of urban space. We are concerned here with describing the spatial structure of the city. Spatial arrangements are intrinsically interesting to every urbanite because the use of space conveys information about innumerable unknown others. Although the city dweller often uses these cues in everyday settings, he or she is nevertheless unaware of how and why this information is used. Chapters 2 to 5 provide an understanding of the spatial aspects of the urban experience. These chapters apply both psychological (microecological) and structural (macroecological) views of the urban space.

In order to provide the student with sufficient information on the structuring of city space, we pose four basic sets of questions:

1. What is the nature of the human-space relationship? That is, how and in what ways does space affect human behavior?

2. What is the nature of urban space? How has the urban container structured the urban experience?

3. In a historical frame of reference, what is the relationship between cultural and social structure and city space?

4. How do social scientists describe the internal structure of the city?

The second theme, developed in Chapters 6 to 8, deals with how social space changes in the city. While the first theme deals with statics, the second deals with the dynamics of the urban space. The emergence of spatial arrangements is considered at two levels: the psychological and the communal. At the psychological level the urban landscape is taken as the result of innumerable choices made by the individual under certain constraints. This approach studies urban space from the perspective of the potential migrant seeking a residence in the city. At the level of the community, the social, cultural, and economic factors that encourage population shifts between urban neighborhoods are identified. The information within the two approaches is integrated to develop a better understanding of why people become segregated in the city.

Several questions bear directly on the nature of spatial dynamics:

1. How do the individual's images of the urban space form, and how do these images affect spatial behavior?

2. Why do people change their place of residence?

3. How and why do neighborhoods change?

The third theme of this book, that spatial arrangements both indicate and cause social structure, is developed in Chapters 9 to 12. Space is discussed as a reflection of urban structure and as a social force that must be dealt with both by the urbanite and by the city. When one knows the spatial structure of a community, one can better see the community's underlying organization and the role and position of various groups within it. Space, however, does not just mirror the urban society; it actually reshapes it. Although we humans have built the urban container, it shapes our very thoughts and actions. Manipulating space is therefore a powerful tool in reordering urban society. Relevant questions include:

1. What can a city's spatial arrangement tell us about its value system and basic orientation?
2. How does housing design affect human behavior?
3. How does the physical layout of the whole city, with its segregated settings, affect social welfare?
4. How can the urban space be redesigned to meet in a more just way the needs of cities and their people?

The issues discussed in this book, then, are obviously not just of scholarly concern. Everyone interested in the city and its future must deal with the themes presented here. We believe that the social sciences can inform the urban planning process. We hope that this book contributes intelligently to that process.

PART ONE
Spatial Patterns in the Urban Area

The central theme of this book is that space orders—and thus has consequences for—both the urban system and urban behavior. Without spatial structure the city would be plunged into chaotic disarray.

To demonstrate the importance of spatial structure, several basic issues are considered in Part One. Chapter 2 reviews the questions surrounding human territorial behavior and examines the nature of the spatial relationship in humans. Following this investigation of the "nature of human nature" we then detail in Chapter 3 the unique qualities of the city. The theme of Chapter 3 is that throughout human history urban space has served as a basic mechanism for promoting social order. Chapter 4 provides a historical account of urban space, suggesting basic differences between the spatial order of preindustrial and industrial societies. Finally, Chapter 5 presents the major social science models for describing the spatial structure of cities.

Chapter 2

Humans as Spatial Animals

INTRODUCTION

The poet Robert Frost observed that "good fences make good neighbors." This conventional wisdom appears to hold true for a significant portion of the animal world. For many species, including humans, life is played out in bounded spatial arenas that affect and are affected by the behavior within them. On the Ugandan plains the male kob, a species of antelope, aggressively protects his mating territory against potential invaders. In the freshwaters of Europe, the stickleback fish carves out a small portion of the riverbed and with great feats of acrobatics and bubbling rage chases off intruding males. The musical *West Side Story*, whose plot revolves around the animosity between two street gangs, deals with a comparable tendency among humans to claim space and vigorously defend it. To some observers the similarities between these behaviors in humans and other animal forms is so striking that it implies a shared instinctive urge to claim and defend portions of space (Ardrey, 1966; Greenbie, 1976; Wilson, 1975). Others have argued that this view is oversimplified (Klopfer, 1969). If this idea is true, it promises to modify much of our social and political thought and to have a profound impact on the study of social space.

This chapter attempts to clarify the nature of the relationships between spatial structure and human behavior. It provides necessary background for an understanding of the impact of spatial arrangements on urban behavior. First, the controversy surrounding human territoriality is outlined. The second part of the chapter deals specifically with human social behavior—considering the impact of spatial settings on everyday actions.

SPATIAL ASPECTS OF ANIMAL BEHAVIOR

Ethology is the study of animal behavior. During the past fifty years ethologists have studied the impact of space and territory in numerous animal species.

One of the earliest studies was Howard's classic analysis of bird territories (1920). Since then an enormous variety of spatial behaviors has been described, and the biological and social functions of this behavior have begun to be clarified. Research shows that spatial behaviors vary widely from one species to another. One reason for this variation is that different kinds of animals require different spatial environments in order to survive and reproduce. Natural selection tailors species to particular habitats. Competition tends to exclude all but the most successful species from each particular niche, or portion of the habitat (Klopfer, 1969). According to this principle of competitive exclusion, the enormous diversity of animal species and behavior patterns is partly a function of the diversity of the environment itself. A diverse and complex environment leads to a richer array of behaviors among species.

Not only do the environmental requirements of species vary, but also the sense mechanisms used to experience the environment differ as well (Hinde, 1970). A few behaviors such as reflexes are essentially nonspatial, but most actions involve locomotion in space and response to specific environmental stimuli. The sensory apparatus of all animals is highly selective, orienting them to different features of the environment. In lower animals the selectivity may be extreme, so that the frog, for example, only sees insects that are moving. It does not ignore motionless insects; it simply does not register their existence in the first place. Also, various species emphasize different senses. Small ground-dwelling mammals inhabit a world dominated by the sense of smell; birds of prey depend on enormously precise vision; while bats and dolphins use a sound spectrum outside human perception. Thus not only are physical environments diverse but so, too, are the "subjective" environments that guide behavior.

Perhaps the most interesting class of spatial behavior is territoriality. Although some animals drift through space without fixed reference points and interact with others of their species only fleetingly, many forms, including most vertebrates, behave according to rather precise rules of spacing and landholding. Boundaries and tenure patterns indicate *territory*. In biological terms, territory is "an area occupied more or less exclusively by an animal or group of animals by means of repulsion through overt defense or advertisement" (Wilson, 1975:256). *Territoriality* is the complex of behaviors associated with territory. It has been defined as "animals' habitual use of a circumscribed area; behavior characterized by recognition of, use of, and some kind of defensive reactions toward a specific area" (Buettner-Janusch, 1973:553).

It is possible to detect and study territory by observing others entering the space in question, for territory is inextricably bound up with the urge to defend it. In most but not all territorial animals, the defender is aggressive only against members of the same species.

Another type of spatial behavior closely allied to territoriality is *individual distance*. This is a critical area, or "bubble," surrounding the individual animal. When its bounds are violated by another animal, discomfort and some overt reaction follow. Individual distance differs from territory in the sense that it moves with the individual animal. It is space not anchored to a given place. For example, individual distance can be seen in operation when birds arrive in groups at a temporary perch such as a telephone wire. Bickering and movement occur until the birds are spaced an appropriate distance apart. A German fable clarifies the concept:

> One very cold night a group of porcupines huddled together for warmth. However, their spines made proximity uncomfortable, so they moved apart again and got cold. After shuffling repeatedly in and out, they eventually found a distance at which they could still be comfortably warm without getting pricked. This distance they henceforth called decency and good manners (Leyhausen, cited by Wilson, 1975:257).

Types of territory and modes of territorial defense vary across species. Nice (1941) classifies territory types as mating, feeding, nesting, or winter-roosting areas. Klopfer (1969) adds to this list of individual territories the communal spaces groups, such as packs of wolves and troops of baboons, defend. Maintaining territory and individual distance may involve direct attack (dragonflies), vocal signaling (birds, crickets, frogs), odor signatures (cats, dogs), aggressive display (deer, stickleback, baboon, rhesus monkey), or some combination of these actions.

It was once thought that all these nonhuman territorial behaviors were exclusively instinctive. In 1868 J. B. Altum insisted that "animals do not act, they are acted upon; that is they respond to stimuli and drives, including the territorial drive" (cited by Wilson, 1975:260). Certainly some territorial responses in lower animals can be accounted for in very simple stimulus-response terms. For example, the stickleback, a small spined freshwater fish, responds in a rigid and unvarying way to certain stimuli. Each spring the male carves out a circular territory in the riverbed and builds a nest. His drab color changes to green, and his underside becomes bright red. This coloration attracts females and repels competing males during breeding. When male neighbors engage in a border dispute, they make stylized threats involving a kind of headstand that displays the red patch. Tinbergen (1951) showed that this instinctive response can be elicited automatically by simply exposing the breeding fish to the color red.

In some species territoriality seems to be only partly instinctive; the rest is learned. For example, many birds demarcate their territory by a distinctive song. It has been shown that the young bird must learn the details of the song during a critical susceptible period. Not only do individual species possess distinctive learned songs, but also regional dialects have been distinguished within the same species. It appears that instinct dictates that the bird will sing and provides what have been termed *templates,* or generalized song structures, but learning fills in the details of the song and the local dialect. Much territorial behavior appears to be of this type. It is not purely programmed instinct, nor does it have the enormous flexibility of learned behavior in humans.

In evolution, behaviors do not emerge without purpose. Since so many different species are territorial, we can infer that territoriality provides strong competitive advantages. Many ethologists have addressed this question (Brown, 1964; Ardrey, 1966; Lack, 1966; Hensley and Cope, 1951; Hinde, 1970). Klopfer (1969) catalogues some of the advantages hypothesized:

1. Increased efficiency in exploiting the environment.

In feeding territories an individual becomes more familiar with the home area because it occupies the same space over extended periods of time. This advantage applies to both predator and prey. Predators increase hunting success in familiar environs, while prey is more successful in escaping.

2. Less intense competition for food and regulation of population.

In most but not all territorial animals, the female is sexually unresponsive to males without territory. Thus, the number of territories limits breeding. In a year when food is scarce, territories are large and proprietors few, and fewer offspring are born. In times of plenty, territories are smaller, more females are sexually responsive, and populations grow. Starvation is unlikely, for territoriality limits population density (Wynne-Edwards, 1971).

3. Enhancing the formation and maintenance of pair bonds.

The need to have and defend territory encourages permanence in the parental relation. As Ardrey suggests: "Through isolation of the two in their little world, and their joint antagonism for all others of their kind, nature keeps the pair where they belong, at the service of the next generation" (1966:83).

4. Less time spent in aggression.

Territoriality reduces aggression during the breeding season by encouraging pair formation. Since this stabilizes breeding, the competition for sexual partners is more orderly. Similarly, in the case of feeding territories, members of the same species spend less time fighting for a food source because territories allocate feeding rights to specific individuals.

5. Slowing the spread of disease.

Parceling out land to individuals lowers the density of the community. Such spacing reduces the likelihood of disease spreading within the local population.

These functions of territoriality (and especially the density- or population-regulating function) bear greatly on the natural order. Biologists have long puzzled over the apparent order of the natural world. All creatures are self-interested; all have certain basic biological needs that must be met. How, out of all this self-interest, is the interest of the group maintained and order preserved? The answer for some biologists is simple—certain genetically inherited behavior patterns, such as territoriality, impose order on the natural world. Wilson refers to these behavior patterns as the "morality of the gene." Ardrey writes:

> Territory is . . . the chief mechanism of natural morality, something more than an open instinct, more than a superb defensive instrument—in truth, a natural mediating device between the good of the one and the good of all (1966:73).

FROM ANIMALS TO HUMANS

The debate concerning the relationship between human and animal behavior has gone on since the time of Darwin. It has heated up recently with the publication of controversial books such as Ardrey's *Territorial Imperative* (1966) and with the development of the science of sociobiology (Wilson, 1975). For students of the city, it would be extremely significant if innate spatial behavior patterns in humans could be demonstrated. Unfortunately, no simple way of demonstrating such patterns is available as yet.

At the level of analogy, ethological findings on nonhuman behavior are interesting when applied to humans. Statements about human behavior based on such analogies, however, can be misleading, especially when they have normative or moralistic implications. An extreme example is the use of the pseudo-Darwinian idea of nature "red in tooth and claw" to justify unbridled competition in human affairs, in which "intrinsically superior" types are destined to prevail. This philosophy formed one basis of Nazi racism and territorial aggression.

Beyond question, considerations that may be loosely termed "territorial" play a dominant role in our legal, economic, and political life. All cultures stand in implicitly or explicitly defined relationships to portions of the earth's surface, which they defend physically under certain circumstances. In traditional and tribal societies, communal occupancy of hunting grounds and agricultural land is the norm. The legal basis of the feudal order of the Middle Ages was permanent occupancy of land provided by the lord in exchange for homage and specified military services. At the present time the principle of ownership of land in perpetuity is established worldwide. The territorial sanctity of the nation state evokes national fervor in most people. Patriotism (and local attachments to place) may or may not be innate, but these emotions are certainly deeply rooted in human experience. The question is how much human's economic, political, and social use of territory can be illuminated more than metaphorically by reference to studies of nonhuman behavior. We contend that findings on nonhuman spatial behavior must be applied to humans only very carefully.

The observation that certain animals tenaciously defend individual and group territories appears to apply straightforwardly to human behavior. For example, when urban youth gangs mark and defend their turf, it seems plausible that they are reenacting the age-old ritual of an innately aggressive and territorial primate. Ardrey argues:

> We act as we do for reasons of our evolutionary past, not our cultural present, and our behavior is as much a mark of our species as is the shape of a human thigh bone or the configuration of nerves in a corner of the human brain (1966:4–5).

In fact, although gang warfare is undeniably territorial, there is little evidence that such behaviors are innate in humans. Klopfer writes, "These . . . accounts rest on abysmal ignorance of the diversity of territoriality in general and of the implications of this diversity" (1969:102).

Another example of an often-cited but questionable analogy between human and animal behavior is the inferences drawn from Calhoun's work on overcrowding (1962, 1966). Calhoun showed that in the wild, rat populations stabilize at relatively low levels because territoriality reduces breeding densities. Introducing high densities in artificial laboratory settings resulted in highly abnormal behavior patterns: sexual impotence, homosexuality, cannibalism, violence, "autism," unexplained fatalities, and erratic care of the young. High density produced a *behavioral sink*—a condition of increasing social and psychological disorganization. Wilson later observed that these reactions to high density were not confined to the rat. Most mammals forced into abnormal proximity in cages tended to compensate by spending hours "hiding" and avoiding eye contact.

If humans react like rats to density, then many symptoms of social malaise found in large cities are obviously the result of overcrowding. The city, it may be argued, is much like the experimenter's cage. When high densities encroach on individual distance, the urbanite may behave as the caged animal does. Although the city may, indeed, be viewed in some ways as a behavioral sink, there is little evidence that density itself is the factor at work. Studies of urban density have been unsuccessful in establishing the links between overcrowding and urban disorganization (Freedman, 1976). In fact, Calhoun's work may not hold for primates in general. Recent work on a macaque colony transplanted to Oregon suggests that moderately increased densities may actually inhibit rather than promote aggression (Gray Eaton, 1976). Nobody would deny that crowding 100 people into a single room will cause problems! But at the moderate densities characteristic of even the most crowded cities, the effects of density seem to be both complex and subtle.

A major reason for caution in applying animal findings to humans is the set of learned behavior patterns termed *culture*. Humans differ from other animals in the degree to which learning predominates over instinct. But in abstracting and symbolizing behavior, humans seem to be unique. It is possible that the territorial urges have been reinterpreted symbolically to such an extent that ethological findings on nonhuman territoriality are irrelevant.

To say that humans are cultural animals is to imply that our response to spatial stimuli differs from that of other animals. Human interaction with the environment is mediated by symbols, above all by language. The mediation of culturally determined symbols, particularly language, between the world and our understanding of it casts our ideas of human territoriality in a profoundly new form. The sociologist W. I. Thomas (1951) has argued convincingly that the meanings we attribute to various situations control our response and not the situations themselves. This control is exerted in two different ways. First we only perceive things we are conditioned to see; that is, we only perceive what fits into our existing concepts and symbols. In a sense, we do not think about what we see, but we see what we think. Thus, culturally determined symbols act as a filter. Second, culture assigns relative values to the things that we do perceive. What is evaluated as a comfortable and friendly interaction distance among one group may pass as embarrassing intimacy among another. Thus culture acts as a partially opaque and partially distorting lens focusing or refocusing the stimuli surrounding us.

This difference between human and nonhuman responses to environmental stimuli has several important consequences for the human-space relationship and the concept of territoriality in humans. Because of culture:

1. Human interaction with the environment is active rather than passive.

2. Human response to space is highly variable.

3. The functions of territory in humans vary from one cultural level to another.

We shall elaborate on each of these in turn.

Active Versus Passive Approaches to Environment

Studies of living species and of the fossil record emphasize adaptation, a one-sided process in which plant and animal species evolve to fit the available niches. In the long run, living things have profoundly changed the physical world; for example, the atmospheric oxygen of the earth resulted from the evolution of green plants. But few species modify their environment in an apparently active and purposeful way. Humans are the greatest modifiers. Indeed, since the Industrial Revolution, our interaction with the physical environment has been so active it appears piratical. The idea that human beings are distinct from the rest of nature and that we may do as we will with our environment is common to many philosophies from Christianity to Marxism. Environmentalists have forcefully argued that this idea is false and dangerous.

With culture the human species has significantly extended its biological capacities. Human behavior can change drastically without fundamental alterations in our genetic structure. Because of the symbolic nature of culture, information can be transmittted across generations in a nongenetic fashion such as books or films or oral traditions. Consequently culture becomes a continuum flowing from one generation to the next. At the same time culture is more flexible than genetic structure since culture changes much faster than inheritance. Thus, humans are more adaptable than other species to environmental fluctuation and change (White, 1949). At the same time, because humans are somewhat independent of genetic heritage, we are also somewhat less dependent on the environment than other life forms. Culture permits humans to construct artificial environments. We are not passive receptors of stimuli. Lawton and Nahemow (1973), in their analysis of the spatial behavior of older people, argue that the degree to which environment shapes behavior depends on the physical and mental competence of the individual. This *environmental docility* hypothesis suggests that the greater the degree of individual competence, the less the proportion of change in behavior due to environmental factors. When the individual's ability to use cultural symbols is impaired, as in the case of senility, the environment-behavior relationship becomes less complex.

Although an active and intelligent control over our environment distinguishes us from the nonhuman world, it is absurd to pretend that we are in active and intelligent control of all aspects of the urban environment. Again and again in this book we will discuss situations in which man-made environments control human behavior in undesirable or unknown ways.

The Variable Response of Humans to Space

The immense cross-cultural diversity of human spatial behavior throws a great deal of doubt on the idea that we are bound by a universal set of innate, genetically determined responses. Although different animal species possess quite different responses, spatial behavior tends to be similar within a given species, except for very minor variations such as the local dialects of the birds' song. Patterns of spatial response in humans are largely cultural. Human behaviors are more similar within cultures than between them. Thus in humans, culture performs a role similar to that of the species for other animals.

For example, individual distance is highly variable from one culture to another. What might be seen as an invasion of an individual's space in one culture may be the distance of customary interaction in another. What may be an uncomfortably high living density for one group may be normal for another. In Arab cultures, for example, personal interaction with strangers is often a close-range affair. Also, more pushing and shoving in public is tolerated in Arab countries than in the United States or Western Europe. Even within the European countries, conventional modes of interaction distance vary. George Orwell (1968) observed that the English are among the easiest people in the world to shove off a sidewalk! Edward Hall remarks that such differences lead to problems when, say, an American and an Arab share the same public space:

> As I waited in the deserted lobby, a stranger walked up to where I was sitting and stood close enough so that I could not only easily touch him, but I could hear him

breathing. . . . If the lobby had been crowded with people I would have understood his behavior, but in an empty lobby his presence made me exceedingly uncomfortable (1966:151).

Density ceilings characteristic of the community and society also vary from one culture to another. Culture, in the form of knowledge, beliefs, and practices, determines the minimum and maximum densities that a society must fall within. Wiechel's classification of cultures by density (cited in Hawley, 1950) indicates the cultural variability in territorial spacing (see Table 2.1).

Table 2.1   Average Densities by Type of Culture

Average Persons Per Square Mile	Culture Types
1–8	Hunting and gathering, fishing
8–26	Pastoral
26–64	Early agricultural
64–192	Agricultural
192–381	Early industrial
381+	Industrial

Source: Hawley, 1950:151.

Density ceilings vary from society to society. The more advanced and extensive a society's technology, the better it can absorb large concentrations of population. This evidence suggests that cultures differ in their territorial relations.

Cultural variability is also evident in concepts of territory and modes of territorial defense. In most modern societies the law recognizes and protects individual and corporate ownership of land. Territorial defense is currently organized around the nation state. This form of organization emerged only recently. In the medieval period, for example, conflict was organized in terms of feudal and dynastic alliances in which the concept of nation did not figure. Indeed, for most of human history and prehistory hunting and gathering was the highest form of economic organization. In this system not only was the nation concept undeveloped but also individual land ownership was unknown.

In hunting and gathering societies, war was seldom waged for territorial gain, and the warfare that did result from territorial disputes was highly ritualized. It was more aggressive display than overt aggression. Karl Heider describes the ritual warfare of the Dani, a horticultural people located in western New Guinea.

> Battles . . . are massive affairs which are announced in advance and are rarely fatal.
> The basic front is usually static. Individuals move forward to about 20 yards from the enemy, fire a few arrows, or threaten with spears and then fall back. The rear ranks join in the shouting, threatening and exhibitionistic shaking of feather wands and long hair.
> Lulls in the battle are frequent as both sides draw back to rest, to smoke cigarettes and to shout at each other (1972:21).

In agricultural and industrial societies, on the other hand, territory is defended or expanded more directly with an elaborate technology used to increase the body count of the enemy and reduce the casualties of allies. Organized warfare that endangers the whole civilian population is quite new to history. It gives new urgency to the need to understand what, if any, territorial urges underlie such behavior.

Cross-Cultural Variations in the Functions of Territory

Just as human spatial behavior varies from culture to culture so, too, do the functions of territory. One crucial function of animal territoriality is economic, the regulation of food supplies. Dividing space into individual or communal plots is a rationing device ensuring that the competition for food resources within a species will be minimal. Such spatial divisions also produce intimate knowledge of the immediate area, encouraging more efficient use of the environment. These functions are critical for humans, however, only in hunting and gathering societies, which are related to the environment much as animals are. At this simple level of technology, each community represents a self-sufficient economic unit providing all basic needs within its own territory. In essence, the basic economic unit is the local territory. As such, territory modifies the intensity of competition between hunting and gathering communities. Since all such groups in a given environment exploit similar food sources, territorial regulations reduce the strains of competition by limiting the use of a particular piece of the area to a select group.

In self-sufficient agricultural societies this basic relationship between land and population still holds, although continuing improvements in crops and techniques enhance the productivity of land. Since the Industrial Revolution, however, territorial specialization has occurred and self-sufficient communities have declined. Territorial units, each performing somewhat special tasks, have been integrated into a regional and world economy. Thus, territory has lost its economic function as the world has evolved into an international marketplace.

The function of territory in regulating density has also declined with cultural evolution (Wrigley, 1969). Perhaps the most influential writer on the relation between population growth and territory was Thomas Malthus. His "Essay on the Principle of Population" (1798) suggests that while population increases geometrically (as 1, 2, 4, 8, 16 . . .), the food supply can only grow arithmetically (as 1, 2, 3, 4, 5 . . .). The amount and productivity of the land, then, ultimately checks population. Although Malthus suggests that population growth is limited primarily by the amount of land available to a society, this ceiling effect of territory has little impact in technologically developed societies because of the nonlocal territorial organization of the economy and the large economic surpluses. Malthus's law applies best to nonhuman and preindustrial human populations, whose density is regulated by territory. In preindustrial societies growth is near zero, and this stationary position is maintained by the resource limitations of the local area. In contemporary developing nations, however, such is not the case. Whether densities are high (India, Bangladesh, Bahamas) or low (Brazil, Venezuela, Botswana) population is growing faster than the amount of land in use.

Perhaps the only function of territory that appears to be shared by human and nonhuman animal forms is the impact of territory on aggression. Territory appears to reduce the time spent on aggression against others of the species. Through the development of informal and formal regulations surrounding territorial use, humans have established rights of peaceful residence. The legitimate possession of territory reduces the potential threat of continued aggression and dispute over occupancy. Territorial rights in humans and animals are generally honored, without the necessity of a fight to the death. Humans have legally enforced territorial rights against the intrusion of strangers into home, neighborhood, and nation state.

Considering the variety of human territorial behaviors and territorial functions, are concepts derived from ethology of any value in understanding human spatial responses? Wilson (1975) argues that social scientists are unwilling to view territorial behavior as a universal human trait because they erroneously think about territoriality in terms of a rigid framework of stimulus and response: "the stickleback model." He suggests that in reality most animals respond to their neighbors in a variable manner. The problem with this argument, however, is that the variety of human behavior is so great that it is difficult to make any universal generalizations about human territoriality.

Although the analogies between humans and other animal forms are potentially informative, at present they can be nothing but metaphorical. Humans certainly occupy individual and group territories that they are prepared to defend under certain circumstances, but does territory represent a need basic to all members of the species? Are humans in fact innately territorial? Most vertebrates exhibit some type of territoriality, and it is conceivable and even likely that humans possess genetic traits associated with the use of space. At present such traits have not been identified. And cultural evidence indicates conclusively that whatever human biological drives may exist are channeled and diversified by culture.

SPATIAL STRUCTURE IN EVERYDAY SETTINGS

Distance and Segregation

Although the ways in which humans use and respond to space vary from culture to culture, spatial arrangements exert an enormous influence on day-to-day social behavior. In the remainder of this chapter we will study this influence.

In order to understand the impact of space on everyday activities it is necessary to define the essential characteristics of the spatial variable. We will discuss the nature of space in more detail in Chapter 6. Here, it is sufficient to point out that from a geometrical point of view space regulates social interaction in two ways. It *separates* actors by *distance*. And it *segregates* them with *boundaries*, such as walls of buildings and the intangible limits of neighborhoods and political units.

A tremendous number of studies in geography and human ecology have been conducted on the effects of physical proximity or distance on human interactions of all types. The fundamental observation of these studies is that interaction decreases as distance increases. The term *distance decay* refers to the tendency for a particular behavior to decline as the distance between the activity and the potential participant increases. George Kingsley Zipf (1949) suggests that the distance decay effect is merely one example of the human tendency to operate according to a *principle of least effort*. In short, spatial movement is costly, and the shorter a distance one must move to perform a certain activity, the more likely that activity is. While the costs of such movement vary by type of activity, it is apparent that the frequency of freight flows, telephone calls, shopping, social and commuter trips, marriages, friendships, and many other social or economic relationships decreases in a curvilinear fashion with increasing distance, as shown in Figure 2.1 (Wilson, 1970; Olsson, 1965). Distance molds social interaction.

In similar fashion the boundaries of the urban space affect urban life and

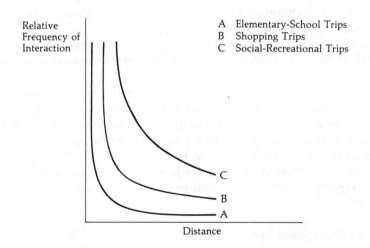

Figure 2.1 *Distance-Decay Curves of Interaction*   Distance decay is the tendency for a particular behavior such as trips to elementary school, shopping, and social or recreational travel to decline as the distance between the activity and the potential participant increases. These curves are hypothetical, but different rates of distance decay have been substantiated for each of the behaviors. The curves indicate that children generally go to schools in the immediate area, while visiting and recreation trips are longer in average length but still limited by distance.

experience. The city itself is a bounded social and physical space containing a set of bounded microspaces (neighborhoods, parks, thoroughfares, and buildings). The urbanite carries out his or her everyday life in prearranged spatial settings. In the city, both people and activities are highly segregated. Everything and everybody has its place, and zoning, trespass, and vagrancy laws enforce the pattern. This spatial structure directs and organizes our everyday lives. It allows for routine or patterned living through the process of exclusion. Our lives are structured spatially so that we can perform our daily routine with little probability of experiencing events or people we view as strange or undesirable. Without any effort at all, a white, middle-class businessman can avoid high-crime areas, ethnic ghettos, and congested tourist areas. If he wishes, he can spend his entire day surrounded by other middle-class businesspeople—in spite of the great variety of functions and persons the city contains.

Not only is the general spatial pattern of the city prearranged, but also the microspace we act in is designed and relatively fixed. We work and live in buildings whose space segregates activities and people from one another. Activities within the home are segregated by room. There are rooms for eating, for cooking, for personal hygiene, for sleeping, for leisure activities, and for socializing with friends. Even our yards are segregated into a public space (the front yard, for interacting casually with neighbors) and a private space (the back yard, for interactions with family and more intimate neighbors). At work separate rooms are provided for each type of activity. There are mail rooms, secretarial pools, offices, and production rooms. Also the place each individual occupies in the organizational hierarchy is reflected by the type and size of the room he or she occupies. In general, the higher the status of the individual, the more spacious the quarters and the higher the floor number. This spatial division of both cities and buildings provides essential structure to our everyday lives.

This situation is rather ironic. We have achieved a nearly complete mastery over our environment, and we carry out our everyday activities in settings that are mainly or exclusively artificial. But these settings have been created haphazardly or at best with only half-conscious recognition of human needs or of the impact of the forms themselves in molding action. Urban planners, engineers, architects, interior decorators, and even furniture designers exert substantial but largely unexplored control over our behavior.

Types of Segregated Spaces

Space is bounded or segregated in a variety of ways. The anthropologist Edward Hall (1966) speaks of three types of spatial structuring. *Fixed-feature spaces* are the areas organized by immovable boundaries such as walls, fences, and streets. *Semifixed-feature spaces* are spaces created by the arrangement of movable objects—furniture, screens, plants, and so forth. Fixed-feature and semifixed-feature space create mechanically maintained distance. In these types of spaces, the proximity between the objects in the space is a function of the external environment. *Individual space,* on the other hand, represents socially maintained distance. Within a given cultural milieu each type of interaction carries with it certain expectations (norms) as to how actors should space themselves in the activity. Friends should be close; strangers should keep their distance.

In all spatial contexts, proximity is relative and never absolute. Nearness is situational. What is considered a great distance in one setting might be viewed as a short distance in another.

The behavioral implications of situational nearness have been studied from two complementary perspectives (Ball, 1973). *Microgeography,* as developed in the work of Steinzor, Sommer, Festinger, Strodtbeck, and others emphasizes the impact of semifixed and fixed-feature space on social behavior. It focuses on space "as it is experienced and as it structures conduct" (Ball, 1973). This approach stresses the interpersonal consequences of spacing. On the other hand, proxemics emphasizes individual space. As defined by Hall, *proxemics* is the study of space as a mode of communication individuals use to send and interpret information. Thus space is one aspect of nonverbal communication, and spatial variables represent elements of social interaction that are learned but taken for granted. In our interactions we either consciously or unconsciously take spatial variables into account in order to assess our relationship with others.

Microgeographic Research

Microgeographic research, conducted in both laboratory and natural settings, has shown that the arrangement of boundaries and of objects in various situations can control who meets whom, when, where, and for how long. Such arrangements can also affect the quality of the interaction.

Which way buildings face, where exits and entrances are located, where stairways and elevators are positioned, as well as how other central meeting places are designed affect the number of potential contacts between individuals in the structure. (Because of its pervasive influence over everyday actions, engineered proximity or architecture will be discussed in Chapter 10.) Proximity not only affects the frequency of interaction but also determines who will fill certain roles in a group. Small-group studies summarized by Bavelas (1968) point out how spatial patterns determine group structure and character. In these studies of communication flows, each subject was given a series of cards printed with a number of symbols. The group's task was to find the symbols all their cards had in common. Each subject was seated in a cubicle so that he or she could communicate with others only by writing messages passed through slots in the cubicle. Cubicles were arranged in a variety of patterns. Figure 2.2 summarizes the four seating arrangements considered in the study. The diagrams show that individuals occupying the most central position in a pattern

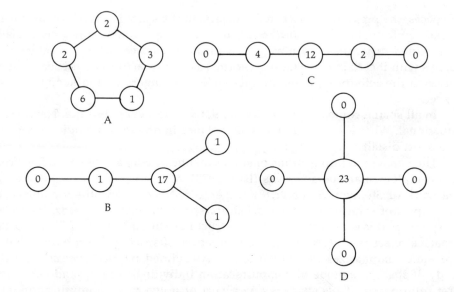

Figure 2.2   *The Emergence of Recognized Leaders in Different Small-Group Spatial Pat-*
terns   Spatial arrangements can affect the emergence of roles in a group. Bavelas's
review of communication studies suggests the effect of seating on the emergence of
leadership roles. The number at each position indicates the frequency with which
group members named the individual at that position as a task leader in the experiment. (*Source:* From A. Bavelas, "Communication Patterns in Task-Oriented
Groups," in D. Lerner and H. D. Lasswell (eds.) *The Policy Sciences*, 1951. Reprinted
by permission of Stanford University Press, Stanford, CA.)

were most likely to be recognized as the group leader. Seating also seemed to
affect group cohesion and efficiency. In highly centralized groups such as C
and D, the morale of individuals in the periphery was quite low. At the same
time, however, these organizational settings developed more quickly and errors in performance were minimal. What these groups lacked in cohesion, they
appeared to gain in achievement.

   Strodtbeck and Hook's experiments with jury room settings came to conclusions similiar to those of Bavelas (1968). They found that in experimental
jury deliberations, the person sitting at the end of the rectangular jury-room table was chosen significantly more often as the leader and was the most active
member of the group. It was not entirely clear from this study whether people
with leadership qualities tended more often to choose the head of the table or
whether people who chose this position gained influence from it. What was
striking, however, was that persons from a higher socioeconomic status picked
the head position more often. This finding was later confirmed by Lott and
Sommer (1967) in another context. It appears to be a cultural norm that leaders
will seat themselves at the head of a table. In many homes the head of the

household tends to sit at the head of the table at dinner, reflecting his or her position in the family.

The quality of relationships can be manipulated simply by rearranging furniture. In the 1950s Sommer began observing elderly women patients in a state hospital. The ward was well furnished, yet doctors noticed that the women very seldom conversed with each other. The source of the problem was obvious to Sommer. Chairs on the ward were arranged in straight lines along the walls and back to back in the center. "They (the women) were like strangers in a train station waiting for a train that never came" (1969:79). As in many institutional settings semifixed feature space had been arranged for the convenience of the institutional workers rather than the inmates. By merely arranging chairs around tables and adding some couches, Sommer increased both the frequency and intensity of interactions. After a short period of adjustment, both brief and sustained conversations nearly doubled. The ward was shortly transformed into a therapeutic community.

Further observations of students in cafeterias and libraries led Sommer to realize that seating arrangement varied with activity. He distinguished four situations: conversation, cooperation, coaction (no mutual interaction), and competition. In order to determine seating norms by task, Sommer asked subjects how they would prefer to seat themselves in each case. The results may be seen in Table 2.2. Side by side choices were favored for cooperative activities, reflecting the "closeness" required for such a task. Conversations, on the other hand, could be maintained either by corner seating or "short" opposite seating, the major factor being maximized eye contact. Visual closeness was extremely important as well in competitive action, but the key in this situation seemed to be the need to maintain some distance from the competitor. One cannot afford

Table 2.2   Preferred Seating Arrangement by Task Type

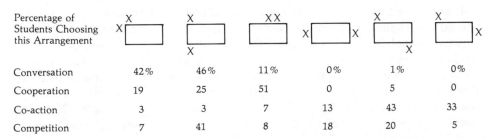

Percentage of Students Choosing this Arrangement					
Conversation	42%	46%	11%	0%	1%	0%
Cooperation	19	25	51	0	5	0
Co-action	3	3	7	13	43	33
Competition	7	41	8	18	20	5

Source: Robert Sommer, *Personal Space: The Behavioral Basis of Design,* © 1969. Reprinted by permission of Prentice-Hall, Inc., Englewood Cliffs, New Jersey.

Robert Sommer's study of student interactions in natural settings suggests that preferred seating arrangements vary by type of interaction. In "close" interactions, students prefer minimal distances and the maintenance of eye contact. Sommer's work is one example of microgeographic research.

to be too close to one's adversary. Coaction—similar activity carried out individually—requires a maximization of distance between individuals and a minimization of eye contact. Such positioning discouraged interference with each other's work. Overall, Sommer's work clearly shows the power architects and interior designers can exert over everyday behavior.

Proxemics Research

The social environment, as well as the elements of the physical environment (such as fixed and semifixed feature space), affects group interaction. Proxemics studies this relationship. The relative location of ourselves and others has important consequences for our behavior in any physical setting. Each type of interaction requires a different individual distance. Hall (1966) argues that there are four zones, or spatial distances, within which social behavior occurs in American culture. The four distances are labelled intimate, personal, social, and public. Each has a near and a far phase.

The decisive factor in the choice of a zone appears to be the degree of intimacy between the actors taking part. *Intimate distance* is the zone from 18 inches to physical contact. The close phase of intimate distance involves either lovemaking or physical aggression. The far phase involves interaction in which touching is permitted and in which conversation takes place with lowered voices. *Personal distance*, from 18 inches to 4 feet, is the zone in which most personal (or what sociologists refer to as primary group relationships) occur. In its close phase, between 18 inches and 30 inches, personal distance is often used by close friends of the same sex. It is also the normal separation for conversation at informal gatherings. The far phase of personal distance is used for ordinary interaction, generally between acquaintances.

Social distance extends from 4 to 7 feet in its close phase and from 7 to 12 feet in its far phase. This is the arena in which most secondary relationships occur. It is referred to by Linder as the business distance (1974:3). The more impersonal the transaction, the greater the distance between parties. Formality characterizes behavior at this distance. Even more formal in character, however, is social behavior at a public distance. *Public distance* is set so that communication is one way; the group includes one or more speakers and an audience. There is no genuine interaction, only presentation and observation. Spatial patterns such as those noted by Hall are similar to what the sociologist Garfinkel called *background expectancies* which are those learned but implicit elements of an actor's social world.

In numerous situations our choice of body position is predetermined. Often the existing spatial structure forces us into distances inappropriate for the social relationship we are trying to maintain. Behavior in elevators is one example. The elevator rider assumes a rigid posture, eyes riveted forward toward some fixed point, conversation polite but minimal. The situation is quite formal, and each individual on the elevator tries to assume a businesslike expression as if to thwart intimate advances in such close quarters. In the classroom, as well, interaction distance and the goals of the educator are sometimes mismatched. In the large lecture hall, the instructor is often removed from the audience by the position of the podium. Educational activities are expected to be somewhat formal, but often students are seated too far away, leaving them with an impression that the teacher is cold and aloof.

Clearly, as Hall insists, space has meaning. It speaks of our intentions toward others. Space is dear to us because it is one of the props we use in managing relationships. When our personal space is invaded or is threatened by external forces, our reaction to such situations tends to be angry or defensive. These defensive maneuvers provide clues to how and why we use personal space.

Lofland (1973) discusses the variety of styles the city dweller has developed to preclude interaction while waiting at a bus depot, airport, and so on. The trick, she says, is to remain inconspicuous and to make clear to everyone that one is not open for interaction. Some of the tactics are:

1. *The Sweet Young Thing.*

This style is most commonly assumed by respectable young women who are anxious to maintain their status. The pattern involves very little movement. Once she takes a position inside the setting, she rarely leaves it. Her posture is straight, her legs or ankles crossed. Inevitably she is casually reading a book or magazine, but never too carefully because she is on constant alert for any intruder. The reading material is a prop to demonstrate that she is tending to her own affairs and is not interested in conversing with others.

2. *The Nester.*

Having established a position, this person seldom leaves it. Instead, such people busy themselves arranging and rearranging props like a bird building its nest. Generally this involves searching for and rearranging articles in a purse or briefcase. This continual fidgeting makes the individual look busy and uninterested in the surrounding social setting.

3. *The Investigator.*

The investigators are as absorbed and unapproachable as the nesters. Unlike nesters, their props are their surroundings. Having reached a position in public space, they survey their environment with some care, then they leave their place and investigate every object in sight. Paintings, ashtrays, pillars, vending machines, even telephone booths—nothing escapes their attention. They are busy, and their business is exploring. The message is clear: Go away, I'm too busy to be bothered with you.

Russo's study of invasions in college libraries provides further evidence of the importance we place on protecting our individual space (Sommer, 1969). Normally newcomers to libraries and waiting rooms space themselves some distance apart. Russo tested the reaction of subjects to an invasion of this space. Her subjects were all women sitting at a table with empty chairs on either side and across from them. Five different invasion techniques were used. The one most successful in producing a response was for the experimenter to sit along-side the subject and move the chair closer to her. After half an hour about 70 percent of the subjects moved. Over all, however, there were wide individual differences in the way victims reacted. Some used defensive gestures such as frowning, head-shaking disapproval, and double takes; others shifted posture or moved away. Few, however, exhibited verbal aggression. Territorial reactions were varied but seldom aggressive.

These studies are important for understanding urban living. In the city, densities in public space are at a maximum and thus the potential for invasion is great. As a result the urbanite develops defensive mechanisms. Perhaps the most common defensive maneuver is to treat others as nonpersons or objects. Nonpersons cannot invade space any more than a chair or a pole can. In high-density situations like a subway or an elevator people commonly react to each other as objects.

> Many subway riders who have adjusted to crowding through psychological with-drawal prefer to treat other riders as nonpersons and keenly resent situations, such as a stop so abrupt that the person alongside pushes into them and then apologizes, when the other rider becomes a person (Sommer, 1969:37).

To this point we have discussed passive reaction to intrusion. But people use proxemic space in an active way, too: It permits them to communicate feelings and intentions. This is often more obvious with the *vertical* than the horizontal dimensions of space and has been frequently cited in manuals for professionals who must maintain a certain degree of dominance over clients.

> To be able to look down on people gives them a great advantage. . . . Therefore the seat of the interrogator's chair should be somewhat higher from the ground than the suspect's chair. . . .
> It is sometimes better to await an invitation to be seated. Standing is . . . more forceful, while sitting places you on more intimate terms with the customer . . . (Ball, 1973:28–29).

In Hall's work, horizontal distance is considered important for creating and maintaining certain expectations of a social situation. Distance communicates liking. It appears that we place ourselves closer to those we wish to either influence or have as friends. Howard Rosenfeld (1965) conducted an experiment in which half the subjects were instructed to seek the approval of a person, actually a stooge, who was seated in a standard position in the experimental room. Before entering the room, the person who was seeking approval was told to imagine the situation as pleasant and friendly. Each subject was then given a chair and allowed to enter the room. Approval-seeking subjects placed their chairs significantly closer to the stooge than did the approval-avoiding subjects (57 inches versus 94 inches on average). In a similar vein, studies by Kleck (1968) suggest that we put ourselves at a greater distance from those whom we see as different. As in the Rosenfeld experiment, Kleck staged an interaction between a naive subject and a confederate. Half the subjects, however, were instructed ahead of time that the confederate was epileptic. Inevitably the subject placed the chair farther away from the supposedly epileptic stooge than from the supposedly normal stooge.

Not only do we structure proxemic space to reveal our intentions, but this use of distance by actors also appears to have some effect on the others in a situation. Mehrabian (1969a) has found that the closer the approach, the greater the degree of positive feelings about the actor communicated to the other. This seems to hold true not only for communication of affection, but for persuasive communication as well. In another study, Mehrabian (1969b) asked subjects to rate the persuasiveness of a video tape segment. The speaker on the video tape was judged most persuasive when standing closest to the television camera (a distance of about 4 feet). Spatial positioning, then, teaches us about each other's intentions and, in turn, somewhat influences our judgments of others.

Microgeographic and proxemic work shows the important role proximity plays in everyday interaction. Existing spatial arrangements structure relationships. They not only reflect group structure but also affect interaction patterns and serve as information for the individual actor. In this sense space molds experience and behavior. This will become especially apparent in the case of the urbanite, for the city, as we will see, is characterized by an intensive spatial structuring.

SUMMARY

Ethological studies demonstrate that many animal species are territorial and that territoriality confers certain advantages to species. Space plays a central role in human institutions and experience, and human beings display many types of behavior that can be accurately termed territorial. However, there is little evidence either that such behaviors are genetically determined or that any such behaviors are common to all humans. On the contrary, cultural diversity seems to be the norm.

Nevertheless, it is accurate to say that humans are spatial animals. The geometry of the urban space expressed in building design, the overall arrangement of land use, and the segregation of populations have important implications for the urban experience. Space separates social actors by distance and by boundaries. While spatial arrangements do not determine the frequency and nature of interactions, spatial proximity does encourage or facilitate interaction and thus influence its quantity and quality. Microgeography suggests the crucial role of space in channeling the interaction process. Proxemic studies indicate how the nonphysical features of space are used in communicating information in such interactions.

Chapter 3

Spatial Structure and the Urban Experience

INTRODUCTION

Our concern with the city involves a specific interest in the effect of community context on social structure and individual behavior. If spatial structure has behavioral consequences, then we must ask the central question: What unique aspect of the city context makes urban life styles differ from others?

In one sense, the city can be described as the most human of environments, for the city more than any other ecosystem bears a distinct human imprint. Indeed, the city is in many ways an artificial environment—a man-made and controlled setting. Yet at the same time, the urban environment is often characterized as unlivable and dehumanizing. In much of American literature the city is portrayed as an evil force. The works of Twain, Poe, Hawthorne, Dreiser, Norris, James, and Lewis describe the city as a place of personal frustration, exploitative commercialism, loneliness, miserable poverty, vice, and corruption. For them the city is the setting for deviation. Contemporary music has been equally unkind. Blues, a city-spawned genre, sings of the despair of the black urbanite. Country and western lyrics, with their "sin-sex-booze" themes, express the problems of the urban hillbilly as a recent migrant to the city (Gist and Fava, 1974). These contemporary reflections on urban life represent the love-hate affair Westerners have had with cities. On the one hand, the city is seen as an exciting place where civilization's fruits are to be found; on the other hand, it is viewed as a lonely and anonymous setting.

What are these things we call cities, and why have they generated such ambivalence? In the modern world almost everyone has some understanding of the city. After all, our lives are controlled by decisions made in such places. That the city and the urbanite differ from the rural area and the country dweller seems obvious. Less obvious, however, is what makes them different. Neither social scientists nor governmental bodies can agree on a precise definition of the urban area. The "urbanness" of a community is a matter of degree. Certainly Peoria and New York City provide different urban experiences. Thus, it is often necessary to speak of a rural-urban continuum, with communities placed on this scale at various points.

City scholars have long attempted to distill the essence of the urban quality in concise definitions. Max Weber in *Die Stadt* suggests that the city is a place ". . . where the local inhabitants satisfy an economically substantial part of their daily wants in the local market, and to an essential extent by products which the local population and that of the immediate hinterland produced for sale in the market or acquired in other ways" (1958:67). For Weber, the city is a *permanent marketplace* with a specialized class of traders. Urban scholars such as Gras, Jacobs, Pirenne, and Childe essentially concur with Weber. The city's position as a market center generates its urbane and rational character.

The market-oriented nature of the city is, of course, a matter of degree. In some societies the urban community organizes economic relations and becomes the place for free exchange. As Keyfitz (1967) points out, many of the ancient communities we identify as cities were not true market centers. They gained the surpluses necessary to sustain an urban population through sheer force rather than organized exchange. All roads may have led to Rome in the ancient world, but these roads were primarily for the army.

Mumford, on the other hand, emphasizes the *contextual qualities* of the city. The city is a physical thing, "a permanent container and an institutional structure, capable of storing and handing on the contents of civilization" (1961:93). Early cities are identifiable by "the walled enclosure, the street, the house block, the market, the temple precinct with its inner courts, the administrative precinct, the workshop precinct . . ." (1961:90). This physical structure is seen as a first clue to an urban culture.

Perhaps the most common definition, however, centers on the *demographic qualities*, or population characteristics, of the community. Wirth (1938) defines the city as a relatively large, dense, and permanent settlement of socially heterogeneous individuals. Similarly, Sjoberg (1960) sees it as a community of large size and population density that contains a variety of nonagricultural specialists, including a literate elite. The official censuses of most nations recognize cities as population aggregates exceeding a minimum size or density. These official definitions can be somewhat arbitrary. As Hawley (1971) suggests, in Japan a number of "cities" in the 100,000 to 500,000 population range have over half their lands devoted to agricultural use. When these quantitative criteria, however, are coupled with a qualitative variable such as Wirth's recognition that urban populations are heterogeneous in occupation and culture, we have sufficient information for identifying urban areas.

This chapter deals with the sociological impact of urban qualities on individual behavior. The urbanization of society produces potentially serious consequences for the urban actor. We contend that the spatial structure of the city modifies potentially negative consequences and thus maintains the urban order. The city has been described as a "collection of strangers" (Lofland, 1973). Based on that description we show the difficulties that this situation has produced historically and the adaptations that have been made to this environment, including an intensive use of spatial cues to avoid strange or unpredictable situations.

THE URBAN EXPERIENCE AS
UNIQUE: THEORY AND RESEARCH

The city experience differs fundamentally from the rural. Because of the city's large size, density, and heterogeneity, social organization and interaction are more complex and problematic. The sheer immensity of the modern urban setting encourages unique experiences. Hauser vividly portrays the importance of variations in population density for the urban experience.

> Let us consider the differences in potential social interaction in a community with a fixed land area but varying population density. Let the land area be that which lies within a circle with a 10-mile radius, namely 314 square miles. In such an area the size of the population under different density conditions is shown below.

Population density (population/square mile)	Number of persons (circle of 10-mile radius)
1	314
50	15,700
8000	2,512,000
17,000	5,338,000
25,000	7,850,000

> The density of one person per square mile is not too far from the density of the United States when occupied by the Indians. The density of 50 is approximately that of the United States today, and also that of the world as a whole. The density of 8000 in round numbers, was that of central cities in metropolitan areas in 1950, the density figure of 17,000 was that of Chicago in 1950, and the 25,000 density figure that of New York.
>
> Thus, in aboriginal America the person moving about within a circle of 10-mile radius could potentially make only 313 different contacts. In contrast the density of the U.S. as a whole today would make possible well over 15,000 contacts in the same land area; the density of central cities in the U.S., in 1950, would permit over 2.5 million contacts; the density of Chicago over 5.3 million contacts; and the density of New York City about 7.9 million contacts. These differences in density and therefore in potential social interaction necessarily affect the nature of collective activity and social organization (1963:4).

The changes in social life Hauser alludes to include:

1. *Complex patterns of interaction.* The city dweller has the potential for initiating an enormous number of social ties (Milgram, 1972).

2. *Exposure to strangers.* Because the city contains a large number of people, the urbanite shares the community with a multitude of unknown others (Lofland, 1973).

3. *Exposure to unconventional norms.* The city is large and heterogeneous. As a result it is more likely than other community forms to foster unconventional behavior patterns (Fischer, 1975).

These likely conditions of urban life offer the potential for increased pathology. A variety of theoretical perspectives have addressed the negative consequences of urban life, particularly the social change theories of Tönnies and Durkheim and the urbanism theses of Wirth, Lofland, and Milgram.

In the mid-1880s, Tönnies used the terms *Gemeinschaft* and *Gesellschaft* to characterize the change from old to new community forms produced by urbanization. For Tönnies, *Gemeinschaft* represents a condition characteristic of rural community life. It involves a life pattern in which concerns for calculation, efficiency, and goal maximization are subordinated to a concern for the social relationships themselves. This setting creates a sense of belongingness. Community members refer to themselves as "we," and personal attachment to the social setting is characteristic. The residents share "a community of feeling . . . that results from likeness and from shared life experiences" (Miner, 1968:175). In the *Gesellschaft*, on the other hand, individual self-interests dominate over the community's interest. In this community form the individuals pursue their goals as efficiently as possible with little regard for community involvement. For these individuals, the task to be performed becomes most important, and personal relationships are of secondary interest. This type of community, Tönnies argues, is characteristic of the modern city.

Durkheim suggests much the same theme in *The Division of Labor in Society* (1947). In Durkheim's view urbanizing societies change from a social order based on *mechanical solidarity* to a social order based on *organic solidarity*. In the society characterized by mechanical solidarity, individuals are held together by similarities—that is, by the values and beliefs they share. The cohesion of the social fabric is maintained by this commonality. Strangers are an anomaly in such settings; a sense of belongingness is the rule. As societies modernize (that is, as they become more urban), the basis of social order shifts to organic solidarity. The division of labor, or the differentiation of tasks, makes order both possible and necessary in the modern city. Specialization creates dependencies. Skills and knowledge become so specialized that the urbanite depends on innumerable others just to get by. This dependency is at the heart of the urban order. Such a solidarity represents a delicate, almost precarious order. It is a community prone to anonymity and strangeness—as a result, disorder is always imminent.

Louis Wirth's classic article on the city, "Urbanism as a Way of Life" (1938), incorporates many of the earlier arguments of Tönnies and Durkheim. Wirth suggests that the demographic variables that encourage complex levels of interaction, exposure to strangers, and unconventional norms also create social isolation, alienation, and impersonalization. Wirth's view of the city as anonymous and impersonal appears as well in popular music and literature.

There are several reasons why certain population variables may lead to anonymity and impersonalism. First of all, it is apparent that no animal can process all of the stimuli present in a given context (see Chapter 2). All creatures live in a perceptual world that screens or filters the phenomena they experience. In the city the stimuli are overwhelming. Milgram (1972) claims that the urban experience produces *stimulus overload*. He suggests that the capacity of human beings to recognize a potentially large number of their fellow urban travelers is biophysically limited. The overloaded individual is unable to process all inputs from the environment either because there are too many inputs for the individual information receptor to cope with or because inputs come so fast that a given input cannot be processed before another is presented. When overload occurs, the individual can adapt by preventing certain stimuli from reaching the receptor. As a result, innumerable urban others are essentially ignored. The blank, nearly expressionless faces of urban pedestrians provide one example of this adaptive ability. For urbanites, most of the people sharing public space with them, whether it be in a subway, sidewalk or market place, are nonpersons—objects to be maneuvered around.

Urban demographics may contribute to the anonymous character of the city in another way. Following Durkheim's thesis, Wirth (1938) argues that high densities encourage social differentiation and, most significantly, increased division of labor. In a large, differentiated society where people do not know one another personally it is difficult to maintain a consensus of interests, values, and life styles (Fischer, 1976). As a result, social cohesion is precarious. Individual freedom expands but at the expense of communal order and intimate personal ties.

Wirth suggests that as places continue to grow and therefore increase in density and heterogeneity, the setting becomes more anonymous. Thus the more urban the community, the greater the difference between that community's experiential order and the order of past communities.

What the theories of Durkheim, Tönnies, and Wirth describe, however, is not some actual condition of cities but a potential condition. The city is not necessarily anonymous or impersonal. Yet because it is a community whose members know little personally about the vast number of others sharing its space, anonymity and impersonality are more likely in cities than in other community forms.

A number of social scientists (Fischer, 1976; Gans, 1962; Lewis, 1952; Reiss, 1955) have criticized the conception of the city as an anonymous setting. In particular, these critics dispute Wirth's hypothesis that the city's size, density, and heterogeneity weaken interpersonal ties and diminish close, personal interactions. After all, they argue, Wirth himself describes the city as a collection of social worlds. In these "worlds" one can find intimate social ties based on neighborhood, kinship, status, life style, and ethnic attributes.

Claude Fischer's (1971, 1973, 1975, 1976) empirical and theoretical work on the urban experience provides a telling criticism of Wirth's original thesis. Wirth lists alienation and social isolation as major effects of dense, heterogeneous communities. Yet Fischer's research suggests that communities with different demographic properties have much the same social-psychological characteristics. When the social and cultural backgrounds of the urbanite are taken into account, big-city dwellers are no more alienated or socially isolated than people in much smaller communities. It is certainly refreshing to find that urbanites are not the dispossessed persons they are often thought to be. At the same time, it is highly doubtful that the urban and rural experiences are comparable or that the urbanite is merely a ruralite in a business suit. Urban residents do differ from their rural counterparts in ways that cannot be accounted for by mere differences in their cultural backgrounds. The urbanite is more likely to behave in an unconventional manner (Fischer, 1975). Cities are the sources of invention; they are also the seedbeds for behaviors and attitudes usually defined as deviant. Criminal activity, political dissent, irreligiosity, and antiestablishment beliefs and behaviors in general are more characteristic of the urbanite than the ruralite.

Fischer emphasizes the point that size does not destroy cultural and social ties. Alienation and isolation are not direct products of urbanization. At the same time, the demographic qualities of the city do permit and even foster unconventionality. Indeed, size actually creates and strengthens social ties, and it does this by multiplying diverse social worlds or subcultures. Large size promotes a variety of social worlds (and thus unconventional behavior and attitudes) in the following ways:

1. Large communities attract migrants from a wider area than smaller communities. The wider the territory migrants come from, the greater the probability that these migrants have different cultural backgrounds.

2. Large size produces greater structural differentiation in the form of occupational specialization and the growth of highly specialized institutions and special interest groups. As Fischer indicates, each of these special structural units has its own unique set of life experiences and interests.

3. Increased size, however, does more than merely create a variety of social worlds. It intensifies subcultures. It provides the *critical mass* that permits "what could otherwise be a small group of individuals to become a vital, active subculture" (Fischer, 1976:37). For a culture to survive, certain minimum numbers are necessary to support the institutions that give the group its identity. In the case of an ethnic enclave the minimum might simply mean enough people to keep alive the specialty stores, churches, newspapers, and clubs that service the group.

Important as it is, this critical mass thesis fails to acknowledge the significance of spatial structures in fostering urban diversity. The theory suggests that size makes urban life different. Ultimately, of course, such a position is indisputable, but unconventional worlds cannot emerge and flourish in the city without spatial structures. Segregation makes unconventional behavior possible by removing the smaller community from the social controls and expectations of the larger, more traditional society.

At the same time, the spatial anatomy of the city prevents the social isolation and anonymity Wirth predicts. His picture of the urbanite as socially isolated and culturally alienated is exaggerated. Essentially a great portion of our urban existence is spent in close, personal interactions. All but the most socially detached of us are surrounded by a group of personally known others with whom we interact regularly. Indeed, Reiss (1959) finds that these primary group contacts are far more extensive for the urbanite than the rural villager. The urbanite is not alone. Yet he is a stranger in a land of strangers, for every time he leaves his home territory he must travel through space occupied by perfect strangers. This lack of personal knowledge concerning those in the immediate area is made all the more problematic by the unconventional and therefore unpredictable behavior characteristic of city life.

In this sense, then, the city can be described as a collection of *Gemeinschaft*-like areas that are spatially distinct from one another and together form a loosely knit *Gesellschaft* (Berger, 1978). Tightly segregated local communities lessen the likelihood of social isolation and alienation. At the same time, they promote cultural isolation and nontraditional behavior. Thus, the urbanite who participates extensively in nonlocal social networks is likely to engage in *Gesellschaft*-like relationships (Berger, 1978). This will be especially true in the city's public spaces (its parks, shopping districts, etc.), to which all have legal access. It is in such spaces that we can speak of the city as a world of strangers.

Although urbanites are no more isolated or alienated than people in other settings, the unique demographic qualities of the city place them in a somewhat perilous social position. Necessarily, they can be morally and socially involved only with a small fragment of the community. The ultimate adaptation to the stimulus overload of the modern city is for the urbanite to totally disregard the needs and interests of those irrelevant to the satisfaction of their personal needs (Milgram, 1972). Much like the caged rats of the Calhoun experiments, the city dweller is susceptible to a behavioral sink phenomenon. Such extreme forms of adaptation are rare, but the city appears to be precariously balanced between order and anomie, or normlessness. Wirth's article alerts us to the potential danger of declining social and moral order.

THE STRANGER IN NONURBAN SETTINGS

Throughout most history and prehistory, humans have lived in rural communities where *Gemeinschaft* and mechanical solidarity prevailed. For contemporary humans there is nothing unusual in living out a portion of our lives amid people whom we do not know personally. But for most humans who at one time or another have occupied the earth, such a setting would seem peculiar. Generally *Homo sapiens* has inhabited only small, isolated social worlds in which personal acquaintance is the rule rather than the exception. In these settings, society and community were organized around kinship rules that tightly defined one's relationship to others. Kinship organization was synonymous with social organization.

As Lyn Lofland suggests, "the arrival of a stranger or a group of strangers in these little enclaves of personal knowing was (and in some parts of the world still is) a truly remarkable and momentous event" (1973:4). Of course, the trauma of such an event was greater for some groups than for others. The degree of isolation from other cultures had great bearing on the nature of the reaction to strangers. In all cases, however, such moments were far from routine.

It is instructive to note that some primitive peoples refer only to themselves as human. People occupying adjacent territories are given names that imply less than human qualities. Such a classification scheme suggests just how unusual the experience of sharing a common space with strangers actually was for these people.

For some cultures, strangers posed such a problem that the only logical solution was to kill them. Since they knew nothing of these humanlike intruders, they were unable to anticipate how they would behave, creating a potentially disruptive situation. This kind of situation appeared commonly in the science fiction movies made in the United States during the 1950s and 1960s. Faced with an invasion of alien creatures, people sought either to repel or to destroy the intruders. In the real world, the Tiwi of Australia reacted in similar fashion:

> Tiwi treatment of outsiders prior to 1900 had been to rob them, spear them, kill them. . . . Their own traditions and what little written history there is of "Malay" penetration into the Arafura Sea both tell the same story. Outsiders who landed on the island were massacred or vigorously resisted. Whether they were classified as Malai-ui ("Malays") or Wona-rui (Australian aborigines from the mainland) they were not Tiwi and hence not real people, or at least not human enough to share the islands with the chosen people who owned them (Hart and Pilling, 1966:99, 9-10).

Not all groups, of course, react so violently to strangers. Less isolated people, with less ethnocentric views of other cultures and societies, nevertheless treated the arrival of strangers with great caution and even fear.

> The accounts of early European voyagers to out-of-the-way parts of the globe tell again and again of their being received by the native populations with fear, astonishment, apprehension, ceremonies of propitiation, protective rituals, fainting, and so forth—the exact emotion and behavior of the hosts depending on just what they conceived these strange white objects to be (Lofland, 1973:5).

In some cases these people were viewed as the ghosts of ancestors; in others they were seen as gods of either benign or malevolent nature.

Even when the humanity of the stranger was not doubted, the response was cautious. In many groups with strong kinship systems, before nonnatives could be dealt with they had to be placed in the kinship network and their relationship to each man and woman in the village had to be specified. Although such devotion to establishing kin ties is rare in the contemporary world, the principle behind it is universal. To carry out our daily activity in an orderly fashion, actors must be able to anticipate two related sets of phenomena: They must know what others expect of them in a given situation, and they must know what to expect of others in that setting (Lofland, 1973). If you do not personally know the other, this situation becomes problematic. You must rely on established rules for coding and defining the unknown person under such conditions.

As Erving Goffman (1959) suggests, we are prisoners of our language. While language frees humans from the bondage of a simple stimulus-response mode of behavior, at the same time it forces us to organize stimuli into a set matrix of conceptual categories. In order to act, individuals must first define not only the situation they find themselves in but also the other actors in that situation. Although language offers freedom because it necessitates self-awareness in individuals, this self-awareness also makes them conscious of their separation from the environment. This separation, in turn, makes classification necessary.

The individual with language, therefore, can "know" another in two ways—*personal knowledge* or *categoric knowledge* (Lofland, 1973). Categoric knowing refers to understanding another through information about the individual's roles and statuses. This type of knowledge is generally acquired through visual and verbal cues. It is indirect and relies heavily on cultural stereotypes. Personal knowing, on the other hand, is based on information, no matter how slight, about the individual's history as well as statuses and roles. The importance of this distinction is that strangers cannot remain completely unknown for long. Every culture provides categories, or stereotypes, by which they will eventually become "known."

In *Gemeinschaft* or rural cultures, the community remains intact primarily because of the individual's sense of belonging to a personal community that extends through time and space. As Lofland suggests:

> For these people continued coexistence without personal knowing was impossible. In order to relate to strangers beyond the initial seconds of the encounter, the people living in small personal worlds had to transform them into the only kind of human objects they were familiar with—personally known others (1973:21).

With the city this situation ended. Personal knowing became less and less possible as community sizes grew and as communities began to fill with peoples of diverse culture and occupational pursuit. As a result categoric knowing became necessary.

THE STRANGER IN
PREINDUSTRIAL AND INDUSTRIAL CITIES

We must ask as Wirth, Milgram, and Lofland have: How can it be? How can urban life continue in an orderly fashion if its public space is composed of unknown others? We have just seen that strangeness is intolerable. Before we can act, we must know what we are dealing with. In everyday life we do this by applying culturally acquired categories to our world. What categories does our urban culture provide for us?

For Lofland the answer is at once obvious and profound: "City life was made possible by an 'ordering' of the urban populace in terms of *appearance* and *spatial location* such that those within the city could know a great deal by simply looking" (1973:22). Knowledge of others, then, became primarily visual, and the major categories of knowing were physical appearance and location. One could anticipate the status and roles of others merely by the way they dressed and acted and by where they lived.

Spatial cues provide one means for categorical knowing (Hall, 1966). They supply knowledge of the stranger that can be used to anticipate his or her behavior. Space communicates information that the urbanite uses in everyday encounters with innumerable unknown others. Not only does the spatial order of the city communicate, or provide cues, but also it modifies the stimulus input to the urban dweller (Milgram, 1972). In this sense, anonymity is not a necessary outcome of the demographic characteristics of the city. Because the city is highly segregated—a mosaic of social worlds—it actually simplifies the task of being urban by cutting off many stimuli before they can enter the individual's perceptual field. As we suggested in Chapter 2, the urban dweller can, on a daily basis, avoid undesirable others by choosing the proper travel pattern. We can miss pockets of poverty and districts of crime merely by anticipating the sociophysical layout of the city. To some extent we are all aware that where people reside in physical space adequately indicates where they reside in social space.

Space, then, is especially important in understanding the urban experience. In this heavily populated world of strangers, we can move through urban spaces relatively freely because the city is spatially structured. By merely "knowing" a city's spatial layout, we can know or at least anticipate the expectations and behaviors of countless strangers. Without such apparent order in space, everyday existence in the city would itself be less orderly. We would be bombarded by so many stimuli as to be rendered incapable of action. In order to understand the "urban experience," then, it is necessary to understand urban spatial arrangement.

In the preindustrial city, however, space played less of a role in urban life than it does in the industrial city. In the preindustrial city, order by appearance predominated over the spatial order (Lofland, 1973). As Sjoberg (1960) suggests, the preindustrial setting combined work and residence at a single site.

Because of the limited specialization of tasks and the prominent economic role of the family, artisans and merchants plied their trade at home.

The heterogeneity of spatial use in the preindustrial city went far beyond the melding together of public and private space. Indeed, the modern urbanite would be overwhelmed by the diversity of public space use. As Lofland explains:

> Suddenly you feel tired. The multiplicity of sights and sounds, the pushing and shoving and shouting of the crowd, the smells—particularly the smells—all of this begins to seem "too much." Too many people are crowded into too small a space; too many odors, most of them offensive; too many sights, most of them vile. You can't get away from the beggars and vendors. They accost you wherever you go. You can't escape the crippled limbs, the scarred faces, the running sores. Your person seems never safe from the constant assaults of the pickpockets. Everything seems jumbled together. Rich and poor, health and disease, young and old, house and business, public and private. All seems disorder. All seems chaos. Dizzy, frightened, confused, you step back into the time machine and are returned again to what now seems the orderliness and cleanliness of your own crowded, car-congested, smog-ridden, crime-obsessed modern city (1973:33).

This composite description sounds much like the historian's picture of urban life in the Greek agora and the Roman forum. In such centers you could find a temple or shrine in the midst of workshops and open market stalls. Here the peasant coaxing unwilling livestock to the market might jostle a philosopher pausing to take note of an artisan at work. Students attentively listening to their teacher might find their thoughts momentarily interrupted by the cries of the lame and disfigured beggars sitting close by (Mumford, 1961).

With this mixed character of preindustrial urban space, the city dweller had to rely more on how others looked rather than where they were located. Appearance in the preindustrial order was an extremely important indicator of social status. It was so important, in fact, that in many societies dress codes were legally enforced by *sumptuary laws,* which dictated the proper attire for each social station. While in contemporary societies the norms surrounding dress have the status of folkways (minimally sanctioned norms), in preindustrial societies these norms often had the status of mores (or more formally sanctioned norms).

In such societies the style and quality of clothing were among the most obvious symbols of social class (Barber, 1957:146). Clothing was a means of conspicuously indicating one's consumption habits (Veblen, 1899). In Rome, the citizen class indicated its position by wearing the white toga. In China, the upper-class mandarin symbolized his social standing by ankle-length silk gowns and long fingernails. In India, castes were distinguished by the type of fibre used in their clothing; the sacred thread of the Vishnaya was wool, and for the Brahmin it was cotton. In Inca civilization, the nobility could wear the finer alpaca vicuña wools, but commoners were permitted to wear only the coarser wool of the llama. Additionally, only the nobility could wear gems and feathers, and rings and armbands of precious metals. Even in Elizabethan England commoners were forbidden by law from wearing luxurious fabric such as fur pieces and velvet.

While class differences were signaled by clothing, moral differences were symbolized by body markings (Lofland, 1973). In colonial America the wrongdoer's offense was indicated by a letter placed conspicuously on the body or the clothing of the offender. (Recall Hester's punishment in *The Scarlet Letter*.) In many Middle Eastern and African societies the criminal was either branded or mutilated. A thief might be marked by a missing finger or hand.

Order by appearance, however, represents a very fragile structuring of perceptions. Things are not always what they appear to be. We learn this as a child in the old fairy tales that warn us to be wary of wolves in sheep's clothing. The delicate nature of outward appearances is further indicated by the need in many societies to legally enforce dress codes.

Order by appearance has essentially changed with industrialization (Lofland, 1973). It is still present in the industrial city, but it is certainly more subtle. In contemporary American society Barber suggests:

> The most noticeable features of a "fashion," its hem length, silhouette and color, are the same for all social classes. In this way a certain egalitarianism is satisfied. But the subtle differences are there too . . . The differences are those of material, of workmanship, and of timing (1957:150).

Several features of industrialization led to the demise of the appearential order. One obvious factor was the mass production of clothing. With mechanization good-quality clothing could be produced quickly. Expensive hand-tailored items could be copied and reproduced in large supply, making them available to all classes, not just the rich.

More important, industrialization brings increasing social mobility and the growth of the middle classes. As Lenski (1966) notes, industrial society with its highly specialized labor force distributes wealth more evenly than agricultural societies do. This expanding middle class means simply that a larger proportion of the population than ever before can afford to spend money on the symbols of leisure. Thus, appearance means less in the industrial city.

At the same time, space means more in the industrial city. In the preindustrial city residences were distributed in a cellular fashion, each neighborhood representing a self-contained district with its own shops, industries, schools, and churches. Within these neighborhoods classes were not clearly segregated. Employer and employee lived either together or side by side. Because these were essentially pedestrian cities, in which long treks were quite difficult, spatial segregation was more subtle. The cellular pattern, however, began to fade with industrialization. Industrialization brought greater mobility in the form of more efficient transportation both within and between cities. With this enhanced mobility, spatial separation between the classes became more feasible.

The primary factors in the spatial reorganization of the city were the steam railroad and the electric street car. During the nineteenth century these vehicles essentially reordered the distribution of population and activity in space.

Since that time the city has become a mosaic of social worlds in which people are segregated on the basis of life-cycle characteristics, socioeconomic status, and ethnicity. This distinctive structuring of people with territories is of great importance to the order of the modern city. Space organizes in the modern city to a far greater extent than it did in previous times. It eases the potential strain of the large, dense, and heterogeneous world in which modern urbanites live. Thus, knowledge of the spatial order of the contemporary city provides the social scientist with an understanding of the urban experience itself and how that experience is made possible.

While spatial structure organizes the diverse activities and populations of the modern city, not everyone benefits equally from this imposed order. It is obvious that these segregation patterns maintain the status quo. The urban space reflects and promotes injustices inherent in a society (see Chapters 9 and 11). Perhaps space means more in the industrial city, but in addition to creating order, it also feeds our stereotypes and misunderstandings of others. Intolerance and ethnocentrism are fostered by allowing the average urbanite to avoid the social and cultural diversity characteristic of the city.

SUMMARY

The appearance of the city changed the very nature of human experience. Because of its size, density, and heterogeneity, social interaction in the city is more complex, unconventional norms are more likely, and exposure to countless unknown others increases. Many theorists have viewed these changes in the urban experience as potentially pathological. Little evidence, however, can be given to support Wirth's portrait of the urbanite as socially detached and alienated. Indeed, large population size may actually stimulate the development of small personal worlds.

As a world of strangers, the city encourages unique means of anticipating the behaviors of countless unknown urban others. Strangers' behavior is made predictable by an ordering of population according to appearance and spatial location. In the preindustrial city spatial usage was more heterogeneous—public and private spaces were not clearly segregated. Although these places were ordered spatially, the mixed character of preindustrial urban space meant that the urbanite had to rely primarily on the appearance of others rather than where they were located. Sumptuary laws enforced order by appearance.

Industrialization permitted the mass production of clothing and the growth of the middle classes, both of which led to the demise of appearential ordering. With the growth of more efficient transportation, on the other hand, spatial segregation increased. The spatial structuring of the industrial city gave order to an otherwise disorderly and anonymous situation by creating minia- ture subcultural spheres in which a great part of the urbanite's day could be played out. Such an ordering allowed the city dweller to avoid unpredictable and therefore dangerous situations.

Chapter 4

Historical Perspectives on the Spatial Structure of Urban Society

INTRODUCTION

The arguments of Sjoberg, Wirth, and Lofland, as discussed in Chapter 3, suggest that we can generalize about two basic types of cities: the preindustrial and the industrial. In Lewis Mumford's (1961) terminology, the city ceased to be a relatively small, compact, and exclusive *container* of civilization at the time of the Industrial Revolution. Instead, it became a dispersed and socially inclusive *magnet* drawing great waves of population to itself. Since the Industrial Revolution, the Western city has changed continuously and ever faster. Much of this change results from technological advances with a variety of economic and social repercussions. The industrial urban container bears the distinct imprint of these sociocultural changes.

This chapter examines the interrelationship between the social structure and the physical form of cities. It provides historical evidence that supports a concept shared by most archeologists: The physical form of the city symbolizes and makes concrete the preoccupations of its culture.

There are several reasons why the study of the historic city is indispensable for a study of the contemporary city. The most obvious is that the maturity of many modern world cities makes it impossible to fully understand their physical and institutional structure in contemporary terms. Most cities contain "fossil" features. In the United States, Boston is perhaps the best known example of an urban fabric formed around such relic features as the Common, the colonial graveyards, and Beacon Hill.

Also, the study of social structures in urban space is nonexperimental. To some extent urban history provides the researcher with the necessary means to perform mental experiments in which historical comparisons take the place of the experimental controls used by other sciences.

Finally, urban history provides us with an array of information that is conceptually simpler and more manageable than information from the modern city. With such data we can discern processes more clearly than we can in contemporary urban places.

THE PREINDUSTRIAL CITY

The Urban Revolution and the First Cities

Describing urban origins precisely requires two basic types of knowledge: a suitable definition of the city, and some understanding of city-hinterland relationships. Traditionally, urban archeologists have distinguished the city from the noncity with criteria similar to Sjoberg's, which were discussed in Chapter 3. Sjoberg's definition is economic and cultural, and its major condition is the existence of a large, permanent settlement with nonagricultural specialists and a literate elite. Urban society requires an agricultural surplus sufficient to support social classes that are not directly engaged in producing food.

There are two conflicting theories of how this surplus developed and cities began (Geruson and McGrath, 1977). The first and most widely accepted account rests on the notion of agricultural primacy and urban piracy. The historical and prehistorical evidence suggests very clearly that the economy of the preindustrial town, whether ancient or medieval, was parasitic. Without the established market mechanisms of the commercial or industrial city, the town had to rely exclusively on its hinterland to survive and grow. Usually a surplus of produce was exacted from agriculturalists through coercion, in the form of taxes or tribute to a ruler. The town-country dichotomy represents one of the oldest and most prolonged class struggles in human history, as Marx recognizes in *The Communist Manifesto* (1848). Inequality is at the heart of the urbanization process. The early town thrived because of these inequities. It grew because it subjugated the countryside. Fernand Braudel, an historian, writes, "The town only exists as a town in relation to a form of life lower than its own. There are no exceptions to this rule . . . It has to dominate an empire, however tiny, in order to exist" (1973:374). It is not surprising then that until the Renaissance, cities were walled, defensive structures—symbols of this political and economic struggle against the outside world.

This generally accepted view of early city-hinterland relationships has some opponents. Its most vocal critic is Jane Jacobs (1969), who argues that the early town did not depend totally on rural areas for its survival. Instead, it actually stimulated the development of agriculture. Cities provided the technological innovation and goods and services that agriculturalists used to improve their own standards of living. Although this argument certainly holds true for industrial societies, very few urban historians find evidence for it in more ancient towns. The production of marketable goods and the exchange of such products was sufficiently underdeveloped to make the city-hinterland relationship one-sided. Jacobs's observation that the most thoroughly urbanized countries are precisely those that produce food most abundantly is probably true only for contemporary societies.

Nevertheless, the assertion that early cities stood in a parasitic relationship to their hinterlands is true only in an economic and political sense. In more general cultural terms, the earliest cities were sources of intense innovation. Essentially all cultural, religious, political, artistic, and social institutions of the ancient civilizations were urban.

> It is not now, and never has been, in the rugged and invigorating atmospheres of the woods, the seashores, or the mountains that the greatest achievements of our species have been made. Rather, they have been and are being made in Tyre, Carthage, Constantinople, Cairo, Jerusalem, Seville, Damascus, Florence, Calcutta, Peking, Tokyo, Rome, London, Paris and New York (Buettner-Janusch, 1973:511).

These cultural achievements were possible only when a critical mass of nonproducers could be supported by the excess production of nonurban areas. Authors with a cultural rather than an economic orientation have therefore emphasized the productive rather than the parasitic role of the early city. Lewis Mumford, for example, speaks of the ancient city as "a permanent container and an institutional structure, capable of storing and handing on the contents of civilization" (1961:93).

The Urban Revolution in Mesopotamia

The earliest known cities that satisfy Sjoberg's definition appeared as a result of several agricultural, technological, and political developments in Sumeria, an area in southern Mesopotamia at the mouths of the Tigris and Euphrates rivers in modern Iraq. The urban revolution here began with the Bronze Age, around 3500 B.C.

These early cities exercised military and religious influence over a population who lived under primitive (Neolithic) agricultural technologies and social systems and whose lives were scarcely changed by the urban revolution. In the very earliest Sumerian centers trade was not very important. Basic commodities were taken by force, and the military ranged over large areas in order to insure the stability of urban resources. Urban nonagricultural classes were supported by a surplus of nonperishable grain crops (emmer and barley) achieved through large-scale irrigation projects made possible by a highly organized, city-centered political system deeply rooted in religious belief. The traditional tribal or clan societies of the surrounding Neolithic villages were incapable of organizing communal irrigation or forcing surplus production.

The emergence of several new social classes accompanied the growth of the highly centralized political system in the city. At the top, the warrior kings controlled a military establishment and an administrative class of scribes, priests, astronomers, overseers, and accountants. Lower down the social scale

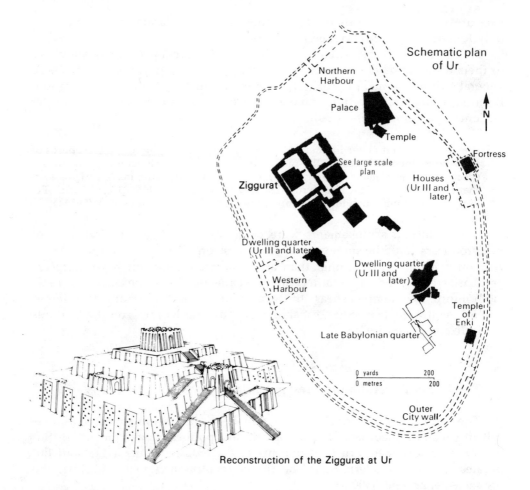

Reconstruction of the Ziggurat at Ur

Figure 4.1 *Schematic Plan of Ur*   The walled city stood on the mound formed by the ruins of older buildings. The temenos was the religious citadel and included the ziggurat, temples, and the palace. It was walled off from the rest of the city and it contained densely populated residential quarters. (*Source:* From J. Hawkes, *Atlas of Ancient Archaeology*, 1974. Reprinted by permission of Rainbird Publishing/Robert Harding Associates, London.)

were a variety of artisans and laborers and a class of slaves. Organizational change was supported and made possible by rapid cultural innovation. Written language, arithmetic, and the calendar were invented during this period, probably to meet the dual needs of accurate record keeping required for the new taxation activities and for the astronomy associated with religious practices.

The physical structure of the early Sumerian cities is quite well known. Ur, famous as the birthplace of the Biblical patriarch Abraham, was typical (see Figure 4.1). The city, located on the Euphrates River, was small, probably never ex-

Figure 4.2   *Erbil in Northeastern Iraq*   This site has been inhabited for nearly 6000 years. The closely knit grain epitomizes organic growth. The residential area of Ur would have looked very much the same from the air. (*Source:* Morris, 1972:9; reprinted by permission of Aerofilms, Ltd., England.)

ceeding 25,000 inhabitants, but it was densely populated. It was oval in form, about three-quarters mile by one-half mile, surrounded by a defensive wall indicating its warlike status. Figure 4.2 shows a modern example of how Ur might have looked from the air. Typical of many ancient towns, Ur was dominated by a religious fortress containing a step pyramid, or ziggurat, and prominent grain storage facilities. This fortress was surrounded by two-story housing with quite sophisticated amenities such as plaster walls and airy central paved courts (Morris, 1972:8). The outer city contained the hovels of the poorer classes. This social gradient from the elite in the city center to the poor at or beyond the limits of the city wall is one common to most preindustrial cities.

The relatively small size of the Sumerian city and the compact intensity of its political, cultural, religious, and economic activity led Lewis Mumford (1961) to speak of this initial phase of urbanism as an *implosion,* or spatial concentration, to be contrasted with the urban *explosion,* or dispersal, of the nineteenth and twentieth centuries. The "imploded" city with its characteristic high population densities and mainly pedestrian movement, usually grew without plan. Unlike the modern city, which represents a center of communications and production in a nationwide and even worldwide network of communities, these ancient cities were basically parochial and inward looking. They were preoccupied with their own theology and customs. The city was aloof from the outside world.

Besides the Mesopotamian area there were three other "primary hearths" of urbanism in the Old World (see Figure 4.3). They were the Egyptian culture (the Nile Valley, around 3000 B.C.), the Harappan culture (the Indus Valley, around 2200 B.C.) and the Shang civilization (the Hwang Ho Basin, around 2100 B.C.). The socioeconomic mechanisms in the evolution of urban culture in these

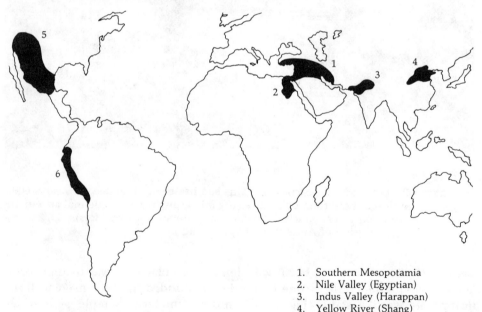

1. Southern Mesopotamia
2. Nile Valley (Egyptian)
3. Indus Valley (Harappan)
4. Yellow River (Shang)
5. Mesoamerica (Aztec and Maya)
6. Peru (Inca)

Figure 4.3   *The Locations of the First Civilizations*

areas were similar to those in Mesopotamia. In each case a highly autocratic military elite developed, along with an associated literate and priestly caste. In each, Neolithic farming societies were transformed by the collection of a non-perishable grain crop produced on fertile and irrigated land in the valleys of major rivers. The details of urban form, however, differed by area. For example, the cities of the Harappan culture had strict grid-plan street patterns, while those of Egypt were dispersed over larger areas and were unwalled.

The Greek Polis

The period between the fifth and the third centuries B.C. in Greece is often held up as a high point in urban history. During the Golden Age, between the defeat of the Persians in 479 B.C. and the Macedonian conquest in 338 B.C., the key political and cultural institution was the *polis*, the independent city-state. The populations of these few dozen states were small, usually in the tens of thousands. Athens, by far the largest of the city-states, did not exceed 100,000 people in the fifth century B.C., well over three-quarters of whom were nonciti-zens—females, slaves, or foreigners (Mumford, 1961:130).

In the Golden Age, Greece exhibited a peculiar blend of unity and disuni-ty. Politically, until Athens established its dominance, each city-state was com-pletely autonomous. As a result, Greek-speaking peoples were constantly fight-ing, and even in the Persian wars the armies of Xerxes that fought against the confederacy led by Athens and Sparta contained Greek contingents. This char-acteristic divisiveness probably resulted from extremely parochial religious in-stitutions (the gods worshipped varied from one city-state to another) and the marginal level of agricultural production. The very limited potential of Greek farmlands forced cities to turn to plunder and piracy in order to support their populations. Although these militaristic attempts to solve the resource problem were eventually supplemented by an extensive trade network headquartered in Athens, the growing population could not be supported in the existing cities. As a consequence, the period 700–500 B.C. witnessed extensive colonial foundations in Italy, Sicily, Ionia (the western part of modern Turkey), and even southern France. These colonial towns, while retaining all the elements of civic symbolism characteristic of the older centers, had a less haphazard spa-tial structure. Their internal street pattern was based on the grid plan, which was rigidly adhered to no matter what the local topography was like.

Despite the growth of a colonial empire and the expansion of its interna-tional commercial activity, most Greek citizens owned and operated farms (Thomlinson, 1969). As Braudel (1976) points out, this semipeasant status typi-fies many preindustrial towns. The underdeveloped agricultural technology severely limited the number of truly urban occupations. Liberal estimates sug-gest that during this period it took the efforts of about twenty farmers to meet the needs of one average urbanite (Hawley, 1971:36).

The principles governing the organization of space in the polis differed fundamentally from those at work in the modern city. Religious rather than secular forces profoundly influenced all aspects of Greek urban culture. The entire social structure, and in particular the special status of citizen, can be understood only in religious terms.

Greek religion was founded on strict observance of rites honoring ancestors and local gods. This fact explains the attachment of citizens to particular locations and the extreme severity of exile, a common form of punishment. The Greek citizen was enmeshed in a local hierarchy of religious obligations, which began with the domestic household gods, including the ancestors, and ended with the gods of the city, who usually represented versions of the Olympic deities. All social interactions, particularly those of marriage and democratic participation, occurred in the context of religiously defined groups. Slaves, foreigners, and women had either limited rights or no rights at all within this highly particularistic and localized theology. Fustel de Coulanges writes:

> A comparison of beliefs and laws shows that a primitive religion constituted the Greek and Roman family, established marriage and paternal authority, fixed the order of relationships, and consecrated the right of property, and the right of inheritance. This same religion, after having enlarged and extended the family, formed a still larger association, the city, and reigned in that as it had reigned in the family. From it came all the institutions, as well as all the private law, of the ancients (1956:13).

We moderns can scarcely understand how much religious rites pervaded urban life. Even the supposedly rational, urbane Athenians condemned Socrates for subverting these beliefs.

However, another characteristic of the polis—its participatory democracy—is greatly valued today. It is important to note that only the citizen—the individual with legal rights and responsibilities to the polis—could participate in the political system. The citizens, in turn, represented only a fraction of the urban population. Nevertheless, this minority of free, franchised males participated in a cultural setting oriented toward public rather than private pursuits, which was reflected in the physical form of the Greek city.

Civil life focused on the public space formed by a variety of structures. Religious activity was represented in complexes of temples and shrines—the Acropolis, in the case of Athens. Stadiums and theatres were typically found on the outskirts of cities, sometimes beyond the defensive wall. The life of the citizenry, however, revolved around the *agora*, a combined market and meeting place. Wycherly says of the agora:

> The word agora is quite untranslatable, since it stands for something as peculiarly Hellenic as polis . . . One may doubt whether the public places of any other city have ever seen such an intense and sustained concentration of varied activities. The agora was in fact no mere public place, but the central zone of the city—its living heart. In spite of an inevitable diffusion and specialization of functions, it retained a real share of its own miscellaneous functions. It remained essentially a single whole, or at least strongly resisted division. It was the constant resort of all citizens,

and it did not spring to life on occasions but was the daily scene of social life, business and politics (cited in Morris, 1972:25).

Greek public space was grand, but the residential areas themselves were deplorable. "The Athenians lived under the Acropolis, as many generations lived under the spires of Oxford, in squalid magnificence" (Zimmern, 1931:300). Private space contrasted vividly with the institutional space on which citizens lavished their invention and funds. Private residences, where most women and many slaves spent their time, were extremely squalid. Constructed largely of mud along very narrow alleys, with no sanitation or water arrangements, the dwellings of the Greek citizenry differed markedly from the comfort of the Roman elite classes. Mumford writes:

> The highest culture of the ancient world, that of Athens, reached its apex in what was, from the standpoint of town planning and hygiene, a deplorably backward municipality. The varied sanitary facilities that Ur and Harappa had boasted two thousand years before hardly existed even in vestigial form in fifth-century Athens. The streets of any Greek city, down to Hellenistic times, were little more than alleys, and many of these alleys were only passageways, a few feet wide. Refuse and ordure accumulated at the city's outskirts, inviting disease and multiplying the victims of the plague (1961:130).

For the most part, city growth was organic and haphazard. Because religion exerted such great control over public behavior, social segregation was not crucial to the urban order in Greece (recall Lofland's explanation of the importance of spatial order in Chapter 3). As a result, residential space was less highly organized than in the modern city.

The Hellenic city-states of the period immediately before the Macedonian conquest established norms and ideals of urban structure and organization that were to dominate the Mediterranean world until the collapse of ancient civilization. They still exert substantial influence today. The ideals of the Greek city were later diffused widely by the Romans. These norms included physical ideals of architecture and grid-plan layouts, religious ideals of a stable and sanctified pattern of land use, and democratic political ideals. Another norm, which declined during the Roman period, was the rigid and highly exclusive definition of citizenship.

The Roman City

By the time of the Macedonian conquest and the decline of Athens (about 340 B.C.), weaknesses in the political and economic organization of the Greek polis were apparent. One problem was that participation in urban government was forbidden to the merchant class. Many writers have argued that this constituted a fatal economic weakness: Only encouragement of long-range and reciprocal commercial exchange could have prevented the chronic economic crises and the political parochialism of the city-states in their decline. These problems of political and economic integration of vast areas of space were solved, at least for several centuries, by the Romans.

Some writers have claimed that in the Roman, or Hellenistic, period urbanism advanced little. The distinctive contributions of the Romans, they claimed, were essentially organizational and engineering embellishments on the Hellenic ideal. Mumford writes scathingly, "The special Roman contribution to planning was chiefly a matter of sturdy engineering and flatulent exhibitionism" (1961:214). Indeed, the extreme poverty of the ancient world in technological inventiveness is one reason for the lack of any truly radical advances in urban living. However, a balanced view must take into account the phenomenal organizational and civil-engineering capacity that enabled the Romans to establish the Hellenistic city throughout most of the known world.

The Romans succeeded where the Greeks had failed in establishing firm commercial ties between cities and hinterlands over great distances. For example, imperial Rome itself was fed largely by North African grain. At the same time, the merchant class achieved unprecedented respectability and political power. Although extensive agricultural landholdings were the primary source of wealth, a class of wealthy enterpreneurs wielded substantial political power.

The growing influence of the merchants was made possible by another significant sociological difference from the Greek polis. In the period of Rome's expansion, citizenship was treated as an honor to be bestowed on successively larger groups until finally in 212 A.D. the emperor Caracalla gave citizenship to all freeborn males in the empire. Citizenship resulted from urban residence rather than membership in an exclusive religious group. Thus, legal participation in urban life was far more open. Under the impetus of the expanding empire and the wider definition of citizenship, Rome and other major cities grew to unprecedented size.

In part this extensive urban growth was made possible by the engineering achievements of Rome. Roman cities far excelled their Greek predecessors in municipal and domestic engineering. Sewage disposal and water supply, baths, heating systems, and domestic comfort, at least for the wealthy, were the best in history to date. Equally impressive were the excellent and extensive road systems, which made large-scale overland commercial exchange and military government feasible for the first time.

The physical form of the typical Roman city adhered very closely to the ideals of the Greek colonial town rather than the polis. (Even temporary military camps were laid out on this general scheme.) A square or rectangular area bounded by a defensive wall contained a rectangular grid plan of streets including two major intersecting thoroughfares called the *via principalis*, which ran east to west, and the *cardo*, which ran north to south. At the center was the forum, the political and market center analogous to the Greek agora. Other prominent features in the landscape were temples and theatres, or arenas, which were frequently located beyond the wall because of the normally peaceful conditions.

The social space of Rome itself was unsegregated, partly because of its hap-hazard growth over an extended period. Two distinct types of residence were often mixed together in the urban space. Most common people, or plebians, lived in multistory tenement blocks (*insulae*). The wealthy elite lived in exten-sive single-story dwellings (*domus*) focused inward upon an open courtyard. Perhaps this inward-looking character of the *domus* (with its blank outer walls) provided sufficient social distance between its inhabitants and the squalor sur-rounding them.

A number of authors, including Lewis Mumford, have drawn very close analogies between the urban problems that beset ancient Rome and problems of the modern American city. Rome was the scene of a laissez-faire and specu-lative urban land market complete with deteriorating buildings and slum land-lords; it had a spatially organized voting system complete with ward bosses and gerrymandering; it suffered from a transportation problem so severe that finally vehicular traffic was banned from the city in daylight hours; and it pos-sessed enormous "welfare rolls" of idle poor (mostly freehold farmers pushed off the land by capitalistically organized, slave-worked agriculture). Despite the closeness of some of these analogies, we should not forget that the growth of metropolitan Rome resulted from far-reaching and highly centralized politi-cal and economic ties quite unique in the ancient world. The process, as we will see later, was in no way comparable to the urbanization that accompanied the Industrial Revolution. Specifically, urbanization was not the result of the radical changes in the structure of urban productive activity that are described later for the industrial city.

The Medieval City

After the demise of the western Roman Empire in the fifth century A.D., Eu-ropean life focused on the land. From four hundred years of turmoil, in which urban life and commerce declined, the feudal system emerged. Feudalism was a rural system organized around agricultural landholding. In this system the nonproducing elites of the church and the nobility were supported by the farmer. The legal structure of landholding in the feudal period was based on delegation of tenancy rights from the king downward. Instead of owning land outright, barons and other large landowners held the land in fief from the king. That is, they obtained the right to occupy the land in exchange for doing homage to the king and for assuming the obligation to perform specified mili-tary services for him. At the lowest end of the scale serfs and villeins worked land for themselves, in exchange for specified obligations to their lord of the manor.

With feudalism the long-distance exchange relationships of the Roman pe-riod declined, and local subsistence economies became universal in the West. The road system decayed, reflecting the demise of trade in all but a few luxury items for the wealthy. The Mediterranean Sea, which had in earlier centuries been a scene of commercial exchange, became a frontier zone of piracy and conflict between three cultures: the Latin West, Greek Byzantium in the East, and the newly conquered Islamic lands of North Africa and Spain.

In this context the city as a viable form of community organization did not emerge until the tenth century. The rebirth of the city was rooted in both political and economic necessity. The lord, first of all, required fortresses for defense, since in this intensely parochial society enemies were numerous. The populations of these walled settlements represented a cheap substitute for a standing army.

Also, cities grew in importance because an urban middle class of traders and craftsmen expanded (Pirenne, 1925). The growth of this new urban class has been attributed to changes in agricultural technology, which improved yields and made feeding cities possible, and a system of inheritance termed *primogeniture*. In primogeniture, the first son inherited property, and the second and later-born sons were thrust out of the family household at the death of the father. This system created a substantial pool of potential urban migrants, and in time many of these dispossessed persons became traders, the core of the new middle class.

As this middle class enlarged, it began to challenge the power of the clergy and the nobility. Since the middle class brought substantial wealth to the city through its commercial activity, it was able to bargain effectively for power in the feudal system. The merchants required secure and stable marketplaces and an easing of the travel restrictions imposed by the lords. The lords, in turn, required tax revenues from trade to finance their continual wars. Thus the urban merchants had the upper hand, and their commanding bargaining position brought substantial political autonomy to the early medieval city. To ensure continued commercial activity, the middle class demanded the establishment of a set of municipal rights that amounted to local self-government under the control of the merchants. These demands included the right to move from area to area, the right to hold regular markets, and the right to organize a court and town council. These rights were obtained by royal charters, in which the king granted the city protection, freedom of trade, and exemption from certain feudal obligations in exchange for specified services (often including military obligations) in addition to taxes and tolls. The effect of these charters was to confer a special extrafeudal status on the city. Indeed, in the early medieval period European cities had an independence they never enjoyed before or since. At first this autonomy was jealously guarded and membership in the urban group was very exclusively defined. The advantages of urban living were very evident. One specific attraction was the freedom that a runaway manorial serf gained if he could demonstrate residence in a city for a specified period (traditionally a year and a day). This gave rise to the medieval German saying, "City air makes one free."

Because of the attraction of urban life, intense pressure on urban living space developed. Frequently settlements (faubourgs) grew up beyond the city walls. Often the burghers (the ruling class of merchants) were torn between maintaining exclusivity and enjoying the obvious financial (tax) advantages that would accrue from incorporating the faubourgs. Incorporation was frequently accomplished by moving the city wall outward.

As the medieval period proceeded, cities grew and immigrants were socially assimilated. This process accelerated as the rural feudal system began to break down. However, the medieval city never experienced large immigrations as the industrial city has, partly because the small scale and exclusive guild structures of urban industry severely restricted employment opportunities. (Guilds, or exclusive organizations of craftsmen, were forerunners of modern unions.)

The physical form of the early medieval city mirrored the social dominance of the merchant class. Cities were small. A defensive wall (see Figure 4.4) contained a haphazard (organic) plan of narrow streets focused on the city center. At the center was the market place, the guildhall, and the residences of the well-to-do, in addition to the church or cathedral. The most prestigious residential space was closest to the city center; the least, farthest away.

Social space in the medieval city revolved around a clearly maintained distinction between public and private space. Private space embraced the dwelling and working space of those who had a legal foothold in the city. Frequently large families with servants lived under the same roof with craftsmen and apprentices, for economic activity was small scale and craft based. No clear-cut distinction between residential and work space existed. Despite this economic integration, residential space in the city was finely segregated by wealth, and sometimes distinctive ethnic ghettos grew up close to the city wall or beyond it.

Public space in the medieval city was accessible to many transient classes who had a right to pass by and to do business but who had no legal foothold in the residential space. Public space included the narrow thoroughfares and the marketplace. It intruded very closely on the private space, and social distance was maintained by terracing housefronts and by focusing social life in rear gardens. Thomas More in his *Utopia* describes the ideal of medieval urban living:

> Built on the side of a hill covering some four square miles down to the river's edge, with streets very commodious and handsome, twenty feet broad . . . the houses of fair and gorgeous building . . . joined together in a long row through the whole street without any partition or separation. On the back side of the houses lie large gardens. Every house hath two doors, one into the street and a postern door on the back side into the garden. The houses have three storeys, one over another, the outsides made of flint, plaster or brick and the inner sides strengthened with timber work and the roofs are plain and flat, covered with a kind of plaster so tempered that no fire can hurt or perish it and able to withstand the violence of the wind. And after supper the people bestow one hour in play, in summer in their gardens, in winter in their common halls where they exercise themselves in music or in honest and wholesome communication (cited in Schaffer, 1972:19-20).

Figure 4.4 *Caernarvon, Wales*   Caernarvon is a medieval bastide town. Unlike
organic growth towns, bastides were built by royal authority to extend and control
its domain. Welsh bastides were built as military garrisons and had only minor
trade functions. (*Source:* Morris, 1972:92; reprinted by permission of Aerofilms Ltd.,
England.)

The Renaissance and Baroque Cities

The typical medieval town possessed a high degree of political autonomy
by royal grant, an arrangement benefiting both king and citizens. But later in
the medieval period municipal power waned. With the demise of feudalism,
royal power was consolidated across Europe in nation states such as France and
England or in regional states such as the German principalities. Sometimes, as
in Holland, the corporate city survived and was integrated into the nation.
More often, towns lost their autonomy to the royal government. This political

centralization was one in a series of changes that eroded the economic, political, and social bases of the medieval city, profoundly modifying its form.

The Catholic Church, which was the only effective cosmopolitan force in the Middle Ages, lost much of its authority because of schisms and the Protestant Reformation. While the church waned as a centralizing influence, mercantile capitalism reached new heights. Mercantilist philosophy, under which the state sought control of trade and economic growth, became a dominant principle guiding political action. Mercantilism stimulated trade, and as a result cities grew. London quadrupled in size between 1530 and 1630, and by the end of the seventeenth century London and Paris had surpassed the half-million mark.

The growth of centralized political power led to a growing concern with urban design. Renaissance and baroque urban forms resulted from conscious and large-scale design on behalf of a small minority of wealthy citizens. In the independent city-states of Renaissance Italy, banking, trading, and aristocratic families patronized art and architecture. The later and more ambitious forms of the baroque embodied the ostentation of despotic royalty, exemplified in the enormous palace of the French king Louis XIV at Versailles.

The dominant feature of Renaissance and baroque urbanism was conscious manipulation of the whole urban space, with individual structures contributing to an overall design. Both before and after the Renaissance, architecture tended to focus on the esthetics and the practicality of individual buildings. The concerted and unified manipulation of the whole urban space in the Renaissance-baroque city rested on the exercise of centralized power unhindered by the individual property rights that constrain planning today. The difference between Renaissance and baroque forms is an ill-defined distinction of time and degree. Although art historians make fine distinctions between the two, the most significant difference is scale. In Renaissance design the concern was to organize and embellish small, closed spaces, whereas baroque design attempted to create an illusion of infinity with its large-scale forms and open vistas (Morris, 1972:106).

Mumford enumerates some of the symbols of the Renaissance-baroque design including "the straight street, the unbroken horizontal roof line, the round arch, and the repetition of uniform elements, cornice, lintel, window and column . . ." (1961:348). To these we might add an almost obsessive concern with symmetry, both in the architectural details of individual buildings and in the juxtaposition of buildings in the urban space. A concern for the sheer scale and size of buildings appeared in the later baroque period.

Design themes included the long straight street, the gridiron plan of secondary streets, a variety of enclosed open spaces including plazas, piazzas, traffic hubs (e.g., Place de l'Etoile in Paris), and purely residential squares focused on a small square park (Morris, 1972). Many such squares are to be found in northern London. This period also saw the introduction of many buildings and functions absent in the medieval city and still present in modern cities, such as parks, squares, ornamental gardens, theaters, zoos, palaces, and museums.

The horse-drawn carriage became a dominant feature of urban traffic in the Renaissance period, producing an extremely high casualty rate. Stagecoach accidents in France killed more people than railroads did (Mumford, 1961:370). One problem was that speed of movement was related to prestige—royalty sped along at a gallop, "as if they were in the open country."

The excellent street plans of the later baroque city would appear to have the potential for greatly increased mobility and functional differentiation of the urban space. Mumford, however, emphasizes the nonfunctional character of much urban road building, designed, if for any purpose beyond ostentation, only for the easy movement and parade of large bodies of troops.

In many cases, baroque principles led to the abrogation of individual property rights and the destruction of numerous well-designed localities, for baroque rulers planned as they wished and displaced people at will. Mumford writes:

> The baroque cliches of power, hardly even with the decency of a disguise, lingered right into the twentieth century: witness the plowing of the Seventh Avenue extension through the one historic quarter of New York that had integrity and character . . . (1961:388).

Many authors have indicated the relationship between dictatorial government and the construction of banal, large-scale architecture even at the present time. Albert Speer in *Inside the Third Reich* (1970) describes Hitler's elaborate plans for Linz and Berlin, including a triumphal arch planned (with obvious symbolism) to be much larger than the Arc de Triomphe in Paris.

In summary, Renaissance and baroque urban forms arose from the large-scale implementation of the desires of capricious and even despotic minorities. Although some esthetic features of the designs are still highly prized, the autocratic philosophy and many of the grandiose pretensions of baroque design are now considered wholly inappropriate. Nevertheless, baroque principles are frequently invoked in the few modern contexts where large-scale unconstrained plans are possible, including the design of national capitals from L'Enfant's plan for Washington, D.C. (1790s) to Canberra (1920s) and Brasilia (1960s). Precisely because baroque forms symbolize the values of ruling minorities, it is fruitless to search for detailed relationships between urban form and the evolving structure of mass society.

In many ways the baroque conception of the city was diametrically opposed to the direction in which the Western city was evolving. To give two specific examples: Commerce and industry were entirely neglected in the baroque ideal city precisely when mercantile capitalism was laying the institutional foundations of the Industrial Revolution. Also, baroque planning was predicated on autocratic power precisely in the epoch of the English, American, and French democratic revolutions. The continuing recurrence of baroque motifs in the organization of urban space (even in socialist systems) attests to their esthetic power rather than to their functional appropriateness. People like them because they are handsome, not because they work well.

Trends in the Preindustrial City

The Renaissance-baroque city was the final expression of Western urbanism before the Industrial Revolution. It is customary to refer to all cities before this time and to contemporary cities in nonindustrialized countries as preindustrial. Sjoberg (1960) and Berry (1973a), among others, argue that certain common features distinguish preindustrial cities from later urban places.

Size and Stability   With few exceptions preindustrial cities were small. During the entire preindustrial period the overwhelming majority of people were nonurban. In England and the United States immediately before industrialization, no more than 5 percent of the population was urban.

The small size of cities indicates the strong economic, technological, and social constraints on urban growth. Simply, the preindustrial city grew little. It was not a scene of significant migrations from rural areas, nor did it witness great bursts of growth through natural increase. Cities were often dangerous places to live—mortality rates were high—and immigration served only to offset these very high death rates. Because of this stability, boundaries in the urban space were durable, and the uses of specific areas became traditional and permanent. This contrasts vividly with the modern city. For the past 150 years, cities have continuously grown and constantly readjusted in pattern. A substantial part of the theory and vocabulary of modern urban studies concerns dynamic processes—such as succession, filtering, and transition—all of which were largely absent before the Industrial Revolution.

Security was a major concern in the preindustrial city, walled off as it was from the bulk of the population. As Braudel (1973) points out, however, the ramparts were socioeconomic dividing lines as well as protective devices. Indeed, the walls symbolized the aloofness and social separation of the town and the country.

Economic Organization   Economic activity occurred on a relatively small scale, and much of it was decidedly nonurban. Even large cities in England on the eve of the Industrial Revolution continued to engage in agriculture (Braudel, 1973). In the West such cities housed shepherds, vine growers, farmers, and herdsmen. Many such towns owned surrounding fields and pasturage. During the harvest townsmen were expected to work in the fields. Domesticated animals, usually pigs, were tended in the streets. Indeed, streets were so covered with the dung of such animals that people occasionally used stilts to cross them!

Industrial production was small scale and craft based, a fact we will explore in more detail soon. As a result, cities during this era were spatially organized in a manner quite different from contemporary cities. The town's economic activity was not organized into a variety of districts, as is common today. Functional specialization of different parts of the urban space was unknown. The various stages of the productive process were carried out under one roof. Masters, craftsmen, laborers, and merchants frequently lived and worked on the same premises. The spatial separation of home and work with its complicated commuting patterns were absent.

The economic function of the city increased in scope and complexity through the preindustrial period. In the earliest city-states of the Middle East, the dominance over the hinterland was military and religious. In later periods the interchange between city and hinterland became more explicitly economic. Throughout much of preindustrial history, the nonurban populations were essentially self-sufficient and the cities exported intangibles such as defense and religion.

As suggested earlier, trade was extremely limited in the first cities. The Hellenic period, however, witnessed steady growth in the importance and social recognition of the merchant class, from the early Greek city in which trade had been the concern of disdained and unfranchised foreigners, to the enormous trading class of late Rome. The growing significance of trade was indicated by the changes in the city's physical form. The prominent religious and political gathering places of earlier cities gave way in the medieval and Renaissance periods to the economic landmarks of the marketplace and the guildhall.

Not only did the emphasis on economic exchange shift during the preindustrial era, but also the very nature of economic relationships changed as well. Before the Golden Age of Greece the idea of purely economic exchange did not exist. As Karl Polanyi (1957) suggests, transactions were public acts designed to reinforce prestige and obligation. Exchange was more like gift giving aimed at reinforcing networks of social obligation than a purely economic transaction. "Brides, slaves, and plots of land were among the objects exchanged, and the laws of reciprocity that governed the transactions tended to be embedded in the kinship organization" (Abrahamson, 1976:38). Early cities were organized around kinship rather than market principles. Economic concepts such as profit, interest, and supply and demand were foreign. Social relations were controlled by kinship rather than by individualistic and rational economic concerns. These were truly places governed by mechanical solidarity, which declined only with the increasing respectability and political dominance of the trading classes.

Citizen Status in the Preindustrial City   The merchant class's rise to respectability is actually only one instance of a broader process of social assimilation that evolved slowly through preindustrial history. This trend, which accelerated with industrialization, is the source of the great transformations in the urban experience identified by Wirth and Lofland (see Chapter 3). In the earliest cities, membership in the civil body—citizenship—was a rare privilege, prescribed by religion and jealously guarded against outsiders. Citizens were a homogeneous lot, quite different from the heterogeneous populations of modern cities. The lack of citizenship severely restricted one's ability to participate in public activities. Participation in the celebrated democracy of Greece was limited to the citizen class. Many city dwellers were unenfranchised, and some groups were forbidden even to live in the city. In the later Hellenistic world, citizenship came to be conferred simply by residence, rather than by religious or traditional qualification.

Medieval European urbanism witnessed the same process: An exclusive definition of citizenship gave way to one based only on residence. In the early period, residence in the chartered and independent towns was a privilege rigidly guarded. The early medieval faubourgs that grew up beyond the city walls symbolized the aspirations of those who wished to participate in civic life but were relegated to live beyond the walls. Later these sanctions were relaxed as the economic advantages of city life and the demands for urban workers grew. Finally, citizenship was conferred solely by residence. Thus, the preindustrial period saw a trend toward cosmopolitan definitions of citizenship, setting the stage for the massive demographic urbanization that accompanied industrialization and that produced the large and socially heterogeneous urban populations on which the concepts of Wirth and Lofland depend.

Social Organization and Mobility   The major unit of the preindustrial social organization was the family, which usually involved large extended-family groupings (a family including members of at least three generations). Because of this arrangement, households were generally unlikely to relocate. Not only were residential areas more stable than in the modern city, but also they were often less segregated along class and ethnic lines. In many cities rich and poor alike lived in the same areas in what Berry refers to as a "cellular net" (1973a). Since most economic activity took place in the home, the urban pattern was often a collection of self-contained districts, each with its own shops, institutions, and services. Also, because different parts of the production process were carried out in a single household, people in a variety of social stations often lived in the same place.

This is not to imply, however, that segregation by social class did not exist. In fact, almost all preindustrial cities shared a similar pattern of residential location. Typically the most prestigious locations were close to the symbolic centers of urban life (the palaces, temples, or in later years the market and guildhalls). Successively poorer groups lived farther away from these centers, and certain outcast groups such as the merchants lived in ghettos near or even beyond the walls. The ethnic ghetto was a common feature in such cities. In some cases the ghettos were bounded by physical barriers. Hawley (1971) cites the case of Ratisbon where cell-like structures closed off by gates divided the city into three separate sections: one for royalty, one for clergy, and a third for the merchants.

Another feature common to preindustrial cities was the limited mobility of its inhabitants. Horse-drawn or pedestrian travel was the only means of movement available, and thus the city was a highly compact place. This acted as an additional constraint on interactions, which were also rigidly bounded by the social system.

Modern geographic analysis of urban travel suggests three major categories of intraurban travel: journey to work, shopping, and social-recreational trips. Each of these was minimal in the preindustrial city. The work trip was almost nonexistent since home and workplace almost always coincided. "Shopping travel" existed, although the demand for consumer goods was limited and was typically satisfied in local markets. Social-recreational travel was also minimal in part because many social interactions occurred within the extended family. Essentially the only classes that customarily ranged over great distances were the military and the merchants.

THE INDUSTRIAL CITY

The Industrial Revolution and Urban Social Space

The distinguishing features of the industrial city lie in the technological and organizational changes accompanying industrialization. This second urban revolution first occurred in England in the second half of the eighteenth century because of unique political, technological, and demographic factors.

First, England was unusually politically cohesive and centralized. The late eighteenth century witnessed the beginnings of the colonial empire in Africa and Asia and thus increasing access to new sources of raw materials and markets. Second, a series of advances in the organization and techniques of farm production were under way; these included innovations in agricultural methods and the reorganization of land tenure produced by the program of Parliamentary Enclosure. Third, far-reaching demographic changes had occurred, specifically, a decline in the death rate and the beginnings of streams of migrants from countryside to city. (These changes occurred partly as a consequence of the reorganization of agriculture and the subsequent decrease in the farm population.) Fourth, the last half of the eighteenth century saw the beginnings of the transportation revolution, involving extensive highway financing, the construction of turnpikes, and the initiation of a canal system. At the same time, a cluster of technological innovations occurred (steam engine, cotton gin, spinning jenny) that embodied the Industrial Revolution itself. Finally, the institutional means necessary for large-scale enterprise were emerging, including credit, extended banking facilities, limited liability, and the joint stock company.

Against this background vast increases in industrial production and urban population occurred. Each of these changes exerted enormous impact on the physical form of the urban space and on the social structure within it.

Impact of Changes in Productive Activity

The original economic base for the Industrial Revolution was the exploitation first of water power and later of coal in textiles and iron and steel manufacture. The impact of early industry on the city's form can be understood by considering how industries operate most efficiently. Economists speak of two ways industries achieve efficiency: scale economies and agglomeration economies.

Scale economies refer to the savings involved in large-scale production—as the quantity of industrial products increases, the cost per unit decreases. The heavy industries, so prominent in the early industrial period, yield particularly impressive scale economies. For example, one large blast furnace is much cheaper to operate than several small ones totaling the same capacity. Thus, the organization of industries into a few large-scale concerns greatly improved productive efficiency.

Working the new large-scale plants required an extensive pool of hired laborers. The resulting housing problem constituted the most obvious legacy of the early industrial city. Large numbers of working-class families were housed in northern England in terraced cottages. The extreme poverty and desolation of these grimy communities is well known. Lewis Mumford (1961) speaks critically of these settlements as "coketown," "mechanicville," and "manheap." Extensive slums and a large class of urban poor thus appeared in the city for the first time since Rome in the second and third centuries. These centrally located ghettos became characteristic of the industrial city.

Scale economies also produced economic and functional specializations in the use of urban space. For the first time, place of residence and place of work became separate—producing large-scale daily movements of commuters. Initially workers commuted by foot, and as a result working-class housing clustered close to the place of employment. Later, subsidized commuter transportation separated home and work farther.

Close proximity to the factories and mills made the city an undesirable place to live. For the first time in urban history the city became repulsive to the upper classes. As a result, the elite classes of owners and industrialists eventually moved to locations some distance from the towns. Thus the gradient of social classes was reversed: The city turned inside out.

Because scale economies operate within a single firm, they are termed *internal economies*. The other means of industrial savings are *agglomeration economies*. These arise from the firm's overall context and location, and hence they are referred to as *external economies*. These efficiencies arise through savings from proximity to other industries, to a trained labor pool, to specialized transport facilities, to resources and energy supplies. Partly because of agglomeration economies and partly because of local coal supplies, early heavy industries clustered in industrial belts such as the coalfields of northern England and the German Ruhr Valley. Such specialized clusters of interrelated industrial activity have been termed *conurbations* by Patrick Geddes (1915). Large cities close together constitute a spatial form unique to the industrial and modern periods; in previous epochs they would not have been economically viable. The textile towns of New England represented a small-scale conurbation of the early American industrial period. Clusters of cities devoted to aerospace industries in Texas and California are modern examples.

Impact of Demographic Urbanization

A second major force in the early industrial city was rural-urban migration on an unprecedented scale. Table 4.1 shows the change. In Mumford's terminology, the Industrial Revolution transformed the city from a container to a magnet. During most of the nineteenth and early twentieth century, urban populations grew significantly more by net migration than by natural increase (births minus deaths). Adna Weber (1899) found that in the great cities of the nineteenth century as much as 80 percent of the adult population had been born outside the city and two-thirds of these had lived in these cities less than fifteen years. Only in the most recent censuses of industrial countries has it become clear that these great migrant streams have all but ceased. In developing countries they continue unabated.

This continuous and large urban migration has had major consequences for the industrial city. Urban space has become dynamic and ever changing. During the past two centuries the Western city has grown without pause, producing an intense competition for urban space.

This theme of urban process and dynamics is reflected in all contemporary theories of urban space in human ecology and urban geography, which view growth in the city's population and area as the major factors in increasing segregation. The industrial city, with its teeming numbers, is a highly segregated place.

Table 4.1   The Urban Proportion of the World's Population: How it Changed from 1800 to 1970

	Percentage of World Population		
Year	In All Urban Places	In Places 20,000+	In Cities 100,000+
1800	3.0	2.4	1.7
1850	6.4	4.3	2.3
1900	13.6	9.2	5.5
1950	28.2	22.7	16.2
1970	38.6	32.2	23.8
Percentage Change per Decade			
1800–1850	16.4	12.4	6.3
1850–1900	16.3	16.4	19.1
1900–1950	15.7	19.7	24.1
1950–1970	16.9	19.3	21.1

Source: From K. Davis, *World Urbanization 1950–1970,* Vol. II, 1972. Reprinted by permission of Kingsley Davis.

The unprecedented growth of cities in the nineteenth and twentieth centuries is a product of the industrial era. The industrial city acts like a magnet, drawing people to it. These figures show the continuous and high rate of change during the past two centuries.

Immigrants to the city arrived in a space that was already highly segregated. Typically, first-generation migrants chose residences in a specific area of the city—usually near people of similar ethnic or social background. These migrants generally clustered around the central area of the city—the locus for most urban employment. The large number of migrants produced great pressure for population movements outward from this center. Connected with these pressures was the intensified competition among different groups for space. Since each social group migrated to a different area, and since the volume of migration also varied from one group to another, various areas of the city grew at different rates. As a result, neighborhoods changed relatively rapidly. As one group began leaving an area, another would quickly displace it. The contrast between this situation and that of the preindustrial city could not be more marked.

These continuing waves of in-migration created the intense pressures of size, density, and heterogeneity described in Chapter 3. As cities became larger and more dense and consisted of a greater variety of peoples, certain pressures toward social change emerged. Among the most important was the growth of secondary, or impersonal, relationships, producing the changes detailed in Chapter 3.

The Role of Transportation Technology

Industrial activity encouraged an increasing specialization of land use and a reversal of the old residential pattern by social class. Although these shifts in the urban spatial pattern were implicit in the nature of the industrial economy, changes in transportation technology actually made them real. Indeed, each major innovation in transportation during the industrial era was marked by a distinctive phase in the history of urban space. In North America the evolution of the industrial city involved four stages: the *pedestrian*, the *railroad*, the *streetcar*, and the *automobile* city (Yeates and Garner, 1976; Warner, 1962).

In the early industrial city people basically moved around the city on foot, accentuating the clustered activity produced by scale economies. While place of work and residence was beginning to separate during this period, the distance between the two points was small. In New York City at the turn of the century, the average commuting distance was approximately one-quarter of a mile (Pred, 1966). The limitations on travel imposed by the pedestrian city created a cellular city pattern similar to that of the preindustrial period. Residential areas were segregated more by industrial employment than social class. Often employer and employee lived close both to one another and the factory. The first real separation of the classes in the early industrial city can be traced to the horsecar (Ward, 1971), which was first introduced in New York City in 1832 and was extensively used in eastern cities until the 1870s.

After 1860 the railroad began to profoundly affect the form of the American city. Rail transport exerted both centripetal and centrifugal pressures on the urban spatial pattern. The railroad permitted some population dispersion (centrifugal movements), but mostly for the wealthy. With the growth of rail transport, concentrations of wealth grew at points distant from the city. These communities are termed *exurbs* to distinguish them from *suburbs*, which are communities physically contiguous to the main city.

However, the major spatial effect of the railroad was not dispersion but concentration (centripetal movement). Railroad travel is fixed and inflexible, and short-distance travel is costly. As a result, the railroad encouraged the growth of towns along its routes and thus cities grew up in the interior of the nation. More important, however, because of the diseconomies of short-distance travel, both economic activity and populations within the city tended to concentrate during this period. Hawley attributes the emergence of the central business district in the nineteenth-century American city to the steam railway.

> The establishment of the steam railway terminal in the interior of the city . . . set in motion a redistribution process that ultimately produced a well-defined centralization of activities. Public buildings, central offices, banks, services to business and industry, hotels, and retail and personal service establishments gathered about the terminal to take advantage of the quick communication with hinterlands and with other centers (1971:91).

The first major decentralization of urban populations came from the electric streetcar, which by the 1890s had grown to 850 systems operating in over fifty American cities (Hawley, 1971:92). The electric streetcar permitted extensive middle-class suburbanization. Warner (1962) suggests several significant effects of this early suburbanization. First, it improved housing and health standards for the middle class. More significant from our point of view, however, it permitted greater segregation of the middle and lower classes. The new evenness of wealth in the suburbs meant a greater uniformity of community membership and life style. The middle classes saw this homogeneity as desirable.

The suburbanization processes initiated by the streetcar were reinforced and extended by the automobile. The automobile differs qualitatively from commuter railroads and rapid transit systems because it has unlimited access. Unlike earlier forms of travel, which produced starshaped patterns of settlement by expansion along a few arterials, the automobile allowed the city to spread out in all directions. Gottmann (1961) argues that this process involves a dissolution of the traditional urban form.

Since the early 1900s the auto has been the major force in reshaping the urban community. Its main impact has been to expand the city over ever wider areas. More particularly, however, it has led to a growing separation of the middle and upper classes from the central city. The urban space became highly parochial and segregated, to the point where the problems of the city proper have largely become the problems of the poor and disadvantaged.

THEMES IN THE
EVOLUTION OF URBAN SPACE

This brief summary of urban history has dealt almost exclusively with the Western European and North American city. No mention has been made of other urban cultures such as those of China, Africa, India, and the Moslem lands, nor have we described indigenous New World urbanism in Mexico, Peru, and Guatemala. Despite this limited historical perspective, however, it is clear that the historical variety of social and physical forms is enormous. This history entails several major themes.

The City as a Cultural Artifact   We have already discussed our unique ability to mold environments and create new ones. The city may, therefore, be viewed as a cultural artifact and urban space as a physical and symbolic manifestation of the interests and aspirations of a culture. Historical examples are many. The ancient cities of Egypt and Mesopotamia were dominated by the symbols of religion. In Athens the Acropolis symbolized ancient religious themes, while the agora, the stadium, and the theaters attested to the subsequent concern for civic participation. For a great part of the feudal period in Europe, the church was prominent in the cityscape, indicating its role as a centralizing force among the scattered fragments of feudal isolation. As the merchant class grew in power and influence in the later Middle Ages, however, the city took on imprints of the new commercial interests. The guildhall and the marketplace were visible symbols of the new priorities. In later periods the baroque and industrial cities made tangible the aspirations of autocratic rulers and industrial capitalists. It is instructive to attempt to deduce the priorities of contemporary American culture from the physical fabric of its cities.

Economic Transformations and Spatial Form   Economic factors contribute substantially to our understanding of the reasons for the existence of cities, their external relationships, and their internal structure. An economic division of labor and the emergence of a nonfarming elite were the foundation of the early cities and of their social structures. An early exchange relationship was established in which agricultural hinterlands provided food and cities provided certain nontangibles such as religious, cultural, and administrative functions.

The main distinction in the spatial organization of economic activity is between the preindustrial and the industrial periods. In the preindustrial city small-scale, craft-based manufacturing industry was highly segregated in the urban space. This segregation was an essentially social segregation of the manufacturers into quarters associated with particular crafts rather than a functional segregation of the different components of the manufacturing process. In the industrial city three major changes occurred. First, great increases in the scale of activity generated a new class—an industrial proletariat—that came to dominate many cities numerically. Second, large-scale commuting of workers began, increasing the strangers encountered in the public space. Third, complicated patterns of industrial location in the urban space led to vast clusters of associated activities and to functional specialization in space.

Social Transformations and Spatial Form   The city has been the locus of social and technical change for the society. Thus urban space has reflected periods of great social transformation. The city has been the site of evolution to a more complex division of labor and the growth of new social classes, the site of great waves of immigration, and the source of potential psychological crises for urbanites.

Permanent settlement with a stable resource base permits a more complex division of labor to develop. Under such conditions groups of individuals are freed from the normal requirements of food production and can thus follow nonagricultural life pursuits. In the preindustrial city this meant the growth of craft and merchant groups. In the industrial city industrial production required the growth of an extensive middle class to manage large-scale factory production.

The city has thus been the source for a growing distinction among peoples. In its initial stages the basic distinction was between the town and the country, as Karl Marx insisted. In the ancient city this difference was evident in the legal distinction between citizens and noncitizens. Most preindustrial cities had proletarian classes, yet only a relatively small "middle class" of entrepreneurs and officials. In the industrial city the working class grew and differentiated. But the most distinctive social change of the industrial city was a differentiation of roles and functions and an enormous expansion of the middle class. With this growth, urban space became more segregated and mosaic-like. Indeed, the division of residential space into miniature worlds with homogeneous life styles became characteristic of the industrial city.

Extensive residential segregation is also a response to the enormous variety of ethnic and socioeconomic subgroups in the industrial city. The city has always magnetically attracted hinterland populations, but since the Industrial Revolution rural to urban migration has been phenomenal. In the United States up until the 1960s, the urban scene has been one of continual migration and assimilation. The result has been a steady pattern of neighborhood change as new ethnic groups invade the communities of established populations, and these populations in turn move to other areas.

Another major result of the growth in the number and variety of people in the modern city has been an ever greater threat to the psychological well-being of the urbanite. As Lofland suggests, this threat stimulated the dispersion of middle- and upper-class families away from the city center. The new city is distinguished by its unattractiveness for certain categories of the population.

Proximity in the City   The impact of physical distance on urban organization depends upon the transportation technology. The preindustrial city was essentially pedestrian. It was therefore extremely compact. Lofland's description of the resulting colorful and crowded public space (Chapter 3) highlights the close juxtaposition of rich and poor and of citizen and outsider this compactness produced. Consequently the lines of social demarcation were clearly drawn and rigidly enforced. Often the social areas, ethnic ghettos, and quarters devoted to various crafts were physically separated by walls.

The impact of the successive advances in transportation technology was to reduce drastically the friction of distance on activity. This had two main effects: economic integration and social segregation, both of which occurred over greater and greater distances. The *economic integration* of urban space over great distances resulted in complex patterns of movement and commuting, and the existence of specialized areas of industry, commerce, and residences in the modern city. *Social segregation* processes also came to operate over greater distances. The history of transportation innovation quite closely parallels the dispersion of successively lower social classes. The railroads generated exurbs of the wealthy; the streetcar is associated with suburbanization of the middle classes, and modern automobile transport has made suburban living accessible to all except disadvantaged classes such as ethnic minorities, the elderly, and the inner-city poor. The greater areal scope of segregation in the modern city has produced an extensive suburban landscape in which very fine shades of social distinction are drawn and in which specific localities tend to be extremely homogeneous.

Modes of Change in the Urban Landscape   The modern city, in contrast to its ancient counterpart, is the scene of dynamic change in land uses and in spatio-social structures. Ultimately, all changes in the physical and social structures of the city flow from human decisions. These decisions may be made by individuals responding to long-established traditions and customs or to social pressures to conform or seek profit, or they may be group decisions or the edicts of autocratic governments. In the most ancient cities the occupancy and use of plots of land was sanctioned by religion and reinforced by tradition and custom. The unchanging nature of the custom-based spatio-social structure of the preindustrial city reflected the strength of tradition (and the lack of any significant forces of change). However, as early as the Roman period, a quite different principle became evident: the speculative development of urban land for individual gain by private capitalists. Finally, throughout urban history we find periods in which the urban space has been deliberately planned, perhaps reaching its most extreme manifestation in the comprehensive and autocratically conceived plans of the baroque period.

Modern and westernized cultures reveal a variety of modes of change in the urban landscape. In the United States the decisions of entrepreneurs and consumers in a relatively free land market limited by mild regulations such as zoning produce a situation in which large-scale and comprehensive planning is both impractical and politically unacceptable. Allocation of urban land is left, within the bounds of regulation, to free-market mechanisms. By contrast, in the welfare states of Western Europe and to a still higher degree in the socialist countries, activity within the urban space is closely regulated and comprehensively planned. These alternate modes of controlling change will be discussed in more detail in Chapter 12.

SUMMARY

In Mesopotamia collecting and administering a food surplus permitted development of specialized, nonagricultural classes. Literacy, arithmetic, astronomy, bronze-working, and other cultural innovations occurred, and the first true cities emerged as small, compact, fortified settlements focused on monumental temples, palaces, and granaries. Three thousand years later in Greece, elaborate public buildings contrasted with squalid private space. Norms of architecture and democracy developed, but citizenship was defined as a restricted privilege. The Romans dispersed the classical geometry of urban form over wide areas and evolved an inclusive, residential definition of citizenship.

After the Dark Ages, trading connections gradually resumed and the chartered cities of the Middle Ages emerged. The chartered city symbolized the power and political autonomy of the merchant class. Compact cities focused on the marketplace, the cathedral, or the guildhall. With the rise of the nation-state, the autonomy of cities declined and baroque ideals of urban form emerged, including symmetry, monumentality, and integrated design of the whole urban space by autocratic power without regard for functionality or individual property rights.

The Industrial Revolution was accompanied by far-reaching changes in economic organization, agriculture, demographics and transportation. Scale and agglomeration economies and massive migration into cities led to an explosion in the size of towns and to a reversal of the social gradient. Elite classes moved centrifugally, leaving the poor close to the city center. Continuing transportation innovations—railroad, streetcar and private automobile—continuing shifts in productive activity, and increased economic and social complexity led to the characteristic dispersed and segregated form of the modern city.

Chapter 5

Descriptive Models of Residential Structure

INTRODUCTION

The experience of flying over a great city at night is unforgettable. From this vantage point the order of the city stands out. You see the intense activity at the city's heart spilling over into rivulets of light radiating out in all directions. Farther away from the city's core, these streams tend to diminish, ending in shallow pools of diffused light. As the plane comes closer to earth, the city's various districts become apparent: certain sections show by their lighting a mixture of residential and commercial use, others are more predominantly residential in character. The major residential sections themselves differ greatly; certain areas have homes spaced at moderate distances from one another along cul-de-sacs; others have homes, sometimes duplexes, spaced close together in gridlike fashion. From the ground the city may appear disorderly, but from the air it reveals itself as a marvelously ordered spatial unit.

The structure of urban space has been a subject of study in sociology and geography for many years. In this chapter we review these descriptions of density and sociodemographic patterns within the city. Why should we be concerned with these population and social heterogeneity criteria in the study of spatial organization? For Wirth, Milgram, and Lofland, at least, the answer is simple. These factors are the very bases of urbanism. Thus the arrangement of populations and social groups in the urban space should affect city life, with each area of the city providing a somewhat different experience.

The first part of this chapter deals with models that describe the distribution of the population in the urban space. The second section is concerned with the social patterning of the urban residents who live at various points in this space.

Our primary interest here is with residential patterns in the city. Where and with whom people share a neighborhood space says something about the very nature of urban social organization. It speaks directly of the structural inequality inherent in the city's institutional makeup. Also, residential space is critical to an understanding of the overall land-use pattern because residential

Table 5.1   Mean Percentage of Land Devoted
to Various Uses in 48 Large American Cities

Type of Use	Total Land	Developed Land
Total developed	77%	100%
Residential	29.6	39
Industrial	8.6	10.9
Commercial	3.7	4.8
Roads & highways	19.9	25.7
Other public	15.2	19.6
Total undeveloped	23.0	—
Vacant	20.7	—
Underwater	2.3	—

Source: From J. H. Neidercorn and E. F. R. Hearle, "Recent
Landuse Trends in 48 Large American Cities." *Land Economics,*
40, 1964, pp. 105–110. Reprinted by permission.

land use consumes by far the largest portion—about 40 percent (Neidercorn
and Hearle, 1964)—of all land within the city (see Table 5.1).

DENSITY MODELS

The Basic Regularity: Clark's Law

Perhaps the most basic question we can ask about urban residential space
concerns the overall distribution of population densities in the city. *Population
density* refers simply to the number of persons per unit of space. Density should
not be confused with *crowding.* While density is usually regarded as a physical
condition of limited space, crowding is the psychological experience of such
spatial limitations. High density is not a sufficient condition for crowding (Stokols, 1972). Crowding is specific to certain situations and cultures. Later chapters will discuss the behavioral implications of crowding. For now, however,
we will deal with the purely descriptive concept of density.

A variety of density measures have been used for specific research purposes. *Internal density* (populations per unit of floor space) can be distinguished
from *external density* (populations per unit of ground area). On a citywide scale
one can speak of *gross density* (density for the whole city) and *net density* (density for residential areas of the city only). Since the distribution of people in a
large city varies by time of day, further distinction can be made between *employment density* and *residential density.* For example, it is estimated that at the
end of each working day nearly a quarter of a million people leave Chicago's
central business district (Meyer et al., 1965:37). Residential density is the most
extensively studied. Usually residential density refers to gross, external mea-

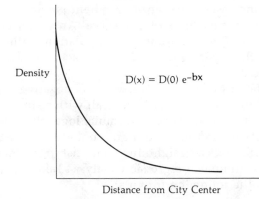

Density

$$D(x) = D(0)\,e^{-bx}$$

Distance from City Center

Figure 5.1 *The Density-Distance Relationship*   Colin Clark demonstrated the mathematical relationship between density and distance from the city's core. The form of this relationship is termed the negative exponential. The curve suggests that density declines in a greater than linear fashion with increasing distance from the center. (*Source:* From C. Clark, "Urban Population Densities." *Journal of the Royal Statistical Society,* Series A, 1951, pp. 490–496. Reprinted by permission.)

sures of population concentration. In this section we use density only in this sense: the number of residents per unit of total ground area.

You probably already have some notion of how density is patterned in cities. For example, you are aware that center city areas contain large numbers of people on relatively small amounts of land. High-rise apartments and multiple-family homes are common in these areas. Farther away from the center, in the suburbs, homes are spaced farther apart and are predominantly single-family detached dwellings. There is obviously, then, some relationship between distance and density—a pattern that is even more apparent when viewed from the air.

This density-distance relationship is described mathematically by Colin Clark (1951). According to Clark, cities' overall density patterns approximate the form shown in Figure 5.1. The form of this curve can be represented by a mathematical function called the *negative exponential*. It has been substantiated for many different cultures and time periods, and is thus sometimes referred to as *Clark's Law*. Mathematically the law is:

$$D(x) = D(0)e^{-bx}$$

In this equation *D(x)* represents the density at some distance *x* from the city's center. *D(0),* termed the *central density parameter,* is the density at this center. It indicates the degree of *congestion* in the urban core. The value *e* is a mathematical constant, 2.7182. . . . The parameter *b, the density gradient parameter,* varies from city to city and governs the rate at which density decreases as distance from the city's core increases. The density gradient parameter measures urban *deconcentration*, or the compactness of city space. An urban area with a large density gradient has a highly concentrated population. Cities with a smaller density gradient, on the other hand, are less compact and have a deconcentrated population distribution.

Because it is difficult to test Clark's Law in its negative exponential form, almost all empirical studies of density have dealt with a simpler, modified version of the equation. To get the simpler formula, logarithms are taken of each side of the equation. This transformation does not affect the empirical content of the model, but it produces a straight line relationship that may be readily fitted to data with the technique of regression analysis. Taking natural logarithms in Clark's Law gives the following formula:

$$\log D(x) = \log D(0)^{-bx}$$

This equation expresses the logarithm of density as a straight-line, or linear, function of distance, and b measures the slope of the line.

Clark's mathematical equations suggest that although the form of the density-distance relationship remains the same for all cities and time periods, the

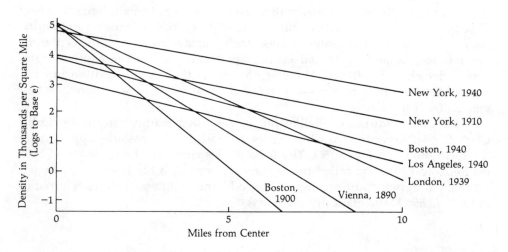

Figure 5.2 *Density-Distance Gradients for Selected Cities and Time Periods* Clark's data for a number of cities at different periods of time indicate that the density gradient *b* declines with time. The value of both *b* and *D(0)* varies for different cities at the same time period and for the same cities at different times. (*Source:* From C. Clark, "Urban Population Densities." *Journal of the Royal Statistical Society,* Series A, 1951, pp. 490–496. Reprinted by permission.)

congestion in the urban core and the rate at which density declines from the urban core can vary considerably for the same city at different time periods and for different cities at the same time period (see Figure 5.2).

Some Explanations of the Regularity and Its Significance

Clark's Law indicates that all cities are most congested at the center, and density in areas away from this core declines in a greater than linear fashion with increasing distance. This pattern is corroborated by the history of the urban form. In both the preindustrial and industrial city the range and intensity of cultural, economic, and social activity decrease away from the city center. In both, there is great contrast in the intensity of activity between center and periphery. This relationship highlights the distinction between inner city and outer city. Since high densities encourage complex interaction patterns and greater subcultural variety (see Chapter 3), the density-distance pattern suggests that substantially different life ways and experiences may distinguish these two areas.

Why do the congested center and the uncongested periphery occur universally? For most macro-oriented ecologists and geographers the regularity can be accounted for by considering the economics of the urban land market, which will be discussed in more detail in a later chapter. For now, however, we simply point out that the value of land increases very steeply toward the city center. This gradient applies primarily to commercial rather than industrial land use, but the competition between land uses for space in this core results in higher values per unit area for all land use types, including residences. Higher land values encourage more intensive (or profitable) use of each unit of area. In the case of residential uses this increased intensity appears in housing construction. High-rise apartment buildings and condominiums, townhouses, and duplexes are built instead of the space-consuming single-family dwellings found on suburban lots. Such developments increase residential densities enormously and tend to offset the diminished proportion of residential land in city centers.

Casetti (1967) explains the dynamics of the land market in terms of the choices people must make in moving to any site in the city. He shows that Clark's Law can result from differing migration patterns at varying distances from the city center. Casetti assumes that potential migrants experience a conflict between two opposing preferences. On the one hand, a *centrality preference* leads people to choose sites that are as central as possible. At the same time, a *congestion disutility* discourages people from choosing sites that are too crowded. While access to people and activities is desirable, crowded housing and congested streets are not. Migration to or away from an area is an attempt to balance these positive and negative forces. The result is a congested center, with congestion declining at a more than linear rate with increasing distance from this core.

Congestion and Deconcentration: Variations by Time and Place

Although the form of the density-distance relationship is universal, the amount of congestion and deconcentration varies substantially by time and place. These variations in the density model parameters can provide a key to understanding spatial dynamics as well as structure.

Temporal variations in urban density patterns seem to be very systematic. The processes of concentration and decentralization are so regular that Schnore (1965b) suggests predictable stages for industrial cities as they age.

Stage 1   The central city gains population, while outer portions of the metropolis lose population.

Stage 2   Both center and outer portions gain numbers, but the center gains at a faster rate.

Stage 3   Both center and periphery gain population, but periphery gains population faster.

Stage 4   The periphery gains numbers as the center loses.

This stage theory of urban density patterns is supported by studies of changes in the density parameters themselves. In the case of the industrial city, congestion at first increases and then peaks and begins to decline. The density gradient, on the other hand, appears to decrease continuously (Newling, 1966; 1969).

Data for Chicago in Table 5.2 clearly show both these tendencies. $D(0)$ reached its height in the first decade of the century, while b has steadily de-

Table 5.2   Density Parameters for Chicago 1860–1950

Year	b	D(0)
1860	.91	30.0
1870	.87	70.8
1880	.79	96.6
1890	.50	86.3
1900	.40	100.0
1910	.36	100.0
1920	.25	73.0
1930	.21	72.8
1940	.20	71.1
1950	.18	63.7

Source: Berry et al., 1963:396. Reprinted from the *Geographical Review*, Vol. 53, 1963, with permission of the American Geographical Society.

Chicago's density pattern closely follows Schnore's prediction concerning the change in values for $D(0)$ and b with time. The density gradient declines continuously with time, while central densities first increase and then decline with the growth of suburbia.

**Table 5.3   Percentage Change in Populations and
Areas of Selected Urbanized Areas, 1950 and 1970**

Urbanized Area	% Population Change	% Land Area Change
Baltimore	36.0	104.0
Denver	110.0	178.3
Milwaukee	51.0	348.9
Philadelphia	37.6	141.3
Rochester	47.0	125.5
Toledo	33.9	137.1

Source: From *The Changing Spatial Structure of American Cities* by John R.
Ottensmann. Copyright 1975, D. C. Heath and Company, Lexington, MA.
Reprinted by permission of the publisher.

The percentage change in metropolitan land area between 1950 and 1970
has been significantly greater than the rate of population growth during
that period. The central city has spilled over into surrounding areas with
suburbanization. This spill-over makes the task of defining the urban
area difficult. The Census Bureau's *urbanized area* concept gives a reasonably accurate picture of the auto-age urban area. An urbanized area consists of a city of at least 50,000 people together with all the continuously
settled territory surrounding this city or cities. The data in the table are
reported for this type of areal unit.

clined. The initial increase in density was due to the concentration of immigrant streams near the city center. The subsequent dispersal resulted from the
advances in transportation technology discussed in Chapter 4, as the railroad,
the streetcar, and the automobile successively extended the commuting range
of the urban community. Indeed, in recent years, the area covered by the modern metropolis has increased many times faster than population growth (see
Table 5.3).

Although industrial cities generally show the same trends in congestion
and decentralization, not all industrial cities change at the same rate. Additionally, industrial cities have patterns of congestion and decentralization which
differ considerably from nonindustrial cities.

Several factors affect the nature and rate of congestion and concentration
in a particular city (Schwirian, 1977). We have already described the influence
of transportation facilities and technology on spatial dispersion. Additionally,
the general growth context of the city and its spatial configuration contribute
to the density pattern.

The *general growth context* includes two aspects: the current rate of population increase, and the rate of housing starts or new residential construction.
Population growth necessitates some basic change in the urban space. This
change involves either concentrating populations at the city core or redistributing these populations in hinterland areas. Each city's spatial response to
growth depends on the nature of the housing market in that city. For rapid decentralization to occur, new housing must be constructed at a rate comparable

to population growth. If construction fails to keep pace with this growth, then the added population must be housed in the older residences of the city, increasing congestion.

The *spatial configuration* of the city also affects the rates of congestion and decentralization. Large cities have shallower, or smaller, density gradients than smaller places (Berry et al., 1963). In essence, large cities are spread out over a wide area. This great territorial expanse means that living at or near the edge of the metropolis is extremely costly in terms of the time and money spent in urban travel (Schwirian, 1977). Because of that cost, the rate of decentralization is slower in the large city. Cities characterized by high densities, on the other hand, should have higher rates of decentralization. As Casetti (1967) argues, in these cities the preference for central location is counterbalanced by the general distaste for congestion. To escape these undesirable consequences, many people move to the suburbs. Indeed, one of the better predictors of suburbanization in United States cities between 1960 and 1970 was the population density in central cities (Weiser, 1977).

Cross-Cultural Variation: Industrial and Third-World Cities

The nature and the direction of the relationship between these forces and urban dynamics differ considerably for industrial and nonindustrial (or Third-World) cities. While the density-distance pattern is the same in both types of cities at any one time, the values of the parameters $D(0)$ and b change differently through time. In industrial cities density gradients decrease continuously, whereas in nonindustrial cities the gradients remain constant. Similarly, in industrial cities, central densities increase and then decline, while in nonindustrial cities central densities increase (see Figure 5.3). This evidence suggests that the nonindustrial city responds to urban population growth differently from the industrial city. As Western cities grow, crowding declines and the city spreads out. In the nonindustrial city, growth simply means overcrowding. These cities remain compact in spite of population expansion, and population growth does not induce urban sprawl.

These cross-cultural differences in spatial dynamics can be clarified by recalling the nature of residential patterns in the preindustrial city. Prior to the growth of industry in cities the most highly valued residential sites were central ones. With industrialization, however, central residential sites became less desirable because of the concentration of heavy industry. This basic shift in site preference encouraged an eventual decline in central densities and a deconcentration of population. Without industrialization, cities in the Third World will encounter rapidly increasing densities and constant compactness. The negative consequences of this implosion are apparent, for example, on the streets of Calcutta, where as many as 400,000 homeless people sleep in the open each night.

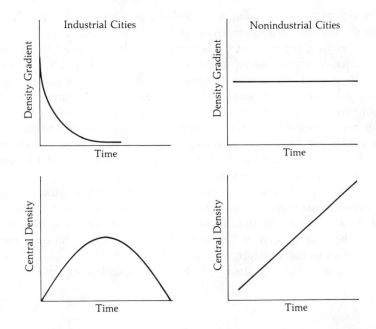

Figure 5.3 *Temporal Comparisons in Density Parameters for Industrial and Nonindustrial Cities* Industrial and preindustrial cities differ significantly in the changes in their density parameters over time. Preindustrial cities continually increase in terms of congestion, while spatial dispersion remains constant. Industrial cities, on the other hand, eventually become less congested and the population continuously disperses. (*Source:* Berry et al., 1963:389–405. Reprinted from the *Geographical Review, Vol. 53, 1963,* with permission of the American Geographical Society.)

Realistic Models of Density Patterns

Over the whole city, Clark's Law provides a good average representation of residential density. However, in the modern industrial city Clark's model over-estimates residential densities at the city center. In this zone it better approximates employment density than residential density. The reason is simply that the urban core specializes in nonresidential activity.

A more accurate model would follow the form of the negative exponential in areas away from the center and would show a marked decrease in density at the core. Newling (1969) presents such a model and describes density as a quadratic rather than a linear exponential function of distance:

$$D(x) = D(0)e^{bx-cx^2}$$

Here *D(0)* represents central density, as before, but now there are two density gradient parameters, *b* and *c*.

This model generates a variety of density patterns including the original Clark formulation and other patterns that portray population decline in the urban center. Newling argues that these forms may be arranged to show the historical sequence of urban configurations in the Western city, as shown in Figure 5.4. In the periods of *youth* and *early maturity* density peaks at the core. In *late maturity* and *old age* this core becomes more and more nonresidential. As the city continues to age, the density peak moves progressively outward, and population becomes more evenly distributed throughout the urban area. This aging process, as has been noted, does not seem to have occurred in preindustrial or contemporary Third-World cities, which seem to be fixed at one of the first two stages of spatial evolution.

Neither Clark's nor Newling's model is a completely satisfactory portrayal of urban density-distance patterns. In each of these simplified accounts, the density of the city at any particular point is a function of the distance between that point and the city's center. Distance, however, is not the only factor producing the urban density pattern (Guest, 1973).

Rees (1968), in a detailed study of Chicago, indicates that the density of an

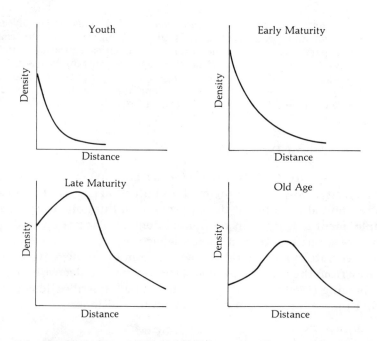

Figure 5.4 *Newling's Stages of Spatial Development*   The actual density-distance relation is best represented by a quadratic rather than linear exponential function. Newling suggests that with age, density peaks farther and farther away from the center. (*Source:* Newling, 1969:242–252. Reprinted from the *Geographical Review*, Vol. 53, 1963, with permission of the American Geographical Society.)

area within the city depends upon the social class of the neighborhood. Originally, the Clark and Newling models were fitted to density averages taken over circular bands of the entire city at various distances from the center. Such averaging masks sectoral variation in density patterns. However, it is possible to fit the models separately to various sectors of the city. Rees provides such an analysis for Chicago, where central densities are highest on the south side in the area of the black ghetto (see Table 5.4). This sector also has the steepest density gradient, indicating heavily concentrated population. Here suburbanization has not occurred to the extent it has in other sectors. This contrasts greatly with the density gradient for the northern sector. The areas on the outer edges of this district are more prestigious than those on the southern edge; as a result, more deconcentration has occurred north of the city. Thus, the variation in density patterns by area seems to be associated with areal differences in socioeconomic status. Prestigious areas tend to have less congestion and a more deconcentrated population distribution.

When distance from city center is controlled, social class appears to be inversely related to density. People in the lowest social classes tend to live in congested areas, whereas people in the upper classes live in areas of low density (Amato, 1970; La Greca and Schwirian, 1974).

The age of an area is also a good predictor of density (Berry et al., 1963). In older areas of the city, housing was constructed with less efficient transportation technologies in mind. Residences were built on smaller lots and tended to be of either the multistoried or townhouse variety.

Although, as we are about to discover, the social class and the age of an area are themselves highly related to distance, neither factor is a perfect function of distance. Each variable independently affects density. For reasons of simplicity, however, the Clark and Newling descriptions of urban structure are taken as adequate for many research purposes.

Table 5.4   Density Parameters by
Sector for the Chicago Metropolitan Area

Parameter	Metropolitan Area	Sector				
		N	NW	W	SW	S
b	.056	.037	.05	.062	.063	.08
D(0)	33.0	39.0	27.7	37.5	29.2	81.1

Source: Rees, 1968, cited in Berry and Horton, 1970:277. Reprinted by permission of Philip Rees.

Density parameters vary by sector in Chicago. This variation is significant because it suggests the influence of social class on the distribution of populations. On the south side extreme congestion with high degrees of population concentration prevail. The south side is the locus for the black ghetto. On the north side congestion is lower and dispersal is greatest. This area generally contains more prestigious homes.

SEGREGATION MODELS

The City as a Mosaic of Social Worlds

Just as areas vary in size and compactness from one portion of the city to the next, they also vary in social character. Indeed, the deconcentration pattern tends to accentuate this variation. As cities decentralize, the social characteristics of core city and hinterland populations become more and more polarized.

The city, as Louis Wirth (1938) observed, is a mosaic of social worlds—an area of great diversity characterized by an equally intensive pattern of residential segregation. Many of the earliest works of human ecologists contend that this pattern of segregation permits the city to function in an orderly fashion. For example, Park writes: "The organization of the city, the character of the urban environment and of the discipline it imposes is finally determined by the size of the population, its concentration and distribution in the urban area" (1925:6). Park's viewpoint is still widely accepted.

Thus the neighborhood, the local social world for the city dweller, is a central concept in urban studies. Before we discuss the patterning of neighborhoods in the urban area, we need to review the varied understandings of this basic social unit.

During the 1920s and 1930s human ecologists saw the city as an organization with a life of its own.

> The city is curiously resistant to the fiats of man. Like the Robot, created by man, it goes its own way indifferent to the will of its creator . . . It becomes apparent that the city has a natural organization that must be taken into account. (Zorbaugh, 1926:188).

Thus the city was viewed not as an artifact of human creation but as a natural phenomenon. So too, its neighborhoods were viewed as *natural areas*. By this term ecologists meant to suggest that the social solidarity of the neighborhood was uninfluenced by political decisions or the norms and values of the larger urban culture. Rather, neighborhood organization directly resulted from individual decisions to locate there. Each area by virtue of its proximity to industry or transportation, or its natural advantages had a distinct physical individuality reflected in land values. This difference in land values tended to sort out the population and produce areas of distinct social character. Because individuals with similar social and cultural backgrounds found themselves living in the same area, a social order emerged in the local community. These unplanned neighborhoods occurred, then, not simply because individuals shared a common home territory but because they also shared a similar social past.

The natural areas conception of the neighborhood has been criticized on several counts. Firey (1945) and Gans (1962a), both of whom looked at specific areas of Boston, suggest that the neighborhood can be viewed more properly as a *cultural area*. Firey criticizes human ecology's emphasis on residential location as an "economizing," or fiscal, activity. Neighborhood space, he points out, symbolizes a cultural heritage; sentiment is attached to space. Neighborhood organization is not simply the result of an accident of location. People choose to live in certain areas of the city because of the particular cultural heritage they bring with them. Christen Jonassen (1949) shows this to be true of the Norwegian community in New York City. He suggests that the primary motive for the relocation of Norwegian neighborhoods since the mid-1800s has been the Norwegians' preference for low-density settings. This distaste for high-density areas is rooted in the very culture of Norway. Of all the industrialized countries of the world, Norway has one of the most scattered populations. Similarly, Gans's work in the west end of Boston suggests that first-generation Italian immigrant enclaves resulted from cultural rather than fiscal consider-ations. Many of the remnants of Italian rural village life survive in these neigh-borhoods.

The cultural areas concept, while critical of the earlier notion of the neigh-borhood, leaves intact one of the basic assumptions of the natural areas ap-proach. Both tend to overemphasize the point that neighbors eventually devel-op ties of loyalty and mutual obligation with their coresidents because of their common backgrounds (Suttles, 1972). This assumption has led many urban crit-ics to claim that neighborhoods are no longer viable social units but mere col-lections of population. Gerald Suttles claims that these critics are misguided. Their conception of a viable neighborhood rests on two naive assumptions:

1. It assumes a "golden age" in which neighbors personally identified with each other. In reality, the neighbor relationship in many rural soci-eties is more aptly characterized as businesslike or secondary than pri-mary (Heberle, 1960). In these communities a person is related to neigh-bors by specific rights and duties established by custom and law. For example, during the Middle Ages in Germany a neighbor could not even leave the area overnight without giving his neighbors advance no-tice. Failure to give such notice cost the offender a fine.

2. It assumes that the local community needs the allegiance of most of its members to be an influential social unit. It is more likely, however, that the modern urban neighborhood acquires its corporate identity and via-bility not so much from a similarity of sentiment as from the fact that its residents are held jointly responsible by other communities for the ac-tivities of its members. "It is in their foreign relations that communities come into existence and have to settle on an identity..." (Suttles, 1972:13). Suttles refers to this concept as the *defended community*.

Both of these faulty assumptions stem from the natural and cultural areas idea that a local community emerges from the sentimental ties to an area and its coresidents. Suttles's concept of the defended community is an important conception of the local community. Unlike the cultural and natural areas ap-proach, it does not insist that common social and cultural background is necessary for a viable neighborhood organization. In essence, cultural and ethnic purity is not essential to the organization's health. Thus, even if segregation were to decline in the city, the neighborhood could survive as a political and social unit.

Traditional Models of Urban Neighborhood Structure

Still, the city is a mosaic of social worlds. The degree of homogeneity within these local social worlds, however, has long been a point of contention. The Chicago School, which produced the natural areas concept, certainly overemphasized the social similarity of neighborhoods in its classic *concentric zone model*. In reaction to this simplistic picture, urban geographers and economists developed two alternative descriptions of the urban space: the *sectoral* and the *multiple nuclei* models. Each of these three models is concerned with describing the geometry or shape of the urban space—a space constructed of individual pockets of homogeneous population and activity (see Figure 5.5).

The Concentric Zone Model   In 1923 Ernest W. Burgess wrote "The Growth of the City: An Introduction to a Research Project," a paper whose impact on the direction of urban social science has been phenomenal. Simply, Burgess suggested that the unplanned or organic city grew in a patterned way. That is, although urban location resulted from individual decisions, land use in the city was orderly and even predictable. As Burgess put it:

> The typical processes of the expansion of the city can best be illustrated, perhaps, by a series of concentric circles which may be numbered to designate both the successive zones of urban extension and the types of areas differentiated in the process of expansion (1923:86).

Thus, the modern city, as it expanded in space, tended to assume a pattern of concentric zones each characterized by a distinct type of land use. This is the basis of the concentric zone model (see Figure 5.5).

In its ideal form, land use in the concentric zone model follows this pattern:

Zone 1: *The Central Business District.* This area is the focus of the city's commercial, civic, and social life. At its heart is the downtown commercial district. Surrounding this area is the wholesale district with its warehouses and markets. While Zone 1 is an area of intense activity, it occupies only a small fraction of urban land. It is the central public space.

Zone 2: *The Zone in Transition.* This is composed of an inner factory district and an outer ring of deteriorating housing. At one time it had been a suburban fringe area housing many of the city's successful members. As the city expanded, however, business and industry began to locate here, and

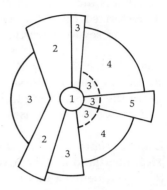

Concentric Zone Theory

Sector Theory

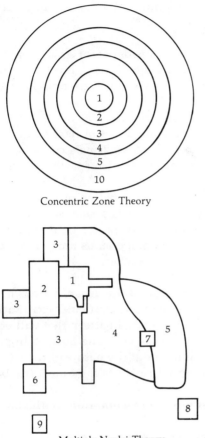

Multiple Nuclei Theory

District

1. Central business district
2. Wholesale light manufacturing
3. Low-class residential
4. Medium-class residential
5. High-class residential
6. Heavy manufacturing
7. Outlying business district
8. Residential suburb
9. Industrial suburb
10. Commuters' zone

Figure 5.5 *Schematic Illustration of Early Theories of Spatial Structure*   The three classic geometric theories of spatial structure are shown, each arguing for a different urban geometry. Both concentric zone and sector theory assume a single-centered city but differ in the amount of homogeneity within residential zones defined by distance. Multiple nuclei theory does not accept the monocentric assumption. It portrays a less clear-cut spatial pattern than the other two. (*Source:* From C. Harris and E. Ullman, "The Nature of Cities." *The Annals of The American Academy of Political and Social Science*, Vol. 242, 1945, pp. 7–17. Reprinted by permission.)

living in this zone became undesirable. Much of the land in this area was bought up by speculators anticipating long-term profits from expanding commerce and industry. In essence, this land lay fallow. Absentee landlords did little to improve residences since they anticipated far greater profits in selling these sites for commercial use.

This is the area of first-generation immigrants and social isolates. It is characterized by a highly mobile population, bad housing, high crime rates, and severe poverty.

Zone 3: *The Zone of Workingmen's Homes.* Residents of this area have achieved enough occupational mobility to escape Zone 2, but they cannot afford the costs of long treks to their place of work. It is predominantly an area of two-family houses.

Zone 4: *The Zone of Better Residences.* This zone and the next contain the great heartland of urban America—the middle class. Zone 4 consists of hotels, apartments, and single-family dwelling units with spacious yards.

Zone 5: *The Commuters' Zone.* Beyond the zone of better residences is an area outside of the legal boundaries of the city. It is a ring of small cities, towns, and villages, most of which are dormitory rather than employing suburbs. The commuters' zone is the least homogeneous area of the city, each suburb having a distinctive residential character.

Burgess makes it very clear that this description of the urban space is not to be taken as an accurate portrait of urban land use in any particular city. Rather, it represents an *ideal type;*[1] that is, it describes the spatial pattern that will occur if certain processes operate without constraint in the city. The Burgess hypothesis is thus couched in a number of assumptions about the nature of the city being described. Cities follow the ideal type only insofar as they meet the basic assumptions of the model.

Schnore (1965a) outlines the stated and unstated assumptions of the model.

1. The central assumption of the zonal hypothesis is that the city is growing. The model is intended to describe the reorganization of space that occurs as the city expands outward radially.

2. In turn, the process of radial expansion is assumed to occur under certain ideal conditions, unaffected by potentially distorting influences. Essentially Burgess assumes that the city lies on a perfectly uniform plane. In such a situation spatial growth is unaffected by natural and artificial barriers to growth such as rivers and mountains, railroad tracks and highways.

   Besides these physical barriers to growth, Burgess ignores other historical and administrative factors that might distort the spatial pattern. These include the survival of an earlier use of a district (because of its historical value or because of the economics involved in changing an al-

---

[1] The ideal type is a theoretical concept developed by Max Weber. It is a mental construct formed by exaggerating a trait or traits found in some real-life situation. It represents an idealized state from which one can measure deviations or variants.

ready built-up area) and the existence of a city master plan to regulate expansion.

3. In addition to the assumed absence of distorting features, the city is understood to be of a particular historical type. Essentially the zonal hypothesis refers only to Western industrial cities. The model presumes an economic system that encourages economic competition and the private ownership of property. In such a system freedom of residential choice depends on economic status. With respect to transportation, Burgess further assumes that in this modern industrial city movement is equally easy, rapid, and cheap in every direction.

4. The model rests on certain assumptions about the geometry of space. In particular, it assumes a single center of commerce and industry.

5. Finally, the hypothesis also assumes the city's population to be particularly diverse. It must be a population with sufficient ethnic and racial variety. There should also be a variety of occupational groups in the population.

Even with these qualifications, the Burgess hypothesis has received a great deal of criticism. Perhaps the most persistent objections to the model involve criticisms of the zonal concept itself. Numerous critics suggest that Burgess's five zones are arbitrary, each zone in fact being considerably more heterogeneous than the model predicts. On the basis of this objection, two alternative descriptions of the urban geometry have been developed.

Sector Theory   The city of sector theory can be divided into pie-shaped wedges or sectors (see Figure 5.5). In this model the socioeconomic characteristics of residents vary most between these sectors rather than between the concentric zones. Like the Burgess model, the theory assumes a growing city and thus actually describes the dynamics of radial expansion. The theory was developed by Homer Hoyt (1939) to describe the internal residential structure of 142 American cities in 1900, 1915, and 1936. From an analysis of this extensive array of data, Hoyt made the following observations:

1. The most highly valued residential areas are located in wedges on one side of the city. Generally, these sectors are located on the city's periphery, but at times a high-rent sector extends out continuously from the center.

2. High-rent areas originate at the periphery of the central business district near the retail, financial, and office districts. This point is always farthest removed from the side of the city with industrial concentrations.

3. Middle-class areas are usually found on either side of the highest-rent areas.

4. Some cities have middle-class housing on the edges of lower-class as well as upper-class areas.

5. Low-rent areas are frequently found opposite the high-rent areas. Usually low-rent areas are in relatively central locations.

On the basis of these observations, Hoyt concludes that the gradient pattern of residence discovered by Park and Burgess holds, but only in specific sectors of the city. According to the gradient pattern, the socioeconomic status of residents rises as distance from the central business district increases. Hoyt, however, argues that the concentric zones mask a great deal of heterogeneity in socioeconomic status. In many cities a single zone may include wedges of lower-, middle-, and upper-class housing.

Essential to Hoyt's model is the dynamics of urban space. While Burgess emphasizes central growth as the key to spatial expansion, Hoyt emphasizes axial growth; that is, socioeconomic differences in sectors built up around the original central business district persist. Thus, high-rent areas do not skip about randomly in the urban space but rather follow definite paths. Movement of these areas over time tends to follow established routes of travel (usually along the fastest transportation lines) or aim toward new concentrations of office buildings, banks, and retail stores. Also, according to Hoyt, high-rent areas tend to move toward high ground, which is free from flood risks, along waterfronts not used by industry, and toward those social groups perceived as the community elite.

The Multiple Nuclei Theory   One of the assumptions common to the concentric zone and sector theories is the existence of single-centered cities; that is, cities in which business and production activity is located at a common point. In many cities, however, the pattern of land use is not built around a single center but rather around several distinct nuclei (see Figure 5.5). Some cities have had this multiple-center pattern almost since their beginnings, but these patterns of multinucleation have proliferated with transportation improvements in the twentieth-century American city.

The Burgess and Hoyt models describe city space at the early stages of the automobile age. In 1920 there was only one auto for every 13 people, whereas in 1970 that ratio dropped to 2.3 persons per auto. This great increase in the number of private passenger cars was a major force in the reshaping of the city space—after Burgess and Hoyt had described the city's spatial pattern. It is not surprising then, that Hoyt later wrote an article citing the recent alterations in the urban form that dated the classical models (1964). The most frequently discussed changes have been the tendency of retail trade and manufacturing to move away from the city center and into the suburbs (see Table 5.5).

The domination of the central business district over retail sales in the metropolis has been seriously weakened by the growth of the suburban shopping center. By the 1960s general merchandise sales were increasing over seventeen times faster in the suburbs than in the central business districts, and suburban

**Table 5.5   Suburban Share of
Metropolitan Employment and Population
for Forty Metropolitan Areas, 1948–1963**

	1948	1954	1958	1963
Employment	%	%	%	%
Manufacturing	33.1	38.6	42.0	51.8
Wholesaling	8.2	14.5	20.7	28.6
Retailing	24.7	30.6	37.2	45.4
Services	15.2	21.6	26.1	31.3
Population	36.0	43.5	48.2	54.3

Source: From J. Kain, "The Distribution and Movement of Jobs and Industry" in J. Q. Wilson, *The Metropolitan Enigma*, 1968. Reprinted by permission of Harvard University Press.

The data on the suburban share of metropolitan employment show that the suburbs have acquired a significant share of metropolitan industry over time. The greatest gains have been in manufacturing and retail trade. Such information suggests that the auto-age city is best characterized by multiple nuclei. Industry has dispersed continually over time with the growth of the suburbs.

shopping centers covered more area than the combined areas of all metropolitan business centers (Hoyt, 1964).

Manufacturing activities in central areas of the city have also seriously eroded. Because of the high building densities and the expense of central area space, manufacturing has decentralized. For example, in Kain's study (1968) of forty metropolitan areas between 1954 and 1963, the central cities experienced a net manufacturing loss of 1,031,920 jobs while the suburbs gained nearly that many jobs.

Harris and Ullman (1945) addressed some of the deficiencies of the concentric and sectoral models by proposing a *multiple nuclei* model of urban geometry. This model suggests that cities develop a number of districts that grow up around distinct centers, each specializing in a particular activity. The growth of these separate districts results from four factors:

1. Certain activities need special facilities. Manufacturing districts require lots of space and access to regional transportation networks, whereas retail districts require less space and more accessibility to local than regional markets.

2. Certain like activities benefit from close proximity to one another. Most important, financial and office districts require close communications with other offices in the area. Retail stores of a particular type also increase potential customers by clustering. Thus we find in the city "automobile row," furniture and carpet districts, and so forth.

3. Although some like activities benefit from proximity, certain unlike activities tend to repel one another. Heavy-industry areas make residence undesirable, and thus high-status residence is atypical in these areas. Manufacturing and warehousing activities also require close proximity to rail facilities and truck terminals. These transport facilities cannot concentrate in retail districts where pedestrian and automobile traffic are heavy.

4. Not all activities can afford the expense of locating in the most desirable areas. Certain activities like warehousing and heavy manufacturing require great expanses of space. In areas where space is at a premium these activities cannot function economically.

Inherent in the Harris-Ullman description is the view that each city's spatial structure is distinctive. The number, variety, and arrangement of districts in the city depend upon the city's history, its current population, and its economic activity. While urban geometry is highly variable from city to city, Harris and Ullman suggest that certain districts commonly occur in all large cities. All these cities have a *central business district*, but, because cities tend to grow asymmetrically (as Hoyt suggested), this commercial area is usually near an edge of the city rather than at its geometric center. Within this district separate centers develop for retail trade, finance, and government activities. Near the central business district an area of *wholesale and light manufacturing* usually emerges. This district locates near interregional transportation facilities. *Heavy industry*, on the other hand, locates near the present or former boundary of the city because of its undesirable effects on the local environ and because of its need for large spaces. *Lower-class residential districts* are likely to occur near this area and near wholesale and light-manufacturing areas. *Upper-class residential districts*, on the other hand, are likely to occur in areas far removed from industry.

The Harris-Ullman model should be treated as a kind of footnote to the two classical theories of residential location. It accepts the Burgess theory's general description of residential distribution; that is, residential social status is decentralized, with higher-status residential areas more likely on the periphery of cities. At the same time, it views sector theory as somewhat more precisely describing the overall geometry of residential distribution. However, because both theories assume a simple urban geometry (a monocentric city), neither portrays the urban shape accurately.

Contemporary Research on Urban Geometry

Although Harris, Ullman, and later critics find fault with both concentric zone and sector models, current research suggests that certain generalizations in these classical theories still hold true. A great deal of empirical research has dealt with the observation in both theories that socioeconomic status tends to increase with distance from the central business district (Duncan and Duncan, 1955; Uyeki, 1964; Schnore, 1965b, 1972; Yeates, 1972). These analyses find at least qualified support for the decentralization hypothesis. Schnore's work (1965b) is most instructive. His study of 200 urbanized areas finds that older cities are most likely to have a decentralized residential status pattern (see Table 5.6). This result does not contradict the Burgess and Hoyt models. Indeed, both theories were intended to describe the change in housing patterns as cities grew. Thus, as cities evolve—and get older—residential status decentralizes (Haggerty, 1971).

What of the disagreement between the two models? Each model suggests a somewhat different geometric pattern of residential distribution. How can the two descriptions be reconciled? Brian Berry (1965), summarizing data collected on the internal structure of a number of cities, suggests that the models are not alternative descriptions but together give a more precise picture of the urban space. Socioeconomic characteristics of urban residents are distributed according to a sector pattern. The educational levels of neighborhoods as well as their occupational and income statuses are arranged along axes drawn from the center of the city to the periphery. Areas of homogeneous socioeconomic status are thus most like Hoyt's pie-shaped wedges.

Areas with similar life-cycle characteristics, however, are best described by

Table 5.6   City-Suburb Differentials in Socioeconomic Status, by Age of Central City, 1960

	Percentage of Urbanized Areas with Higher Suburban Values in:			
Census year in which central city reached 50,000	Median family income	Percentage completing high school	Percentage in white-collar occupations	Number of areas
1800 to 1860	100	100	100	14
1870 or 1880	100	100	100	17
1890 or 1900	86	75	58	36
1910 or 1920	75	75	54	48
1930 or 1940	72	56	31	32
1950 or 1960	51	47	24	53
All areas	74	69	50	200

Source: From *The Urban Scene* by Leo Schnore. Copyright © 1955 by The Free Press. Reprinted with permission of Macmillan Publishing Company, Inc., New York, N.Y.

When information on city-suburban status differentials is arranged according to the age of the city, an evolutionary pattern is apparent. Older urbanized areas are characterized by high-status suburban populations and low-status central city populations. This pattern fits well with Burgess's concentric zone model. The model describes an evolutionary path—as cities grow, high-status populations will eventually be found on the outskirts of the city, while low-status populations will be left behind in the core area.

the concentric zone pattern. The age of the population in an area, the type of housing (single-family owned or rented versus multiple dwelling units), the size of family, and the percentage of women working vary by zones. At the edge of the city and outside it are newer, single-family houses in which larger, younger families reside and where the wife stays at home. These areas are family-oriented places. Toward the center of the city one is more likely to find career-oriented areas with clusters of apartment complexes and concentrations of older, smaller families with working wives.

When the sector and concentric zone patterns are overlaid on a city, one can more accurately describe the neighborhoods of the urban space. Within each sector there is a mix of career- and family-oriented areas but great similarity in social status. Around each concentric zone, on the other hand, there are a variety of status areas but little difference in the life-cycle character of these neighborhoods.

Recent Models of City Structure

Social Area Analysis   The major problem with the classical models of urban geometry appears in attempts to synthesize them. Both the Hoyt and Burgess descriptions assume that people are distributed across neighborhoods according to a single criterion—status. People, however, are segregated in space according to several criteria, each of which produces a somewhat different distribution (Berry, 1965). The first attempt to describe the multidimensional character of the urban space was Shevky and Williams's (1949) analysis of Los Angeles. This research and later work by Shevky and Bell (1955) developed a new approach to urban space called *social area analysis.*

Social area analysis is designed to classify the communities of the city. It is more concerned with the social characteristics of small areas than with their location in the urban space. From an elaborate and sometimes confusing array of hypotheses about the nature of urban societies and the communities they contain, Shevky, Williams, and Bell arrive at three basic constructs that, they argue, describe the social differences among urban neighborhoods. These three constructs are social rank (or economic status), urbanization (or family status), and segregation (or ethnic status). To measure these basic dimensions of residential differentiation, a number of sociodemographic variables reported by *census tracts* (the Census's attempt to define urban neighborhoods) are selected. The *social rank* dimension includes statistics on occupation and education in the tract. The *urbanization* construct is indexed by data on fertility, the proportion of women working outside the home, and the proportion of single-family homes. *Segregation* is measured by the proportion of nonwhite people.

This approach has received considerable criticism. Its most serious critics (Hawley and Duncan, 1957; Udry, 1964) point to Shevky's weak justifications for using the three constructs as a description of neighborhood social structure. As Hawley and Duncan (1957:340) point out, "One searches in vain among these materials for a statement explaining why residential areas should differ one from the other or be homogeneous." Thus, in the view of many social scientists, this deductive approach to the city space fails to provide a convincing description of neighborhood structure. While these criticisms are useful, the theoretical framework of social area analysis can be restated in such a way that it is salvageable, at least in part.

The theory behind social area analysis is based on an interesting premise: "We conceive of the city as a product of the complex whole of modern society; thus the social forms of urban life are to be understood within the context of the changing character of the larger containing society" (Shevky and Bell, 1955:3). This premise runs contrary to Wirth's understanding of the sources of urbanism. Whereas Wirth looked to unique qualities in the city context to explain urban life, Shevky suggests that urbanism is a product of the larger urban society. Thus, the social structure of urban neighborhoods can ultimately be traced to changes in the society itself. The residential differentiation of the city results from society's evolving social differentiation.

As societies modernize, certain changes occur in their social organizations that are eventually translated into local community change. According to the Shevky-Bell theory, modernization results in increasing societal *scale*. By this they mean that as a society modernizes, the social and economic interchanges within that society increase in both extent and intensity. At the local level, economically productive individuals depend more on one another. At the societal level, the society, which was once composed of a number of loosely connected, economically independent communities, is transformed into a network of interacting and interdependent communities. These changes are accomplished by increasing specialization in the division of labor and by improvements in communication and transportation technology. In turn, these changes lead to new bases for differentiation in the modern society. The growing specialization of tasks leads to the development of a status system based on achieved (e.g., occupation, education) rather than ascribed (e.g., ethnicity, family social position) criteria. Occupational status rather than the ownership of land becomes the key to stratification in the modern industrial society. Under such conditions the family declines in importance as an economic unit. While historically the family could control the ownership of land, it had little influence over occupational placement. This results in the spread of alternative family patterns. Since the family is no longer the basic producing unit, households can opt for the more traditional large family or they can choose to reduce family size in order to increase their chances for social mobility. Finally, improved transportation and communication capabilities increase the mobility of the population. This allows for a greater diversity of populations within a given community. Freedom of mobility also makes residential choice more feasible for the masses. Ironically, freedom of choice results in the segregation of these diverse populations in the local community.

Thus, an increase in societal scale socially differentiates people along dimensions of social class, life style, and culture. In the Shevky-Bell thesis these three dimensions are translated as social rank, urbanization, and segregation, which are the bases of local residential differentiation. The social character of urban neighborhoods can then be described with reference to the three Shevky-Bell constructs.

Just how accurate is the Shevky-Bell typology? As we have seen, its justification is theoretical. Unlike the earlier models of Burgess and Hoyt, it is not based on empirical observations. Van Arsdol et al. (1958) studied ten large American cities in an attempt to assess the validity of the classification scheme and found that only six cities conformed to Shevky's indexes. That four cities did not fit the pattern seemed to suggest that the types of differentiation should be empirically derived rather than logically deduced from some grand theory of social change. This led students of the city to a different approach to the urban space—factorial ecology.

Factorial Ecology   Factorial ecology uses a statistical technique called factor analysis to describe the social character of urban neighborhoods. The chief aim of factor analysis is economy of description. Given a large set of variables and their correlations with one another, factor analysis enables us to see the pattern of relationships among variables. This pattern is expressed by categorizing sets of variables into factors or dimensions that are empirically independent of one another. In essence it creates a multidimensional typology from the existing data rather than from some underlying theory (as in the case of social area analysis). Factorial ecology involves applying this technique to large data sets describing the differences among residential areas of the city. Typically, the data analyzed include a range of demographic, socioeconomic, and housing variables reported for small areas (usually census tracts). The model aims to account for the great differences in neighborhood characteristics through a much smaller number of factors.

The growing criticism of social area analysis coupled with tremendous improvement in computer technology has led to a great expansion in factorial ecology research. What is most striking about this research is the general consistency of findings. A great deal of the variety in residential patterns within cities of the Western world can be explained by three underlying factors. A factor referring to *socioeconomic status* has been found in almost all cities and cultures studied. A *family characteristics* dimension is also typically discovered, although for cities in less-developed countries this factor cannot be separated from socioeconomic status. A third factor emerges with sufficient regularity to suggest that it is a usual characteristic in residential differentiation. This dimension, *ethnic composition*, occurs most frequently in the ethnically heterogeneous cities of the Western world.

In considering the earlier work of social area analysis, these findings raise two important points. First, for cities in the Western world the empirical results of factorial ecology and the logically deduced typology of social area analysis are strikingly similar. As the theory predicts, the local areas of Western world cities are segregated according to socioeconomic, family, and ethnic criteria.

But what of the dissimilarity between the cities of economically advanced and disadvantaged nations? Here, too, social area analysis is instructive. In the Shevky-Bell thesis, the residential differentiation of the city varies according to the scale of the particular society. It is not surprising, then, that in the underdeveloped nations of the world the dimensions of residential structure do not separate as they do in the West.

> In small-scale societies, or societies that are low on modernization indicators, there is little social differentiation of these three [major] dimensions; that is, social status is highly related to family patterns and both are related to ethnicity. In such a society to know one's status is also to be able to successfully predict one's family patterns and ethnic standing (Schwirian, 1977:193).

As societies modernize, segregation patterns within cities become more complex and thus more subtle.

Schwirian and Smith's (1974) cross-cultural analysis of Puerto Rican and Canadian cities suggests the nature of the relationship between modernization and urban segregation patterns. In the highly modernized Canadian society city size and areal differentiation do not appear to be related. Canadian cities, in general, are arranged according to social rank, family status, and ethnic factors. In the economically developing Puerto Rican society, however, the arrangement of the city's space depends on its size. The largest city in Puerto Rico, San Juan, shows a pattern of areal differences comparable to those of cities in economically advanced nations. The smaller cities in Puerto Rico, however, reflect the less subtle segregation pattern of cities in the Third World. Schwirian explains this difference in terms of the typical path of economic development: .

> In societies in the midst of the economic development process, the rates of social change are not uniform across the whole society. Change proceeds at a much faster pace in the region of the primate city (the largest city) . . . Change comes first to the primate city and then diffuses throughout the rest of the society (Schwirian and Smith, 1974:325).

Modernization leads to an increasing variety in neighborhood areas, but what characteristics in a society make this growing differentiation within the city possible? Unless there is almost no relationship between social class and family characteristics, three factors must be present to permit a separation of social rank and family status factors (Abu-Lughod,1968):

1. Each stage of the life cycle must be associated with a change in residence.

2. For every economic level, the city must have neighborhoods with hous-

ing accommodations suitable to families at particular points in their life cycle.

3. The values of the culture should encourage mobility as the means of suiting individuals to housing needs; sanctions against movement should be minimal.

In the underdeveloped nations such conditions simply do not exist. Kinship is the very basis of social organization, and the extended family is a key institution. Status and identity, in the larger society and in the local community, are determined largely by kinship structure. Under such conditions, spatial mobility is limited, and segregation is clear-cut.

Factorial ecology provides the urban researcher with an acceptable method for mapping the social areas of the city. However, as we will see in later chapters, the theoretical framework of Shevky and Bell is useful in understanding the role of societal change in the segregation process. It traces urban segregation to the nature of the society rather than the individual urban community.

SUMMARY

The urban space is highly structured. Social scientists disagree somewhat about the exact features of this structure, but all would hold the following ideas:

1. In all cities populations are distributed unevenly in the urban space. The differential distribution of populations within the city is at least in part predicted by distance from the city center.

2. As population deconcentration accelerates, social status and distance from the city center become directly related. This relationship between distance and social status is more accurately expressed by a sector, rather than concentric zone pattern.

3. The residential space of preindustrial and industrial cities differs in systematic ways. While the preindustrial city is congested and compact, the industrial city is spread over a wider territory and is less congested. In terms of social space the industrial city is also more finely segregated than the preindustrial city since the bases for residential segregation are more varied in the industrial city.

4. Perhaps the major factors in any reorganization of city space are the overall society's level of modernization, the city's general growth context, and its dominant modes of transportation.

PART TWO

The Process of Spatial Change

In previous chapters we attempted to describe the structural features of urban space. The chapters in this section deal with the processes that generate these spatial patterns. We begin in Chapter 6 with a discussion of the most fundamental of all such processes: the way people form and use mental images of their environment. We already know from Chapter 2 that spatial structure influences behavior through the shared images people have of their environment. These images condition spatial decision making in activities such as shopping, recreation, and house or apartment hunting. Images thus ultimately influence how city spaces change.

In Chapter 7 we consider why individuals shift residences in the city. Here we focus on individual decision making itself—or the patterns of behavior influenced by human cognition. Ultimately all spatial changes can be linked to these individual decisions concerning spatial mobility. Although this individual (or disaggregate) approach provides important clues to why neighborhoods change, most studies of such changes have adopted an aggregate (or ecological) perspective. Chapter 8 views spatial evolution in these terms, as a process of neighborhood change, and emphasizes the collective movement decisions of populations rather than individuals.

The chapters in Part Two are arranged hierarchically. We begin by analyzing spatial experience and behavior as a basic psychological process—human cognition. Then spatial change is viewed as the result of social psychological processes—individual movement decisions made within social contexts. Finally spatial change is considered as a group process in which some neighborhood populations are more likely to change than others. Each of the three approaches provides somewhat different information about spatial evolution. The end of Chapter 8 combines information from these perspectives to provide a synthetic account of areal change.

Chapter 6

Images of the Urban Space

INTRODUCTION

The entire urban fabric and all the behavior within it are ultimately products of human *decision making*. We may define decision making as a process of choice that leads to the selection of certain types of behavior over others. Decision making occurs at many levels. Decisions are made by individuals carrying out their everyday pursuits, by businesses attempting to maximize profits, by governments attempting to balance individual and business interests, and by planners who are consciously manipulating the urban space.

In each case, these decisions are guided by urban images. We may loosely define *image* as the sum total of an individual's knowledge and beliefs about an environment—in this case, a city. The study of image and image formation is central to urban social science. The city is an immensely complex physical and social space. To appreciate it and to live in it, the urbanite must make sense of it. In Chapter 3 we suggested that personal knowledge could not effectively guide the city dweller through the urban experience. Categorical knowledge, or urban imagery, is necessary to guide the urbanite's behavior. "The city, as a whole, is inaccessible to the imagination unless it can be reduced and simplified. Even the oldest resident and the best-informed citizen can scarcely hope to know even a fair-sized city in all its rich and subtle detail" (Strauss, 1961:8). Images simplify this complex environment and make the cityscape comprehensible.

Image formation and decision making underlie almost all behavior in the urban space. In turn, most of these behaviors can be understood as some kind of *spatial problem solving* (goal-directed activity in a spatial setting). Space puts distance between actors and/or objects. Thus, to satisfy basic interests and needs, we must move toward potential sources of satisfaction or have them move toward us. Urban social scientists generally deal with two basic types of spatial problem solving: *repetitive* or *recurrent* travel, which embraces shopping, commuting, social and recreational travel; and *residential mobility*, which refers to the most important spatial decision most of us ever make—where to live.

This chapter contains information on spatial images and their role in spatial decision making in general and recurrent travel in particular. Chapter 7 addresses the topic of residential decision making in more detail.

COGNITIVE VERSUS RATIONALISTIC MODELS OF DECISION MAKING

We defined decision making as involving choice and indicated that choices are influenced by images of the urban environment. On closer examination, however, the idea of choice in many everyday situations is elusive. It is customary to reserve the term *choice* (and the term *decision making*) for situations involving conscious selection. In fact, many types of urban spatial behavior may be characterized as *habitual* (such as driving to work every day along the same route or frequenting the same set of shops). The borderline between choice behavior and habitual behavior is not clear-cut. While a habit may result from decisions made earlier, habitual behavior involves no immediate decision making. Also, we tend to think that acts of choice involve volition, or free will. In fact, we probably use free will less often than we would like to believe.

Within the social sciences two distinct and contrasting accounts of decision making are in use—the *rationalistic* and *cognitive*. This chapter will deal exclusively with the cognitive approach. However, the rationalistic approach has produced important classes of models in urban economics, urban geography, and human ecology. Because we will deal with these models in later chapters, we will take time to compare the two approaches now.

Urban economics, human ecology, regional science, and traditional urban geography frequently employ assumptions about rationalistic behavior drawn from the theory of economics. The assumptions involve a mythological creature called *economic man*. This person has the following characteristics:

1. *Perfect knowledge.* He or she is assumed to have a mental image of reality that is complete and accurate in all respects and that includes a complete knowledge of all economic values and prices.

2. *Optimizing behavior.* The rational individual is assumed to seek tirelessly for the "best" alternatives, using unlimited abilities to evaluate and compute.

3. *Profit maximization.* As a producer the rational individual is assumed to be concerned only with maximizing profit. As a consumer, the individual seeks only to maximize utility.

To appreciate the value of these seemingly absurd assumptions, you must understand the difference between descriptive and normative models. *Descriptive* models attempt to reproduce reality as closely as possible. As descriptive models of human behavior, the assumptions above are obviously unacceptable. No one actually behaves this way. *Normative* accounts, on the other hand, begin with an idealized account of reality and deduce its consequences. The power of normative models lies in analyzing the discrepancy between the idealized results and the actual empirical results. This approach is useful in measuring the efficiency of actual behavior by comparing it to some optimal behavior or in prescribing goals for planning purposes. Normative models are widely used in urban planning, for example. Despite their usefulness, it is obvious that the rationality assumptions do not accurately describe real behavior. They represent a good normative model but a poor descriptive one.

Many economists and other social scientists are dissatisfied with the descriptive power of the rationality assumptions. H. A. Simon (1957), for example, developed the idea of *bounded rationality*, which proposes that individuals are rational but within the bounds of their imperfect knowledge. For example, in seeking a new home they choose the best available, but their set of known alternatives is a very small subset of the total existing set. Bounded rationality relaxes the "perfect knowledge" assumption. A different modification of the rationality assumptions discussed by Simon involves the idea of *satisficing* rather than *optimizing* behavior. He argues that individuals do not necessarily seek the best in any sense. Instead, they seek an adequate alternative, determined by some internal *aspiration level* (Siegel, 1957). This modification relaxes the "profit-maximization" assumption. The question of whether choice behavior is boundedly rational or satisficing when seeking a new home will be discussed in the next chapter.

The account of behavior that underlies most work in sociology, behavioral geography, environmental psychology, and related fields may be called *cognitive*. It has its roots in psychological theory, and it represents a descriptive rather than a normative approach. Instead of assuming rationality, this approach acknowledges that reality can only affect behavior insofar as the individual perceives and experiences it. Because of human limitations to knowing, the *experiential environment* is imperfect and incomplete, yet its image guides behavior (Boulding, 1956).

The cognitive approach recognizes that our knowledge of reality and our specific images of the urban environment are acquired by perception and cognition. The primary source of information for these images is physical *perception*, which involves the reception of information through the sense organs. The experiences provided by perception are organized internally through what psychologists call *cognitive processes*. The term *cognitive* refers to the knowledge or belief elements of mental images. Our mental images of urban space are imperfect. These imperfections, or distortions, are not in the least surprising, since reality contains an immeasurable amount of information, of which our sense organs can only process a part. Some of this selectivity is purely perceptual, determined by the physical limitations of these sensing mechanisms (for example, we do not see infrared). A more important type of selectivity occurs at a cognitive rather than a perceptual level. Cognitive selectivity is determined primarily by culture. Culture structures our cognitive processes, making them very selective. The senses, especially vision, receive enormous amounts of information, only a small portion of which ever reaches the conscious mind. There is evidence that filtering and selection are governed by language and previous experience. Whorf (1956) argues that language structures the way we think about the world. Also, Gestalt psychologists suggest that we view our world in unified wholes, or patterns, that are learned. For example, blind adults who recover their vision surgically have to undergo long training before they can "see." To understand the perception and cognition of urban space, we need to investigate these filtering mechanisms.

Intimately associated with cognitive aspects of image but logically distinct from them are *preferences.* Preferences are called *affective* because they represent feelings about the components of an imaged real world. Cognitive and affective processes together lead to the formation of *attitudes* which predispose us to behave in particular ways.

The formation of preferences is related to an individual's underlying structure of values, which results from innumerable cultural, social, and personal determinants. The step from internal attitudes to the actual preferences revealed in overt behavior is very complicated. It involves the decision-making process by which an individual's actions are related to his or her value structure. The rationalistic account of the decision process is naive. It assumes that the individual is perfectly knowledgeable, that preferences are viewed in profit and loss terms, and that the individual always behaves so as to maximize these profits. In reality, however, our preferences may only be vaguely defined; from force of habit, social pressure, or for expediency we may even act contrary to what we ourselves judge to be our optimal course of action.

Most of this chapter deals with cognitive image rather than with decision processes. The next section addresses the nature of space and of spatial imaging.

THE NATURE OF THE SPATIAL IMAGE: HUMAN PERCEPTION AND COGNITION

The Nature of Space

All cognitive and rationalistic models of urban spatial behavior contain basic assumptions about the nature of space. Usually these assumptions are implicit, and space is not precisely defined. Space and concern for its mathematical representation is of such great concern in the natural sciences that philosophers have devoted a good deal of attention to just what space is.

Two profoundly different approaches to space are the *absolutist* and the *relativist* accounts. The absolute view of space is associated with Isaac Newton. He saw space as a container, as a kind of ultimate frame of reference. Newton's contemporary Leibniz disagreed with this view and argued that space can only be defined in terms of the relative positions of material objects. The idea that space would somehow remain behind if all matter were removed does not make sense in this view, which has been confirmed by Einstein's theory of relativity. Today the absolutist view of space is not accepted. For example, the word *motionless* can only be defined with reference to other objects, and not in any absolute sense. As you sit reading this book, you may be sitting still but you are not motionless relative to the sun!

Such philosophical discussions are related to another contemporary question concerning space. Which geometry best describes reality? From an abstract point of view each geometry may be regarded as a set of axioms and theorems about entities termed points, lines, and so forth. In the nineteenth century it was realized that many consistent geometries can be constructed. Although Euclid's geometry is still used and taught for everyday purposes, it appears that the universe on a large scale is best described by a geometry developed by Riemann. This apparently abstract issue of alternate geometries has had a profound impact on recent geographical studies of space perception. Although the surface of the earth itself is adequately described by Euclid, this is not necessarily true of our mental or perceptual maps (Tobler, 1976). Consider, for example, three points A, B, and C along a straight highway. In reality it must be true that the distance AC is the sum of the distances AB and BC. However, an individual may perceive and cognize these three portions of the highway quite separately. There is no logical reason why the perceived distances need satisfy AC = AB + BC. As we will see in a subsequent section, work on the perception of distance has tended to confirm these ideas. People do not always perceive space in Euclidean ways.

Our primary concern here is with distinguishing the basic properties of space. Space has both metric and topological components. *Metric* properties of space are qualities that can be measured numerically; they depend ultimately upon distance. Examples are lines, curves, directions, and angles that can be measured by a ruler or protractor. *Topological* properties of space are more abstract qualities that do not depend upon distance. Examples are the order in which points are interconnected, the identity of regions with insides and outsides, and other properties of points, lines, and regions that do not depend upon distance. For example, a triangle has three vertices, each one of which connects exactly two sides, and the triangle has a meaningful inside and outside no matter what the metric properties of its sides and angles. There is evidence that we organize our perception of space more topologically than metrically.

Cognition of Space

The German philosopher Kant has greatly influenced our understanding of space perception. He argued that we do not build up our spatial images purely from sense perception. Instead, he claimed, we come equipped with a "prior" intuition of space (that is, a built-in method of organizing our experience spatially). Although Kant's philosophy is not widely accepted today, his idea that we are predisposed to structure experience in spatial ways remains important. Jones writes:

> Though it seems clear that Kant was mistaken in believing that such-and-such specific forms of spatial putting together are a priori, it does not follow that he was mistaken about space being a form of the mind's apprehension of its world. Space might be a mode of ordering contributed by the mind and the various geometries might be accounts of the various possible types of such ordering (1952:825).

About two-thirds of all sensory nerve fibers entering the central nervous system come from the eyes. This is significant because the eye primarily detects patterns of space. Therefore we perceive our universe in essentially spatial terms.

Gestalt psychology emphasizes the importance of space in perception, particularly the role of bounded spaces in organizing visual experience. This concept is demonstrated in Figure 6.1. In A lines of different lengths converge at a point, and the figure lacks pattern. When the drawing is bounded as in B, however, you can discern two patterns, both crosses, one with slender arms. As the observer concentrates on the central point, one cross emerges and becomes dominant, while the other becomes part of the background. This effect is termed the *figure-ground relationship*. It shows that the bounds of a space affect the perception and cognition of objects within it.

All human self-identity and action is linked to the formation of mental cat-

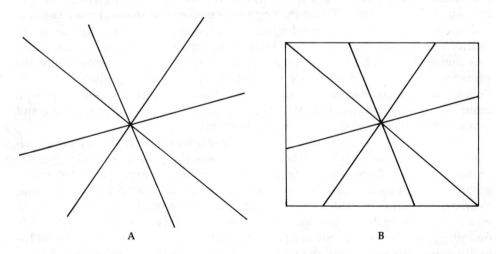

A   B

Figure 6.1 *The Figure-Ground Relationship*   This example from Gestalt psychology indicates the importance of boundaries in the perception and cognitive organization of space. A appears to be devoid of pattern. When boundaries are imposed in B, a crosslike form emerges. This example is referred to as a figure-ground relationship. It hints at the major role boundaries seem to play in cognition of urban space.

egories—what psychologists term *concept formation*. We think in terms of wholes, and these wholes must be bounded (a beautiful painting is not considered aesthetically pleasing until it has been framed).

> In organizing sensory phenomena, the individual responds to stimuli in terms of patterns—and it is the segregation of circumscribed wholes which enables the sensory world to appear imbued with meaning. Studies have shown that the organization of wholes is affected by such factors as proximity and the presence of closed areas (Taylor, 1972:243).

With this in mind, recall some of the conclusions of Chapter 3. As the city became more complex (larger, denser, and more heterogeneous), it also became more segregated. Our cognitive processes strive to create coherent wholes out of the city's diversity. We endow neighborhoods and districts with uniformity (which may be partly imaginary). The result is a cognitively manageable mosaic. In essence, spatial segregation both real and imagined produces an understandable environment.

How do people form and use such images? The discussion of animal behavior in Chapter 2 indicated that spatial location and locomotion underlie virtually all behavior in territorial animals, and that intimate familiarity with territory has great survival value. In most species these behaviors seem to be inherited. The ethologist Lorenz, however, has argued that in higher animals (including primates) these mechanisms may be learned. Primates can make "imagined" movements; an animal can "visualize" certain potential movements, such as reaching for food or moving along a branch, without physically performing them. Such an ability clearly requires a detailed knowledge of spatial relationships. Lorenz terms the cognitive element of spatial image the *central spatial model* (1971). Archeological evidence suggests that humans spent millions of years as hunters in the featureless grasslands of East Africa, in direct competition with far stronger predators. During that time strong selective pressures for efficient mechanisms of spatial behavior were probably at work. To survive, humans had to develop a detailed understanding of their environment. In humans the central spatial model appears to be more far reaching and more highly organized than in any other animal.

Our cognition of space presumably shares features with that of other primates, but it also has symbolic and verbal aspects that seen to be unique in the animal kingdom. Lorenz and others have described a surprisingly large segment of human mental activity in terms of the central spatial model. We tend to interpret many variables that are aspatial in a spatial way. For example, many of our images and metaphors for time are phrased in spatial terms. We describe time as occurring in intervals. The Latin roots of the word *interval* literally mean "space between the walls." We speak of a long time or a short time, midday, and afternoon.

Thus evidence indicates that human beings possess a very highly developed sense of space, one that is intimately related both to their heritage of primate evolution and to uniquely human conceptual and symbolic abilities.

Some relevant modern research on the brain indicates that the two hemispheres of the human brain perform different functions (Gazzaniga, 1972). In right-handed people the left hemisphere tends to perform analytic functions associated with reasoning, calculation, language, and symbolism, while the right hemisphere performs synthetic functions including the processing of pictorial images, the governing of emotions, and aesthetic appreciation. Apparently humans are unique among animals in this respect. The point that concerns us is that both hemispheres are involved in forming and using mental maps. The anatomical complexity of the process partly accounts for the great complexity of our concepts of space.

Try the following experiment. Ask yourself a number of questions about a city you know well, such as: How would I get from A to B? Roughly how far is it from C to D? How well do I know the following neighborhoods . . . ? What are the most prominent features of a given area? In attempting to answer these questions you will discover that a variety of different processes are involved. You will find yourself visualizing areas, maps, pictures, and diagrams you may have seen. You will at the same time systematically reconstruct a setting; for example, attempting to count blocks, or asking yourself "Where would I go at this intersection?" and you might find yourself using items of local knowledge in a fashion that is very hard to classify as either pictorial or verbal.

Downs and Stea (1977) have attempted to identify the basic elements of space cognition that arise in spatial problem solving. They argue that to solve the spatial problems of everyday behavior, people need to know certain properties of place. They summarize these properties under the term *whereness*. The essential components of the whereness of places are:

1. *Identity.* The distinctive identifiers of a place: its name, or its street number, the name of an area or locality. Downs and Stea point out that place names frequently carry overtones of meaning, symbolism, and value. In spite of what Shakespeare said about "a rose by any other name," the particular identifiers we attach to places play an extremely important role in our images of space. Iceland sounds like a cold, infertile wasteland, whereas Greenland suggests a land of verdant hillsides and warmth. We have these images of the two areas because of their place names. Actually, Greenland is not green, and Iceland is a lot less forbidding than it sounds.

2. *Location.* This attribute of place, which is logically quite distinct from its identity, concerns relative or absolute location in space. It could be specified, for example, by map coordinates or by latitude and longitude. Such an abstract characterization of location is unusual under ordinary situations. We are more likely to describe location in terms of proximity to other places or in terms of a sequence of path-finding instructions that indicate how to get to a particular place.

3. *Distance.* Distance plays a more important role in spatial image or behavior than absolute location. People cognize distance in many ways, which

are not limited to measures of feet or miles. In fact, most people are rather hazy about the precise distances they cover every day. We tend to think of distance in terms of effort, travel time, travel cost (e.g., bus fare). A subsequent section deals in more detail with cognition of this spatial variable.

4. *Direction.* Direction, like distance, is a metric property of space. Our sensitivity to it, our "sense of direction," varies considerably from individual to individual. In prehistory and even in modern hunting societies such as the Eskimos, a sense of direction is a crucial survival trait. Many "primitive" peoples are skillful in orienting themselves by the direction of the stars, the wind, the sun, and by clues from vegetation. In modern cities a sense of direction is much less crucial to survival! In fact, almost all urban routes are so roundabout that in proceeding from A to B, we move successively in various compass directions. Still, a sense of the relative orientation of major urban landmarks is required to create accurate mental images, at least for areas of urban space that are too large to be taken in at a single glance. Identity, location, distance, and direction are basic elements of spatial understanding. These elements meld together to form an integrated image of place—what is frequently referred to as a *cognitive map* (Downs and Stea, 1977).

Cultural Variables and the Cognition of Space

Despite Kant's suggestion that it is human nature to view our world in a spatial way, and despite Downs and Stea's suggestion that our understanding of space contains certain universal elements, spatial understanding varies by culture. Before we consider the Western image of the city, we will attempt to portray some of the cultural variations.

We can, of course, perceive spatial phenomena with all of our senses. Our images and memories of particular places are composites of past sights, sounds, and smells. A particular taste or smell can call back remembrances of past events and places. Proust's enormous novel *Remembrance of Things Past* consists of reminiscences sparked by the taste of a particular long-forgotten confectionery. Cities themselves have distinct smells often associated with particular districts. The dank, musty smells of the French Quarter in New Orleans are unforgettable, as are the aromas of the ethnic neighborhoods of New York and the sickening stench of carcasses in the slaughter house districts of Chicago and Cincinnati. A striking example of such association is found in Waldo Frank's description of Chicago: "The spirit of the place—perhaps its soul: an indescribable stench. It is composed of mangled meat, crushed bones, blood soaking the floor, corroding the steel, and sweat. A stench that is warm and thick, and stubborn" (cited in Strauss, 1961:15). Despite the primitive power of smell and taste, and their association with particular places and values (bakeries, home cooking, farmyards, railroad stations, etc.), they normally play only a minor role in forming useful images of place.

Although the modern Western city is an extremely noisy place, we make little use of sound in finding our way or in regulating our behavior. Acoustically, places in the preindustrial city were more clearly differentiated than they are today. Street noise was at a far lower level, and purposeful sounds, such as curfews and church bells, played an important role in regulating urban life.

Vision vastly exceeds all our other senses in its capacity to transmit information about the environment. A number of interesting intercultural differences in visual cognition have been detected. Since seeing is learned, it is reasonable to expect differences between groups that live in widely differing environments. An astonishing example is found in Colin Turnbull's *Forest People* (1961), a classic study of African pygmies. A group of pygmies, who spend their lives in dense forests, were brought out onto the plains. A herd of buffalo were grazing in the far distance. A pygmy asked Turnbull, "What insects are those?" and refused to believe that they were buffalo. Lacking a sense that size diminishes with distance, he thought the creatures were much too small to be buffalo!

Another far more general difference in visual cognition exists between peoples who live in carpentered and noncarpentered environments (Segall et al., 1966). Americans live in a world dominated by straight lines and right angles in our cities and in the rooms where we live and work. You need only glance around to be convinced of this. By contrast, in many preindustrial cultures angles and straight lines are very rare in everyday life. The Zulu of South Africa, for example, have a traditional culture entirely without words or concepts for squares or rectangles. Their doors, windows, houses, and villages are round (Ittelson et al., 1974:117). Experiments with optical illusions suggest that such peoples lack the sense of perpendicularity and linear perspective that we develop from early childhood (Allport and Pettigrew, 1957). These examples suggest cultural differences in our visual knowledge of the environment. Though interesting, such differences are insignificant by comparison with cultural variations in the meanings and values ascribed to the environment.

Basic spatial attributes of environment assume extraspatial or symbolic meaning in many cultures. Compass direction is a good example. Tuan (1974) provides many examples of the association of symbols, values, and colors with the principal compass directions. Among the Oglala Sioux the associations are: north, white, wind; south, yellow, summer, growth; west, black, thunder, rain; east, red, light, wisdom. In the traditional culture of China, similar associations were interpreted specifically in terms of city plans and played a role in regulating activity in the "ideal" city. Chang'an, capital of the T'ang dynasty, was partially laid out in accord with these principles (Tuan, 1974). The associations were: south, red, summer, happiness (petitioners approached the palace from the south); center, yellow, desire; west, white, autumn, sorrow; east, green, spring, anger; north, black, winter, fear.

Closely associated with the meanings ascribed to items in the landscape are the values we attach to certain spatial structures. Despite our complex and sometimes contradictory evaluation of the city, it is clear that our cultural values influence the urban experience. A given value system may cause an almost imperceptible feature of the environment to become a prominent item in the mental landscape. For example, it would be impossible to discover visually the enormous symbolic significance of the battle site at Bunker Hill in Boston. Members of a single culture share more than common environmental values and knowledge. They share language, and this, too, has been shown to enormously influence the formation of cognitive images. The hypothesis of *linguistic relativity* (Whorf, 1956) goes further, suggesting significant variations in cognition between speakers of different languages. This is plausible, since many of our concepts (cognitive categories) are linguistic. It is known, for example, that languages develop rich vocabularies for the most common experiences of the speakers. Thus Eskimos have many descriptive terms for snow, as do Arabs for camels or Americans for the parts of an automobile (Bourne et al., 1971).

Finally, our culture differs qualitatively from all others in urban history in the variety of sources of information incorporated in urban images. Direct sense perception and verbal information from personally known others have been supplemented by information from the mass media. Most literate people in the world have some mental picture of Paris, New York, or Jerusalem, though they may never have been within a thousand miles of these places. In large cities people are as likely to experience changes in the urban space (e. g., new construction) through reports of local media as by personal observation.

Images of Urban Space

The first widely read study of the urban spatial image was done by the architect-planner Kevin Lynch. Although the methodology was crude by today's standards, Lynch's *Image of the City* (1960) represented a revolutionary approach to the study of urban imagery.

Lynch studied residents' images of three contrasting cities: Boston, Los Angeles, and Jersey City. A long interview was conducted with a small sample of residents in each city. In Boston additional information was gathered both in the field and the laboratory. A variety of "image elicitation" questions were asked in these settings. Respondents provided information that included quickly drawn maps of the city, lists of the city's distinctive features, descriptions of various types of trips through the city, and descriptions of particular urban features. Lynch concedes that the small size of these samples (which were biased toward the managerial-professional class) restricts the generality of his findings. However, Lynch's data have proved valuable in setting guidelines for future studies and in yielding general ideas that have been supported in subsequent research.

Lynch was primarily concerned with visual image. He hypothesized that despite the vagaries of individual perception, different people's images of the same area share many common features. Thus it is possible to speak of a group or public image of a locale. According to Lynch a group image is the product of the environment's imageability, which he defines as "that quality in a physical object which gives it a high probability of evoking a strong image in any given observer" (1960:9). Lynch argues that imageability is closely related to a quality of *legibility*. He defines a legible city as one "whose districts, or landmarks, or pathways are easily identifiable and are easily grouped into an overall pattern" (1960:3).

In Lynch's view, a high degree of legibility in the urban landscape is desirable for the following reasons:

1. Clarity is intrinsically desirable for esthetic reasons; cluttered images are generally deemed ugly. A plesasing image is focused and simple, whether the image is a photograph, painting, or city.

2. A legible city is easy to use. It readily provides the environmental cues people need for successful orientation and efficient spatial behavior. This is especially vital because of the size, complexity, and potential confusion of the modern city (see Chapter 3). As Milgram and Lofland suggest, we organize our lives spatially to prevent the heterogeneity of the city from overwhelming us. Caryl River's description of a personal experience in Washington vividly and honestly portrays the importance of legible spatial organizations in everyday activity.

> The world of black Washington might as well have been on Mars, for all we knew of it. We drove through it, peering from behind locked car doors at dark people sitting on the stoops of redbrick row houses. We felt insulated on the other side of the District line, but we understood how things were. I remember one of the jokes we used to tell:
> A white Washingtonian picks up a black hitchhiker in Alabama. The man is shuffling, servile. "Please, sir, can I have a ride, sir?"
> In Atlanta, the white man opens the door and says: "Get out now, boy."
> "Oh, please, sir, let me ride a little further, sir."
> This goes on through the major cities of the South until the driver crosses Memorial Bridge from Virginia into Washington. He opens the door again and says: "Get out now, boy."
> The black man grabs him, pulls a knife and snarls: "Who you calling 'boy,' white man?"
> Implicit in the joke was a concept of territory we all accepted without really understanding it. I first became aware of it in more than a subliminal way when I was driving through Southeast Washington one night with some of my high-school friends. We were coming home from a Chesapeake Bay beach (white, gentiles only). We made a wrong turn, and at the same instant everyone in the car realized that outside there were nothing but black people for miles and miles and miles. We were all suddenly and irrationally afraid. No one had looked at us in a hostile way; few people even noticed us. But I felt, for the first time in my life, that I was not on my own ground. I had assumed, I suppose, that every place in the United States of America was "my turf." I had a glimpse, in those few nervous moments, of what it must be like so often to be black in white America (Rivers, 1972, quoted in Downs and Stea, 1977:136).

3. In addition to guiding actual behavior, an orderly image provides a broader frame of reference within which activity as well as beliefs and knowledge can be organized. "Like any good framework, such a struc-

ture gives the individual a possibility of choice and a starting point for the acquisition of further information. A clear image of the surroundings is thus a useful basis for individual growth" (Lynch, 1960:5).

4. Clarity of image also performs a social function. It provides symbols of collective experience and an orderly background for social communication. If all members share clear and similar images of their environment, then their security and their basis for social cohesion are enhanced.

These four arguments in favor of clarity in the urban landscape can be described as *esthetic, behavioral, conceptual* and *social*. The historical summary of the city in Chapter 4 provides instances in which visually clear images symbolize basic cultural values. For example, the forceful and stark organization of baroque urban space constituted a political statement, while the monumental architecture of various ancient cities symbolized and made concrete civil and religious values.

Given the importance of legible images, what elements in the landscape determine its degree of legibility? Lynch detected five recurrent elements in his respondents' images of the three cities. These were *paths, edges, districts, nodes,* and *landmarks.* Each of these is a purely topological rather than a metric construct, suggesting that topological features provide a basis for the cognitive structuring of space.

1. *Paths* represent linear features in the landscape along which vehicular or pedestrian movement occurs.

2. *Edges* are also linear landscape elements. However, they are seen as boundaries such as walls, edges of development, and railroad tracks. Movement does not always occur along edges; indeed, edges may bar movement. Sometimes edges coincide with paths; for example, where a major route skirts a distinctive district and serves as its boundary.

3. *Districts* are distinctive areas of urban space that have some underlying character or unity about them. Individuals can recognize when they are "inside" or "outside" such a district.

4. *Nodes* are points, or "strategic spots," in a city. They are often defined as the intersection or cross-point of movement paths. Other nodes constitute the core or identifiable center of districts.

5. *Landmarks* are also point locations. However, the observer may not necessarily enter them. They may be viewed externally; they can usually be seen from great distances; and they serve to orient the observer and to coordinate his images of different areas. They are used as reference points for finding one's way.

Lynch found paths to be the dominant feature of most people's images, particularly people who were most familiar with the area. This probably reflects the highly mobile nature of industrial urban populations. We tend to ex-

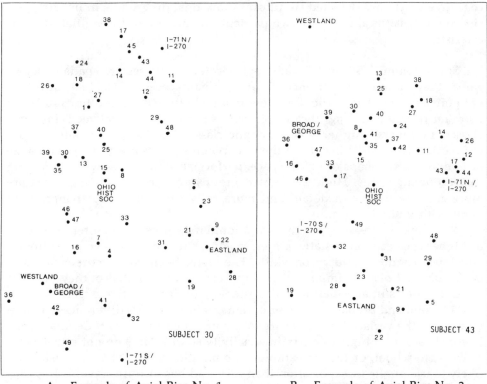

A.   Example of Axial Bias No. 1   B.   Example of Axial Bias No. 2

Figure 6.2 *Individual Configurations of Columbus, Ohio* These diagrams represent the cognitive images of Columbus, Ohio, for two subjects. The numbered locations are point cues—identifiable locations in the city—for which the subjects made a series of distance judgments. The technique of multidimensional scaling was used to reconstruct the overall configuration of points implicit in the distance judgments. The two examples illustrate the diversity of the inferred mental maps for different individuals. For instance, subject number 30 reveals a pronounced north-south bias. (*Source:* Rivizzigno, 1976; cited in Golledge, 1978:181. Reprinted by permission.)

perience most of urban space, except for our neighborhood, while we are in motion. This suggests that our images of most places will be quite sketchy and strongly path oriented.

Further research by behavioral geographers employs techniques that provide more detailed information on the structure of cognitive images (Golledge, 1978a; Golledge and Rushton, 1976; Golledge and Rayner, 1975, 1977). Subjects are asked to judge the distances between a specified set of points. From these data and the technique of multidimensional scaling, a *cognitive configuration* is constructed that shows the relative location of the points in a maplike form. Figure 6.2 shows two such configurations. Different systematic distortions in mental imagery are apparent for each of the subjects. This and other work on cognitive spaces has detected significant individual differences in imaging. Socioeconomic status and sex are two particularly important differentiating characteristics.

Socioeconomic Status   Because socioeconomic classes are spatially segregated, they naturally experience different urban spaces. Individuals at different points in the social structure know relatively little of each other's turf. But more far-reaching and significant differences in image exist between the social classes. In general, higher socioeconomic classes have more accurate and far more extensive mental images of the city. When subjects are asked to verbalize or to draw sketch maps of urban space, performance improves with increasing socioeconomic status. Highly educated groups produce sketch maps that are more accurate, richer in detail, and more fully interconnected than respondents with limited education.

There are two reasons for this variation. First, in very broad terms, people of higher socioeconomic status are more educated and thus have more highly developed cognitive and verbal skills. They have been much more exposed to the media that play an important role in image formation. Also, they have far fewer problems in articulating and expressing their subjective experience.

A second and probably more important reason for class differences in mental maps is the variation in exposure to the urban environment. Generally, the lower classes have highly constrained activity spaces. They do not travel as far to work, to school, or for recreation as the middle classes. They are also more likely to use public transportation than cars, and bus or train travel is less conducive to forming extensive images than travel by auto (primarily because the car offers greater spatial freedom than the fixed routes of public transit). The extreme case of a space-bound group is the ethnic ghetto. Here people only rarely travel beyond a few blocks of their home, particularly if they are elderly or unemployed.

Florence Ladd (1967) provides poignant evidence of the influence of ghetto life on spatial imagery. She asked a number of black children to draw a map of the area around their home (see Figure 6.3). Most of the children drew a very detailed picture of the area immediately surrounding their home and school, but depicted the nearby white housing project as the largest completely blank area on the map. One child's map suggested the extent of the psychological barrier between black and white areas. On his map the street dividing the neighborhoods is depicted as a wide boulevard nearly five times bigger than any other such path.

The hypothesis that class differences depend more on exposure and activity space than on intrinsic differences in ability received support in work by Goodchild (1974). Dealing with British data, Goodchild divided a sample into working-class and middle-class groups. He found no differences in the intrinsic cognitive ability to recall details of imageable objects. However, maps drawn by the middle-class group were more extensive than those of the other

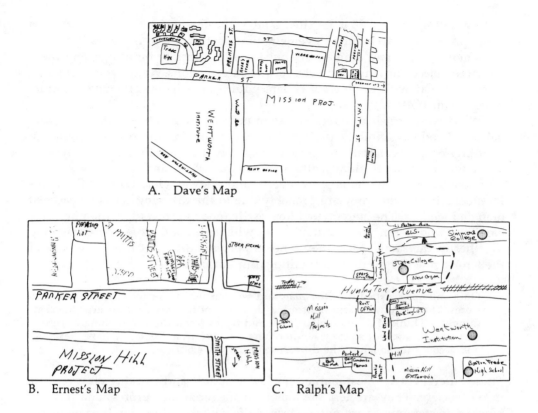

A.   Dave's Map

B.   Ernest's Map   C.   Ralph's Map

Figure 6.3 *A Child's View of the Ghetto* Florence Ladd asked a number of black children around the Mission Hill area of Boston to draw a map of their neighborhood. From his conversation it was apparent that Dave was afraid of venturing into the white Mission Hill project. His map detailed only the area immediately surrounding his home. Ernest emphasizes the dividing line between the white and black areas. Like Dave he has never ventured across Parker Street. Ralph, on the other hand, attends the prestigious Boston Latin School. His map is very detailed and emphasizes the schools in the area. His action space is much less restricted. (*Source:* From F. Ladd, "A Note on the World Across the Street." *Harvard Graduate School of Education Association Bulletin*, Vol. 12, 1967, pp. 47–48. Reprinted by permission.)

group, and they displayed a more detailed knowledge of the road network. Goodchild's results also indicated more concern with attractive surroundings and a greater emotional investment in the environment among the middle class.

Sex   Child development research suggests that sex differences in spatial preference emerge relatively early. Based on observations of children at play,

Erikson (1974) argued that females tend to prefer enclosed spaces, whereas males prefer open areas and movement along pathways. In the boys' constructions more people and animals are outside enclosures or buildings, and there are more objects moving along streets and intersections. Along with tall structures boys play with the idea of collapse; ruins are exclusively male constructions (Tuan, 1974).

Whatever intrinsic differences may or may not exist between the sexes, sexual socialization definitely produces sexual variations in spatial imaging in later life. Women generally seem to draw area-based maps rather than ones emphasizing movements along paths (Appleyard, 1970), and housewives' maps tend to exaggerate the home area (Everitt and Cadwallader, 1972). If these differences are genuine, they are probably due to the differing activity spaces of men and women: The stereotyped housewife tends to travel less than her husband and to different destinations. Even when men and women are traveling together in the same space, they tend to perceive different things because of the strong role differentiation traditional in our culture.

> On a shopping expedition the man and woman will want to look into different stores. They may walk arm in arm but they do not thereby see and hear the same things ... Think of a frequented street and try to recall the shops along it: certain shops will stand out sharply while others dissolve in a dreamlike haze. Sex roles will account for much of the difference (Tuan, 1974:62).

These differences are most marked for lower-middle and working-class couples in our society. They are less obvious in managerial and professional classes, where role stereotypes are not as clear. As female role stereotypes come under attack, sexual differences in spatial imaging may be expected to lessen.

The Cognition of Distance

As we have just seen, we structure our images of urban space primarily in a topological way. Many more detailed explanations of spatial behavior, however, involve the metric property of *distance*. Of the abstract properties of "whereness" identified by Downs and Stea (1973), distance is by far the most important. Indeed, it is difficult to study spatial structure or spatial behavior without considering distance. For example, distance variables are implicit in the models of residential segregation discussed in Chapter 5. Essentially, it is argued, communities organize themselves so that groups that are socially separate become spatially separate. Social distance coincides with spatial distance (a notion especially apparent in the concentric-zone model).

In models of everyday travel, distance variables play an even more crucial role than they do in the literature on segregation. One time-honored approach is to assume that individuals organize their behavior so as to minimize total distance traveled (according to a general principle of least effort). Like the oth-

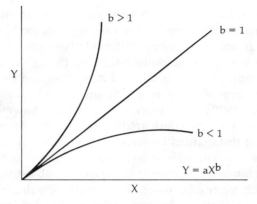

Figure 6.4 *Psychophysical Relationships Between Real and Cognized Distance (power function with various parameter values)* The power function relationship is of the form $Y = aX^b$ where Y is cognitive distance, X is real distance, and the values of the parameters a and b determine the form of the curve. Values of b both less than and greater than 1 have been estimated in various contexts (Briggs, 1973), but the most frequently observed relationship is $b < 1$. This implies that under most circumstances far distances tend to be underestimated, relative to short ones. Other research on urban cognitive distances has shown that such psychophysical representations are often an oversimplification. The cognition of specific distances is liable to be affected by numerous contextual and individual variables.

er rationalistic assumptions described above, this is simply untenable as a description of actual behavior.

Our cognition of distance is influenced by a variety of social and environmental factors that modify the relationship between imagined and real distance. In the modern city, with its complex and indirect road networks, physical distance is clearly difficult to estimate, even if we discount the social and psychological factors that distort our images of distance. Geographers and others have attempted to clarify this relationship between cognized and physical distance by establishing simple mathematical relationships between the two. A long established area of psychology known as psychophysics approaches this task. *Psychophysics* deals with the relationship between the subjective sensation of a stimulus and the physical magnitude of the stimulus itself. Mathematical relationships have been found between subjective sensation and such simple physical stimuli as light intensity or the pitch of sound (Stevens and Galanter, 1957). Although cognitive distance is more complicated than basic laboratory stimuli, several simple mathematical functions have been fitted to cognitive distance (Lowrey, 1970; Ekman and Bratfisch, 1965; Briggs, 1973). Power functions appear to perform best, as they do for other types of stimulus (Stevens, 1958) (see Figure 6.4).

Although the power function appears to best describe the relation between cognitive and real distance, this research is still far from conclusive. It can generally be assumed that any simple psychophysical relationship between cognitive and real distance must be qualified to take into account the effects of social and environmental factors. For example, the relative location of the downtown district has been shown to bias distance estimates, though research in this topic appears somewhat contradictory. Studies of American and British cities discovered a tendency for subjects to overestimate distances in the uptown direction (Brennan, 1948; Lee, 1970). In a more recent study, however, Briggs (1973) found that people tend to overestimate distances in the downtown direction.

How can such contradictions be resolved? We have already indicated that mental images consist of complex interwoven cognitive and affective components. Cognitive distance is not independent of the subjective values or preferences associated with places. In short, the growth of suburban shopping centers and the public's shift in buying patterns toward such locations has probably changed uptown-downtown cognitive distances. Several studies supply further evidence of the importance of individual preferences for the cognition of distance. Ekman and Bratfisch (1965) asked students to rate cities according to both their distance from them and the degree of emotional involvement they felt with events occurring in these places. They found that the more involved people are with a particular place, the less distance they are likely to estimate. This finding indicates a relationship between the affective and the cognitive components of distance, and it implies that we tend to live in small social and psychological worlds in which knowledge and emotional commitment are intertwined. For retail stores there is also evidence that retail preferences lead to systematic underestimation of distances—the more you like to shop at a particular location, the closer you think it is (Thompson, 1965).

Preference is not the only factor that may distort our estimation of distance. Places where we prefer to shop, go to school, or satisfy our recreational and cultural interests are also places we are familiar with. There is general agreement that familiarity breeds accuracy (Downs and Stea, 1977). The more familiar we are with an area, the longer we have lived at a place, the less likely we are to make errors in judging distance.

Canter and Tagg (1975) suggest another variable in distance distortion. Accuracy, they argue, is a function of a city's legibility.

> In order to cope with everyday urban life, people try to fit their spatial experience into some simple cognitive structure that serves as a ready basis for the storage and manipulation of information . . . The more readily a city lends itself to developing a simple cognitive structure, the more accurate are the distance estimates that its inhabitants generate (Downs and Stea, 1977:143).

Our estimates of distance result from complex social, psychological, and environmental influences. The world in our heads does not necessarily accurately reproduce the geometrical space that surrounds us. Image directly affects behavior, and image is itself a social product, a product of our urban experiences.

DEVELOPMENTAL AND
LEARNING PROCESSES IN SPATIAL IMAGING

The Development of Space Cognition

It should be apparent by now that cognitive mapping and using these maps in everyday situations involves many complicated processes. We use a variety of skills in mental map making, including abstract conceptualization, pictorial imaging, verbal and nonverbal memory, as well as analysis and synthesis. To investigate how the individual forms such images, we must deal with two related but logically separate processes. We must first ask how the individual develops a sense of space, and then we must ask how specific images of space are learned. *Learning* refers to the acquisition and retention of specific facts about a particular space. *Development*, on the other hand, describes changes in the organization of behavior, including learning, that produce a capacity to understand space.

One starting point for the study of the development of imaging skills is a fact familiar to everyone: A child's view of the world is very different from that of an adult. The developmental psychologist Piaget takes this as a basic tenet: A young child's cognition is both qualitatively and quantitatively different from an adult's. Charles Dickens and Mark Twain both brilliantly captured the world view of the young. Dickens, through the eyes of children, created a world of dark and light populated by irrational adults, in which the protagonist is tortured by dreads that would be neurotic in an adult but are probably truthful to children's experience. Twain, by contrast, created a boundless unknown world of opportunity in which his more mature and conniving Huck Finn and Tom Sawyer make their way, in a continous process of exploration. Both authors accurately describe three basic characteristics of a child's perception of his environment. It is exploratory, as its bounds continually expand with increased mobility. It is uncritical. Children apprehend and accept things before they fully understand their purposes. And it is immensely detailed. Our own memories of childhood contain far more sensory detail than maturer memories though, because we lacked discrimination, the details we recall are often incongruous and inconsequential.

Obviously, the dominant theme in an infant's world is exploration and growth. Very young children actively explore their surroundings in a fashion that has little connection with their immediate needs of hunger or warmth. They value novelty. They are positively reinforced by exploration and reveal obvious enthusiasm for nonfrightening change (Kessen et al., 1970). In these initial encounters with the world, three processes occur. First, children learn the trustworthiness or the *consistency* of reality; for example, they will eventually show surprise when a magician makes an object disappear from where it "ought" to be. Second, they begin to understand the distinction between *self* and external reality. Third, *language skills* begin to develop as verbal labels are attached to new objects encountered in the exploration process (Ittelson et al.,

1974). Because of the evident conflict or tension between trustworthiness and novelty, many child psychologists emphasize the need for a delicate balance between novelty and security in an infant's environment.

These basic facts from developmental psychology, however, tell us little about the development of mapping abilities. It is quite difficult to establish a precise timetable for the growth of topological and metric concepts. One fruitful line of approach has been to observe children in constructive play and to attempt to deduce what spatial concepts they possess. For example, Blaut and Stea (1971) report an ability in three-to-five year olds to construct landscapes with models of houses, trees, and so forth. They do this in a way that reflects understanding of the basic principles of the spatial organization of communities. In short, they can conceive of a bird's-eye view of an urban environment.

Even more surprising results have been obtained from techniques that bypass the inability of children to sketch or interpret the highly abstract symbolism of conventional maps. Stea and Blaut (1971) experimented with aerial photography. They found that children were able to interpret these images, even before school age. These results indicated a previously unsuspected ability in spatial abstraction and cognitive mapping among the very young. Further cross-cultural research in Puerto Rican communities suggested that these skills were "independent of a specific location, culture or educational system" (Downs and Stea, 1977:192).

There have been various attempts by developmental psychologists to provide a systematic theory of child learning processes, and these schemes throw some light on the development of spatial imaging abilities. By far the best-known of such theories is Piaget's. His model involves an account of the interaction between the infant and its environment. The infant is presumed to be

Table 6.1 Stages in the Development of Spatial Imaging: Piaget's Account

1. *Sensorimotor* (birth to 1½ or 2 years). No linguistic or conceptual symbols mediate between the infant and reality. Presumably no cognitive map exists at this point.

2. *Preoperational* (1½ to 7 years). The child is able to internalize or image interactions with its environment through the use of symbols. It exhibits behavior similar to the imagined movements postulated by Lorenz in all higher mammals (recall the discusson of the central spatial model).

3. *Concrete operational* (7 to 11 years). At this stage the child is capable of mental acts such as arithmetic but is incapable of thinking about abstractions. The work of Blaut and Stea suggests that cognitive maps and mental spatial operations are highly developed by this time.

4. *Formal operations* (11 to 14 years). The child's mental processes are emancipated from the concrete; abstract thought in adult form is present. The child possesses all aspects of cognitive mapping ability, including all analytic or left-hemisphere capability.

Source: Modified from Piaget and Inhelder, 1967.

actively involved (motivated) in the exploration of its environment (Hart and Moore, 1973:259). This process is punctuated by *equilibria,* when the infant temporarily achieves a unified and integrated understanding of its relationship to its surroundings. The driving force in this development is *adaptation.* Adaptation possesses two complementary aspects: *assimilation* (as external reality is incorporated into existing intellectual schemas), and *accommodation* (as the schemas are modified to accord with external reality). The principal developmental stages postulated by Piaget are four: *sensorimotor, preoperational, concrete operational,* and *formal operations* (Piaget and Inhelder, 1967) (see Table 6.1).

Work in the tradition of Piaget by Blaut, Stea and others clearly shows that by about the age of seven children have the capacity to create and use spatial imagery in everyday spatial problem solving. This capacity appears to be a function of the maturation process. Thus the capacity is not culture bound; apparently only the content of our imagery is culturally influenced.

Spatial Learning

Everyone is familiar with the frustration of trying to give complicated instructions to a stranger who asks for directions. We know how to get to where he or she wants to go, but expressing it simply is very difficult. It is even more frustrating to be on the receiving end of such instruction. Often the direction giver, in an effort to be helpful, hopelessly confuses us by telling us too much or by assuming we have much local knowledge. This problem vividly illustrates the results of spatial learning. Residents and newcomers have such different cognitive maps that even a serious and well-meaning attempt to bridge the gap may fail. How, then, does a newcomer develop the spatial images necessary to become a functioning resident of a place?

It is clear that the learning process is not continuous. Local areas of a cognitive map may grow smoothly as a few more details are learned about an area that is already quite familiar. But abrupt "quantum jumps" in information occur. A visit to a new acquaintance or to an unfamiliar part of town can sketch in large areas of the map on a single day. One crucial aspect of the development of image is the cognitive fusing of local perceptual components. We can summon up visual recollections of extremely local areas, including the environs of home or of downtown. On a larger scale, though, direct perceptions cannot provide us with an overview. A map of the city can, and we are all familiar with the integration that occurs when we learn how the jigsaw of locally perceived fragments fits together.

Spatial learning involves many distinct sources of information, three of which are especially important: direct perception, social networks, and media sources such as newspapers, radio and television. Horton and Reynolds (1971) argue that a newcomer moves through three distinct stages of image formation in the process of understanding the new community of residence. The first stage is one of *distance bias*. Newcomers have no established local social networks and are not familiar enough with local place names for media references to contribute to their mental image. They rely heavily on personal observation. A strong distance-decay effect operates: The individual's knowledge is confined to areas he or she physically perceives. The second temporal stage is the period of *community socialization*. Personal observation ceases to be the primary source of image. Integration into social networks and growing familiarity with local media, together with the saturation or overload effect of visual perception, increase social and media inputs to image. The third stage is *equilibrium*. Social and media inputs are still the principal sources of the mental image, but the image is changing much more slowly. The time frame associated with the stages varies greatly. In the case of a young, mobile, and socially oriented household, the transition into stage two may occur in a few weeks. In the case of a relatively immobile, single retiree, it may take much longer. It is very clear that the equilibrium state of spatial learning is far from the ideal or perfect knowledge assumed by the rationalistic decision-making model. To be convinced of this you should try to recall the exact sequence of stores on a well-known street that you have traveled maybe hundreds of times! Learning stops far short of perfect knowledge, obviously because of information overload. Just as Lofland (see Chapter 3) claims that we react to a host of strangers, so, too, we react to myriad places in a city through categoric knowledge rather than extensive personal knowledge. It is, however, an error to assume that we only learn what we need to carry out our daily behavior. Even in maze-running experiments with animals, *latent learning* is known to occur (Tolman, 1948). That is, certain aspects of the landscape that are of no immediate practical utility are "noticed," and they may later be used readily if the need arises. If we suddenly need to buy Italian bakery products, we will go to a store we have seen but not observed as being useful before.

Besides using various sorts of information at different stages of familiarity with a place, Downs and Stea (1977) suggest that we also use varying learning styles. To solve some immediate spatial problems, for example, in shopping or in getting to work, we need to learn the *responses* to particular stimuli (for example, "at the end of the road turn left," "to catch a downtown bus wait at intersection A"). The cognitive result of this response learning is termed *route mapping*. By contrast, the process of acquiring detailed personal knowledge of places is referred to as *place learning*. The cognitive result is *survey mapping*—detailed knowledge of a series of places (place learning) and interconnections (route mapping). Although both types of learning occur continuously, it is obvious that with increased familiarity place learning naturally dominates the later stages of image formation. Different types of learning are required for different types of behavior. Far deeper knowledge is required for the residential mobility decision; an individual will certainly perform place learning of potential residential neighborhoods but not necessarily of the areas where they shop, work, or go to the doctor.

Attempts at a General Theory of Spatial Behavior

Despite the importance of space for everyday learning and behavior, very few attempts have been made to develop a unified theory of spatial behavior. Perhaps the most notable effort has been the work of the psychologist Kurt Lewin (1951). Lewin's *field theory* describes human behavior as the product of the interaction among psychological states (needs, tensions, and changing personality states), cognitive images, and values associated with the external environment. The theory is phrased in abstract language and is relatively imprecise in its predictions of spatial behavior. In spite of these shortcomings, it has had an important influence on ideas and terminology in behavioral geography.

Lewin's model is based on Gestalt psychology. He argued that to understand behavior we must delineate the regions within which that behavior occurs. These three basic spatial arenas are: the life space, the perceptual-motor region, and the foreign hull. *Life space* refers to the area for which the individual possesses knowledge and in which he or she is potentially capable of interacting. The area the person knows directly from ongoing perception is a much more restricted area called the *perceptual-motor* region. Somewhat like individual distance, this region immediately surrounds the individual, wherever he or she may be within the life space. The rest of the world—the region beyond the cognition of the individual—is termed the *foreign hull of the life space.*

Lewin views human behavior as spatial problem solving. Space separates objects and persons from one another. People behave according to sets of goals. These goals can only be met by movement toward the objects in the life space that are potentially satisfying. The goals themselves are set by the needs, drives, and life-cycle stage of the individual actor. Lewin's account of human behavior is topological. Goals are met by movement, and movement within the life space is conditioned by the paths and barriers that either permit or impede it.

A number of behavioral geographers have translated Lewin's abstract concepts into operational terms in order to guide research on spatial behavior. Wolpert (1965) developed a Lewinian account of migration, which will be discussed in the next chapter. A slight reformulation of Wolpert's ideas was applied by Horton and Reynolds (1971) in analyzing *repetitive* or *recurrent* travel behavior.

Since Horton and Reynolds were primarily interested in spatial behavior within urban communities, they adapted Lewin's general spatial terminology to the urban context. They spoke of action space and activity space, rather than life space and perceptual-motor regions. *Activity space* refers to the set of places with which an individual has direct, personal contact in the course of everyday travel. *Action space* is a broader construct, embracing the set of urban locations about which the individual has information. This cognitively defined set is closely analogous to Lewin's life space. Inseparable from the action space is the affective component: the subjective utility or preference associated with places.

Like Lewin, Horton and Reynolds emphasize the changing nature of place utility. It depends upon the shifting needs and social characteristics of the individual. Action space is viewed as dynamic; it changes for reasons internal and external to the individual. The urban space evolves, and the individual learns of these changes. Also, old established but unfamiliar regions of the city are incorporated into action space. These processes lead to a continuous growth in action space. More abrupt changes might also occur, as the individual's life stage, job, marital status, or place of residence change. Eventually the individual's activity space approximates his or her action space as spatial learning progresses. The path to this equilibrium, however, could be abruptly set back if residence changes.

Horton and Reynolds (1971) tested some of these ideas. They confirmed that similar individuals have similar images and that differences in location and income lead to variations in image. Middle-income groups were familiar with more extensive areas than low-income groups, but each group was most familiar with its own home area. This *local effect* is found almost universally in studies of cognitive space.

SPATIAL PREFERENCE

Most work on mental maps and urban images has addressed cognitive rather than affective issues. One drawback associated with a purely cognitive account of mental maps is that it cannot accommodate decision making and spatial problem solving. No one undertakes overt spatial behavior as a consequence of his or her knowledge, though knowledge guides behavior. We behave in response to needs, evaluations, and preferences. In short, our spatial behavior represents a sequence of explicit or implicit choices that are governed by affective aspects—urban images. In some cases choices are conscious and overt, as when we visit a new supermarket for the first time. More often, our behavior is repetitive and habitual. Such behavior is still governed by preferences—in this case, the preferences that led us to form particular spatial habits in the first place.

Previous discussions in this chapter provide some hint of the complexity of subjective spatial evaluations. We like and dislike areas of the city for many reasons: personal experience, the reports of others, categorical knowing, or detailed personal knowing. Above all, preferences must be related to the specific spatial problems an individual is attempting to solve. We may evaluate a particular area positively for one purpose and negatively for another. According to the old joke, New York City is a nice place to visit but a terrible place to live. We certainly have far more exacting requirements for our home area than we do for sites we visit briefly for shopping or recreation. Place utility therefore varies with trip purpose.

The Lewin/Horton and Reynolds action space formulation is exceptional in that it attempts to explicitly fuse cognitive and affective components of image. Although their theory has been applied empirically, it is primarily useful as a general conceptual scheme. You should realize that developing models capable of predicting urban spatial behavior requires a far more detailed account of spatial choice.

Models of spatial preference assume that place utility consists of two elements. Places have intrinsic degrees of desirability that vary according to trip purpose (*site utility*). At the same time, since a place is simply one point in a network of other places, there is a distance cost that involves the distance between the place and the current location of the decision maker (*distance disutility*). These two components combine to give *aggregate place utility*.

Much has been written about the disutility of distance. For example, Zipf (1949) argues that our aversion to distance derives from a general principle of least effort. Walter Isard (1956) points to a close analogy between the disutilities we associate with time and space. If we defer consumption of goods and services for one year, we require a premium to be paid in the form of an annual interest rate. An interest rate of 5 percent indicates that we equate $1 now with $1.05 in a year's time—or that a bird in the hand is worth 1.05 birds in the bush! This process is called time discounting. Isard (1956) argues that space has a precisely similar effect on our preferences. Items close by are valued more highly than the identical items located at a distance, because of the negative economic and psychological effects of covering the intervening distance. Time preferences and space preferences are closely analogous; at the very least, it costs us time to travel. It is generally accepted that we are less sensitive to physical distance or to the dollar cost of covering it, than we are to this time cost.

The precise interrelationship between the site and distance components of place utility is quite complicated, depending, among other things, on the type of spatial behavior under study. For example, if we are considering a crosstown residential move, the costs of overcoming distance are completely negligible compared with the utility of finding a suitable neighborhood and acquiring a suitable site. In this case site utility completely outweighs distance disutility. By contrast, in a repetitive travel activity such as grocery shopping, the distance component is far from negligible. Time costs (or bus fares, or gas costs) form a significant component of total costs. We frequently patronize close-by stores instead of traveling long distances to stores we would actually prefer on the basis of site utility alone.

This discussion of site and distance preferences assumes that these two elements can be measured and treated separately. The separability of site and distance aspects of place has, however, been questioned. For example, Thompson's work on distance perception (mentioned above) suggests that if we have a low site evaluation of a place, we will tend to exaggerate its cognitive distance. Thus, site and distance effects interact statistically, and it is logically impossible to measure them separately. Few spatial choice models have successfully met this very serious logical problem although recent work by Rushton has attempted to solve these measurement difficulties (1969, 1976).

The study of space preference is at an early stage. Efforts have not been made as yet to address the full psychological and social complexity of place evaluations. They have focused rather specifically on only two types of preference: residential desirability and the place utility of retail opportunities. In the next two sections some findings on each type of preference are outlined.

Residential Preferences

Peter Gould and his associates (1965, 1974) explored the residential preferences of college students. Students in various places were asked to rank the forty-eight contiguous states as desirable places to live. There was clear evidence of local consensus and interregional disagreement on residential desirability. For students in the North, East, and West the patterns of preference were roughly similar; the highest ratings were for the home state and immediately adjoining states (what Gould calls the local dome of desirability). The West coast received uniformly high ratings as did the New England coastal areas. Moving from west to east ratings declined precipitously, but the direction of declining ratings shifts in the Great Plains. From the plains on, the preference direction was north to south with high ratings in the north and very low ratings in the south. These similarities can be seen in Figure 6.5.

The southern viewpoint, however, deviates significantly from the overall pattern. In contrast to students from other regions, Alabama students discriminate very carefully among states in the South. Neighboring Louisiana and North Carolina receive high ratings, but Mississippi and South Carolina receive very low evaluations. Alabamians, unlike other students in Gould's sample, made fine distinctions among southern states. They had more information about these areas than other students, and this information is obviously critical in forming preferences. Places about which we have little information (the foreign hull of the life space) tend to be underevaluated. Also, Gould and White (1974) suggest that distant places are negatively evaluated. That is, distance in cognitive space and physical space are positively related—most students viewed distant states as least like their home state.

Gould's work and the efforts of a number of other geographers dealing with regional preferences (e.g., Aangenbrug, 1968; White, 1967) promise to throw light on the cognitive dimensions of interregional migration. Residential desirability and place utility concerns have also been studied at the intra-urban level (Brown and Moore, 1970; Johnston, 1968; Peterson, 1967). The objective has been to develop usable models for predicting residential choice. This work will be discussed in detail in the next chapter.

Dimensions of Retail Desirability

Much work in behavioral geography has focused on shopping behavior, a particular variety of recurrent travel. This research has identified the factors that make an area attractive, with an eye to adequately predicting retail patron-age. Rationalistic models of retail choice have been relatively unsuccessful in this endeavor (Berry, 1967; Clark, 1968; Yuill, 1967), and cognitive approaches have been emphasized in the more recent studies. We will focus on two specific studies by Downs and Burnett.

Downs (1970) examined people's attitudes toward a shopping center in Bristol, England. He was interested in determining and ranking the various factors people considered in assessing site utility. Using questionnaires employing a semantic differential technique, he asked people to rate the facility according to a number of categories. He found eight aspects to be important. In order of importance they were:

1. Service quality

2. Price

3. Structure and design

4. Shopping hours

5. Internal pedestrian movement

6. Shopping range and quality

7. Visual appearance

8. Traffic conditions

In another attempt to understand the bases of retail stores' site utility, Burnett (1973) assessed the importance of a number of evaluative criteria for two small samples of shoppers (recent arrivals to the city living in a new residential development versus established residents living in an older neighborhood). Shoppers of similar social and economic background and of similar length of residence use the same criteria to choose among alternative shopping places. The low-information group (the new residents) stressed parking facilities, merchandise quality, and distance as crucial factors in their choice. The high-information group placed far less emphasis on distance. Apparently they were willing to travel farther to locations they found attractive in terms of site characteristics. We would, of course, expect the action space of the longer-term resident to be more extensive and complete.

The two groups in Burnett's study differed in other respects than the relative importance they attributed to physical distance. The less informed consumers tended to use previously learned generalizations and to evaluate unknown locations in terms of their perceived likeness to known locations in the city center. Long-time residents chose on the basis of more detailed local information.

In an unfamiliar environment it appears that individuals pass through two distinct stages in preference formation. First, they transfer to the new environ-

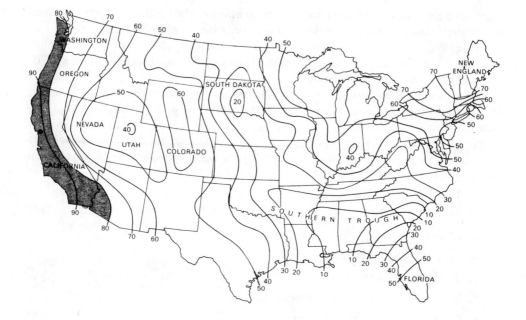

The View from California

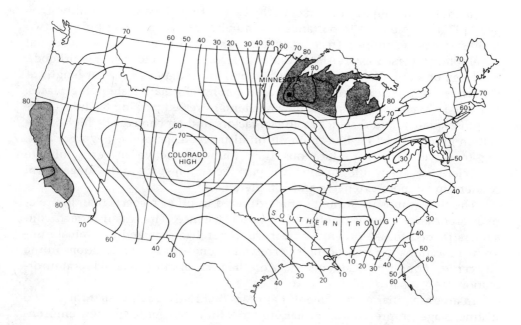

The View from Minnesota

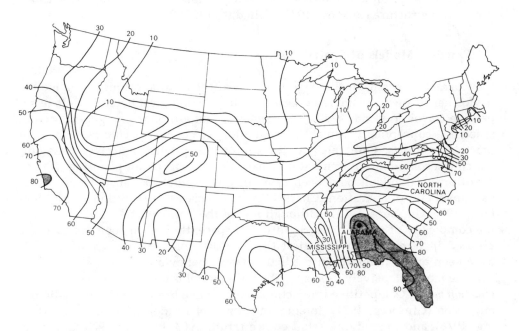

The View from Alabama

Figure 6.5 *Residential Preference Maps of the United States* These contour maps show the residential desirability of American states as perceived by samples of students in each of the three locations indicated. High values indicate a high degree of residential preference. Colorado, for example, is quite highly rated by each group. Each group also tends to perceive as desirable their present location in California, Minnesota, or Alabama. Gould terms this a local desirability effect. The groups show significant differences in their perception of certain areas. For example, the Alabama group draws an important difference between their own state and neighboring Mississippi, a fine distinction that is lost on the Californians and Minnesotans! (*Source:* From Abler, Adams, Gould, *Spatial Organization: The Geographer's View of the World,* 1971. Reprinted by permission of Prentice-Hall, Inc., Englewood Cliffs, New Jersey.)

ment previously learned generalizations about spatial structure, which we have all built up from everyday experience. We know, for example, that it is much easier to park in suburbia than downtown. These "borrowed" preferences guide us in our initial evaluations. Later, as we acquire more detailed local knowledge through the spatial learning process, we discriminate alternatives through specific knowledge of their desirability. In a sense we begin with categorical knowing (preferences based on general stereotypes) and evolve toward more specific personal knowledge of places in our action space. It may be argued that in the long run consumers cease to exercise any overt ongoing choice; instead, they carry out their repetitive spatial behavior in a stereotyped or habitual way, in accordance with a fairly stable and perhaps unconscious preference structure (Burnett, 1973; Golledge, 1967; Bucklin, 1967).

Practical Models of Spatial Choice

Current research on the cognitive and affective dimensions of choice behavior has thrown considerable light on the psychological determinants of repetitive travel. You may well feel, however, that although the general action space is a conceptually valuable formulation, it has no specific usefulness in practical contexts. One relevant test context is predicting travel behavior, which is a common requirement in urban and transportation planning. A variety of practical models have been developed to predict spatial choice in everyday travel and in migration (Charles River Associates, 1976; Stopher and Meyburg, 1976; Ginsberg, 1971). Although few of these models take full account of the complexity of individuals' cognition of space, they have been increasingly phrased in terms of psychological theories of choice. Spatial choice models have been quite successful in predicting travel behavior.

The most extensively used spatial choice model is termed the *competitive interaction model*. Competitive interaction models have been applied to predicting migration (Ginsberg, 1971), to studying regional residential desirability (Ewing, 1976), and to studying retail choice (Huff, 1963; Burnett, 1973; Louviere, 1976; Stanley and Sewall, 1976). One of the earliest versions of the model, described in Table 6.2, was used to predict consumers' retail choices (Huff, 1963;

Table 6.2   Huff's Competitive Spatial Choice Model

1. The attractiveness of a given store to a consumer is assumed to be directly proportional to the size of the store, and inversely proportional to the distance between the store and the consumer, modified by a parameter measuring the rate of distance decay in attractiveness (see Chapter 2).

$$A_i = \frac{S_i}{d_i^{\lambda}}$$

   A_i = attractiveness of i—th store. S_i = size of i—th store (this might be measured by area of floor space or payroll). d_i = distance between the store and the consumer (this is often measured as travel time). λ = parameter calibrating the effect of distance on attractiveness; it varies according to the type of interaction.

2. The probability p_i that a consumer travels to store i is assumed to be directly proportional to A_i and inversely proportional to the sum attractiveness of all stores.

$$P_i = \frac{A_i}{\sum_k A_k}$$

Source: Modified from Huff, 1963.

Lakshmanan and Hansen, 1965). The theory formulates choice over a set of competing alternative destinations such as retail stores. It is assumed that the probability of an individual choosing a particular destination is proportional to some subjectively perceived utility. This utility, in turn, directly depends on the intrinsic characteristics of the site and is inversely related to its distance from the consumer. The model, therefore, combines the ideas of place utility and spatial disutility (or discounting), which we defined earlier. In its simplest form, site attractiveness is measured by size (e.g., floor space), and distance disutility is measured as travel time. It is possible, in more elaborate forms of the model, to measure and incorporate distinct perceived dimensions of retail attractiveness such as those described by Burnett and Downs. La Rue (1978) predicted drugstore patronage using a variant of this model modified to take into account price, convenience of store hours, confidence in the pharmacist, proximity to other shopping objects, and extra services provided by the store. Although our understanding of space preference and choice processes is still crude, it has proved possible to incorporate cognitive and affective information into successful predictive models of spatial choice.

SUMMARY

Behavior in urban space is governed by decision making. Two fundamentally different accounts of human decision making are the rationalistic and the cognitive approaches. The cognitive account assumes that behavior is guided by images that are always incomplete and imperfect. All images are built from physical perception through sense organs which are highly selective and from complicated learning processes. Cognitive components of image represent knowledge or beliefs, while affective components reflect preferences and evaluations. Urban behavior is governed by spatial images, which are sometimes referred to as mental maps.

Absolute and relativist views of space have been outlined. The relative view is more useful in understanding spatial behavior. Space has metric and topological properties. Mathematical descriptions of space are called geometries. No one geometry provides a uniquely correct description of mental maps. Human cognition of space is complicated. We are innately disposed to structure our experience in spatial ways, probably as a result of our evolutionary heritage. Space cognition involves analytic (left hemisphere) and synthetic (right hemisphere) processes that combine linguistic symbols and visual patterns in a complex way. Identity, location, distance, and direction are fundamental to mental maps. Lynch's work suggests that our principal organization of urban space is topological rather than metric. Key structural elements are paths, edges, districts, nodes, and landmarks. Mental maps are conditioned by general cultural differences and by more specific effects such as sex and socioeconomic status. Distance cognition is especially important. It may be crudely described by psychophysical relations such as a power function, but in detail it is controlled by many variables including social determinants and evaluations of place.

Spatial images grow by processes of development and learning. A child's capacity to image space has been described in terms of Piaget's stages: sensorimotor, preoperational, concrete operational, and formal operational. Learning of cities occurs discontinuously. One theory classifies the stages as: distance bias, community socialization, and equilibrium. Response learning and place learning are two functionally distinct learning styles.

No integrated and fully successful theories of spatial behavior are available. Lewin's field theory represents an abstract and topological effort to formulate such a theory, while Horton and Reynolds provide an operational formulation of urban action space.

Although cognitive aspects of image guide behavior, choices are made with respect to preferences. Two main areas in the study of space preferences are repetitive travel and migration (residential preferences). The competitive interaction model is a simple operational model of choice which has been successfully applied in both areas.

Chapter 7

Residential Location: The Decision-Making Process

INTRODUCTION

Ethologists have shown that maintaining and defending a home base is common to a large number of vertebrate species. It is unquestionable that the fixed space termed *home* is also of primary psychological and social significance for humans. The home is a kind of "backstage" area (Goffman, 1959) where individuals can relax their concern with projecting the proper self-image and enjoy more intimate social relationships. Everyday phrases such as "a man's home is his castle" indicate the significance we attach to the home. To be "at home" with a topic or activity is to be comfortable with it. A home, according to Webster's Dictionary, is "a place where one likes to be; (it is) a restful or congenial place." It is a place of great personal significance. Witness how many millions of people subscribe to magazines such as *Better Homes and Gardens, House and Garden,* and *House Beautiful.*

When a family purchases or rents a house or apartment, it is buying more than a physical structure to provide shelter. It is buying a supply of local services and a certain degree of accessibility to school, workplace, and friends (Leven et al., 1976). Perhaps even more important, in making a residential location decision a family makes a conscious statement of its perceived social position. It is buying a symbol of social status and managing its social image.

In this chapter we analyze the motivating forces that encourage a family to forsake their present residence and search for alternative housing. In terms of the decision-making perspective of Chapter 6, this *residential mobility decision* is the most important spatial decision most of us ever make. Detailed study of residential moves is crucial to understanding the urban space. To know why people move is to appreciate the basic needs of the space-consuming public. Such knowledge can be used to build better residences—residences attuned to human spatial requirements. At the same time, to understand the process of residential mobility is to gain insight into the shifting residential sector of the urban landscape.

The historical survey in Chapter 4 demonstrated the crucial role played by migration in industrial urbanization. Residential mobility is a distinguishing feature of industrial society, and the United States is, more than most contemporary nations, a product of recent migration. Without this mobility, urbanization could not have occurred (although since about 1930 natural increase in the United States has played an increasing role in urban growth).

Indeed, a number of authors have termed America a nation of movers. Rossi (1955) points out that many Americans, for at least a period of their lives, discard their residences about as often as they dispose of their automobiles. Census data indicate that for the last few decades, 20 percent of the United States population changed residence annually. Over five-year intervals, approximately 50 to 60 percent of the population changed their dwelling at least once. Most of these moves, however, are only short-distance ones, indicating a change of neighborhood but not of community. In fact, approximately 60 percent of all moves are to places less than 5 miles away from the previous residence.

While such moves are insignificant in terms of distance, their significance both for the subjective urban experience and for the physical fabric of the city is unquestionable. Because of our own mobility and because the city is in flux around us, our images of urban space evolve continually. More than any other culture we have learned to live with continuing change, and if we require constancy and stability, we seek it elsewhere than in our physical surroundings (Toffler, 1970).

Mobility is evidently a topic of great practical interest to the urban planner. The spatial configuration of the metropolis is a product of population movements. The growth of the suburbs and the accompanying decline of the central city is ultimately the result of population redistribution, as is the characteristic urban mosaic described in Chapter 5. It is only through such mobility that populations come to live in the segregated neighborhood (Butler, 1976). Movement is both a consequence and a cause of the urban condition. If we can develop some appreciation of the movement decision at the individual level, we can begin to understand why neighborhoods change. Building such explanations will lead to an informed theory of the process of urban spatial change.

AN APPROACH TO MIGRATION STUDY

Migration is not easily defined. If an individual moves across the street, down the block, or even to another apartment in the same building, is that person a migrant in the same sense as the individual who moves to another city or nation? Also, are certain types of spatially mobile people such as students, migrant workers, visiting businesspeople, vacationers, and members of the armed forces migrants? Such groups are economically and socially important in some communities, yet their moves differ radically from the mobility of the average household. Are there moves that should not be considered migration and people who should not be considered migrants? In answering these questions, two aspects of the move should be considered: the distance covered, and the degree of permanence in the relocation (Goldscheider, 1971).

Typically, demographers have been rather restrictive in their conception of migration. As Thomlinson suggests:

> In order to be considered a migrant, one must make a move of some consequence. Demographers, thus, define persons as migrant if they change their place of normal habitation for a substantial period of time, crossing a political boundary in the process (1976:267).

This conception closely follows the Census Bureau's definition of migration as a move across a county boundary. Such conservative approaches to migration are designed to ensure that only significant moves are counted. That is, only moves that represent some basic change in surroundings and require a certain minimum effort on the part of the movers should be considered migration.

This definition, however, is defective in two respects. First, by restricting migration to moves across political boundaries it assumes that crossing administrative boundaries involves greater changes for the migrants and the communities than movement within such political units (Goldscheider, 1971). This, of course, is not necessarily the case at all. Movement between two neighborhoods of different social status, life style, or ethnic character can take place within the same administrative unit. Similarly, a move between political units does not automatically imply any change in neighborhood status. Such distinctions are arbitrary.

A second and more serious weakness of the conservative definition of migration is that by restricting migration study to passage across political boundaries, the researcher ignores the most typical of moves—the short-distance move (what demographers call *residential mobility*). If for no other reason, such moves are significant because they are the most common and therefore have the greatest potential for altering the spatial structure of a community.

Perhaps the most useful definition of migration is less restrictive. Everett Lee (1966) defines migration as a permanent or semipermanent change in residence. No restrictions are placed on the distance of the move or on its voluntary or involuntary nature. The only moves excluded are continual or cyclic movement of a nonpermanent type such as the seasonal wanderings of the nomad, the annual jaunts of the vacationer, or the daily treks of the commuter.

Migration refers to a single act, but viewing it as a single behavior oversimplifies the decision making involved. In fact, two distinct decisions arise in any household's movement.

1. The mobility decision itself—the decision to seek a new residence. This decision can be viewed as the result of several interacting forces: the characteristics of the place of origin, the social characteristics of the po-

tential migrant, current residential satisfaction, and the perceived costs of moving.

2. The search for a new residence. This involves active spatial search. This search is governed by a potential migrant's continually changing image as well as the household's social characteristics and the characteristics of the destination area.

There are many fundamental differences between the conditions at area of origin and of destination. Persons living in a particular place are immediately acquainted with the area and thus are able to make unhurried judgments about it. The mental picture of their local activity space is fairly complete. Information about potential destinations is far less complete. Because of the personal importance of the movement decision, potential movers typically undertake a conscious search, endeavoring to become better acquainted with possible new neighborhoods. In the terminology of the previous chapter, they attempt to develop place knowing of potential home sites. Because of the enormous complexity of urban space, this search is usually satisficing rather than rationalistic. People seek not the "best of all possible worlds" but a home site that is good enough to meet certain basic requirements. The common checklist of requirements is surprisingly simple, as we will see.

THE DECISION TO MOVE

Residential Dissatisfaction and the Decision to Move

Why do people decide to seek a new place of residence? The most obvious answer is that people decide to move when they are no longer satisfied with their present dwelling or, in Julian Wolpert's (1965) terms, when a certain threshold of dissatisfaction is exceeded. Although level of satisfaction has proved to be an adequate predictor of migration (Speare, 1974; Bach and Smith, 1977), it is equally apparent that not all satisfied residents remain in their present homes nor do all dissatisfied residents pack up their belongings and move. This lack of total congruence between satisfaction and mobility expectations results from several features inherent in the decision-making process.

Perhaps the most obvious of these features is the nature of the various forces that can motivate movement. Simply put, not all moves are voluntary or open to individual choice. Eric Moore (1972) suggests that the decision to seek a new residence may be motivated by one of four possibilities:

1. The decision to move may be out of the hands of the individual household. An example of this situation is eviction by local government mandate or the decision of a landlord.

2. Certain changes may arise that affect a household and thus lower the evaluation of the present residence so that migration is encouraged. These situations include marriage, divorce, a death in the family, a long-distance job reassignment, or some sudden change in finances.

3. Changes in housing requirements or in the immediate environment often lead to some dissatisfaction with present housing. These changes in circumstances are not of the magnitude of those described under number 2 and, thus, more options are available to the household.

4. Sometimes the awareness of other available housing opportunities may lead a household to become dissatisfied with its present dwelling; that is, comparisons with other available opportunities may lead a household to reevaluate its present home.

The first two motives discussed by Moore represent situations where the household is forced to move. Under such circumstances, dissatisfaction with present housing plays almost no role in the decision to move. Indeed, it is difficult to talk about a residential mobility decision at all. Most studies of migration ignore these two instances because the household has no option other than moving.

At first thought, this omission might be construed as a weakness inherent in the decision-making approach to migration. After all, doesn't it seem that such an approach might ignore a significant motive for movement, especially among groups susceptible to forced moves such as renters in general and the poor in particular? While the lower classes may be more likely to be evicted, the middle and upper classes are more likely to experience forced moves of another type—job transfers. Thus, the mixture of motivating factors behind forced moves produces a situation in which the probability of experiencing this problem is roughly equal for all classes. Also, forced moves are less typical than moves by choice. In Rossi's study of Philadelphia, 61 percent of all moves were voluntary (1955). A decision-making approach to mobility is adequate, therefore, to account for the most common motivating forces in movement.

Even when considering voluntary migration alone, it is apparent that not all dissatisfied residents move. All home spaces have costs intermingled with benefits. As a result, urban economists have described migration as the result of a decision to make certain trade-offs such as more congestion, dirt, and noise for greater accessibility (Casetti, 1967) or more land and space for less accessibility (Alonso, 1960). The resident of Long Island puts up with the unpleasant two-hour commute to Manhattan to get a two-story house with green space in the suburbs. Thus, dissatisfactions must be weighed against benefits as well as against the costs and unpleasantness associated with the move itself.

Julian Wolpert (1965) elaborates the complex relationships between dissatisfaction and movement. His theory is based directly on Lewin's field theory of spatial behavior described in Chapter 6. Wolpert points out that when a household changes its dwelling place, it incurs considerable cost in time, effort, and inconvenience. Although motivated by a desire for greater long-run satisfaction, the move itself is universally considered to be unpleasant. This reluctance to move suggests that mobility is a reaction to a significant perceived change in the satisfaction derived from present housing or to a change in potential satisfaction elsewhere. A certain threshold of dissatisfaction must be overcome before a move will be made. The satisfaction (or what Wolpert terms the *place utility*) derived from a residence depends on a variety of factors: individual factors such as age, race, education, and income; locational variables such as neighborhood quality, access to work, schools, shopping, and other amenities; site characteristics such as the quality of the residence and the number of rooms; and social factors including a household's degree of integration into local social networks.

In his analysis of threshold formation, Wolpert simply emphasizes that the evaluation of alternatives depends upon the potential movers' current *life-cycle stage*—that is, their ages and the ages of their children. This account of an individual's reaction to thresholds assumes satisficing behavior. If satisfaction with present housing exceeds this minimum threshold, the household does not consider the move, even if it is aware of slightly better residences, or even if satisfaction with the present dwelling deteriorates slightly. In essence, the perceived value of moving has to be enough to overcome the negative aspects of the move itself. Because of this basic resistance to moving, the perceived gain has to be substantial.

In this regard Wolpert distinguishes between the *stresses* and the *strains* that may result from the mix of costs and benefits inherent in urban housing. People are willing to tolerate stress because they receive some important benefits in return. If, however, the costs of gaining these benefits become intolerable, then strain results and strain encourages migration. The threshold between stress and strain varies among individual households.

These points are better understood when migration is viewed as a long-term process in which movers progress through a series of stages toward some housing ideal. Michelson (1977) suggests that people may have different residence rationales at different points in their lifetime. They may move a number of times, each time progressing toward some eventual goal. Thus, early in their careers, people may not be completely satisfied with their present housing simply because their ideals cannot yet be realized. Foote et al. (1960) point out that 90 percent of the nonfarm population considers owning the preferable form of tenancy. Despite this fact, only about 65 percent of all housing units are owner occupied (U.S. Bureau of the Census, 1973). Clearly, a significant number of renters will be dissatisfied regardless of housing quality. This dissatisfaction with current housing may not be immediately translated into action because the threshold of dissatisfaction has not been reached: The disutility of the present dwelling is outweighed by the costs and personal worries involved in the move itself. Also, there are certain circumstances in which dissatisfaction cannot be resolved by movement. A rise in housing costs or a housing shortage lowers the chances of moving even when dissatisfaction is high. These problems are accentuated for the lower classes, whose housing options are normally so limited that they may simply be forced to reevaluate their current residence.

Dissatisfaction obviously is something people can learn to tolerate to a degree. Even in periods of normal vacancy there is evidence that less than 50 percent of all households convert their dissatisfaction into movement (Foote et al., 1960). For many, dissatisfaction changes before migration ever takes place. Brown and Moore (1970) show that "strain" may be resolved through some change in the existing environment such as redecorating or remodeling the home or getting more actively involved in local community activities. Another way to reduce strain is to alter the needs creating the dissatisfaction, perhaps by reassessing the importance of the need or by altering the household that created the need in the first place (e.g., encouraging older children to seek their own place of residence or by placing an aged member of an extended family into a nursing home). The pool of potential movers, people who would like to move when the opportunity arises, may be termed *latent movers*. A change in the national economic climate may cause many latent movers to enter the market at the same time.

The act of moving to a new home, then, involves a complex decision-making process, which cannot be understood in simple rationalistic terms. We have emphasized the satisficing nature of the decision and the crucial importance of the threshold concept. A certain threshold of dissatisfaction must be exceeded before the costly move process is undertaken. As we have indicated, it is clear that knowledge of an individual's level of satisfaction with the present dwelling is inadequate to predict movement. Bach and Smith (1977) show that the most likely group of movers are not those people expecting to move nor those dissatisfied with their present location. Rather, movers tend to come from a special subset of both of these groups—the dissatisfied resident planning to move.

The Sociology of the Migrant: Sources of Residential Dissatisfaction and Inertia

What factors produce this group of unhappy residents and willing movers? Figure 7.1 presents a very general explanation of the forces behind this process. It is apparent from this simple portrayal of the decision-making process that to understand satisfaction and movement desires, the social scientist must consider both the characteristics of the home environment as well as the social characteristics of the decision maker.

To predict migration, then, it is important to construct a sociology of the migrant. A large portion of the population moves in any single year. But it is obvious that not everyone migrates, and it is well established that those who do move differ sociologically from those who remain in their present household (Goldscheider, 1971). Migration is selective. This point is itself of great relevance to an understanding of the process of urban spatial change. Because

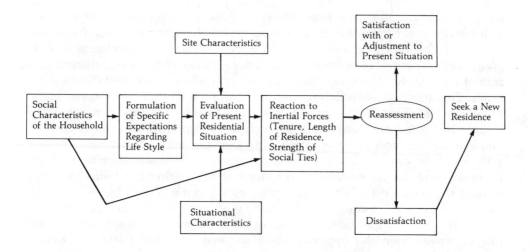

Figure 7.1 *The Decision to Move* (*Source:* Adapted from Eric Moore, "Residential Mobility in the City," Resource Paper 13, Commission on College Geography, Association of American Geographers, 1972. Reprinted by permission.)

migrants do not represent a cross-section of the population, it is clear that movement has patterned social determinants and consequences. In areas with a concentration of people likely to move, one might expect more rapid turnover and potential for neighborhood change.

The probability of movement depends in part on the social characteristics of the household. Families at different stages of the life cycle, with different career patterns and varying positions in the stratification system, have distinct life-style preferences. These variations in life-style expectations, in turn, lead people of diverse backgrounds to judge their current housing by different sets of standards. Also, such differences in household characteristics lead to a variety of reactions to the costs of movement. For some these costs are too high. For others the costs when weighed against the advantages are immaterial.

Spatial mobility is a status-conferring, or at least a status-maintaining, activity. Housing is thus viewed as an opportunity to maintain and enhance life-style aspirations. Wendell Bell (1958) recognizes three types of life-style aspirations as possible reasons for moving. Some households are consumption oriented, while others are either prestige or family oriented. The *consumption-oriented household* stresses the desire to have housing that provides quick access to urban amenities and services. This life-style expectation is most common among moderately affluent single-person households, young childless couples, or older couples whose children have left home. The *social prestige aspiration* is likely to be found in the young, upwardly mobile household with few children. Such households primarily emphasize a life style appropriate to their station. *Family-oriented aspirations,* on the other hand, are most common among households with a moderate to large family. Here housing should provide a healthy environment for the raising of children. Moore (1972) adds to this list a fourth type of life-style aspiration—the *community-directed aspiration.* This value emphasizes the need for interaction with others of a similar value orientation. It could be found in many varieties in the communes of California in the 1960s.

While these life-style aspirations are significant for mobility, Butler's (1969) national survey of movers finds no direct relationship between aspirations and movement. It is most likely that life style plays a more complex role in mobility decisions. As the work of Michelson (1977) suggests, life-style orientation extends its influence over the span of the mobility career; that is, aspirations are satisfied in stages rather than in a single move.

That aspirations are satisfied in stages suggests the importance of a life-cycle approach to migration, as Wolpert's field theory advocates. In migration studies, age appears to be the strongest predictor of movement propensity. Indeed, life-cycle changes may compel mobility. Younger people are more likely to move than older people. The highest rates of mobility for the United States population occur between the ages of eighteen and thirty-four. Young adults are at the stage in the life cycle that normally involves leaving the parental home, establishing a family of their own in a new location, entering the labor force, starting a career, and having children. Marriage, family expansion, and occupational mobility are all usually associated with spatial mobility. Older persons, then, because they are at the end of the career and family cycles tend to be nonmobile. Not all older people, however, are residentially stable, and not all younger persons are mobile. In the United States approximately 10 percent of people over fifty change residence annually. Age does not determine migration; it merely facilitates or discourages it. While almost one-third of the older population wants to move, only about 25 percent of the group desiring to move actually do migrate (Goldscheider, 1971). Older people experience serious obstacles to moving such as limited budgets, restricted housing options, strong social bonds with an area, familiarity with neighborhood facilities and services, all of which younger households are less likely to encounter. In short, movement for them is costly.

The age-migration relationship implies a more general connection between social characteristics and residential mobility. The correlation between age and migration is not direct. Age has sociological significance. It is the most basic element of stratification. People at different ages perform different roles. Age integrates individuals differentially into kinship networks and the occupational system.

Goldscheider (1971) argues that age is important for migration because it affects how much individuals are tied to their community. Age influences kinship and occupational links to a local community and thus affects the propensity to move. Generally, older persons are more integrated in the community through local kin ties, friends, social organizations, and housing investments.

They are, in short, more prone to be residentially stable. These social characteristics, which tap community bonds, should affect an individual's migration probabilities.

The Goldscheider thesis represents the first step toward a general sociological theory of migration. Existing evidence appears to support the underlying principle of the thesis. In addition to age, ethnic and socioeconomic stratification modify participation in social roles. These two aspects of class structure limit access to the goals and resources competed for in any given community. Both race and socioeconomic status influence residential mobility, although not in any simple or clear-cut fashion. Nonwhites in the United States seem to express a greater desire to move than whites. Census data, however, suggest that these desires are not likely to be translated into mobility. (White and black mobile groups between 1970 and 1974 both equaled 57 percent of their respective populations.) Migration varies by race only in terms of the length of the move. Whites are more likely to make long-distance moves out of the metropolis, whereas nonwhites are more likely to move between neighborhoods in the metropolitan area. The mobility differences by socioeconomic status reflect a similar situation. Higher-status groups exhibit a greater propensity to undertake long-distance moves, whereas lower-status groups exhibit a greater amount of intrametropolitan movement.

Race and class differentials do not directly support the community integration thesis. To substantiate this thesis, we must consider that portion of the population with the lowest migration propensities—those persons over sixty-five—and ask just who among this population does move (Goldscheider, 1971). The answer is enlightening. It is precisely that segment of the elderly without family, housing investments, or other social and economic ties to the area who move most frequently. Among the older population, married persons plan and desire to move less often than either the single, widowed, or divorced. Also, members of one-person households are twice as likely to move as those from three-person households. Satisfaction with the current home and the desire to move appear to be related to the social linkages with the surrounding community. Moving is done at the expense of established social ties; when these bonds are strong, dissatisfaction is unlikely and migration is difficult.

The effects of age on the decision to migrate appear to be at least twofold. On the one hand, societies are age graded—each age representing a distinct phase of the life cycle. In this sense, a person's arrival at some new stage in the life cycle may force a reevaluation of the appropriateness of current housing for the new age role. At the same time residential mobility is costly, and these costs vary from one stage in the life cycle to the next. Families are tied to their neighborhoods because of financial, social and individual commitments (Bach and Smith, 1977). Some people are freer to move than others. Homeowners have greater commitment to their current residence than renters. People with school-age children have ties to a neighborhood they may be reluctant to break for their children's sake. Individuals who have lived in their present house for a long time have social and psychic bonds to the area that more recent households lack. One simple generalization has been suggested: The longer a household lives in an area, the less likely it is to move, regardless of any other factors. McGinnis (1968) calls this the *axiom of cumulative inertia.* The dissatisfaction threshold grows larger over time. Financial and social ties cloud the possibilities and probabilities for migration. Since people in the aggregate tend to solve problems by choosing the least costly alternative, many dissatisfied households seek to alter their dissatisfaction without moving.

The Rationale for Movement: Site and Situational Characteristics of the Residence

The household decision maker's threshold of dissatisfaction depends upon his or her current life-cycle stage. The level of dissatisfaction itself, however, results from a complex interaction between the household's current life-style aspirations and the site and situational characteristics of the present home. Studies of the individual migration decision indicate that the reasons given for moving usually refer to these site and situational pushes rather than to the pulls due to life-style aspirations.

These findings must be interpreted with care. Sometimes we ourselves do not appreciate the motives for our behavior, and we are unlikely to give a full account of ourselves in a questionnaire. Many psychologists and sociologists have been extremely critical of explanations based on verbal rationalizations of behavior (Fishbein, 1967). Attitudes elicited verbally, in interviews, are termed *reported preferences,* while those inferred from direct observation of behavior are termed *revealed preferences.* A full understanding of the movement decision must be based upon judiciously integrating observations of the reasons people give and what they actually do when moving.

A large number of studies have contributed to our understanding of the rationales for moving (Rossi, 1955; Leslie and Richardson, 1961; Wolpert, 1965; Butler, 1969; Redding, 1970; Speare, 1974; Bach and Smith, 1977). Moore (1972) summarizes the push factors that may influence a movement decision. Among them are spatial requirements, housing costs, the general condition of the home and neighborhood, accessibility to work and services, and the social composition of the neighborhood.

Rossi's 1955 study of residential mobility in Philadelphia represents the first comprehensive social psychological account of residential decision making. He found that mobility most often serves to adjust housing to the shifting requirements of the family as it changes over time. As families form, grow, stabilize, and then disperse, their housing needs change. Preeminent among these life-cycle changes are dwelling space needs. Almost every subsequent survey has found spatial requirements to be a major consideration in residential dissatisfaction. As we would expect from the cognitive account of decision making, perceived needs are more critical than actual requirements. Rossi's data suggest that objective measures of need based on rooms-per-person figures predict satisfaction less accurately than the individual's perception of the adequacy of dwelling space.

Michelson's (1977) study of residential mobility in Toronto somewhat qualifies past findings. He discovered that when the types of present housing (either apartment or house) are distinguished, dwelling space is less important for the apartment resident than for the homeowner. Moving to a house to gain interior space is more often used as a rationale for migration among previous homedwellers than by previous apartment dwellers. Michelson believes this difference suggests a hierarchy of needs in which the desires for ownership and for a single-family dwelling outrank living space as a motivator for movement until they have been satisfied.

In addition to the spatial requirements push, many people are dissatisfied and want to move from their present location because of the general physical condition of their own home or the neighborhood. The home's interior and exterior appearance, its state of repair, as well as the state of repair of other housing in the neighborhood influence a household's satisfaction with the present residence. Noise and pollution levels in the neighborhood are also quite often given as a primary reason for movement plans (Michelson, 1977).

To this point, at least, the research on the social psychology of migration has produced no surprises. With regard to housing costs and accessibility, however, current research challenges social science's previous view of the mobility decision.

Individual households apparently do not view residential mobility in standard economic terms. Housing costs are seldom cited as a primary reason for movement. "In fact Lansing et al. (1964) showed that over 55 percent of movers spent more on housing after the move than they did before" (Moore, 1972:6). This does not suggest, however, that economic considerations are not built into the movement decision. Rather, economic decisions may involve a series of complex trade-offs between price and other features such as space, congestion, and so forth that do not show up in simple cost calculations. The purchase or rental of a residence is, after all, not simple. The family is not just buying shelter but social standing, access, neighborhood services, and companions for themselves and their children.

Central to macro or aggregate theories of migration is the idea that the journey to work is an important factor in selecting a residence. J. D. Carroll (1950) suggests that the residential pattern of cities can only be understood as the consequence of a "principle of least effort" underlying the spatial choice of residents:

> While many factors are involved in the selection of homes and places of work, the persistence of the desire to minimize the distance separating workplace from home acting through each individual worker may be the single element which can create pattern out of the aggregate choices of large numbers of workers (1950:24).

Studies of the individual decision-making process, however, have to this point produced little evidence that accessibility is important for the household's movement decision. Butler et al. (1969) found that accessibility is a significant push only for people living forty minutes or more from work. This is an interesting example of a specific threshold in the mobility decision. In a more recent analysis, Michelson (1977) shows that only those people moving to the downtown area cite access as a primary consideration in migrating. His data also suggest that travel time, rather than actual distance to work, is the major motivating factor in these centralized moves. In fact, very few studies of residential mobility have taken into account the full cognitive complexity of the distance variable, as outlined in Chapter 6.

Is accessibility, then, a relatively minor factor in movement? The answer is unclear. Macroeconomic models of migration very accurately predict overall movement with accessibility variables. Still, at least until recently, people seldom cited accessibility as a primary point of dissatisfaction with current housing. Melvin Webber (1970) argues that in the auto age metropolis of the 1960s and early 1970s distance had become less constraining, and thus the importance of accessibility for households and firms had declined. With vast improvements in transportation and communication technology, the urban area became dispersed and ever more space consuming than in the past. While very few families and businesses chose to locate at great distances from the metropolis, they were locating farther away than before because the cost of movement was minimal. In Webber's scenario, new locational determinants were emerging that were not directly related to accessibility.

There are two reasons for rejecting this view of urban residential change. The most obvious is that since the Arab oil embargo of 1973 the cost of movement has increased drastically, and soaring prices for gasoline are likely to make accessibility more salient in future movement decisions. In addition, it is not that accessibility was ever unimportant, but that its effect on location was more subtle than previously assumed (Moore, 1972). One cannot only be too far away from work and various services, but too close as well. As Casetti (1967) argues, people who maximize accessibility in residential movement must also be willing to accept greater levels of congestion. The noise and pollution levels as well as traffic conditions associated with proximity have immediate costs attached to them. Redding (1970) points out that these costs moderate the profits of access. People want to be close to work, shopping, and recreation, but not too close.

A final push factor in the movement decision is the social composition of the neighborhood. A home, after all, encompasses the immediate social and physical environment. Complaints about neighborhood people or the changing social structure of the immediate area are a source of dissatisfaction for a significant portion of those moving. However, they rank below concerns for space and for physical conditions of the home and neighborhood, which appear to be the primary motives for moving. Of course, what people say they do and what they actually do are two different things. It is unlikely anymore that people will openly admit that they are contemplating a move because of the changing ethnic composition of an area. The issue is sensitive. Enough empirical evidence does exist to suggest that despite what people say, ethnic transition of a neighborhood produces considerable migration among the area's original tenants.

Ironically, it is the mobility level of the neighborhood itself that makes this factor prominent in individual decisions to leave. Rossi's early study indicates that more mobile neighborhoods tend to produce a belief among residents that their social status clearly differs from the neighborhood's. Additionally, high-mobility areas are seen as less friendly places than stable neighborhoods. In essence, the transitional quality of some places tends to encourage dissatisfaction.

SELECTING A NEW RESIDENCE

Once a person decides to move, the decision-making process shifts to a new phase involving a different set of considerations. While the decision to move is a function of generally negative features pushing people out of their current residence, the selection of a new residence results from pulls or attractions to a new home space. Moore (1972) divides this second phase of the migration into three stages: (1) establishing criteria for evaluating a potential residence, (2) searching for attainable alternative housing, (3) evaluating alternatives and the final selection. The choice of a new residence (rather than the decision to move) involves distinctively spatial problem solving. It is at this stage that the numerous cognitive and affective aspects of spatial image come into play. The process is typically described as a *search*, according to a satisficing rather than a rationalistic criterion.

This choice process is, of course, highly constrained. People must choose housing within a range of available sites. The array of sites available and the knowledge of such places (cognitive image) is conditioned by a set of urban agents whose interests may or may not be similar to those of the individual resident.

> If we consider the series of events associated with each change of residence, it is readily evident that a number of different actors are involved. Although the household occupies the center of the stage, the actions of individuals and groups such as friends and acquaintances, real estate agents, land developers, financial institutions, and particularly urban planners and politicians, influence the outcome of the individual decision by providing limits on the range of available opportunities (Moore, 1972:3).

Choice is, then, to a degree affected by all of these actors as well as by the characteristics of the individual household. These constraints are perhaps most apparent during the search process.

Developing Criteria for Evaluation

Generally, the reasons people give for deciding to move are also primary criteria for evaluating alternative housing. Thus the adequacy of living space, the physical condition of the home, the condition of the neighborhood, accessibility, and life-style aspirations are factors the potential migrant uses in evaluating a future home site. Not all of these criteria, however, will be employed by the individual migrant. Rossi (1955) suggests that the family will keep the number of situational and site factors small in order to make comparisons between alternatives simpler.

A long shopping list of criteria makes for a long and difficult search process, one in which most people would be unwilling to participate. Studies by Rossi (1955) and Butler et al. (1969) suggest the most important criteria to be the interior space of the home and the physical and social quality of the neighborhood. The exterior appearance of the home, on the other hand, is a feature most people are willing to trade for other advantages. A home with a very nice inside appearance and less desirable exterior appearance is overwhelmingly favored over a home with a better exterior than interior (Butler et al., 1969). People are also more willing to accept a less desirable home in a good neighborhood than a more desirable home in a less desirable neighborhood.

Although the individual decision maker uses highly simplified choice criteria, different movers emphasize different criteria. Michelson's research (1977) suggests that motivating forces may differ among people moving to different housing types and locations. Those choosing downtown locations tend to stress accessibility criteria more often than those considering suburban sites. Families moving downtown cite public transportation and access to work twice as often as those moving to the suburbs. Additionally, those moving to houses are more likely to stress interior space and appearance benefits than those moving to apartments. In short, the residentially mobile population is composed of individuals with varying social and physical requirements that must be met by a range of choices in the existing housing stock.

Searching for Attainable Alternatives

Once the required benefits of a move are decided upon, the household begins the search process. This search is primarily an information-gathering activity. The prospective migrant usually relies on three sources of information to find vacancies: the newspaper, the real estate agent, and social contacts within the community. People most frequently use the newspaper to discover listings, but the most effective information source (that is, the one most often used in actually finding the new home) is the individual's network of friends and acquaintances (Rossi, 1955).

The use of acquaintances suggests the parochial nature of the housing search (Wolpert, 1965). The social network of the average household is limited in a patterned fashion in the city. People of similar social class background and occupation tend to be delimited spatially in the city (see Chapter 5). The result is a distinct sectoral bias in the interaction and travel patterns of the average city dweller—action space and activity space are intimately related. In a moderately large city, an urbanite living on the east side of town knows little about the residential areas and commercial facilities on the west side. People tend disproportionately to associate with others living in the same sector of the city as themselves. As a result, spatial choice is limited by the sectoral activity space of the potential migrant (Johnston, 1972). Simply, the household bent on moving is likely to remain within a given general area of the city. There are two basic reasons for this: (1) Most of the personal information about other neighborhoods comes from people living in the same general area; (2) people perceive the sectoral pattern of segregation in the urban area, and they judge their own sector to be suitable to their social requirements.

The choice of a new home is one particular instance of spatial problem solving, as discussed in Chapter 6. Thus the search is organized in locational terms (Brown and Moore, 1970). Areas of the city are selected or rejected on the basis of their perceived social and locational advantages, as well as the degree of information available about the area. The search for new housing is therefore not just a function of the range of available vacancies; more importantly, it results from the family's awareness of vacancies.

While social contacts appear to represent the major supplier of this information among the total pool of migrants, the real estate agent is an effective source for a significant segment of this pool—the homebuyer. Approximately 50 percent of all home purchasers see the agent as the most effective source consulted (Michelson, 1977). Although the social sciences have generally neglected the study of real estate agents, their influence over the homebuyer and the spatial composition of the city is potentially profound.

Real estate agents are primarily information managers (House, 1977). Their role is to establish communication between buyer and seller to facilitate the sale of real property. They do not passively manage data, but rather they select the information that is passed between both parties. It is this information-screening activity that has significance for individual choice.

Real estate agents can dramatically change neighborhood composition—most blatantly illustrated by the practice of blockbusting. While blockbusting is not the typical case, under more normal circumstances the agent exercises considerable control. Agents want to find clients homes they can afford in areas they will like. While most people know ahead of time where they want to live, for people unfamiliar with a city the agent's role is to find a suitable neighborhood. In so doing real estate agents are cultural brokers interpreting local prejudices, life styles, and so on (House, 1977). Most agents view their role as one of finding the proper social environment for the client. To carry out this duty they preselect vacancies according to sets of expectations they hold regarding a client's needs, further simplifying the individual's information field. At times this information simplification is governed by ethnic stereotype and prejudice, as a Canadian agent suggests: "We help purchasers end up in the right area. It would be a tragedy if an English Canadian from out of town ended up in a French area" (House, 1977:114).

The information both social contact fields and real estate agencies provide about residential opportunities is far from complete. The limitations themselves constrain choice and conserve the existing spatial patterns within the urban area. The constraint on choice is most obvious for the lower classes. Because of limited spatial mobility their social networks are geographically limited. In addition very few real estate agencies are willing to take lower-class clients, because of the small commissions such potential buyers can produce.

Evaluating Alternatives

The basic feature of the choice process when compared to the mobility decision is that considerations are more limited in scope. People spend longer, on the average, deciding to look for new housing than they do actually choosing a new house (Michelson, 1977). The limited information field coupled with the establishment of certain criteria severely restrict choices. The residential sites actually visited tend to be few in number and are usually concentrated in small areas around the site finally chosen (Moore, 1972). Current research suggests that households adopt a conservative strategy that involves taking an acceptable home rather than searching for the best possible choice.

Many movers, then, take the first acceptable opportunity (indicating that residential mobility is more accurately described as a satisficing rather than boundedly rational behavior). Such conservatism undoubtedly contributes to the fact that recent movers have the highest probability of moving again. Whenever several alternatives are available, once again the stance is conserva-

Table 7.1   The Compatibility of Different Dwelling Qualities: The Index of Incompatibility[a]

Qualities as Inferior	Transportation	Neighborhood Reputation	Costs	Outside Appearance	Number of Rooms
Transportation	—	1.27	1.09	1.30	.73
Neighborhood Reputation	1.09	—	1.27	.55	.36
Costs	.82	.94	—	1.29	1.18
Outside Appearance	1.18	.68	1.46	—	.64
Number of Rooms	1.29	.82	1.18	.76	—

[a]An index value greater than 1.00 indicates that the two qualities tend to be incompatible. A value less than 1.00 indicates compatibility.

Source: From *Why Families Move* by Peter Rossi. Copyright © 1962 by The Free Press of Glencoe, a division of The Macmillan Company. Reprinted with permission of Macmillan Publishing Company, Inc., New York, N.Y.

The residence provides a complex bundle of services to the individual household. Because of this complexity, dwellings are not normally attractive in all respects. Residential decisions usually involve some trade-offs (e.g., less space for greater access). Rossi's Philadelphia data suggest some of the variables involved in the trade-off. Maximizing one quality usually implies sacrificing others.

tive. Cost is apparently the major "clinching" factor in making a decision between two or more acceptable places (Rossi, 1955). Approximately 60 percent of
movers cite cost as a major consideration.

Since dwellings are not normally attractive in all respects, residential
choice involves trade-offs. Maximizing one criterion means minimizing others.
A house with cost advantages is less likely to be accessible to work and other
activities. It is more likely to be smaller, to have a poorer exterior appearance,
and to be located in a neighborhood of lower repute (see Table 7.1). Given the
wealth of potential considerations and trade-offs, as well as the limited time
spent in the search, such a conservative strategy is functional. This strategy,
however, promotes mobility and spatial change within the city. "We know that
many households make poor choices of new dwellings; much of this is due to
having to make a decision based on very limited information and highly inefficient and personalized search procedures within a short period of time"
(Moore, 1972:19).

SUMMARY

The home base is of great psychological and social significance to the urban
family. As a social space it is the basic building block for the neighborhood
unit. In turn, the neighborhoods of an urban area form the basic social mosaic
that characterizes the city space. To understand the evolution of the city mosaic, you must first have some comprehension of the rationale behind the decision of city dwellers to move from one home base to another.

Several factors affect a movement decision: the social characteristics of the
household, the social and financial costs of movement, and the extent of dissatisfaction with the current residence. Dissatisfaction is not enough to prompt a
move. People at different stages of the life cycle and at different points in the
social structure react to these dissatisfactions in a variety of ways. Older and
poorer residents may experience fewer alternatives, and higher costs. For them
dissatisfaction must often either continue or decline without migration.

Curiously, while the home territory is of critical social importance, once a
person has decided to move, he or she spends little time searching for a new
residence. The search appears to be constrained by a whole range of factors that
limit choices. This constraint may lead to further dissatisfaction and more residential mobility.

Chapter 8

Community and Neighborhood Change

INTRODUCTION

Chapter 7 developed an understanding of the individual's mobility decision. We will now consider community and neighborhood change: the impact of large numbers of residential moves on the urban mosaic. Although these changes result from individual mobility decisions, neighborhood change is usually studied from an aggregate (or ecological) perspective. At this level of analysis, the neighborhoods themselves are the units under scrutiny rather than the individuals who make the decision to move.

The chapter is organized into two major sections. The first describes neighborhood change by outlining the pattern of mobility in cities and considering the relationship between aggregate mobility and changing neighborhood characteristics. It emphasizes the traditional ecological concept of succession. The second section of this chapter tries to explain neighborhood change. Three contrasting and complementary explanations are outlined: the rent model, the cultural ecology perspective, and the institutional interaction account. The concluding portion of the chapter brings these models together with the earlier social-psychological explanations of mobility to provide a unified account of urban spatial dynamics.

DESCRIBING NEIGHBORHOOD CHANGE

An Aggregate Picture of Mobility

Roughly 20 percent of the American population changes residence each year. Within the city, however, mobility rates vary greatly for different areas. In a large metropolis, turnover rates in the area around the center may exceed 70 percent per year, while in stable, established suburban communities rates may approach 5 percent, a figure close to the absolute minimum of mobility generated by birth, death, and family formation.

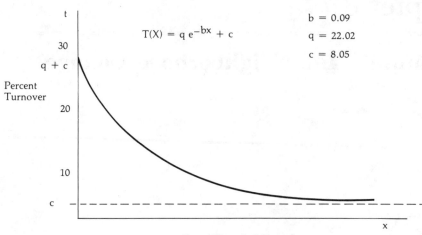

Figure 8.1 *General Form of Urban Turnover Rates* Moore's model indicates that residential mobility declines sharply with distance from the city center, shallowing out until it approaches a minimal, or asymptotic, level of turnover in the most stable suburbs. The parameter c measures this lower limit of mobility. The parameter q measures how much mobility in the city center exceeds c, so that the value $q + c$ gives the total turnover at the city center. The parameter b is a gradient parameter governing the rate of decline of mobility with increasing distance from the center. In this study of Brisbane, Australia, distance was measured in minutes of travel time. The graph shows the numerical values of the parameters for one year. (*Source:* From Eric Moore, "Residential Mobility in the City," Resource Paper 13, Commission on College Geography, Association of American Geographers, 1972. Reprinted by permission.)

A simple portrayal of turnover rates in large cities is provided by Moore (1971, 1972) in a mathematical model that closely resembles Clark's Law. The model was developed for the Australian city of Brisbane with 1961 census data for 171 small areal units (see Figure 8.1). The form of the model is

$$t\,(x) = q\,e^{-bx} + c$$

where $t\,(x)$ represents the turnover at a travel time of x minutes from the center. The parameter c measures the minimum turnover rate in the most stable outlying suburbs. In this study c equaled 8.05 percent. This figure is somewhat higher than the 5 percent lower limit on mobility found in American suburbs, perhaps reflecting a slightly higher level of mobility among the Australian middle class. The parameter b is equivalent to the density parameter in Clark's Law; it regulates the rate of decline in mobility with increasing distance from the center. In Moore's study b equals .09. The parameter q represents the additional increment to turnover (over and above the value of c) found at the center. Here q equals 22.02, and thus mobility at the center was approximately 30 percent—a figure much below that found in the largest United States cities.

Moore found that the parameters q and b were sensitive to the availability of credit for new home construction, while c, as you would expect from its interpretation, remained fairly stable during the study period. As mortgage credit became hard to get, dwelling turnover occurred more rapidly in the inner (rental) portion of the city, increasing the q value and also, because the turnover profile got steeper, increasing the value of b.

The model is significant in that it suggests the parallel between ecological organization and mobility: Both migration and density are distance dependent. Moore's study goes one step further in illuminating this relationship. His analysis looks at the neighborhood correlates of mobility and their relationship to the distance variable. The results for five predictors are summarized in Table 8.1. These data tend to support the following propositions:

1. Population turnover is low in areas with many young dependents (i.e., in areas with strong family-oriented life styles such as stable suburbs).

2. Population turnover is high in areas with many single adults (i.e., areas with low family status, including some inner-city areas).

3. Population turnover is low in areas with a high proportion of single-family dwelling units.

4. Population turnover is low in areas with a high proportion of owner-

Table 8.1   Correlation of Five Socioeconomic
Variables with Population Turnover for Brisbane, Australia

Variable	Correlation with Turnover	Correlation with Distance to Center
Dependency ratio	−.533	+.822
Percentage of single adults	+.570	−.656
Percentage of single dwelling units	−.718	+.856
Percentage of owner-occupied dwellings	−.210	+.655
Percentage of Australian-born population	−.666	+.700

Source: Eric Moore, "Residential Mobility in the City," Resource Paper 13, Commission on College Geography, Association of American Geographers, 1972. Reprinted by permission.

Population turnover is highest in areas with low levels of familism, such as single-family dwellings, owner-occupied buildings and areas with high levels of ethnicity. These characteristics are most likely to occur in areas close to the city center. Neighborhood change is clearly a function of distance from the center.

occupied dwelling units. (This proposition summarizes the effects of one of the most powerful statistical predictors of neighborhood change: the proportion of dwelling units that are renter occupied. Such neighborhoods change at rates several times higher than those in areas that are mainly owner occupied.)

5. Population turnover is low in areas with a high proportion of native-born (Australian) population. (Conversely, change rates are high in neighborhoods with many foreigners, including inner-city ethnic areas.)

The correlations of these predictors with distance to the center are high (in each case actually greater than the correlation with the dependent variable, mobility). The strong distance correlations with the independent variables are consistent with our understanding of the spatial configuration of cities. The independent variables are analogous to the social area analysis constructs that define the dimensions of spatial segregation (see Chapter 5). This provides a clue to the highly systematic behavior of turnover rates in urban space. Mobility is related to a number of ecological variables that themselves are highly correlated with central distance. Thus neighborhood change is strongly related to central accessibility, not because mobility depends intrinsically on distance, but because of the intermediate effect of a number of distance-dependent factors. This also seems to suggest that neighborhood change, as reflected in mobility rates, will tend to produce a pattern of change in keeping with existing ecological models of spatial description.

The Chicago School and the Concept of Succession

While it is useful to think about mobility in terms of continuous profiles such as Moore's model, this perspective obscures the fact that neighborhoods form a patchwork of discrete entities and that they tend to change abruptly rather than continuously. A more elaborate description was formulated by Park and Burgess in the 1920s and 1930s. They called this process *invasion-succession*. This concept links mobility rates with changes in the social characteristics of neighborhoods. As such, it goes one step further than Moore's analysis in describing neighborhood change.

In the Park-Burgess theory the series of events involved in the replacement of one neighborhood group with another is termed *ecological succession*. The concept is borrowed from biology, where it is used to describe the sequence of ecosystem changes in which one community of species replaces another. Biologists see succession as the product of environmental changes. As the habitat changes, new organisms and new relationships between organisms better adapted to the altered environment emerge.

Park and Burgess relied heavily on the work of the biologist Frederick Clements (1916) in adapting the succession concept to the study of city space. Clements argued that a community of organisms "reacted" with its habitat, consequently altering the environment and setting up the conditions necessary for the invasion of a new set of organisms. Burgess reinterpreted the term *reaction* in a sociological sense, suggesting that in human communities the reaction was social rather than environmental. Essentially the redefined concept described the resistance, or the expressed antagonism, of the established occupants of an area toward the invading population (Van Liere, 1977).

In its broadest sense, residential succession simply involves the replacement of one population group in an area with another. The differences between the two groups may comprise occupation, income, ethnicity, race, age, family status, or some combination of these characteristics. Most empirical studies of succession, however, have focused on racial transition.

Despite the emphasis on resistance and racial change, succession is viewed as a normal and orderly process resulting from urban growth. As suggested in Chapter 5, urban growth is accompanied by areal expansion in the cities of developed societies. In such places, the expansion of commerce and industry that results from an increase in the city's population leads to the spread of these activities into residential areas. Since commerce and industry can afford to pay more for space than the individual resident, succession occurs. This succession, in turn, sets off a series of subsequent invasions and successions in a ripplelike pattern. The process accounts for the high number of successions, and the more frequent residential turnover inherent in neighborhoods closest to the central business district.

Yet, even in neighborhoods where residential moves are frequent, succession is orderly. Neighborhoods apparently change in steps. The initial change usually involves the penetration of a small number of in-migrants from some nontraditional group, who are usually upwardly mobile and may actually have higher incomes than the established population. This initial *penetration* is then followed by an *invasion*, in which larger numbers of the new group replace members of the established population group (Duncan and Duncan, 1957). Eventually such migrations lead to a condition termed *consolidation*, with the proportion of the new group rising until they take over nearly completely. Thereafter, when the new group is of lower socioeconomic status than the traditional group, a *piling up* of the new group sometimes results. During this final stage, population densities are higher than at any other period in the succession process.

Most evidence suggests that these changes do not occur rapidly, but rather over an extended time. They do not usually result from panic selling or flight. With regard to racial succession, for example, researchers have found little evidence to suggest that antiblack attitudes influence movement. Racial attitudes are apparently not the key factor in white succession. Whites seem to make their decision out of concern for the future status of the area. Aldrich suggests that "it is highly rational for a white resident to expect that the area will eventually become mostly black, and hence 'undesirable' because whites do not wish to be in a minority, regardless of their pro- or anti-black feelings" (1975:334).

Apparently succession often results from normal mobility patterns, with no more or no fewer moves than in the past. The initial sign that an area is beginning to change appears to be the point at which the established residential group no longer keeps replacing itself. Once this point is reached, succession generally proceeds in an orderly block by block fashion. The pioneers are sprinkled throughout the area, but when residents near these pioneers move, they are replaced by members of the new group. Once such a turnover begins, it is difficult to reverse, even under conditions of strong and organized neighborhood resistance (Duncan and Duncan, 1957; Aldrich, 1975).

Invasion appears to be most common in cities that are experiencing extensive minority population growth and relatively limited majority growth. In this situation there is a high and growing demand for housing by a population whose housing supply is artificially low because of discrimination and monetary constraints on residential choice. The pent-up, or *latent*, demand for housing among urban blacks is a good example. Because blacks have traditionally been denied access to white residential areas, they have a high demand for housing, a demand further exaggerated by urban renewal activities and redlining. (Redlining is an illegal practice whereby banks designate certain neighborhoods, usually with high proportions of blacks, as high risk areas and deny mortgage money to prospective buyers in these areas.) As a result, blacks may be willing to pay more for the same housing than whites. Indeed, studies by Palmore (1966) and Laurenti (1960) suggest that property values may actually rise, in the period of penetration at least. (The dynamics of neighborhood change between ethnic groups will be discussed later.)

Recent Elaborations of the Succession Concept

Although the succession concept is a valuable descriptive tool in assessing neighborhood change, it fails to portray the process of change accurately for two reasons:

1. Rather than focusing on the neighborhood and its evolution through time, it focuses on the process by which one population group replaces another within a residential area. Such a perspective provides only a truncated version of a neighborhood's life cycle; it describes a single population turnover rather than the full history of a neighborhood.

2. Succession is a unidimensional description of a multidimensional process. Since it focuses on population replacement, it deals only with the social dimension of change. It ignores concomitant changes in the physical conditions of residences in the area. This distorts the original biological concept, which stresses environmental as well as population changes.

Each of these problems has been dealt with in detail by subsequent work in the urban social sciences. We shall consider each in turn.

Neighborhood Evolution   Neighborhoods appear to have a natural and predictable life cycle. During this cycle, incomes gradually fall as the neighborhood ages. While the concentric-zone and sector theories incorporated this phenomenon implicitly, Burgess (1923) and Hoyt (1939) showed little interest in formally describing neighborhood evolution. Rather, their emphasis on succession led them to study neighborhood change in a narrow time frame.

Since these early efforts, several students of the city have attempted to refocus this description of neighborhood change. Hoover and Vernon in their study of the New York metropolitan area, *Anatomy of a Metropolis* (1959), suggest that neighborhoods evolve through a sequence of stages in which population densities, population characteristics, and residential structures change predictably. As the physical structures in the neighborhood begin to age and densities increase, resident populations decline in status. Eventually older populations become more predominant.

These observations were based on information at a single time and thus represented nothing more than conjecture about neighborhood change. David Birch (1971), however, took Hoover and Vernon's conceptions and applied them to the study of neighborhood change in New Haven. He found that census tracts evolved through a sequence of stages:

Stage 1:   Rural. This stage is characterized by low population densities and a predominance of single-family units.

Stage 2:   First wave of development. Subdivision begins with high rates of new construction, predominantly single-family units.

Stage 3:   Fully developed, high-quality residential. The initial development has run its full course. In some cases, single-family units still prevail, but densities are considerably higher than in stage 2. In other cases, an increasing number of multiunit structures have been built. In either case, property values and rents are close to their maximum relative to other neighborhoods in the area.

Stage 4:   Packing: As the age of the structures built during stage 3 increases and rents fall, lower-income groups begin to inhabit the dwellings, and, in order to bridge the gap between their old and their new rents, more people pack into the units than they were originally designed to hold. Densities are at their maximum. In many cities these areas might be called "new slums."

Stage 5:   Thinning. By now, the buildings in stage 4 have deteriorated still further, and the children of low-income parents who originally moved into them are leaving, probably for a stage-4 or stage-2 area somewhere else in the city. Population declines absolutely, leaving older couples behind. These areas might be called "old slums."

Stage 6: Recapture. At some point the land occupied by an old slum becomes too valuable to justify its use as an old slum, and its inhabitants become too weak politically to hold on to it. Property is then reacquired, leveled or rehabilitated, and put to more efficient use, such as high-income apartments or office buildings or public housing. When recapture is completed, the area may appear to have many of the properties of a stage-3 area, but with significantly higher densities. At some point there must be a stage 7, as recaptured areas themselves begin to decay, but this has not yet happened in New Haven (Birch, 1971:60).

Explicit in this schema is a notion first developed in the concentric-zone theory—that succession is tied to the physical aging of the neighborhood. Wealthier families tend to live in younger neighborhoods, poorer families in older neighborhoods.

From this notion of neighborhood life cycle, it is easy to see that the same concept can be applied to individual dwelling units within the urban community.

Filtering Birch's data show that as housing ages in a neighborhood, succession takes place. Since aging most often reduces the housing services a dwelling unit can provide and since higher-income groups can demand more housing services, it follows that aging usually leads to lower-income occupancy. This process is known as *downward filtering*; it tends to coincide with succession.

Filtering focuses on the dynamics of the housing market, rather than the social dynamics of population movement. Houses are not typical consumer items. They violate the classic notions of market commodities. Houses are not consumed; rather, when a family moves out, the same house reappears as vacant. Each vacancy is initiated by death, migration out of the area, or by the construction of a new house. This initial vacancy sets up a chain of subsequent vacancies that will eventually be terminated either by demolition or by recruitment of a new household from outside the metropolitan market (White, 1971). Data on specific housing markets indicate that the average length of the chain initiated by a new house is over four vacancies (Lansing et al., 1969). The evidence also points to a relationship between the sequence of vacancies and purchase price. The market value of houses declines steadily with position in the chain. This relationship suggests a gradual filtering down of housing as the existing housing stock ages and new housing is built. In short, downward filtering can be viewed as a source of low-income housing.

The welfare aspects of filtering stem from the fact that the neighborhood container (its buildings) changes at a slower rate than the neighborhood community (its people). Because buildings are extremely durable goods, they are not consumed by a single household but by a succession of households. This difference in change rates suggests that the invading population may benefit. These welfare functions of filtering—that is, its benefits for disadvantaged consumers in the housing market—have been a point of considerable debate. Ratcliff (1949) argues that the construction of new housing releases units to the filtering process and thus leads to improved housing for the lower classes. There is, however, a basic flaw in this argument. Housing values depreciate with age, but at the same time housing quality deteriorates. Since the structural quality of a residence is a function of maintenance, and since a household's ability to maintain a residence is a function of income, it follows that the advantage to the poor can be only temporary. The welfare functions of filtering accrue only when market values decline faster than structural quality. Historically, this has happened only very rarely.

Two factors affect the rate of filtering: the rate of new construction, and the rate at which new households form (Yeates and Garner, 1976). If new construction is going up faster than households are forming, the market value of older housing decreases quickly, providing an advantage to lower-income residents. The existence of such a market condition has led some to argue that better housing can be achieved for all by encouraging the construction of new housing for the middle and upper classes. This argument may have some appeal to local officials who would much prefer to encourage high-income rather than low-income housing in their districts. But it represents, at best, an indirect attack on the housing problems of the poor, and there is no convincing evidence that it has ever worked.

Filtering and succession processes represent the basic dynamics of neighborhood change. They describe maturational changes in the container and community. In combination these parallel processes suggest that the life stage of neighborhoods is determined by the neighborhood's population composition (its average age, ethnicity, and social class), its population density, and its environmental structure (the quality of residences and their availability).

Harlem: A Neighborhood Case History   The simplest way to understand all of this is to look at a specific neighborhood as it has aged. One of the most discussed neighborhood case histories is Harlem's, as recounted by Osofsky (1966).

In the last three decades of the nineteenth century Harlem was a community with great expectations for a solid upper-middle-class future. During previous periods it had been a poor, isolated rural village, but with the growth of New York City, it was annexed and became a popular residence for the established urbanite.

The turning point in Harlem's history came in the 1870s with the expansion of the elevated railway into the area. Almost overnight, rows of brownstones and exclusive apartment buildings appeared. Land speculators made great fortunes buying land, holding it for a short while, and reselling it at a profit. The area became a haven for the upper and upper-middle classes. Many of the houses were equipped with elevators and servants' quarters. Cultural activities flourished. Harlem had its own music hall (the Harlem Opera House built by Oscar Hammerstein) and a great many theaters.

The bubble soon burst, however. At the turn of the century a new wave of land speculation was set off by plans for the construction of new subway routes into the area. Speculators bought up huge chunks of undeveloped land, marshes, and garbage dumps and built a number of new residences. Buyers were paying ten to thirty times what they could gross in rentals in a year. Because of the overbuilding, rents were low. As Russian Jews replaced German Jews in the proletariat force of the garment industry, the Germans began to move uptown to these new residences. A home in Harlem became a symbol of newly found prosperity for the East European Jew. One local paper protested, "Foreigners are crowding up the whole length of the island." The invasion was on.

The housing market glut continued; vacancies increased. Rent prices plummeted. As a result, black families began moving into west Harlem. Block associations formed, but they all failed to prevent the steady invasion of new, less well-off populations. Between 1907 and 1914 two-thirds of the houses in or near the black neighborhoods were sold at substantial losses. By 1920 two-thirds of Manhattan's black population resided in Harlem. The succession was complete.

Mobility Rates and Neighborhood Change   Succession results from the interplay between population changes and changes in neighborhood characteristics. As we have indicated, rapid population turnover may or may not promote change in the character of the area (succession). An inner-city neighborhood serving as a receiving area for immigrants may, for example, have an extremely high rate of mobility while retaining its stable and distinctive ethnic character. On the other hand, in an area of ethnic transition, one single wave of mobility may radically alter the neighborhood. Thus there is no simple relationship between mobility rates and neighborhood change. The crucial factor is the homogeneity or heterogeneity of the migrants, whose characteristics define, in aggregate, the neighborhood's attributes. It follows that not all changes in a neighborhood's population can be described by the succession concept.

Table 8.2   A Typology of Neighborhood Change

	Change in Selected Population Characteristics	Stability in Selected Population Characteristics
High Mobility	Type 1	Type 2
Low Mobility	Type 3	Type 4

Source: Adapted from Eric Moore, "Residential Mobility in the City," Resource Paper 13, Commission on College Geography, Association of American Geographers, 1972. Reprinted by permission.

Moore (1972) describes four types of neighborhood change (see Table 8.2). His typology rests on the relationship between mobility and neighborhood characteristics. Type-1 neighborhoods combine high mobility rates with changes in socioeconomic characteristics. Neighborhoods undergoing ethnic change exemplify this type. Another subtype described by Moore occurs when the image of an area changes, making it suddenly attractive. Many cases can be found in areas of renovated townhouses that attract the upper middle class and the wealthy (this has been termed regentrification). Other examples can be found where construction (e.g., expressways) drastically changes the desirability of a neighborhood for better or worse.

Type-2 neighborhoods are more common than type 1. They combine high individual mobility rates with aggregate stability of population characteristics. The "receiving" neighborhoods for ethnic minorities are an example. Areas of off-campus student housing and areas of apartment housing for young childless couples are other instances. Type-3 neighborhoods combine changes in socioeconomic character with rather low rates of individual mobility. Moore argues that this type of neighborhood is the most widespread in many urban areas. As the single-family housing stock ages, it filters down to successively lower socioeconomic groups. Type-4 neighborhoods combine low mobility and socioeconomic stability. No areas with low mobility can be entirely stable, because of the aging of both the population and the housing stock. The distinction between type-3 and type-4 neighborhoods is, therefore, only one of degree. Moore (1972) argues that type-4 neighborhoods are exemplified by areas in which highly structured social networks (especially in ethnic communities) tie the individual to the neighborhood even though the area may be physically unattractive.

The biological metaphor of succession provides a useful and suggestive description of type-1 and type-3 changes. However, the invasion-succession account is only an analogy between human and biotic communities. Since it is not a theory in any scientific sense, it cannot explain neighborhood change. In the next several sections we review alternative explanations of how communities change, beginning with explanations based on rationalistic economic theory.

EXPLAINING NEIGHBORHOOD CHANGE

The Rent Model of Urban Land Use

The rent theory of urban land use has been elaborated, independent of the tradition of sociological ecology, by urban economists, regional scientists, and geographers (Alonso, 1960, 1964b; Muth, 1969, 1975; Wingo, 1961; Casetti, 1967; Papageorgiou, 1976). It employs terminology that is alien to this tradition. However, its central supposition—that space is allocated according to the ability to pay—is basic to traditional spatial theories in urban ecology (Hawley, 1950).

From this perspective the cityscape may be understood as the result of an urban land market in which the spatial distribution of population and activity results from a competition among groups who have different financial capacities and are all vying for space and location. Rent theory describes this competition between alternative land uses. The assumptions about the nature of this competition come from rational economic theory rather than biology. In a limited sense the rent model explains the competitive process we have been describing.

The rent model is based on a theory of agricultural land use developed in the 1820s by J. H. Von Thünen (1826). The spatial structure of rural land is of no immediate interest to the student of the city, but William Alonso (1960) modified the theory to describe the internal structure of cities. (Earlier, less explicit rent models were developed by Hurd, 1903, and Haig, 1926.) Rent theory rests on three simplifying rationalistic or normative assumptions (see Chapter 6):

1. Human behavior in the land market is rational. Producers are pure profit maximizers, consumers are pure utility maximizers, and all actors in the economy have perfect knowledge of the market conditions.

2. The urban land market is a free market, with no external constraints on land use such as zoning ordinances and planning boards.

3. The urban land market is characterized by intense competition. A great many actors are bidding against one another for a limited supply of space.

Given these basic assumptions, Alonso examines the patterns of land *values* and *rents* in the idealized urban land market. The value of land for specific uses—its profitability for producers or utility for consumers—varies over the urban space simply because different land users possess differing requirements. For example, residential-land owners highly value space, appearance, and neighborhood convenience; industries value access to major roadways; while commercial and business users seek accessibility to consumers.

According to the rent theory, the utility or value of locations for specific uses is eventually reflected in the payments made for land. (Whether land is occupied by owners or tenants is immaterial. We call all such payments *rent*.) In a highly competitive land market, rents closely approximate the value of the land. If, for example, a firm is paying much less for a site than its accessibility to the market warrants, or if a household is underpaying for a lot in a higher-quality neighborhood, then the firm or household is enjoying a *surplus* of profit or utility. In the case of a business or industrial firm, this surplus results in *excess profit*. That is, the firm is acquiring revenue over and above the normal profit required to stay in business. If the urban land market is highly competitive, such surpluses cannot last long. Other business people (or residents) become aware of these "bargains" and intense bidding for the lot occurs. Over the long run the payments made for land closely match the property's potential value. This value is referred to as a *bid rent*.

Each potential land use has somewhat different spatial requirements. As a result, the bid rents for a given plot of land vary with the types of bidders (different types of businesses or different types of residential land developers). The rent model predicts that each lot will be occupied by the type of user who can afford to pay the most.

Thus, rent theory's assumptions have two distinct consequences.

1. Rents on any lot tend to equal its intrinsic value. This is an *equalizing* mechanism that, in the long run, eliminates excess profits. In this sense competition prices space consistently with its value.

2. A single lot is occupied, in the absence of other complicating factors, by the type of development that yields the highest return. This is an *allocation* mechanism. In theory it adjusts land use to the economic environment, ensuring an efficient urban pattern.

Some urban economists have argued that these very powerful economic forces can be relied upon to produce an efficient and humane urban system (Muth, 1975). But two questions arise. First, does the system work? Clearly it does not, at least not perfectly. (We shall address some of the more obvious market imperfections later.) Second, if the system did work, would the results be entirely desirable? This question raises deep issues in welfare economics. Some authors have argued that the competitive mechanisms of economics do not automatically lead to optimal results in spatial contexts (Mills and Lav, 1964). A group of radical geographers have contended that this system is, in fact, conducive to social injustice (Bunge, 1971; Harvey, 1974).

Social inequalities aside, bid rent, or the ability to pay, varies systematically over urban space. Ecological theorists of the urban geometry (e.g., Park and Hoyt) suggest the nature of this pattern. The rent model provides one explanation of the dynamics behind this structure. To understand this model it is helpful to examine the form of the bid rent curve for various land uses.

Commercial Bid Rents   Commercial and service activities tend to occupy the most accessible land in American cities. This is especially true of services (banks, lawyers, accountants, and other professionals) and certain types of retail activity (department stores, specialty shops, etc.). For such enterprises, potential profit is greatly affected by the degree of access to consumers. The spatial structure of urban commercial activity is very finely adjusted to location and centrality. Urban geographers distinguish three principal morphological/ functional types of commercial districts: *nucleations* (ranging from the central business district to suburban shopping centers), *specialized* areas, and *ribbon* developments (along highways in and around the city) (Berry, 1967). Accessibility is clearly a determinant of the first and the last of these three types.

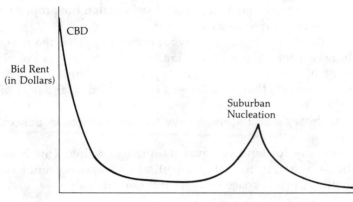

Figure 8.2   *Bid Rent Curve for Commercial Activity*

Figure 8.2 depicts a typical curve for such activity along a major highway. The most notable feature of the curve is its steepness, which suggests that as accessibility declines, potential profits decline disproportionately. Because of this relationship between location and profits, commercial activities have tended to capture the most central land in the modern industrial city.

But what does the bid rent curve for business have to do with neighborhood change? Actually, the spatial dynamics of urban commercial activity influence neighborhood change in several ways. In his concentric-zone model, Burgess (1923) suggests the principal role that commercial growth plays in neighborhood transition and housing stock deterioration. In addition, as we indicated in Chapter 7, access to retail and service activities is sometimes a consideration in the residential location process. Over the long run, of course, commercial activity must service residential demand, and thus it may be expected to adjust location as populations shift in space. In the short run, however, commercial activity may be the attractive force drawing residential development into an area.

Residential Bid Rent Functions   Although the dynamics of commercial bid rent curves have a serious impact on the neighborhood, to understand residential change from the point of view of rent theory we must consider residential bid rent functions in more detail. Like rents for all other types of activity, residential rents vary in highly regular and systematic ways over the urban space.

For the resident, satisfaction (or utility) is the primary determinant of land value, whereas for business, financial profit is the major factor. Human ecologists and economists have placed great emphasis on accessibility as a key factor in the general satisfaction of the resident population. It is important to understand, however, that accessibility may merely be one of many determinants of residential space. The rent model simply implies that under intense competition for space in a free market (i.e., laissez-faire land market), each plot of land will eventually be put to its highest-paying use. These rents depend on the "value" of the land, which may be affected by a variety of factors.

Alonso (1964b) relates residential satisfaction to the household's income and its pattern of tastes and needs. He emphasizes the trade-off between relatively cheap land but high commuting costs on the urban fringe, and expensive land but low commuting costs in more central locations. He discusses the location decision of the household as a *substitution*, or trade-off, process in which the household divides its total income into three categories: *commuting costs, land costs,* and expenditures on a hypothetical *composite good* including all other goods and services the household consumes. The main structure of the model is shown diagrammatically in Figure 8.3. The three lower curves, C, D, and E, show opportunities open to the household, taking two of the options at a time and holding the third constant. The curves suggest a trade-off between distance and land price. These relations correspond well with our general understanding of the city. For example, curve D in Figure 8.3 suggests that a household maintaining the same level of living (consumption of the composite good) can consume more land on the city's periphery. Curve E shows that if residential plot size is held constant, the level of living is greater on the periphery than in the center.

These diagrams only suggest the substitution possibilities open to the household. The actual trade-offs the household makes depend upon associated costs (e.g., mortgage rates, commuting costs, etc.). The amount the household is actually prepared to pay at a given point determines the residential bid rent at that point. As Alonso puts it: "Along any bid rent curve, the price the individual will bid for land will decrease with distance from the center at a rate just sufficient to . . . balance to his satisfaction the increased costs of commuting and the bother of a long trip" (1960:154).

Alonso refines this model to address social stratification over space. His mathematical analysis shows that, for groups of differing income, the wealthier have shallower rent curves than lower-income groups. According to Alonso:

> The reason for this is not that the poor have greater purchasing power, but rather that they have steeper bid rent curves. This stems from the fact that, at any given location, the poor can buy less land than the rich, and since only small quantities of land are involved, changes in its price are not as important for the poor as the costs and inconvenience of commuting. The rich, on the other hand, buy greater quantities of land, and are consequently affected by changes in its price to a great degree (1960:156).

This argument provides one answer to the paradox that has long perplexed urban social scientists: Why do the poor occupy expensive land while the rich occupy the cheaper land?

Given the assumptions of the model, the overall pattern of rent curves in a

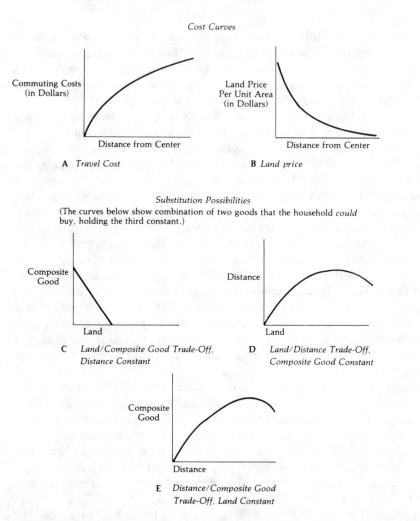

Cost Curves

A *Travel Cost*

B *Land price*

Substitution Possibilities
(The curves below show combination of two goods that the household *could* buy, holding the third constant.)

C *Land/Composite Good Trade-Off,
      Distance Constant*

D *Land/Distance Trade-Off,
      Composite Good Constant*

E *Distance/Composite Good
      Trade-Off, Land Constant*

Figure 8.3 *Alonso's Model of Household Substitution*   Curves A and B represent idealized relationships between commuting costs and land prices as distance from the city center increases. Travel costs increase with distance, but the rate diminishes, as curve A shows. Curve B might seem to run against common knowledge; it seems to indicate that inner-city houses cost more than suburban homes, when in fact the opposite is the case. However, this curve shows land price per unit area, and suburban houses occupy much larger lots than inner-city dwellings. Thus, the relationship holds.

Curves C, D, and E represent the trade-off possibilities a household faces in making a location decision. The shapes of the curves follow from Alonso's mathematical assumptions. Three goods are considered: quantity of residential land consumed, distance from the city center, and a composite good representing all other consumption. The trade-offs are between two goods with the third held constant. These curves suggest that there is an optimal distance from the city center that maximizes either the amount of land or the composite good. (*Source:* Adapted from William Alonso, *Location and Land Use*, Harvard University Press, 1964. Reprinted by permission.)

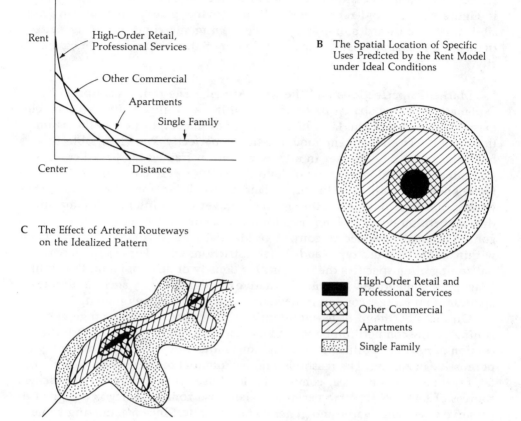

A   The Pattern of Bid Rents for Specific Uses

B   The Spatial Location of Specific Uses Predicted by the Rent Model under Ideal Conditions

C   The Effect of Arterial Routeways on the Idealized Pattern

Figure 8.4 *Bid Rents and Spatial Location*   A shows hypothetical bid rent curves for a number of competing land uses as functions of distance from the city center. It is assumed that the land in any location goes to the use offering the highest bid rent. In a perfectly uniform and symmetrical city, the rent model predicts the pattern of land use in B, which is obviously similar to Burgess's concentric-zone-model. The rent model offers a partial explanation for Burgess's model. The most important single factor in determining the bid rent function of each land use is accessibility to the city center. The radial system of highways in cities modifies the symmetry assumption and leads to the more realistic land use depicted in C. Here each land use extends farther out along the arterials because of the enhanced accessibility.

city should approximate Figure 8.4. In a symmetric city the principle that each plot is devoted to the highest bidding use implies a concentric-ring system of land use. Thus under idealized competitive conditions and in a symmetric landscape, the rent model predicts the same neighborhood morphology implied by traditional urban ecology. In fact, of course, innumerable factors distort the ring system. For example, accessibility is a crucial determinant of bid rents. Differential accessibility around arterial routeways has the effect shown in Figure 8.4C. The bid-rent curves for activities that place a premium on accessibility bend outward along arterials, destroying the concentric-ring pattern that would be characteristic of the rent-determined structure of a homogeneous city.

Market Imperfections and the Rent Model　The rent model provides an explanation of how spatial patterns emerge in an idealized city. No such city exists, however, and the land market is not as uncomplicated as the assumptions imply. The ideal rent model assumes perfectly knowledgeable buyers bidding against one another in a free and unconstrained land market. It goes without saying that consumers of land are neither perfectly rational nor perfectly knowledgeable. And the urban land market is far from free. Zoning ordinances, building codes, and other means of government intervention may limit the competition between land uses for a given site. A zoning variance or a rezoning is usually needed to convert residential land to commercial use. Even within single land-use types additional restrictions exist. For example, residential zoning often specifies the type and/or density of development, thus inhibiting pure competition among alternative residential uses such as duplexes, apartment buildings, condominiums, or single-family development.

On the other hand, it is important to realize that the long–range effect of zoning on the competition between land uses is relatively minor. With the exception of noxious, polluting, or dangerous industries, municipalities are quite permissive in zoning. The reason is simple: Potential bid-rent value is potential tax revenue. Per unit area, commercial land-use types are by far the richest sources of taxes. With some exceptions, land-use zoning policy is designed to preserve or enhance value and generate tax revenue. Since maximizing value is the basic mechanism behind the rent model, it is no surprise that zoning policy does not seriously inhibit the competition for land implied by the rent model. Good evidence for this contention is provided by the city of Houston, which has both no zoning regulations and a distribution of internal land use broadly similar to that of other large cities.

A far more serious qualification of the simple rent model follows from the effects of inertia in the urban land market. Land is an unusual economic commodity in many respects. Unless a city expands its incorporated area, the supply of land remains constant! Also, when development occurs and a particular type of construction takes place, the land becomes committed to that use. Building quality will eventually deteriorate and the utility diminish over time, yet the life expectancy of a typical urban building extends over a range of decades. Thus the kind of adjustments that supposedly occur quickly in the simple rent model are impossible in practice. They occur, but only over relatively long time periods.

Inertial effects are compounded by the American system of land ownership. We place high social evaluation and strong legal sanction on outright ownership of urban land. As Muth indicates (1975), piecemeal ownership of land enormously slows developments requiring *land assembly* (i.e., the consolidation of contiguous lots under one ownership prior to development). This inertial force tends to hamper redevelopment in the urban core. Here land parcels are smaller, and thus land assembly is even more difficult, especially for space-consuming industries.

Another type of government intervention that modifies the process of spatial allocation is *rent control,* usually in deteriorating neighborhoods (Muth, 1975). When a ceiling on rents is imposed on certain properties, a buyer's potential bid is limited and kept artificially low. Thus, there is no incentive for landlords to improve or even to maintain properties. Value consequently declines. A simple supply and demand analysis of rent indicates very adverse effects.

> Rent control produces an excess demand for housing, or a housing shortage. Controlled housing is a good buy for those who can obtain it. Consequently it becomes difficult to obtain. People who might not otherwise do so, especially younger and aged persons, maintain separate households. Others, especially older families whose children have left home, maintain larger dwellings than they otherwise would. Vacancies that do occur are taken quickly. In Paris, it is a common practice for apartment hunters to read the obituary pages early in the morning and rush to a deceased person's apartment in hopes of being able to bribe the concierge and obtain it. . . .
>
> As Milton Friedman once remarked in his *Newsweek* column, anyone advocating rent controls should be made to look for an apartment in New York City (Muth, 1975:129–130, 132).

An Economic Account of Segregation   The rent model provides a simplified account of the forces that produce aggregate patterns of land use and population density. As long as residential values are assumed to derive from simple measures such as space and commuting distance, the rent model provides little insight into the processes of socioeconomic and ethnic segregation that generate distinctive neighborhoods. In the abstract, the rent model merely asserts that use reflects value, without specifying how value arises. We know from our own experience (and from research described in Chapter 7) that a substantial part of our evaluation of residential sites stems from intangibles of "neighborhood quality," which include our assessment of its socioeconomic and ethnic character. In abstract terms the rent model can embrace these evaluations. (Practical measurement of such evaluations is obviously a formidable problem, however.) One simple attempt to extend the rent model to account for segregation processes has been made by Muth (1975).

Muth acknowledges the potential simplicity of an economic account. He makes no assumptions about the roots of sociocultural discrimination. He simply postulates that, for whatever reason, people evaluate each other and that these evaluations reveal themselves in the way people bid for residential land.

Unlike the simpler Alonso model, these land bids depend not only on the intrinsic characteristics of the site but also on the evaluation of the space's proximity to other groups of people (the *externality* characteristic).

Muth describes the segregation process in terms of two unspecified socioeconomic or ethnic groups, which he terms A types and B types. Generally, two rather different situations can occur. In the first case, A types prefer to live in the vicinity of other A types, while B types prefer proximity to other B's. This situation represents attraction within each homogeneous group and repulsion between the groups. The second case applies where only one group is exclusive. A types have an aversion to B types and a preference for nearness to A types. B types share this preference (i.e., they also prefer proximity to A types). This second case applies where most of the members of the B group desire integration. Muth argues that this case may apply to black and white ethnic groups in American cities.

Muth's account of segregation can deal with either case. Starting with a situation of integration (where A's and B's are randomly distributed in space), he suggests that A's and B's make mutually profitable trades of properties because of the externalities of space (differential evaluation of neighborhood quality). Mutually beneficial exchanges will continue as long as any B types remain in A type neighborhoods.

> So long as any B types live in predominantly A neighborhoods, mutually profitable exchanges still exist. Landlords in predominantly A neighborhoods will seek to fill vacancies with A types both to retain their other A tenants and because a new A tenant will offer more than a B type for the vacant space. For these reasons the landlord may even discourage B types who might apply. Similarly, real estate agents would avoid showing B types properties for sale in A neighborhoods ... (Muth, 1975:88).

The long-term outcome of this process is a situation in which A's and B's occupy residences in separate neighborhoods.

This neighborhood structure is stable under conditions of demographic equilibrium between both A and B neighborhoods. In the twentieth-century American city, however, cities swelled with new migrants. As Park (1952) and others have noted, this caused neighborhood boundaries to shift as certain groups grew disproportionately. What happens when population is growing, especially when the relatively less powerful, but integration-seeking group is growing faster? Muth suggests that as the B-type group swells, it begins to encroach on A-type land. This results in several price adjustments in land values. B residents near A-type population concentrations pay more—as an example, nonwhites and slum dwellers pay more if they are in the immediate vicinity of whites and nonslum dwellers. Some evidence suggests that real estate agents will only show minorities housing in white neighborhoods when there is a consensus that the neighborhood is changing (Molotch, 1972). Indeed, Leven et al.'s (1976) study of St. Louis indicates that the expectation that a neighborhood will change, rather than the actual proportion of a minority in an area, best predicts externalities and shifts in the market value of local housing.

> If an identical housing unit were placed in two neighborhoods where one has the mean percent of non-white occupancy (18.8 percent) while the other has one deviation more (27.8 percentage points more nonwhite occupancy), gross price would be about $4,564 less in the latter neighborhood. However, the racial composition of adjacent tracts has an even stronger effect: Gross price will decline more with a one-deviation difference in percent nonwhite occupancy in adjacent tracts—over $5,200 (Leven et al., 1976:77).

Cultural Ecology

It is misleading to speak of the rent model as a unified account of urban structure. Many individuals have contributed to this theory at different times and with different aims. The unifying thread running through studies in urban economics, urban geography, and regional science is that a plot of land is occupied by the use that values it most highly.

Generally, sociologists have criticized the rent model on the grounds that an economic perspective cannot, in principle, capture the psychological, social, and cultural complexity of our evaluations of places. This criticism, however, is unconvincing, because utility (or value) can be defined to embrace any type of place evaluation. As an example, the Muth model addresses ethnic prejudice or cultural differences in place utility. To argue that certain dimensions of place evaluation cannot be captured by an economic model is to say that certain aspects of space do not affect the amount we are prepared to pay for land. It is difficult to decide what these aspects might be.

It is equally difficult to devise meaningful measures of the intangibles of place utility. Many rent model studies, including Alonso's substitution theory, adopt an extremely simplistic account of place evaluation, describing it as a trade-off between residential and commuting expenditures in simple dollar terms. This conception of value is clearly inadequate. Sociological and cognitive research on the intangibles that influence our evaluation of place does not conflict with the abstract version of the rent model. On the contrary, the research enriches our understanding of place utility and facilitates the measurement of value in the rent model.

In this section we consider a perspective that complements the rent model; we term it *cultural ecology*. While the rent model deals in abstract evaluations of place, cultural ecology discusses the way in which specific evaluations derive from membership in cultural and socioeconomic groups. It concerns the cultural evaluations that lead to inertia in neighborhood structure. As the general rent model suggests, residents who value an area highly will bid exceptionally high amounts to stay there (or they will refuse to sell out to high bids from outsiders). Contrary to Alonso's substitution model, these bids may be higher than warranted by the physical condition of the buildings and considerations of accessibility and commuting cost. The reasons for this high evaluation by the residents, however, must be sought in cultural rather than economic terms. As we will see, these values are essentially group values, which can only be defined in social terms. People from differing social and cultural backgrounds value the variety of physical spaces differently and will thus choose neighborhoods accordingly. This indicates the need for developing a cultural ecology—an ecology that views space in both economic and cultural terms.

One of the first social scientists to explore this perspective was Walter Firey in a classic article "Sentiment and Symbolism as Ecological Variables" (1945). He emphasized the inertial effects of cultural values on the normal transition processes in the urban land market. He cited Boston as a case in point. Three areas of Boston have remained relatively unchanged over time despite strong pressures from competing land uses. These areas are the upper-class residential area of Beacon Hill, a set of "sacred sites" scattered throughout the inner city, and a lower-class Italian area known as the North End.

Beacon Hill has maintained its reputation as a fashionable residence in spite of its location in downtown Boston. While business and high rise developments have continually threatened to invade the area, Boston's old families have resisted various attempts by developers to attract them to newer suburban surroundings. As Firey observes:

> Certainly the large apartment-hotels and speciality shops that have sought in vain to locate on the Hill would have represented a fuller capitalization on potential property values than do residences. In all likelihood the attending increase in real estate prices would not only have benefited individual property holders but would have so enhanced the value of adjoining properties as to compensate for whatever depreciation other portions of the Hill might have experienced (1945:144).

This resistance to competing high value land uses is also apparent in the "sacred sites" of downtown Boston. For the Bostonian, the Common (a survival from Colonial days, when many towns allotted a certain portion of space for use as a militia field and common cow pasture), and the colonial burial grounds scattered throughout the inner city are collective symbols of a revolutionary heritage. The result of this high valuation of historical sites is a land-starved central business district. Traffic congestion is high, owing to the narrow streets, and the spacious department stores characteristic of other major cities are virtually nonexistent. Both merchant and consumer pay dearly for the reverence to times past, yet such sacred places remain intact. Clearly space has more than an economic meaning for its occupants.

Space is imbued with sentiment. As a third bit of evidence for this point, Firey considers the Italian ghetto in the North End of Boston. Like the West End area of Boston studied by Gans (1962a), it is an area of classic poverty. To the outsider it is a place of poorly maintained structures, garbage-strewn lots, and vacant buildings—hardly a space toward which one might have sentimental attachments. Yet as Gans and Firey both note, these two areas were urban villages where first-generation immigrants could maintain ties to the old country. Residence here symbolized ethnic loyalty and participation in traditional Italian activities. Such loyalties made the ghetto a difficult place to leave, despite its rundown appearance.

Gans provides the outsider with a firmer basis for understanding these attachments. While ethnic loyalty makes such places more attractive, the selective nature of cognitive maps permits people to suppress many of the ghetto's negative features.

> My first visit to the West End left me with the impression that I was in Europe. Its high buildings set on narrow, irregularly curving streets, its Italian and Jewish restaurants and food stores, and the variety of people who crowded the streets when the weather was good all gave the area a foreign and exotic flavor. At the same time I also noticed the many vacant shops, the vacant and, therefore, dilapidated tenements, the cellars and alleys strewn with garbage, and the desolation on a few streets that were all but deserted. Looking at the area as a tourist, I noted the highly visible and divergent characteristics that set if off from others with which I was familiar.
>
> Subsequently, in wandering through the West End, and in using it as a resident, I developed a kind of selective perception, in which my eye focused only on those parts of the area that were being used by people. Vacant buildings and boarded-up stores were no longer so visible, and the totally deserted alleys or streets were outside the set of paths normally traversed, either by myself or by the West Enders. The dirt and spilled-over garbage remained, but since they were concentrated in street gutters and empty lots, they were not really harmful to anyone and thus were not as noticeable as during my initial observations (Gans, 1962a:11–12).

The ghetto is, then, a social as well as an economic product. David Ward's (1971) analysis of the rise of central immigrant ghettos during the nineteenth and early twentieth centuries provides a historical perspective on this fact. From a strictly economic viewpoint, the tenement districts provided the optimal location for the newly arrived immigrant. Rents were cheap, and accessibility to expanding employment opportunities in the inner city was good. However, when ethnic ghettos became established, this purely economic advantage for the new arrival acquired cultural and social dimensions. Group consciousness encouraged immigrants to flock to these areas. Once the ghetto was established, it provided basic social and cultural structures familiar to the immigrant. The purely economic analysis of the growth of the ghetto characteristically ignored the social benefits of these areas. As a result, early human ecology was inclined to interpret the congested living conditions and dilapidated tenements as a source and symbol of social disorganization. But, despite the poverty, the grime, and the deterioration, this environment offered something to the immigrant that newer, better housing in the suburbs could not.

Firey's work and subsequent studies of neighborhood values and social structure clearly indicate the inertial effect that cultural values have on the operation of the urban land market. In one sense, this perspective provides a picture of neighborhood change quite different from that of orthodox ecology, which, with its concern for the invasion-succession process, emphasizes the changes in the urban mosaic. Cultural ecology, on the other hand, stresses the stability of neighborhoods and their resistance to change even in the face of bids from potentially more profitable uses.

The work of Gans and Firey represents an *idiographic* approach, one based on detailed observations of unique cases. Developing theory, though, requires generalization. Factorial ecology (Chapter 5) provides a solid empirical grounding for a general cultural ecology. Factorial ecology indicates that the modern city is spatially organized not only according to the ability to pay (social class) but also according to ethnicity and family cycle. These factors bear directly on cultural values. Life styles vary by stage in the family cycle, ethnicity, and social class. In effect, each of these dimensions defines a set of "subcultures." Several life styles that are products of these factors have been identified as influencing a person's environmental expectations. These are *familism, careerism, consumerism* and *community orientation*, as discussed in Chapter 7 (Bell, 1958; Moore, 1972).

The variable of occupancy is another crucial indicator of urban subcultures. Broadly speaking, there are two separate housing markets—a single-family dwelling and a multi-family dwelling market. Your life style dictates which of these markets you participate in. Careerism, consumerism, and community orientation are most likely to place you in the multiple-family dwelling market, whereas familism tends to dictate a search in the single-family housing market. As a result, familism flourishes in the suburbs, where densities are low, while consumership, careerism, and community orientation tend to be found in the city.

Low densities and segregated land uses are conducive to nuclear-family activities. Limited access to people outside the nuclear family, coupled with a clear segregation between residential and commercial land uses, encourages a home-centered life style. Apparently people who prefer suburbs to central city neighborhoods tend to be less consumer and career oriented and prefer less extensive neighborhood interaction. They also tend to have children and no particular ethnic identities.

Career and consumer-oriented households, on the other hand, because of their life-style choice tend to have few or no children. Their life style encourages them to minimize the distance between home and work and to be near the centers of commerce and culture. Because they have small families, they are less concerned about yard space and minimum population densities than they are about access to urban amenities.

Michelson (1976) suggests that strong ethnic attachments encourage a "group orientation" emphasizing values of expressiveness and group integration over achievement and nuclear family orientation. As in the case of career and consumer-oriented life styles, the central city is more likely to promote such values. Unlike the other two life styles, however, the environmental forces promoting social interaction (especially among relatives) become para-

mount, while the physical attractiveness of dwellings is of much less significance.

> An emphasis on a life style which includes very strong, frequent, and intense inter-
> actions with a large number of relatives seems to require that they live in some ar-
> rangement of buildings, streets, and open spaces (or the lack of them) that promote
> the easy availability of person to person (Michelson, 1976:66).

While the Boston West Enders, for example, never saw their housing as attractive, they did appear to value the type of buildings they lived in, the arrangement of these buildings with regard to each other and the street, and the particular mix of commercial and residential land use in the neighborhood. The
high densities promoted by heavy concentrations of multistoried dwellings,
coupled with the limited separation between residences and sidewalks, stimulated interaction and thus supported a particular way of life foreign to the suburbanite. Indeed, for the West Ender, suburbs were unfriendly, even lifeless
places. Despite the better quality of housing it offered, the suburban environment was anathema—a threat to the survival of a time-honored way of life. For
these people, the street scene was an essential element in their social activity.

Place evaluations by different urban subcultures thus differentiate the city
into stable, social communities. The physical structure, housing, and layout of
the neighborhood are closely adjusted to the activities and life style of its occupants. Once formed, sentimental and social ties render the neighborhoods re-
sistant to change in the urban land market. The invasion process described by
orthodox ecology represents a threat to these ties. Thus such transitions occur
far less frequently than they would in a truly free and perfectly competitive
land market.

A cultural ecological model of neighborhood structure, then, predicts a
much more complex segregation pattern than that portrayed by Alonso's simple accessibility-based rent model. Alonso suggests a gradient pattern in which
those most able to bear the costs of travel live on the city's outskirts, where
densities are low and distance to the center is high. The cultural model, on the
other hand, foresees a more complex urban space similar to what Berry (1965)
described (see Chapter 5). Here sectors segregated by social class are overlaid
on concentric zones differentiated by family cycle. It should be apparent from
the discussion in Chapter 5 that this prediction more accurately represents the
actual structure of the urban mosaic.

Despite the apparent accuracy of the "stable mosaic" predicted by cultural
ecology, this account has several deficiencies. One, which it shares with the
rent model, is its assumption of *individual autonomy* in decision making. While it
emphasizes the role of subcultures in forming the urban mosaic, it essentially
describes the role of individual choice in the housing market. Although it suggests that housing choice is strongly colored by group evaluations, it ignores
the dominant roles played by institutions in the structuring of social space.

Another deficiency in the cultural approach lies in its expectations concerning the central city population. Taking into account the physical structure of the city and the requirements of various life styles, the cultural approach implies that the central city will be occupied by three groups of people:

1. The cosmopolites and professionals who live in the city to be near its amenities. For the most part this group is either unmarried or childless.

2. The unmarried or childless who do not fall into the first category. These may be temporary members of the group who eventually move to suburbia when children are born or permanent members who never have children.

3. The "ethnic villagers," immigrant groups who live in their own separate communities (Johnston, 1970).

Our own experience with cities, coupled with a great deal of empirical evidence, however, shows that this list is incomplete. The central city is also composed of the deprived. These are the poor or the ethnic minorities who must live in slums because they cannot, or are not allowed to, afford better housing (Johnston, 1970). The cultural ecology model fails to predict this fourth group, because it assumes individual volition and choice. The ability to pay, however, not only limits choice, but also actually dictates a location in the case of the very poor and ethnic minorities. In this instance, location is not a matter of life style but rather of an inherent social structure that closes alternatives.

The failure of the cultural model of neighborhood change to predict a segment of the central city suggests that neighborhood dynamics is actually a function of two distinct processes:

1. A volitional process described by the rent model and qualified by cultural ecology, in which individuals choose from a range of alternative homesites. In some cases accessibility may be the paramount concern. More often the choice is constrained by the household's allegiance to a particular life style.

2. A discrimination process in which the choice of location is not open but is rather a product of decisions beyond the control of the household.

The discrimination process produces racial and ethnic ghettos. These areas are not the product of free-market forces nor of residential decision-making governed by life-style choices. Instead, they are a product of social institutions and overriding cultural values and because of this, the ghetto resident finds it difficult to escape these residential traps.

With one conspicuous exception, the term *melting pot* is an apt description of the American urban ghetto. As we will see in a later chapter, the newest immigrant groups in the nineteenth and twentieth centuries would inevitably spend some time in the urban ghetto, but as their English improved and their incomes increased, they would spread throughout the city (Morrill, 1965). The exception to this pattern is the American black. Banfield (1974) argues that blacks have not experienced the spatial dispersion of other ethnic groups because they arrived in the city too late and in too large a number for the city to absorb them. The black population constitutes the urban area's most recent immigrant group. Since World War I, well over 5 million blacks have migrated to the cities of the North and West (Morrill, 1965). The timing of this move was unfortunate because it occurred as the city began to lose employment. Banfield's explanation of the black ghetto, however, ignores a very simple but important point. The black population is like no other urban ethnic group. Because their ethnicity is visible (a function of race, rather than culture), the assimilation process is more difficult.

Despite tremendous strides in black-white relations during the 1960s, it is apparent that a pervasive "web of discrimination" continues to limit blacks' access to the housing market (Van Valey et al., 1977). Perhaps the best measure of this "pervasive web" is the *segregation index*. It denotes the percentage of the city's population that would have to be redistributed to make the proportion of blacks in each neighborhood equivalent to its percentage in the total city. This percentage is defined as perfect integration. In 1960 the average segregation index for 137 central cities was 75.1, while in 1970 the average index for 237 central cities was 68.3 (Van Valey et al., 1977). This small decline hardly indicates major strides in reducing discrimination.

What factors are at the root of this rather stubborn process? While socioeconomic status is an important basis for the residential distribution of the urban population, it is obvious that it is not low incomes that exclude blacks from better neighborhoods. Racial segregation is more extensive than segregation along either economic or ethnic lines. If racial segregation were merely a function of economic status we would expect segregation levels to be a product of two factors:

1. The extent to which economic groups are segregated in space
2. The extent to which blacks and whites differ by economic status

Taeuber and Taeuber (1972) tested just such a hypothesis by comparing actual racial segregation statistics with those predicted by socioeconomic status (measured by occupational level, a variable assumed to correlate with the ability to pay). The results convincingly indict the simple form of the rent model. In the majority of cities analyzed, the predicted level of segregation was only 30 percent of the actual. These results are consistent with Muth's theory of segregation. In his model, the ability to pay inadequately predicts residential patterns, since two distinct pricing systems operate for the same housing unit, one for each ethnic group.

If racial segregation is more than a product of socioeconomic differences between the races, just what factors are influential in this spatial process? Again, Taeuber and Taeuber (1972) provide some suggestions. In a study of sixty-nine cities for the periods 1940 to 1950 and 1950 to 1960, they found that changes in the nature of the housing market determine segregation patterns by race. They reason that the earlier period was one of severe housing shortages and as a result neither whites nor blacks had enough alternatives to permit a real change in the housing market. Owing to this fact, black growth and black occupational mobility had little effect on spatial change. In the later period, however, the housing supply increased and thus black improvements in income could be translated into better housing. We have just seen from the statistics on racial segregation for 1960 and 1970, however, that this translation tends to be far from perfect. The Taeubers' work, nevertheless, is suggestive. It points to two basic facts:

1. Racial segregation is not merely a function of differences between the races in economic status.
2. Racial segregation is a product of the state of the existing housing market in an area.

This second point is crucial. It suggests that these spatial patterns are less a function of the prejudice of individual white homeowners or of the preference for black households to dwell in black areas than of a set of processes beyond the control of the individual household. Racial segregation is probably best explained by examining the institutions that control access to the housing market.

The results of public opinion polls from 1964 to 1970 support this contention (Guest, 1977). In a national sample, the percentage of whites who felt they had a right to keep blacks out of their neighborhood declined from 29 percent to 21 percent. At the same time, those who believed that blacks should be able to live wherever they could afford a home rose from 53 percent to 67 percent. These data indicate both a decline in segregationist attitudes and at least some support for integrated housing by a majority of whites. It is apparent that the extensive racial segregation suggested by current segregation indexes is not just the result of individual attitudes. To understand racial segregation it is important to examine the role various institutions play in the development and access to housing markets. Such an analysis should provide us with not only a better understanding of racial separation but also of all forms of segregation, whether they be ethnic, socioeconomic, or life cycle.

The Institutional Interaction Perspective

Despite their differences, the rent model and cultural ecology both view neighborhood change as the result of individual choices constrained by economic and social factors. A logical next step in describing the land market is to consider the groups that constrain individual choices. These groups may also be studied as decision-making entities influencing the direction and rate of spatial change (Form, 1954; Long, 1956).

In American society individual choice determines urban structure much more than in socialist countries. But even in our society many formal organizations exert a dominant effect on urban structure and thus on residential choice. While the land market can be described from an organizational perspective, it is not correct to describe it as organized—at least not in the usual sense of that term. There are four basic types of organizations involved in the operation of the land market: real estate and construction agencies, large corporations, government agencies, and small consumers of residential or commercial land (Form, 1954). No single organizational category serves the goal of producing the urban spatial pattern. Rather, each group plays its own "game" with its own set of resources, goals, rules, and judges (Long, 1956). The process of playing out these separate games produces the housing market for a given urban community. This is accomplished not through the self-conscious rationality of any one group but by the interaction of a set of institutional games.

The game metaphor is valuable. Each "game" provides its players with a set of goals and a set of resources to achieve them. In addition, it provides the players with an elite audience and a general public who judge their performance. To understand the operations of the land market it is necessary to compare the goals, resources, judges, and rules under which each game operates.

Real estate and construction agencies together with predevelopment owners play a significant role in the spatial system. They have the greatest interest in and knowledge of the housing market, and they play an intermediary or brokerage role for all the other groups. In a study of the speculative development of surburban land, Sargent (1976) provides a detailed account of the operation of these agencies. His discussion involves the interactions of the following groups: agriculturalists, intervening owners, and land developers.

The agriculturalists and intervening owners are predevelopment landowners. Although they do not build residences on the land, they exert enormous impact on urban growth. If they choose to hold land as a speculative investment, they may delay developments for long periods. Predevelopment owners control both morphology and the timing of suburban growth. Strong incentives exist for the wealthy to hold land as an investment. Land is among the best financial investments because of its rapidly growing value and the tax advantages it provides. Sargent (1976) indicates that distinct institutional structures are emerging to exploit the profitability of predevelopment land investments. These include real estate investment trusts and small-investment clubs.

After the predevelopment holding period, the land passes to the developer. Sargent emphasizes two crucial roles that the developer plays: he or she assembles parcels of land and creates the actual subdivisions. These processes are complex. They are governed by the configuration of parcels the developer obtains, by his or her expectation of the needs of potential buyers, and by a variety of government regulations pertaining to such matters as water, waste, and other utilities.

Once the land is developed, the real estate agents enter the process. This group's role is to allocate homes to potential purchasers. We have emphasized elsewhere how, in their perceived role as social brokers, agents strongly influence neighborhood development. Overall their aim is conservative. By and large they represent a force for the stability and homogeneity of existing neighborhoods. Bankers, as the providers of mortgages, tend to have similar concerns as the illegal process of redlining indicates.

Although the real estate-construction game may not be the biggest game, it is the most persistent. Like other business enterprises its goal is to maximize earnings. Unlike other businesses, however, its profits are derived directly from the land market. It is, therefore, in the interest of both groups to attempt to organize this spatial market and to encourage growth. To achieve this goal the real estate industry has moved from a haphazard collection of local agencies to a "unified professional or fraternal society" (Form, 1954:321).

Big corporations also play a major role in spatial change. Indeed, the big business game is often believed to be the biggest game in town. As a group it owns the most strategic properties in the metropolis, it has the greatest capital resources, and it has a highly rationalized organization with clear-cut goals and a formal division of labor. Its goal in the land market is simple: To operate efficiently, it requires large amounts of contiguous land as close as possible to available markets. This goal puts corporations in direct conflict with other games operating in the urban space. In this game, the judges or scorekeepers are not the general public and the rules are not governed by some vague "common good." Big business is accountable, ultimately, to its stockholders; as a result, it tends to be subject to the control of agents from outside the community. Ironically this, the biggest game in town, is also the most remote from local interests and control. Corporate executives and managers are in some ways inclined to view the city as a dependent partner. They see themselves as significant contributors to the tax base and thus feel that they have the power to demand certain things from the city. Although the business sector may not be actively involved in the dynamics of the urban space on a regular basis, it can have a significant influence on spatial change when it decides to get involved.

Because of their resources and basic goals, both real estate and big business have tremendous influence on the city's spatial organization. Governmental organizations serve as mediators between the interests of these major influences and the weak sister in the land market—the aggregate of local community residents and small businesses. The governmental sector has interests in satisfying both the residential and the big business groups. In order to "win" the political game, a particular administration must garner the votes necessary to stay in office. It is, thus, directly accountable to the resident. At the same time, however, governments must attempt to maximize the tax base in order to operate effectively as a supplier of services. It does this by providing incentives to big business to locate in the area.

In managing the public interest, governments rely on several very powerful tools that can be used to either conserve or change the residential space. By law, local government agencies have the power to change the restrictions on particular types of activity in an area (zoning). These agencies also have the right to expropriate land for public use. At first glance, this seems to suggest that such agencies operate in a position of real strength. This is untrue. Municipal governments are not highly centralized. They are composed of a loosely knit set of agencies (zoning boards, school commissions, planning boards, traffic divisions, park boards, water districts, etc.) that may often be working at cross-purposes with one another. Also, the metropolitan space consists of a number of political entities that may be in direct competition with each other (e.g., cities versus suburbs).

The household sector is the weakest group in the land market. Thus rent and ecological explanations of spatial change that focus on the individual decision maker are, by themselves, inadequate. Residents are the least organized of the groups with interests in the urban space. Although, in the aggregate, they are the biggest consumer of land, they very seldom function as a group and thus have limited influence on the urban mosaic. Their primary interest is in minimizing land use change in order to maximize their investment and conserve whatever social or subcultural attributes made the neighborhood attractive to them in the first place. Residents tend to organize only when these values are threatened. The 1978 victory of Proposition 13 in California indicates the enormous but latent and largely dormant power of organized small landowners.

TOWARD A SYNTHESIS OF INDIVIDUAL AND AGGREGATE THEORIES OF URBAN RESIDENTIAL DYNAMICS

This chapter and Chapter 7 provide two perspectives on neighborhood change. The social psychological account of behavior summarized in Chapter 7 describes the urban mosaic as a product of individual decisions. This chapter has emphasized aggregate concepts such as succession and filtering. Individual decisions are self-seeking and, at least to some degree, autonomous. Despite this fact, it is evident that neighborhoods change in systematic ways. How does the urban pattern emerge out of the seeming chaos of individual decision making? To answer this question we need to consider the interrelationships between individual movement decisions and neighborhood structure.

Neighborhood Structure as a Constraint on Individual Choice

Neighborhood structure channels individual choice, at least in the short run. The actions of a single individual have no perceptible effect on the urban land market. We may love our neighborhood or we may leave it, but we cannot change it singlehandedly. The rent model, orthodox ecology, and cultural ecology all emphasize these constraints. In Burgess's (1923) concentric zone model and in Alonso's (1960, 1964b) rent model, the primary constraint is accessibility, which is usually measured in terms of distance to the city center or to other employment opportunities. In fact, however, data for individual moves reveal no clear relationship between accessibility and either the decision to move or spatial choice. At the same time, a great deal of behavioral research (e.g., Johnston, 1970; Horton and Reynolds, 1971) suggests the crucial importance of accessibility in the formation of individual action spaces. Johnston's work clearly indicates that residential choice is highly constrained by the sectoral action space of the individual. The effects of accessibility on residential mobility are real, but they are more complex than implied in the simple form of the rent model.

The ecological structure of the city restricts the choices considered by the individual mover. Cultural ecology indicates another variety of constraints on individual action. General ethnic, status, and family variables suggest various cultural affiliations within which residential choices will be confined. Within a given affiliation such as an ethnic group or social class, choices are further refined by the household's orientation to consumerism, career, family, or community.

In addition to the constraints of accessibility and subculture, individual choices are further limited by imperfect knowledge of the market and by the constraints of time and effort in the search process itself. As Chapter 7 shows, the search for a home is suboptimizing and extremely limited in scope. For certain groups who are disadvantaged by race, poverty, or age it may be a mockery to speak of choice at all.

In the short run then, it seems that urban structure determines choice. To be sure, individuals have some degree of volition. But residential choice is highly constrained. Most choices appear to confirm and reinforce the status quo as like socioeconomic groups are attracted and unlike groups are repelled within the existing structure of neighborhoods.

Neighborhood Structure as a Product of Choice

In the long term it is an illusion to view the city as a stable mosaic in which individual decisions reinforce the status quo. The system is inherently unstable. To begin with, demographic changes, especially an increase in migrants to the city, intrinsically disturb the system. Even during the life cycle of a single household it is incorrect to speak of stability. The rules of the location game continually change as individuals age. A life-cycle change such as marriage or retirement may well transform satisfaction to dissatisfaction. The physical aging of a neighborhood also continually alters the perceived desirability of an area. As Moore (1972) points out in his taxonomy of neighborhood change, even a neighborhood with little migration changes as its buildings and its inhabitants age. Finally, changes in the nonresidential sector such as commercial blight or expressway construction continually alter the value of neighborhoods, frequently initiating the invasion-succession process. To some degree, we resist change because of the effort and expense of movement. As Wolpert (1965) indicates, dissatisfaction does not automatically induce movement. However, when we do decide to move, genuine options are open to most of us.

Individual households manifest their choices in two basic ways: in the economic and political arenas. The purchase or rental arrangement of households are "votes" in the marketplace. The laws of supply and demand, though modified by the economic peculiarities of the land market, respond to these votes through the chain of decisions involved in development. These decisions are made by predevelopment owners, developers, realtors, and eventually, by the buyers or renters of land. As land is developed, a series of residential vacancies arises through the process of filtering; that is, residences are made available throughout the city because of new development in one particular place.

The second fundamental way in which households exert pressure on neighborhoods is through the political process. As least in theory, voters control utilities, school districts, zoning boards, planning agencies, and other local players in the location game. It is crucial here to distinguish two types of political motivation in urban residents: the *conservative* and the *radical*. We do not use these terms in their usual political sense but only as they pertain to individuals' feelings about their neighborhoods.

In the middle and upper classes, residents are often a strong force for conservatism. Homeowners, especially, are very strongly motivated to preserve a neighborhood's social and physical character. The most conspicuous successes of organized residents are usually in blocking change, through vetoing expressway construction, rezoning, and so on.

Others, particularly the disadvantaged of the inner city, exert pressure for radical change rather than "preservation of neighborhood quality." In the early 1960s ethnic minorities pressed for desegregation. Desegregation remains an important goal, but the late 1960s and 1970s have seen the emergence of other pressures, ranging from radical blacks calling for separate development to neighborhood improvement programs. Proponents of change typically have less political clout than the middle class who, whatever their political affiliation, are profoundly conservative about neighborhood change.

A Synthetic Summary of the Dynamics of the Urban Housing Market and Spatial Change

Any attempt to understand spatial dynamics must incorporate information from both the aggregate and individual accounts of residential change. Spatial dynamics results from a set of interrelated decisions. The amount and quality of land made available for residential development is the product of a series of decisions made by land owners and developers, governmental agencies, and large industrial consumers of land. After this land is developed, a number of residential vacancies appear throughout the city because of filtering. This allows for the operation of residential choice and sets up the potential for a chain of migrations. In turn, the stimulation of residential choice produces some change in urban spatial structure. Thus an accurate description of the city's spatial dynamics must really incorporate the products of at least three separate models: a land development model, a decision-to-move model, and a residential choice model. The skeleton of such a descriptive model is outlined in Figure 8.5. We will consider each segment of this general model step by step.

Housing Supply   The supply of residences in any city results from three separate forces: the age of the city's housing stock, the extent of new residential development within the metropolis, and the dimensions of the vacancy chains generated by filtering. Housing supply is thus, in part, a function of two decision-making processes: the development decision and the resident's decision to move.

Organizational descriptions of the land use market provide at least one account of the dynamics of a land development model. Land development decisions, or the outputs of a real estate-construction game, are the product of three logically separate but interacting games—the residential, big business, and governmental. To convert land to new use, a developer must first convince the present residents of the land that it is to their advantage to sell. The desire to sell results from many interacting factors, including the *landowner's characteristics* (age, years lived at the location, etc.), *the property's characteristics* (its esthetics, topography and soil conditions, its accessibility to various activities, and the site's particular zoning and taxation category), and the *nature of the urban context* (the health of the local economy, the condition of the local housing market, and local policies affecting the costs of services and the location of activities). The latter two characteristics are, in part, a result of outputs from the big business and government games. Big business affects the decision through its general influence on the growth of the urban economy (which affects the value of residential properties) and through its specific location decisions (which may influence accessibility and aesthetics). Government influences the landowner's decision by making policies (taxation and zoning) that affect the land's future income and its market value.

Once a landowner is willing to sell, the developer must make some decision on whether or not to buy. Again, this decision is conditioned by the actions of big business and government. Development occurs if there is a profit to be made; that is, if there is a residential market for the developed properties. The existence of this market is a function of the general growth of the city economically and demographically. In turn, the marketability of a particular site depends on its location in the city with regard to employment, recreation and amenities, and its zoning and taxation category. Government and business elites play a decisive role here.

Obviously, however, urban spatial change does not result directly from the

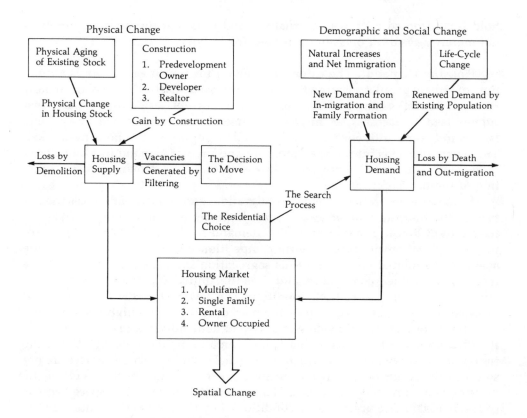

Figure 8.5 *A Synthetic Model of Spatial Change*

decision of developers, nor is the housing supply simply a function of the development decision. Supply is also the result of a series of interrelated residential decisions that are initiated by new development. Through filtering, each family's move changes the context in which others move. Moves occur in chains that may involve five to ten different households (White, 1971). For new houses the average chain's length is approximately four (Lansing et al., 1969). This implies that for every move directly affected by residential development decisions, there are at least three subsequent moves that are only indirectly affected by this process. Therefore, any understanding of the supply side of the housing market must include some consideration of the dynamics behind the individual resident's decision to move.

The question of why people move was dealt with in Chapter 7, which described the movement decision as the result of several factors: the social characteristics of the household, the household's life-style aspirations, the social and financial costs of any move, and the extent of the household's dissatisfaction with its current residence. This explanation suggests that the individual household is confronted with real alternatives and thus that the housing supply is not merely a result of decisions imposed from above.

Housing Demand   The extent of demand for housing in a city is a function of urban population growth (and more particularly the growth of new families) as well as the mobility decisions of current residents. We have just summarized the factors that influence a person's decision to move. These same factors indirectly influence demand as well as supply in the housing market. These variables affect intraurban mobility and predict demand in a city closed to in-migration. No such city exists, however, and thus demand is also a function of the net migration rate.

Urban growth, in the form of net migration, enormously influences the nature of the housing market. A city with high net migration rates is likely to have a tight housing market in which demand for homes outstrips their supply. This situation produces intense competition between individuals for the available residential spaces and thus segregation intensifies. Space becomes a more highly valued commodity, and thus the ability to pay becomes a critical factor in location. Under such conditions the lower classes, the elderly, and blacks essentially get priced out of the market and become highly segregated.

The set of factors influencing supply and demand work together to define the dimensions of the housing market. Given a particular housing market the individual who wishes to move is forced to make choices. These choices are not so much the result of the "real housing market" as they are the result of the housing market in people's minds. That is, changes in the urban space because of residential choice are not only conditioned by the factors that influence the housing market, but also by the action spaces of individuals. Essentially, choice is constrained by a whole set of decisions out of the control of the potential mover as well as by the set of information available to that individual. The spatial dynamics of the city result from a complex, constrained choice process. These constraints on choice produce the urban pattern predicted by the aggregate models of neighborhood change.

SUMMARY

Mobility is related to a number of ecological variables that themselves are highly correlated with distance. The relationship of neighborhood turnover to distance from city center tends to produce a pattern of change in keeping with traditional ecological models.

Neighborhood change has been described by ecologists as an invasion-succession process initiated by the in-migration of a few members of some nontraditional group. This initial penetration is followed by several other stages of change: invasion, consolidation, and piling up. Such descriptions of neighborhood turnover, however, are too simple because succession focuses on only one segment of a neighborhood life cycle and ignores the physical changes that occur in evolving neighborhoods. A better picture of neighborhood change is provided when such areas are described as aging through a predictable life cycle involving filtering as well as social changes.

Such changes have been explained from three approaches—the rent model, cultural ecology, and institutional interaction. Rent theory suggests that space is allocated according to the ability to pay. In a competitive marketplace payments for land eventually match the property's potential value or bid rent. Under idealized conditions such a tendency produces a spatial structure much like that predicted by concentric zone theory. The market, however, is imperfect.

The rent model has been criticized by cultural ecologists who argue that the intangibles of place utility cannot be captured adequately by an economic measure. Places are imbued with sentiment, and these sentimental ties create inertial forces that sometimes inhibit the changes predicted by rent theory. Life style choices greatly influence residential evaluations.

Both rent theory and cultural ecology describe mobility as a product of choice—a description that is unrealistic for certain segments of the population. Among the disadvantaged, choice of location is severely limited by discrimination processes. In short, location decisions are often out of the hands of the individual mover. The institutional interaction perspective describes the organizational dynamics of the residential marketplace. It suggests that decisions made by developers, real estate brokers, big businesses, and government limit the residential choices of the individual household.

PART THREE

The Social Aspects of Urban Space

As we have seen, the city is ordered spatially at both objective and subjective levels. Real urban space is pervaded by regularities, and space also orders the subjective images that guide our behavior. Without this real and cognitive order urban society would be plunged into the disorder envisoned by Wirth (Chapter 3).

Although we have analyzed many features of the urban spatial order, we have not yet inquired into the social significance of space. The chapters in this section address this issue. The theme is posed in a statement by Robert Park:

> Most if not all cultural changes in society are correlated with changes in its territorial organization and every change in the territorial and occupational distribution of the population will effect changes in the existing culture (1952:231).

Space is thus an indicant of social structure and social change, as well as an independent force operating to produce changes of its own. Early human ecology has been criticized for its emphasis on the first view of space while virtually ignoring the second (Michelson, 1976). In Chapter 9 we consider what spatial structure can tell us about the nature of a particular society or community. Here space is treated as a dependent variable, a product of conditions inherent in the city and urban society. In Chapters 10 and 11, on the other hand, we detail the ways in which space, in built and socially evolved environments, influences our everyday lives as well as the everyday operations of the city.

Chapter 9

Spatial Arrangements as an Indicant of Social Structures

INTRODUCTION

The study of urban space provides knowledge of the very nature of cities and urban society. The spatial structure of the city is the product of an amalgam of social factors, and as such, spaces can be read as symbols of these far larger social forces. Like archeologists sifting through the remnants of past societies to gain some indication of the nature of that system, many writers have attempted to "read" the spatial forms of current societies. Suzannah Lessard discusses the symbolic qualities of midtown Manhattan:

> The glass curtain wall stands at a point in history where the optimism and the disillusionment of our age meet, or, to put it another way, where the spirit seeking liberation from the past encounters fear of the future. In 1978, the skyscrapers of midtown—skyscrapers anywhere—are for many people symbols of what is threatening about the time in which we live, a symbolism that may not be universal but is surely closer to being orthodox than to being iconoclastic. The towers are aggressive images of capitalism and technology—forces that are no longer unambiguously associated with goodness. The astounding size of the buildings is as likely to put us in mind of helplessness in a regimented honeycomb as of man's power; their logical simplicity as soon reminds us of the disappearance of warmth and grace as of boldness and purity (1978:32).

In the tradition of the Chicago School, sociologists have also used such spatial cues to make inferences about urbanism and urban structure. The spatial structure of cities provides evidence of the "small social worlds" characteristic of urban organization. Distance reflects the social divisions or distances between groups, as we will soon see.

If spatial distance indicates social distance, it follows that any change in spatial structure in part reflects basic changes in social distance. In the second section we consider this issue specifically in terms of the relation between an ethnic group's social mobility and its spatial dispersion within the city. Finally, the last section of the chapter uses social area analysis and factorial ecology to provide evidence of the changes in the larger society wrought by urbanization.

194

SPATIAL DISTANCE AND SOCIAL DISTANCE

The earliest known written symbol for the city consisted of a cross surrounded by a circle (Orleans and Orleans, 1976). The cross represented the roadways that converged at the city's heart. This convergence stressed the importance of the city's linkages with its surrounding territories. The circle indicated the barriers both symbolic and real that were at the core of the urban order. While the circle was intended to convey the fact that preindustrial cities were walled structures, this earliest known representation of the city says something about the very basis of all urban communities both preindustrial and industrial. Cities from the beginning were founded on differences. In the preindustrial city these differences were primarily between the urban dwellers and the country folk. Hence the need for a wall. The contemporary city embraces almost the whole of society, and is not walled off against outsiders. But with its large, dense, and heterogeneous populations the city is internally divided. Yi-Fu Tuan (1974) describes a highly regimented city of classical China that was almost like a prison. Each district, each ward, and each home was separated by walls, locked doors, and guards. The internal divisions of the modern city are invisible, but hardly less rigid.

Urban worlds in general are diverse, characterized by a variety of life ways and social roles. In the modern urban society, however, specialization of tasks has greatly increased. These differences are what make the city attractive. It is a highly complex social unit offering a variety of work and recreation experiences, a diversity of ideas and life styles. This diversity, however, is also the basis for invidious evaluations (Orleans and Orleans, 1976). Each individual, because of a particular life style, occupation, or social station spends his or her time in segregated settings, and thus each aggregate of people experiences the city in a slightly different way. Segregation is evidence not only of diversity, but also of a social structure that prevents certain individuals from realizing all of their opportunities.

It is Lofland's (1973) contention that space structures or orders the urban experience (see Chapter 3). In the industrial city, the potential for disorder inherent in the overwhelming size and diversity of the urban population is controlled through the spatial segregation of activities and populations. Distance is the building material used to form the walls between the city's diverse cultural groups.

Some physical definition of group boundaries is necessary, because social groups are not concrete entities. Distance and spatial separation provide such a definition and enhance the physical and cognitive cohesion of groups. Because groups are states of mind, boundary maintenance is necessary for the survival of social order (Homans, 1950). Without clear definitions of the insides and outsides of groups, social interaction would be difficult.

In the urban community most individuals participate in a number of social groups. The individual's relationship to each of these groups is defined by a set of status-roles. (Within the group, *status* defines the individual's position relative to other group members, while the *role* elaborates the group's expectations concerning performance within the status.) Because of the highly complex nature and variety of the individual's social participation, role conflict is likely. That is, multiple memberships often place individuals in the delicate position of facing multiple or even conflicting group expectations. One of the means of minimizing such conflict is in the spatial separation of roles. Noncommuting students can attest to the value of some degree of separation between school and family.

It is a great irony of postindustrial urban history that society has become increasingly complex and spatial segregation has become more elaborate and finely graded while transportation technology has almost annihilated physical separation. Ease of movement cuts two ways in the segregation process. It facilitates repulsion; for example, Chapter 4 described the separation of the home and the workplace. On the other hand, it permits social cohesion to be maintained over great distances (Fischer et al., 1978).

The spatial organization of groups not only minimizes the possibilities of conflicting role expectations, but it also makes social life more predictable and comfortable. Because we are evaluative as well as social creatures, we tend to view the world in terms of "us" and "them." Our understanding of the world and thus our sense of place in it is a product of the groups we identify and interact with. To sustain that understanding, it is necessary to distinguish "ingroups" from "outgroups."

Social scientists use the term *social distance* to refer to the subjective sense of being set apart from certain people. Social distance simplifies our group experiences by making clear that certain groups are "off limits." When social distance is low, people feel close to one another and can enter imaginatively into each other's minds and share an experience; in this case, an ingroup is likely to develop (Shibutani and Kwan, 1965). When it is high, people may feel apprehensive and uncertain about others, producing a clearly defined outgroup. Social distance or stereotyping is apparently learned—a product of culture. It does not seem to result from specific personal experiences with outgroups.

In 1925 Emory Bogardus devised a method for measuring the social distance at which members of one group hold the members of another group. The technique involves administering a set of statements about the degrees of social intimacy an individual is willing to have with certain ethnic groups. The degrees of intimacy considered in the scale are presented in Table 9.1. Bogardus (1966) found social distance responses to be remarkably stable over a forty-year period between 1926 and 1966. Although the Bogardus scale is designed to measure social distance between ethnic groups, it is clear that in contemporary industrial societies "ingroup" and "outgroup" designations tend to form around all three of the social area constructs. We tend to identify ourselves with particular ethnic, occupational, and age–family-cycle groups that become central to our own self-definitions.

Since the early work of the Chicago School, perhaps the major hypothesis guiding the efforts of urban ecologists has been the idea that the greater the spatial distance between two groups, the greater their social distance from each

Table 9.1

Degrees of social intimacy in Bogardus's scale of social distance:

1. Would admit to close kinship through marriage
2. Would admit to my club as personal friend
3. Would admit to my street as neighbor
4. Would admit to employment in my occupation
5. Would admit to citizenship in my country
6. Would admit to my country as visitor only
7. Would exclude from my country.

Source: Bogardus, 1925.

The Bogardus scale measures the degree of social distance members of one group customarily place between themselves and the members of another group. Each subject is asked to respond to a set of hypothetical situations with regard to some outgroup. The situations vary in terms of the degree of intimacy involved with the group—item 1 representing the highest degree of intimacy and item 7 the lowest.

other. Basic to this thesis is the assumption that spatial similarity generates social interaction. (This assumption will be reviewed in some detail in the next two chapters.) The notion requires some qualification. Proximity or distance is not the crucial factor in producing community and a sense of "we-ness." As the work of Kevin Lynch (1960) suggests, we do not understand the city in terms of metric distance (see Chapter 6). Instead we view the urban community topologically. This primarily topological image conditions our behavior in the city. Space exerts its influence on the urban experience through boundaries, contents, and structure, rather than through simple distance. Evidence from urban ecology indicates that a group's cohesion is not a function of its contiguity, but its spatial dissimilarity from, and lack of penetration by, other groups (Peach, 1975). This point is made most vividly in Suttles's study of the Addams area of Chicago, an area he calls a defended community (Suttles, 1971).

> For persons in the Addams area only the adjacent neighborhoods are well defined ... Each little section [of the city] is taken to be a self-sufficient world where residents carry out all of their legitimate pursuits. A person who leaves his own area, then, is suspect so long as he has no visible and justifiable reason for straying from his home grounds (1971:15).

The use of the term *spatial distance* to describe the ecological correlate of social distance is ill advised. It is not distance per se, but separation that is the spatial index of group boundaries.

What evidence do we have that spatial structure indicates the existence of ingroups and outgroups? A considerable amount of relevant data has accumulated during the past twenty years. Spatial structure reflects the status arrangements of cities in both preindustrial and industrial societies. In all societies it is apparent that the degree of spatial separation between social classes and ethnic-religious groups reflects their degree of social separation from one another.

The Duncans' (1955) study of occupational segregation was perhaps the first attempt to examine empirically the relationship between spatial structure and the social order of cities. Its motivation stemmed from the early work of Park, who suggested the coincidence of the spatial with the "moral" order. The Duncans' specific concern was how occupational strata were segregated from each other in the city of Chicago. Occupational stratification is one of the ways people distinguish themselves from each other. The Duncans took occupational stratification as an index of social distance. Their measures of spatial distance, or more precisely spatial separation, are similar to the index used by the Taeubers (see Chapter 8). The *index of dissimilarity* calculates the residential differences between two occupational groups. The index is given by the formula:

$$\frac{1}{2} \sum_{k=1}^{n} \left| \frac{X_k}{X_t} - \frac{Y_k}{Y_t} \right|$$

where X_k and Y_k represent the number of persons in occupation X and Y respectively who reside in area k; X_t and Y_t are the total number of persons in the city found in occupation X and occupation Y respectively.

As suggested earlier (see Chapter 8), this index can be interpreted as a measure of displacement suggesting the percentage of persons who would have to move to achieve perfect spatial integration. The following hypothetical example illustrates how this measure is computed.

Area	Occupation X	Occupation Y	Difference
1	20%	30%	10%
2	45%	10%	35%
3	35%	60%	25%
Total	100%	100%	70%

In this example the index of dissimilarity between occupation X and Y is .35. That is, 35 percent of the population would have to be shifted around from one area to another to provide a situation of spatial integration. An additional measure of spatial separation between occupational groups conforms to the same general logic. The *index of segregation* is simply an index of dissimilarity, which is computed between one occupation and all other occupations combined.

In Chicago the index of segregation followed a U-shaped pattern when occupations were ordered by socioeconomic status. This pattern suggests that the

Table 9.2 Indexes of segregation and indexes of dissimilarity for each major occupation group, for employed males in the Chicago metropolitan district, 1950 (Above diagonal, by census tracts; below diagonal, by zone-sector segments)

	Index of Segregation	Index of Dissimilarity for Major Occupation Group							
		Professional, Technical, Kindred	Managers, Officials, Proprietors	Sales Workers	Clerical Kindred Workers	Craftsmen, Foreman	Operatives, Kindred	Service except Private Household	Laborers, except Farm and Mine
Professional, Technical, Kindred Workers	30	–	13	15	28	35	44	41	54
Managers, Officials, and Proprietors, except Farm	29	8	–	13	28	33	41	40	52
Sales Workers	29	11	7	–	27	35	42	38	54
Clerical and Kindred Workers	13	20	18	17	–	16	21	24	38
Craftsmen, Foremen, Kindred Workers	19	26	23	25	12	–	17	35	35
Operatives, Kindred Workers	22	31	29	30	16	14	–	26	25
Service Workers, except Private Household	24	31	31	30	19	25	19	–	28
Laborers, except Farm and Mine	35	42	41	42	32	30	21	24	–

Source: Adapted from O. D. Duncan and B. Duncan, "Residential Distribution and Occupational Stratification." *American Journal of Sociology,* 60, 1955, 497–498. Reprinted by permission of The University of Chicago Press, Chicago, IL.

The table shows a close correlation between the spatial structure of occupational groups and the social ordering of these groups. Data for the index of segregation indicate a U-shaped relationship between occupational prestige and the degree of residential segregation. The most prestigious groups and the least prestigious groups are the most segregated. Data for the index of dissimilarity suggest that the greater the distance in occupational prestige between two groups, the more likely they will be segregated.

occupations at both extremes of the status hierarchy are the most segregated from the rest of the community. A variety of empirical studies since then have clearly demonstrated the lawlike nature of this relationship. When groups are ranked high to low on some socioeconomic dimension (income, education, or occupation), the U-shaped pattern emerges. This occurs whether the city is preindustrial or industrial (Mehta, 1969).

A similar statement about the relationship between social distance and spatial structure can be made for the index of dissimilarity. Chicago's occupational groups exhibited a residential pattern that reflected their status differences (see Table 9.2). This phenomenon is universal and remains unaffected by the society's level of modernization or industrialization. Whether the groups being considered are racial, religious, ethnic, caste, or occupational strata, their residential dissimilarity tends to increase as disparity between the group's socioeconomic status ranking increases (Mehta, 1969).

The indexes of dissimilarity do, however, show some exceptions to this pattern (see Table 9.2). These deviations are themselves enlightening in that they suggest the dynamics behind the spatial-social distance pattern. The deviations seem to result from cross-pressures produced by variation in a group's position on the status dimensions (income, occupation, and education) (Duncan and Duncan, 1955). Perhaps the most significant of these deviant cases occur at or near the boundary between white-collar and blue-collar occupations. Sales workers are very similar to craftsmen and foremen in terms of income, yet their residential dissimilarity from these blue-collar groups is greater than from managers, proprietors, and officials. At the same time, despite their educational similarity with other white-collar groups, clerical workers are residentially more dissimilar from these groups than from craftsmen and foremen.

These exceptional cases can be explained by considering the separate effects of income and education on residential dissimilarity. Education appears to be a far more significant determinant of residential patterns than income (Feldman and Tilly, 1960). Similar education levels indicate shared values concerning the meaning of residence; thus shared culture is more important than shared income in predicting residence. Since sales workers have a higher educational status than managers in the Duncans' study, they are more disassociated from blue-collar groups than managers. But what about the deviant case of craftsmen and foremen? This group has significantly less education than the lower white-collar clerical worker, yet it is residentially very similar. In terms of income craftsmen resemble managers much more than clerical workers, but this similarity fails to appear in their residential pattern. Likewise, the income similarity between clerical and operatives also fails to materialize in residential location. It is clear that the higher incomes of craftsmen and foremen allow them to disassociate from other blue-collar groups. The degree of that disassociation, however, is less than it might be if this group had the same housing-to-total-income budget ratio as clerical workers. In essence, the importance of residential separation for clerical workers appears to be somewhat higher than that for craftsmen. They are willing to spend a greater proportion of their income on housing in order to make clear their social distance from blue-collar groups in spatial terms. Social valuations rather than mere ability to pay are at the heart of the relationship between spatial and social distance.

A relation between spatial structure and social distance exists in the urban community. But why?

The physical isolation of groups may be said to symbolize their social and cultural isolation from one another (Timms, 1971). In simplest terms, spatial separation facilitates social separation by decreasing the chances of undesirable and potentially embarrassing social contact. Residential proximity increases the probability of social interaction. This is, of course, only true to a point. First, social geography has been profoundly affected by developments in communication and transportation technology. The development of the telephone and the automobile has lessened the impact of spatial boundaries. Perhaps prior to such inventions the spatial distance between groups had much the same impact as the moats surrounding medieval castles, but no more is this true. Space is less costly to traverse than ever before. Second, it is socially defined areas rather than distance that is critical to social interaction. Recall the discussion of mental maps in Chapter 6. The black ghetto child drawing a map of the neighborhood imagines the boundary between the ghetto and the contiguous white area to be almost insurmountable—the psychic distance is far greater than the physical distance.

Despite these facts, the physical arrangement of the city indicates more than the social position of groups. It also indicates the boundaries of a complex urban social arena or space. While it may be true that modernization has made location and social interaction less congruent, space still operates to facilitate interaction. Public identity and status are very closely related to the people with whom one associates. Association demands contact, and contact is at least facilitated by spatial propinquity. Residential mobility, then, can be viewed as a strategy for optimizing the probability of desired associations (Timms, 1971). As a particular area acquires an image that reflects the social characteristics of its residents, spatial structure begins to reflect social boundaries (as in the Addams area of Chicago).

Essentially location can be a means of social control. Spatial boundaries between disparate social groups facilitate certain interactions and limit others. Spatial distance maintains social distance. The evidence for this is quite clear in the case of marriage rates. Marriage in the Bogardus scale of social distance ranks first as an indicator of the desire of one group to remain distant from another. Homogamy is the rule; that is, we tend to marry within our own "we" groups.

The choice of a marriage partner and our conception of the marriage market are spatially constrained. Marriage rates are affected by residential proximity and by the spatial similarity of groups. Kennedy's (1943) study of New Haven marriage licenses suggested that 56 percent of the couples applying for licenses lived within ten blocks of each other, and 76 percent lived within twenty blocks. Similar evidence has been gathered for a variety of American cities (Bossard, 1932; Koller, 1948; Catton and Smircich, 1964; Hanson et al., 1972). Catton and Smircich (1964) explain this phenomenon as an example of "least effort" behavior. Using a simple modification of Zipf's principle of least effort, they argue that the marriage rate between two areas is proportional to the product of male and female populations and inversely proportional to the distance intervening between the two populations.

$$M = K \, P_1 \, P_2 / D$$

where P_1 is a population of grooms in area 1, P_2 is a population of brides in area 2, D is the distance between the two areas, M is the number of grooms in area 1 marrying brides residing in area 2, and K is a constant.

The distance limitation on marriage tends to simplify the individual's conceptualization of the marriage market. This market is bounded in a manner similar to the housing markets described by Johnston (1972) (see Chapter 8). Because the city is segregated sectorally by social class, marital as well as spatial choice is limited by the sectoral activity space of the residents. The spatial boundedness of the marriage market is so intense that some students of the family have suggested that the parental controls over romance in the modern society are nearly as strong as those in more traditional societies (Goode, 1972). Spatial segregation by class and ethnicity serves much the same function institutionalized matchmaking did in preindustrial society. In both societies an institution is designed to limit the marital choice of children to "suitable" partners.

Spatial constraints appear to limit many activities in addition to marriage. Boal (1970) provides clear-cut evidence for the coincidence of social and physical space in the city of Belfast, Northern Ireland. He finds that lower- and middle-class areas display a closely knit spatial system in which visiting, residential mobility, and marriage are constrained by the physical space. For these classes a close-knit set of social networks provides evidence for a spatial community. In Belfast space is segregated sectorally along both class and religious dimensions. The dual nature of the social order in Northern Ireland is suggested by the coincidence of social networks with these sectoral patterns. In Belfast, Protestant neighborhoods have social linkages only with other Protestant subsectors while Catholic neighborhoods exhibit similar linkages only with Catholic areas. Linkages occur with areas that are similar in social class and religion. These constraints are a function of an existing spatial order and of mobility limitations, which are class based. Low-status areas in Belfast are characterized by households of whom between two-thirds and three-fourths are without cars. The upper classes experience no such spatial limitations. For the lower and middle classes spatial linkages are a product of mass transport. Bus routes are typically radial or sectoral, and thus spatial linkages are also sectoral.

While Belfast represents an extreme case, such evidence suggests that wherever mobility is limited, social networks will be constrained by physical space. In the American city this points to the particular significance of physical space for the lower classes, the elderly, and the home-bound housewife.

SPATIAL DISPERSION AND ASSIMILATION

The spatial location of groups in the city says much about the relationships among these groups. You might expect, then, that any change in the social position of the group would be reflected in spatial changes—spatial barriers should crumble as the social barriers between two groups diminish. It is easy to see how this relationship between social change and spatial change would manifest itself in the housing market. From Muth's (1975) adaptation of the rent model in Chapter 8, we know that intense segregation between any two groups results from social distance. He describes a situation very similar to the one tapped by the Bogardus scale, in that he assumes that A types have an aversion to B types and prefer nearness to other A types. At the same time B types share this preference for location near A types. Given this assumption two pricing structures occur in the land market, and eventually the A group is totally segregated from the B group. But what if the social distance between A and B diminished? Under this condition a normal market situation would prevail, and people in both the A and B groups would disperse in space solely according to the ability to pay. Thus the spatial position of A and B groups changes as the social distance between them diminishes. Ultimately segregation would decline.

The predictions from Muth's discrimination model accurately reflect the historical situation for ethnic groups in cities characterized by intensive waves of immigration. America is, of course, a nation of immigrants, and its cities bear the distinct imprint of its former status as melting pot for the world. Immigrants were major contributors to the great cityward movements of the nineteenth and early twentieth centuries. Indeed, most immigrants made their original destination a city (Ward, 1971).

The unique ethnic character of American society has led to great interest in understanding the process by which newcomers become Americans. From the late eighteenth century until quite recently, most observers of American society have stressed a *melting pot*, or *assimilationist*, view of this process. This conception implies that a uniformity of culture is the ideal both for the individual ethnic and the society as a whole. The connotation is perhaps made most explicit in Israel Zangwill's play, *The Melting Pot*:

> America is God's crucible, the great Melting-Pot where all races of Europe are melting and re-forming! Here you stand, good folk, think I, when I see them at Ellis Island, here you stand in your fifty groups, with your fifty languages and histories, and your fifty blood hatreds and rivalries. But you won't be long like that, brother, for these are the fires of God you've come to—these are the fires of God. A fig for your feuds and vendettas! Germans and Frenchmen, Irish and Englishmen, Jews

and Russians—into the Crucible with you all! God is making the American (1909:34).

The sociologist's view, though not quite as colorful as Zangwill's, shared the same basic assumption. Until recently most social scientists viewed ethnic status as a dimension of social rank, and thus they saw identification with a particular ethnic group as a temporary indication of the migrant's low status in America. Distinctive ethnic traits, they assumed, would disappear as the migrant was assimilated into the economic structure of the society. "The 'teeming masses' presumably arrived uneducated, unskilled, and uncultured in the United States and then fought their way upward in the social structure over generations" (Guest, 1977:302).

The work of Paul Cressy (1938), updated by Richard Ford (1950), represents the classic ecological statement of the assimilationist perspective. Based on earlier ideas derived from Park and Burgess, Cressy believes that immigrant groups followed a regular sequence of settlement in successive areas of increasing status. This dynamic pattern of invasions and successions represented the spatial context of assimilation. An immigrant group arriving in the city usually settled near the center in the zone of transition. The central concentration of employment in the nineteenth and early twentieth centuries encouraged this centralization of the foreign born. Because they arrived with little status or wealth, they sought low-cost housing near their place of employment. Thus during the waves of great immigration prior to 1920, people of foreign birth dominated the city's central residential quarters (Ward, 1971). After a period of residence in these congested areas, the group, as it improved its economic and social status, moved outward to a more prestigious residential district. With this outward movement and subsequent moves, the group dispersed and became socially assimilated. Thus Cressy and Ford argue that dispersion indicated the disintegration of the group and its absorption into the general American population (an idea that directly parallels the predictions from the Muth model).

Cressy and Ford provide evidence for this decentralization process in the city of Chicago for the period from 1898 to 1940. By computing the median distance from the city center for various ethnic groups at different times, they traced the centrifugal movements. All ethnic groups had made some spatial shift, but the most extensive dispersions had been experienced by the "old immigrant groups" from Northern and Western Europe. The most concentrated groups were the Southern Europeans, a more recent set of immigrants.

The dispersion of ethnic groups continued after 1940 in Chicago (Duncan and Lieberson, 1959). The decentralization was greatest for the "newer immigrant" groups. Despite this decline in centralization, the new groups remained much more highly centralized and segregated than the old. [Studies of Australian cities by F. Lancaster Jones (1967) and I. H. Burnley (1972) suggest a similar pattern of residential distribution.] These differences in residential dispersion reflected basic differences in the social distance of ethnic groups as measured by the Bogardus scale. The older groups were more assimilated into the American mainstream. Not only did they have higher average status on various dimensions of social rank, but they also were seen as more similar to the average American. At least in part, then, the degree of residential concentration can be explained in terms of the group's length of residence.

Assimilation, of course, is not as automatic as this relationship with length of residence seems to suggest. Lieberson (1961) explores in considerable detail the correlates of ethnic residential segregation. He finds that residential segregation correlates with citizenship status, the rate of ethnic intermarriage, the ability to speak English, and the degree of occupational segregation. These factors are not simple functions of length of residence.

The assimilationist portrait of the ethnic's urban experience has been criticized by several current students of ethnicity (Gordon, 1961; Greeley, 1971; Glazer and Moynihan, 1970; Novak, 1971). In this view, sometimes referred to as *cultural pluralism*, American society was strengthened by its *diversity* rather than by its absorption of diverse groups into a homogeneous culture. That ethnic groups do indeed exist and that assimilation is far from complete are indicated by their political viability. Because ethnics apparently still vote as a bloc, politicians attempt to cater to ethnic interests. This is perhaps nowhere more evident than in New York City. The atmosphere of New York and other large metropolitan areas is hospitable to ethnic groupings; it recognizes them and rewards them politically (Glazer and Moynihan, 1970).

The spatial evidence for assimilation is also far from complete. While most ethnic groups appear to disperse with time, ethnic segregation persists. Several social scientists provide evidence that seems to challenge the assimilationist perspective. The contradictory evidence in this regard is twofold:

1. Spatial dispersion, or decentralization, does not by itself indicate a decline in segregation as Cressy and Ford imply.

2. The slight declines in ethnic residential segregation noted by various researchers may be a function of the way ethnic status is measured, which stems, in turn, from limitations in available data.

Comparisons of ethnic residential patterns between central cities and suburbs for several large cities in 1930 and 1950 suggest that surburban ethnics are just as segregated from the native white population as their central city counterpart (Lieberson, 1962). While the most highly segregated central city immigrant groups are also the groups least represented in the suburbs, this does not indicate any clear-cut negative association between segregation and suburbanization. Rather, suburban ethnic segregation exists and it parallels the segregation pattern of the central city.

Nathan Kantrowitz (1973) also provides some evidence that challenges the assimilationist perspective. In an analysis of ethnic segregation for the metropolitan area of New York he shows that ethnic residential segregation for first- and second-generation immigrants is extensive (the average index of dissimilarity was 46.4). While some might argue that New York is a unique case, studies of ethnic segregation have exaggerated how much such patterns have declined over time. These studies' results may be an artifact of the way ethnic status was measured. Ethnicity is usually defined by *foreign stock*—that is, first- or second-generation immigrants. Such a measure is deceptive, because the native white population is constantly changing. Since later generations of a particular ethnic group are defined as natives, indices of dissimilarity cannot detect the true extent of segregation. Third- and fourth-generation Italians, for example, may be living in the same neighborhoods with persons of Italian foreign stock, yet such a situation will not be defined as segregated because these later generations are considered native. Such definitional problems mean that segregation indices automatically decline with time, while undetected segregation may persist.

Thus existing studies provide clear evidence for the spatial dispersion of later generations of an ethnic group. The evidence for desegregation is less clear. Indeed, the data seem to suggest that ethnic segregation persists over time in cities and metropolitan areas, and that it involves many ethnic groups.

Why does segregation of this sort continue? Two sorts of answers can be given: one that is city oriented and the other that is society oriented. The writings of Wirth, Lofland, and Firey provide us with a city-oriented answer to this problem. City life is potentially unpredictable. A shared culture provides us with the ability to predict the behavior of unknown others, but since the urban culture is complex and composed of a variety of subcultures, the urbanite is confronted with a unique problem of prediction. To ensure predictability and stability, therefore, the city dweller is likely to opt for cultural sameness. In spatial terms this means that separate life-style communities emerge in the urban mosaic. That is, to a certain extent, ethnics choose a segregated setting if their subculture is particularly important or salient to them.

Why is the ethnic identity a particularly salient one? The answer to this question is decidedly society-oriented in nature. Glazer and Moynihan (1970) argue that strong structural elements in American society prevent the adoption of a simple American identity. In reality there is no simply American identity. Even the natives have strong regional ties that produce New Englanders, Southerners, Midwesterners, and so forth. But maintaining ethnic identities goes beyond this structural tendency in American society to identify American subcultures. The importance of ethnic identities is a product of a particular history and, perhaps, a particular historical period (e.g., the political success of blacks in the 1960s and 1970s stimulated the emergence of other ethnic identities).

We have a situation in contemporary American cities in which ethnic groups have clearly decentralized, but not necessarily desegregated to any extent. How can this somewhat paradoxical evidence be resolved? One avenue of resolution is to consider the separate components of the assimilation process.

Assimilation can refer to one of a number of subprocesses (Gordon, 1961). At its simplest level assimilation can be divided into behavioral and structural components. *Behavioral assimilation* refers to absorbing the behavior patterns of the host society. This form of assimilation seems to be reflected in the decentralization of ethnic populations through time. As successive generations of ethnics become more middle class in orientation, some of them suburbanize. This decentralization indicates the decline of cultural barriers to residential choice.

At the same time *structural assimilation* involves the entrance of immigrants and their descendants into the cliques, organizations, and general activities of the receiving society. Clearly, structural assimilation is far from complete. In part because of discrimination, but also because of life style preferences, ethnics continue to live apart from natives. This residential association indicates either their inability or their unwillingness to break primary social ties with other ethnics.

The urban mosaic thus reflects the Americanization of ethnics, but not the abandonment of ethnic identities. Here the spatial pattern of cities provides valuable information on the nature of ethnicity in America. Space not only speaks of social distance and changes in this distance over time; it also suggests how these distances are made concrete in American society. Residential choice may tell us more about a person's attitude toward various ethnic groups than their responses to a questionnaire on ethnic attitudes. What we do better indicates how we feel about a particular issue than what we say we feel.

MODERNIZATION AND SPATIAL DIFFERENTIATION

As social area analysts have argued, the urban community exists in the larger context of society. Just as an individual's residential choice indicates who and what that person is, so too the whole urban mosaic expresses the nature and stage of development of society. This point has been missed by most work in urban ecology and the social sciences generally. Traditionally the city has been viewed more as a social force than a social product. It is not enough to state, as the cultural ecologists have, that social rank, familism, and ethnicity are the principal forces in molding social space. We must ask why these criteria are important. With the question posed in this way it is very easy to see why most social scientists have not confronted it: Most work on the city focuses on a particular place and time. This question, however, can only be answered by cross-cultural and historical comparisons. If we recall the historical outline of the city provided in Chapter 4, we can see that transformations in urban form flow from social change. Specifically, the greatest spatial changes in the Western city are correlated with the greatest social changes in our history: industrialization and the associated revolutions in agricultural, political and economic organization, and transportation. That is, the most crucial distinction lies between the preindustrial and the industrial/modern city.

What distinguishes the modern society from past forms? Since Durkheim's *Division of Labor in Society* (1893) most students of social change have argued that the process of modernization involves increasing role specialization and separation. In premodern societies an individual's status in one institutional sphere correlates highly with his or her standing in others. Status is ascribed rather than achieved. This fact coupled with the general coalescence of the criteria for social differentiation (due to the great influence of kinship structures) makes social standing clear-cut. An individual's kinship connections provide a sound basis for predicting place of residence, ethnicity, and social rank. In modern societies this coalescence of status dimensions breaks down. Changes in the organization of society have been accompanied by changes in the dimensions of social differentiation. As societies have modernized, they have become more complex. This complexity has generated a wider range of options and thus produced greater differentiation.

The impact of this differentiation on the factorial ecology of developing cities was described at the end of Chapter 5. It should be recalled that Schwirian and others detected an interesting relationship between size (primacy) and development in actively developing systems. The factorial structures of entirely undeveloped cities are relatively undifferentiated; those of completely developed cities, highly differentiated. But in developing cities factorial differentiation appears to be correlated with size, owing to downward diffusion of the social and economic causes of differentiation from the primate city. Thus San Juan, the largest city in Puerto Rico, has a factorial structure similar to that of developed societies, while smaller cities such as Ponce and Mayaguez have much less differentiated spatial structures (Schwirian and Smith, 1974).

Structural differentiation refers to a process whereby one social role develops into two or more roles that together function more effectively under the new historical conditions. Differentiation thus involves the evolution from a multifunctional role structure to several more specialized structures (Mayer and Buckley, 1970). This growth of specialized structures is indicated and to a degree caused by the simultaneous occurrence of several organizational changes: the growth of public education, urbanization, industrialization, bureaucratization, and rapid communication and transportation. These changes have had special significance for two institutions—the stratification system and the family structure. In turn, changes in these two institutions have greatly affected the nature of the urban space.

The Spatial Impact of Stratification

The nature of stratification in a society depends on its degree of technological advance (Lenski, 1966). As the society's ability to produce goods increases with technological and organizational changes, so the potential for social inequality increases. In simple hunting and gathering societies (societies that also lack cities) the goods and services available are distributed according to need. This is not so in societies where technology is sufficiently advanced to produce a surplus. Once a surplus develops, the society must face the problem of redistributing it. Lenski (1966) suggests two basic "laws" which govern this redistribution:

1. People relinquish control over wealth to the extent necessary to insure the survival and continued productivity of those others whose actions are beneficial to them.
2. Power differences govern the distribution of nearly all of the society's surplus.

Because these two laws tend to operate in all societies, there appears to be a U-shaped relationship between the extent of a society's surplus and its degree of inequality. Hunting and gathering societies generally live at a subsistence level. Lacking a stable surplus, their members are least stratified. Agricultural societies, on the other hand, tend to have the greatest inequality. In these societies, a small group of nobility controls the sources of wealth, while the vast majority of the population lives off the land at a near subsistence level. An example is early medieval feudalism in Europe. The preindustrial city is a product of these circumstances.

   With industrialization, though, surpluses continue to expand and inequality actually declines because of the tremendous societal complexity accompanying industrialization (Lenski, 1966). Industrial production with its factory-based system requires a complex division of labor unnecessary in the premodern society. Assembly-line organization involves a minute division of task, with each person or group contributing a particular service to the final product. In addition, the modern system of production is characterized by formal organization. The bureaucratization of the factory has led to a substantial growth in middle management and clerical positions. These new positions, with the highly specialized knowledge necessary to fill them, have made those in power more dependent on a larger number of others, leading to a more even distribution of wealth.

   Complexity is a basic characteristic of the modern division of labor. Similarly, the modern system of social stratification is multidimensional in character. American students of contemporary stratification systems have generally described it as the result of ranking along a number of continuous linear scales. This description follows Max Weber's conception of stratification. According to Weber (1946), social stratification involves three distinct, but overlapping levels of inequality. These are *prestige classes*, distinguished by an inequality of status or position; *economic classes*, distinguished by unequal income or wealth; and *political classes*, distinguished by an inequality of power. The Weberian conception of inequality differs from that of Karl Marx, who saw the history of society as the history of class struggles. For Marx, inequality is expressed by a series of discrete classes in either potential or open conflict with one another.

Dahrendorf (1959) suggests that Marx's description of inequality is inappropriate for the modern industrial society. Why, he asks, has the proletarian revolt against the owners of production never taken hold in industrial society? Class revolutions, it seems, have occurred only in agrarian societies such as China and Russia. The answer, according to Dahrendorf, lies in the complexity of class systems in modern society. Modern systems are characterized by a multiplicity of organizations and roles that give individuals power on some dimensions, but not on others. Managers and owners, for example, control capital and wages, but it is the labor unions that control the labor force. In our everyday lives most of us exercise some influence over certain spheres of activity, while others appear to be outside of our control. This complex division of authority makes conflict less likely than in a system in which the lines of power are clearly demarcated.

While most American scholars would agree with Dahrendorf's insistence that modern society's inequality is reflected in stratification rather than classes, some evidence suggests that this notion must be qualified. If class is a mythical creature in the modern society, why does residential segregation remain and even intensify in the modern city? We have just seen that real social groups attempt to maintain their groupness by setting spatial bounds between ingroups and outgroups. Social distance manifests itself in spatial segregation. Residential patterns may influence the discreteness of class boundaries through their impact on interpersonal networks (Vanneman, 1977). Marx, for example, cites the isolation of French peasants from one another as inhibiting the development of a group identity and a politically active peasant class (Marx, 1951). Class boundaries become more distinct and class conflict proceeds to the extent that members of a class live in close proximity to one another, but at some distance from opposed classes. This situation already exists in the modern city, yet class conflict is at a minimum.

While it is true that occupational prestige differences appear to be reflected in spatial distance, Marx's version of modern inequality is still not acceptable. Residential patterns in the modern city are multidimensional. The urbanite is segregated not only by ability to pay (a class variable) but also by ethnicity and family cycle position. This complexity prevents clear-cut class distinctions and thus class conflict. In addition to the multidimensional nature of residential location, the great increase in mobility in the industrial society also contributes to the lack of clear-cut class boundaries.

Changes in Family Structure

The institution of the family is also greatly affected by industrialization. The traditional kinship structure fosters reliance upon the security of the extended family, rather than reliance on one's own talents. In the traditional society production is mainly organized within kinship structures. Subsistence farming predominates, and thus exchange and consumption generally occur within the extended family. For this reason market systems are underdeveloped even in the cities. The extended family becomes the major source of security in the premodern system, a fact that is especially important given the high mortality rates in such societies. Because death is an ever-present reality in the traditional society, the nuclear family is not the dominant family unit. The extended family can better care for the needs of its nuclear family units when one of the parents dies (Goldscheider, 1971).

With industrialization the extended family ceases to be the basic source of physical and psychological nurturance. Since economic production is achieved through a factory-based system, the family is no longer the basic economic unit. Extended-family members must leave the household to seek employment in the labor market. The growing spatial separation between nuclear family units lessens the direct control elders can exercize. Actual influence declines in a number of spheres. Family ties in the new economic system are no longer the basis for occupational attainment—*achievement* (statuses that result from individual choice or effort) rather than *ascription* (statuses that result from the accident of birth) becomes the rule. As ascriptive criteria become less significant, love becomes the basis for courtship and marriage rather than kinship considerations. In essence, personal choice becomes more likely in the modern system.

Choice, of course, can only exist if real options are available. As we have already suggested, modern society is characterized by structural differentiation—that is, the multiplication of institutional spheres of influence. Modernization loosens the control kinship structures hold over the society's organization. In the process, life style choices are magnified as a variety of institutions begin to influence the individual. Modernization also leads to a more even distribution of wealth. This also enhances choice, since various life styles become more affordable.

Social area analysis theory suggests the nature of this transformation and shows how this change is reflected in the urban space (see Chapter 5). According to the thesis, the extensive structural differentiation of modern society leads to more complicated patterns of urban residential location. Just as the modernization of society is associated with the emergence of an ever increasing number of axes of differentiation, so also is residential segregation more complex. In the preindustrial city differences in family characteristics are closely associated with differences in social rank. The family tightly controls marriage and occupational attainment. As a result, segregation by social rank reflects segregation by family cycle status. The modernization of society is thus indicated by the growing dissociation between family status and social rank criteria for location.

Studies of ecological structure in the Third World confirm the idea that in the early phases of development social status and familism are closely related. We discussed findings on this relationship by Schwirian and Smith (1974) and Abu Lughod (1968) in Chapter 5.

The independence of social rank from family status appears to result from increasing complexity in the division of labor. As occupations multiply, the functional dependence of individuals upon one another also increases. This fact, coupled with the declining economic control of the family, leads to an increase in upward mobility. Social rank becomes a matter of occupational achievement rather than kinship, and this growing independence between the two institutional spheres is reflected in residential location. Since the extended family is no longer the basic family unit in the society, the characteristics of each nuclear family become important for location. Other than social class, these characteristics usually involve life cycle differences. A city can achieve a residential pattern characterized by an independence between life cycle and social class only if it provides housing accommodations for every social class that are suitable to families at particular points in their life cycle. Also, such separation between factors can occur only if some change in the life cycle stage of the nuclear family encourages movement. These conditions are characteristic of the modern Western city. Limited housing supply may be inhibiting such family-stage segregation in some non-Western contexts. For example, Smith (1976) indicates that in spite of impressive progress toward housing goals in the Soviet Union, a chronic shortage of apartments in Moscow unquestionably inhibits diversification of the urban space along the familism dimension. Newly formed families remain living with their in-laws, and divorced couples have been known to remain living together because they could not obtain separate housing.

Family characteristics may eventually become the most important factor in residential differentiation (Timms, 1971). Cognitive studies of the movement decision indicate that this indeed may already be the case (see Chapter 7). In some developed societies, such as Great Britain, the consumption habits of working-class young people are more similar to those of middle-class young than of their parents (Abrams, 1968). Also, American cities have become increasingly age-segregated (Cowgill, 1978).

Other Dimensions of Differentiation

In addition to separating family and social class factors, factorial ecology finds a separate ethnic dimension for residence in the modern city. Because status is achieved rather than ascribed in modern society, ethnic status no longer predetermines class position. As a result, the members of an ethnic group are at least potentially scattered among the various classes. This fact coupled with the extensive mobility made possible by transportation improvements makes voluntary ethnic segregation possible.

A number of distinct dimensions of spatial differentiation have been detected in developing and developed societies in addition to the well-substantiated factors of social class, familism, and ethnicity. For example, in Finnish cities primogeniture, feminine careerism, and established familism appear as differentiating factors (Sweetser, 1976). In Indian cities the multiethnic and caste-based nature of the society distinguish the factorial pattern from that found in comparably developed cities in ethnically homogeneous societies such as Puerto Rico. Cross-cultural diversity and factorial dimensions of strictly local significance necessarily qualify any generalizations on modernization. But in general an ecological theory of modernization would suggest that the spatial organization of the premodern and modern cities should differ, and that these differences should reflect basic differences between the two types of societies. Modern cities are segregated according to social rank, family, and ethnicity criteria. Premodern cities, on the other hand, are segregated according to social rank criteria alone. A city's ecological pattern, then, indicates the society's level of modernity. Modern societies, with their more differentiated social structure, also have urban communities with more differentiated residential spaces.

Although factorial ecology studies tend to support the modernization thesis, little empirical evidence has been gathered concerning the spatial change in modern cities over time. Timms's (1971) analysis of the New Zealand city of Auckland is an exception. Comparing spatial structures for various time points from 1926 to 1966, he found that social rank, family, and ethnicity factors tended to be independent of each other throughout the period. While the basic ecology was similar throughout, the proportion of variance explained by the factor structure tended to increase. If true in general, this finding implies that as cities modernize the pattern of spatial differentiation becomes more clear-cut.

SUMMARY

Urban spatial structures reliably indicate both the social position and the changing status patterns of various groups. Social distance is reflected in the spatial distribution of populations. Indexes of segregation may be constructed that evidence this relationship. When groups are ranked high to low on some socioeconomic dimension and segregation scores are considered, a U-shaped pattern appears. This pattern of high levels of segregation for both the lowest and highest groups appears to some degree in all cities, both preindustrial and industrial.

Muth's economic model predicts that as the social distance between groups declines, spatial location is more and more likely to become a function of the ability to pay. This prediction reflects the historical situation for American ethnic groups. Ethnic groups have dispersed spatially in American cities, and the rate of dispersion appears to be a function of the group's length of residence in the city. This decentralization reflects behavioral but not structural assimilation. Ethnic groups are still highly segregated. This segregation is, at least in part, a function of choice rather than discrimination. Ethnic identities are maintained and even enhanced by spatial segregation. In the highly complex and diversified urban environment such identities become important.

Just as social distance and change in it are reflected in the spatial order of cities, so also is the very nature of the society symbolized in the urban geography. The spatial structures of modern industrial cities differ greatly from the spatial systems of preindustrial urban communities. Because of weakening kinship ties and the more complex nature of industrial status systems, the social space is itself more complex—a mosaic of small worlds.

The urban space is a product of innumerable social forces. Because space is in part a medium or arena where such forces are played out, we can "read" it as symptomatic or symbolic of less visible processes. Such structures evidence the very nature of societies and cities—their basic inequalities.

Chapter 10

The Social Realities of Housing Design

INTRODUCTION

Cities stand as eloquent testimony to the human species's ability to control and restructure the physical environment. Most of us who live in industrial societies are far closer to, and dependent upon, the built environment than the natural environment (Ittelson et al., 1974:341). Furthermore, most of us who claim the city as home spend almost all of our time in its interior spaces. Architects and planners, then, can exert enormous control over our lives. This has led some social observers to state emphatically that those who manipulate the physical environment can control the actions of its occupants; for example, "Tell me the landscape in which you live, and I will tell you who you are" (Ortega y Gassett cited in Ittelson et al., 1974:17), and "We shape our buildings and afterwards our buildings shape us" (Winston Churchill cited in Merton, 1948:163–217).

The first section of this chapter examines the complex nature of the space-behavior relationship. As such, it serves to qualify the environmental determinism embodied in the claims of Ortega y Gassett and Churchill. The built environment not only reflects the nature of the culture under which it is constructed, but its meanings and thus its influence on behavior are also determined by a set of images that are cultural products. In this sense a particular environment is insufficient to produce a given behavioral outcome. Architects do not have the power that Shelley's Dr. Frankenstein had—we are not products of an engineered setting.

Nevertheless, architects and planners do influence our lives and experiences. This influence is the subject of the rest of the chapter. To put this theme in perspective the reader should recall from Chapter 2 that architectured space is what Hall (1966) referred to as fixed-feature space. Architects can structure the ebb and flow of interactions by erecting boundaries that modify both the topological and metric properties of a space. In so doing they reconstruct the setting of behavior. Ideally, this process should take into account universal spatial requirements as well as culturally conditioned needs. In essence, form should follow function. The problem of which forms suit what activities can

215

only be resolved by instituting a dialogue between social scientists and architects.

THE NATURE OF THE ENVIRONMENT-
BEHAVIOR RELATIONSHIP: ITS
IMPLICATIONS FOR
ARCHITECTURAL DESIGN

As an ideology, planning rests on the belief that by manipulating the physical environment we can control social patterns and experiences (Rosow, 1961). While this belief is to a certain extent correct, it belies the complex nature of the environment-behavior relationship. Space is more than a physical container; it is a social and cultural product as well. Several theories have dealt with this conception of space. Roger Barker (1968) discusses spaces as *behavior settings,* which are spaces with socially defined uses. "A behavior setting is bounded in space and time and has a structure which interrelates physical, social, and cultural properties so that it elicits common or regularized forms of behavior" (Ittelson et al., 1974:70). This conception of behavioral space involves far more than a physical setting with objective topological and metric properties. On the contrary, its character is determined by social definition. Norms are situation specific. That is, we learn to "act specific ways in specific places" (Michelson, 1976:29). We do not normally genuflect in bars or drink beer in churches. Michelson speaks of the space-behavior fit as involving two levels—the mental and the experiential:

> *Mental congruence* exists if an individual thinks that particular spatial patterns will successfully accommodate his personal characteristics, values, and style of life. . . . *Experiential congruence,* on the other hand, deals with how well the environment actually accommodates the characteristics and behavior of people (1976:30–33).

Both types of congruence are a necessary condition for successful design. Clearly, certain design features are unsuitable for certain types of behavior. The central hallway in Western homes affords privacy and personal control that the Oriental home does not. The growing use of the open classroom (a learning area without walls) does not permit teachers to use the same performance styles that educators used in the closed classroom with desks anchored to the floor. The built environment facilitates certain behaviors.

The physical setting is embedded in specific social and cultural systems, so that context and social structure are dynamically interrelated. Because of this complex interrelationship the environment frequently operates below the level of awareness (Ittelson et al., 1974). We become conscious of it only when it changes or is incongruous with other interests. To say that we are generally unaware of the environment is not to imply that it is insignificant to our behavior.

Our ability to adjust to a range of settings is impressive, and it accounts for our continued success and control over evolutionary processes. We can and often do adapt to dysfunctional environments, but this adjustment has physical, psychic, and social costs. Often the adjustments that enable humankind to overcome environmental roadblocks are dearly paid for (Dubos, 1965). Adaptation is perhaps most disturbing because we are so flexible, allowing us to adapt to conditions that are unhealthy both physiologically and socially.

> There are clearly healthy and unhealthy buildings in the medical sense, in the psychological and in the sociological sense. Our ability to adapt is probably why bad elements of architecture are so widely tolerated. . . . This does not mean, however, that adaptation is without cost to humans. It requires energy to move to a new level of adaptation and it requires energy to stay there. Environmental factors that do not conform to some modal value on each of the perceptual dimensions are "expensive" to live with; we pay for "tuning them out" by using more energy or by being less effective in our work or play (Wheeler, 1967:4).

Efficient environments, therefore, are congruent with the basic goals and needs of the species, the group, and the individual. In this sense the setting places certain constraints on the social and cultural content of a localized behavior pattern. It makes some acts more possible than others, and it makes some expectations and preferences more plausible than others.

The influence of environment on behavior, however, is primarily indirect, through already established patterns of behavior and values. As a result, the milieu may facilitate these patterns, but does not usually change the basic direction of a belief or a behavior. Since culture and social structure intervene in the relationship, these patterns are far more important in determining an action than is the immediate arena. Nevertheless, the built environment plays a significant role in our behavior and experiences.

ARCHITECTURAL DESIGN

In one sense, at least, the architect can be viewed as an artist who by erecting barriers sculptures space for social uses. The esthetic role has, however, been overemphasized. During the last twenty years social scientists have provided one important message to the professional architect—treat buildings not as pieces of sculpture, but as sites for behavior.

Although many architects have welcomed this advice, the norms of the profession still stress the artistic role. Beauty remains an overriding goal. We are writing this book on a college campus that gives evidence of the primacy of the esthetic norm. The campus of the State University of New York at Albany was designed by an architect of international reputation. To the outsider it is a very impressive structure with five towered clusters of buildings dotted by fountains and surrounded by geometric plantings. For the user it has numerous design flaws—a lack of central meeting places, inconveniently placed walk-ways, and so much glass that heating and cooling has become a major problem. When questioned on these flaws, the architect replied: "It's so beautiful they won't notice" (Bennett, 1977:19). Nothing, of course, could be further from the truth. The physical plant has impeded the development of a sense of university community and has frustrated many a student and faculty member in the process. It is easy to see the flaws in such an approach to design. It is as if the designer were asked to create a marriage partner. The designer gives the partner an attractive build—a pretty face or a muscular body—but ignores the designed partner's temperament and competence (Bennett, 1977). Such designs can turn out to be monsters haunting our daily lives.

This disregard for user needs is summed up in a single statement by the well-known Swiss architect Le Corbusier: "People have to be educated to appreciate the forms we make" (Lang et al., 1974:4). This high-handed approach to design is easily criticized. The educational process should be reversed—architects should be educated to appreciate user needs. Sociologists such as Herbert Gans (1978) and John Zeisel (1975) suggest that we need a user-oriented architecture. Unfortunately, until quite recently the profession has been peer oriented rather than user oriented. Their audience has been composed of professionals with upper-middle-class tastes. As a result, architects work for the standards of high culture and have made very little effort to address the tastes of low-brow groups (Gans, 1978). Yet different groups have different standards of beauty and good design. Traditionally, architects have cared more about how buildings looked in architectural journals than how they would work in use. Such a notion violates American architectural theorist Louis Sullivan's dictate that form should follow function. Instead, the tail has wagged the dog.

Why have architects traditionally approached the problem in this manner? The reasons appear to be simple:

1. Architects are professionals and thus respond more directly to the norms of the profession than the client.

2. The role of the architect is that of creator and thus has its roots in the art world rather than the social and behavioral sciences.

3. Since the Industrial Revolution and the growth of the profession, most environments have been designed and built for a client other than the user—landlord rather than tenant, the owner of the factory rather than the worker, and so forth.

4. Until recently, space has been viewed by the social scientist as the neutral ground where behavior takes place. Therefore, little information on user needs and the consequences of space existed.

5. Delineating user needs is complicated. What users prefer may not always be what is experientially best for them. Also, it is difficult to design for users because most buildings have a variety of uses and users (Gans, 1978). Which users should be given priority?

Whatever the reasons, however, it is clear that many buildings, particularly large-scale designs, have been conceived as statements. As Gans (1978) suggests, modern societies are simply too diverse and eras are over too quickly for architecture to be used this way. Because buildings are durable goods, we live with relics of past philosophies. Prison architecture indicates this problem. The fortresslike architecture of older prisons is meant to convey the force that society can muster against those who violate its moral codes. The message is clear—here lie society's outcasts, a group that must be segregated from normal society and punished for its wrongdoing. This message, however, is out of touch with current correctional philosophy, which stresses rehabilitation. A publication by the United States Bureau of Prisons points out the lag between correctional ideas and prison construction:

> The very existence of gloomy, thick-walled bastilles invariably produces mental attitudes on the part of both administrator and inmates which militate strongly against the possibility of putting rehabilitation foremost. . . . If the inmates are mentally overwhelmed and dejected by forbidding and repressive surroundings, they can hardly be expected to respond to reformative policies with zest or understanding (cited in Ittelson et al., 1974:376).

This lag between social philosophy and architecture leaves much of the built environment unsuited to current use. To a certain extent this problem is unavoidable, but as long as the architect as artist is committed to making statements in space, that space will be relatively inflexible and incapable of being rearranged to adapt to current user needs. This is especially true when the designer responds to client rather than user interests (Gans, 1978).

In recent years many architects have embraced the user-oriented philosophy. This new architecture identifies three universal requirements:

1. Buildings should be *functional*—that is, they must allow people to accomplish the important and recurrent activities carried out in them.
2. They should be *comfortable*. Lighting, sound, thermal conditions, and furniture should not produce discomfort. Although discomfort is a physiological condition, the factors creating this condition do differ from one culture to the next. At least before the energy crisis, the comfortable heat range for American homes was considerably different from what was considered normal in Great Britain.
3. They should, if possible, be *beautiful*—satisfying the esthetic preferences of a given group of users (Bennett, 1977; Gans, 1978).

Beauty is the least important of the requirements, and functionality is the most crucial. Nevertheless, research by Maslow and Mintz (1956) suggests an interrelationship between "pleasantness" and "functionality." These psychologists had people judge photographs of faces in settings of varying pleasantness. Generally, faces in the pleasant surroundings were judged higher in energy and well-being.

Architects can meet such needs only if their plans provide for some degree of freedom and if they define needs primarily in terms of experiential congruence with the setting (Zeisel, 1975; Michelson, 1976). Environments should not dictate a given behavior. Rather, the physical environment should, within certain limits, maximize the freedom of its users to choose the way they want to live. Baroque forms, which constituted strong political statements, failed to do this—the reason why this particular style is often referred to as the architecture of repression. Without such flexibility, environments may become oppressive. In addition, architects should define the needs of users in terms of the underlying social meaning of behavior rather than in terms of what people claim they want. (For example, in church architecture many congregations express a preference for traditional design, yet such features impede communal worship.) That is, architects must concern themselves with the latent as well as the manifest functions of their design. The concern for functionality is, then, best achieved by evaluating the experiential congruence of the site. This is not to say that concerns for mental congruence are unimportant for evaluating a site. It is, rather, that the underlying social consequences of a space are usually not consciously known to the residents of a particular dwelling (remember Ittelson et al.'s earlier comment about the nature of environment-behavior relations). Survey data must be combined with behavioral observations in adequately evaluating spaces. Thus a user-oriented architecture is more complicated than a client or profession-oriented approach. Unquestionably, however, such an architecture is more desirable.

From the perspective of the social sciences the most important goal of a user-oriented approach is functionality. That is, while design may have important implications for physiological processes or visual stimulation, this is essentially out of our purview. Rather, we are concerned primarily with the built environment's implications for overt individual behavior and group activity. Particular arrangements of boundaries may produce either group inefficiencies or conflict. This is of interest to the social scientist.

In reviewing research on the social consequences of built environments, it is important to consider the variety of territories in which social interaction occurs. Altman (1975:112) distinguishes three such types of fixed-feature spaces:

1. *Primary territories*. These are spaces that are "owned and exclusively used by individuals or groups, are clearly identified as theirs, are controlled on a relatively permanent basis, and are central to the day-to-day lives of the occupants." Examples are the home, school, and office.

2. *Secondary territories*. These are spaces that are less central to the occupants. They are used by a specific group who had less than total control over access to the place by others. Examples are the church and the neighborhood bar.

3. *Public territories*. These are areas available to a great variety of people on a temporary basis.

These territories are not always clearly delimited, as Lofland's (1973) description of the preindustrial city in Chapter 3 suggests. When they cannot be distinguished from each other, problems may emerge.

Since our central concern is with the residential space, our discussion of the design of spaces will focus on the primary territory. It is important to note, however, that a consideration of the site planning of residential areas (the neighborhood) must include all three types of territory.

DESIGNING THE RESIDENTIAL SPACE

The manifest function of the house is to provide shelter. Its latent functions, however, are more complex. The house is not just a physical structure, but also a social unit of space (Rapoport, 1969). A house is then not necessarily a home, for a home is an environment that is congruent with the way of life of its occupants. Only a user-oriented architecture can provide homes.

We have already implied that sound planning must address the questions of human nature and subcultural needs. Are there basic spatial needs that are universal to the human species? Studies in environmental psychology seem to indicate that there are. These basic requirements include the need for *privacy*, the related requirement for *personal space*, the need for easy *access to social interaction*, and the right to safe and *defensible spaces*. However, we must realize that these needs are conditioned by culture. This complicates design, for each group of users achieves these needs according to an established set of lifeways. Thus design should be congruent with the culturally modified needs of particular groups of users. We must, as Greenbie (1976) suggests, design for diversity.

Privacy

Privacy involves the individual's ability to control the behavioral inputs of others and the behavior outputs to others (Ittelson et al., 1974). Westin defines privacy as

> the claim of individuals, groups, or institutions to determine for themselves when, how, and to what extent information about themselves is communicated to others. Viewed in terms of the relation of the individual to social participation, privacy is the voluntary and temporary withdrawal of a person from the general society through physical or psychological means, either in a state of solitude or small group intimacy or, when among larger groups, in a condition of anonymity or reserve (1967:7).

In this sense privacy is both an individual and a group right.

This right, or requirement, satisfies a number of functions (Ittelson et al., 1974). It permits personal autonomy. That is, it provides a sense of individuality and a feeling of control over the environment. We use space to reinforce the sense of self that comes from gaining command over situations. This is the reason why many designers stress the importance of permitting the individualization of spaces (places to hang paintings, pictures, and documents; doors that may lock people in or out, walls that may be changed in color and appearance, and so forth). Altman and Haythorn's (1967) study of sailors in isolation suggested that these men each laid claim to particular spaces as a means of maintaining their sense of personal identity under the trying circumstances of no contact with the outside world and extremely close living arrangements.

In addition, privacy permits emotional release—or a backstage area where image management can be relaxed for a time. In this regard, it also provides an opportunity for self-evaluation, or reflection. Symbolic interactionists stress the importance of reflection in the self-development process. Given the constant stream of information available to each sensory receptor, the individual must from time to time withdraw himself or herself from these events to integrate and assimilate all the available information. In this state of withdrawal, the individual not only processes information, but also recasts it in a way to make plans for subsequent behavior.

Finally, privacy offers opportunities to maintain or attain more intense personal relationships between members of a primary group. Privacy limits and protects communication, enabling individuals to share confidential information with those they trust and providing a means of temporarily cutting off communication with outsiders. Privacy encourages group cohesion and some boundary maintenance between groups.

Ultimately, privacy affords freedom (Westin, 1967). The extent of privacy provided by a particular setting affects the individual's ability to choose or avoid group experiences. In this sense, freedom of choice is not only a function of a particular sociopolitical system, but of physical settings as well.

The allocation of space in the household to certain individuals and activities structures contact between family members. Spatial arrangements modify interaction possibilities (Smith, 1971:55–56).

1. Proximity increases the probability of interaction between persons who occupy the same space.

2. The activities of individuals in a given space that are not directed toward eliciting a response from others may necessitate avoidance behavior.

3. Within this space the behavior of others can be heard or seen immediately, and thus it is available for immediate judgment and evaluation.

4. The others present constitute reference groups whether or not their expectations or evaluations are known.

Imagine the tyranny of a house without rooms! This situation existed up until the eighteenth century in European housing. As Hall (1966) suggests, family members simply did not have privacy as we know it today. Privacy then was socially rather than physically structured. This situation is still quite common in British culture, where each member of the household does not typically have a room of his or her own.

> When the American wants to be alone, he depends on architectural features for screening. For an American to refuse to talk to someone else present in the same room . . . is the ultimate form of rejection and a sure sign of great displeasure. The English, on the other hand, lacking rooms of their own since childhood, never developed the practice of using space as a refuge from others. They have in effect internalized a set of barriers, which they erect and which others are supposed to recognize (Hall, 1966:140).

It is of course more difficult to achieve privacy through "internalized barriers." Given the need for privacy, the opportunities for contact and social evaluation are more easily controlled by spatial arrangements: Just as "good fences make good neighbors," good room design makes for pleasant family interaction in a household. In households with limited space, assigning activities and individuals to specific locations is difficult (Smith, 1971). The great concern among the lower and working classes for discipline in the socialization of children (Bronfenbrenner, 1958) may be a function of the lack of spatial controls over behavior.

Individual Distance and Crowding

The right to privacy and the right to a minimum amount of space to carry out social activity are obviously related. Privacy is much more difficult to achieve in small spaces. We have just argued that minimum levels of privacy are necessary for self-development, emotional health, and group cohesion. Are there, likewise, minimum individual distance requirements necessary for the healthy functioning of the individual and the group?

Hall's (1966) work in proxemics provides convincing evidence that there is no absolute density requirement for *Homo sapiens* (see Chapter 2). The optimal density for social behavior varies from one social situation and from one subculture to the next. This is not to say that crowding has an insignificant effect on social behavior, but that its effects on social behavior are complex. High densities are not a sufficient condition for crowding. Crowding is not a physical concept, but rather an emotional state—a feeling. It is therefore conditioned by both the physical and social setting as well as by the social and psychological characteristics of the individuals within that setting.

Most social scientists have, in the past, viewed high densities as unnatural (Freedman, 1975)—as conflicting with the basic biological needs of the species. This biological approach to density has directed us to search for the pathologies generated by overcrowding (Baldassare, 1976). A number of studies have linked high densities to the incidence of such human pathologies as psychoses, delinquency, communication disorders, and deficient maternal care (Gruenberg, 1954; Chombard de Lauwe and Chombard de Lauwe, 1959; Galle et al., 1972; Bernstein, 1968). But a great deal of contradictory evidence has also been amassed. Winsborough (1965), Gillis (1973), Mitchell (1971), Carnahan et al. (1974), Freedman (1975), Booth and Edwards (1976), and Baldassare (1976) have generally found only weak relationships between density and various forms of social pathology. Once socioeconomic factors are controlled, most of the density effects disappear (Winsborough, 1965). Findings such as these led Carnahan et al. to conclude that "if crowding was ever a major source of pathological behavior, it may now be of only minor import" (1974:14).

There are a number of reasons, both conceptual and methodological, for this confusing state of affairs.

1. Past work has overemphasized biological approaches to the density-behavior relationship at the expense of sociological theory.

2. Density (the physical state) has been confused with crowding (the socioemotional state).

3. Much of the past work has focused on the effects of density on the behavioral statistics of areas. Thus individual responses have often been ignored.

4. Density has been measured in a variety of ways, leading to a variety of conclusions.

Let us review each of these points in turn.

Ethologists in general have stressed the notion that high densities are unnatural and that they conflict with the territorial requirements of most vertebrate species. The evidence from human social evolution disagrees with this conception. Throughout human prehistory and history, the natural tendency for the species has been to live in fairly large groups. Even under the relatively limited technologies of the hunters and gatherers, men and women resided in compact communities although foraging areas were wide. High densities must, at least to a degree, be desirable. Increased density is necessary for a complex division of labor—societies with high densities offer a greater variety of occupational choice and a greater diversity of activity (Durkheim, 1947). This is not to say that density does not produce costs as well, but a certain minimum level of density is actually desirable (Winsborough, 1965).

Is the human species unusual in this respect? A careful review of the ethological literature suggests that the findings are not as clear-cut as Calhoun's rat experiments (see Chapter 2) might indicate (Freedman, 1975). First of all, each species, and even each strain of laboratory animals, responds to density differently. Some rats, for example, do not develop the behavioral sink observed by Calhoun. In addition, there is evidence that the pathological reaction of mice and rats to crowding may be confounded by the population size of the caged group (Freedman, 1975). Work since Calhoun's shows that the amount of cage space per animal is less crucial to subsequent behavior than the number of caged animals. Increased adrenal activity, a physiological indication of stress, results primarily from having to react to a large number of animals—that is, it is due to increased social stimulation. Such findings question the individual distance requirements even of rodent populations!

Even if the biological evidence were more clear-cut, however, the impact of density on behavior must be put in social and cultural context. Since Simmel (1905), sociologists have addressed the issue of population density. Simmel saw high densities as producing excessive "nervous stimulation." Milgram (1972) resurrected this argument and placed it in the context of systems theory. According to Milgram, high densities produce a situation of stimulus overload in which the receptor simply cannot process information fast enough. Overload, however, does not automatically produce pathology. Rather, the individual can adjust to this potentially difficult situation by blocking certain inputs and by altering his or her social relationships. In other words, we can adapt to stressful events by adjusting the social structure.

Stokols (1972) provides perhaps the most sophisticated understanding of crowding's effects in his *equilibrium model of crowding*. The model implies, and subsequent empirical research has confirmed, that crowding does not always produce negative consequences. Since crowding is ultimately an individual state, the factors that influence the image and response to crowding include not only the qualities of the physical and social environment, but also the personal attributes of individuals (Stokols, 1972). The aspects of the physical environment Stokols views as important are the amount of space and its arrangement, as well as the stressors (such as noise, lighting, etc.) that affect the salience of the immediate environment. The social environment involves the characteristics of the group occupying the space (Stokols lists the role structure, stratification system, and group size as being especially important. We might also include factors such as group norms and the quality and frequency of interactions). Finally, the crucial personal attributes of the individual include current physiological states (hunger, fatigue, etc.), individual skills and weaknesses in environmental competence (intelligence, agility, etc.), and personality traits (inner- versus other-directed, achievement motivation, etc.).

These environmental and personal factors combine to produce a particular experience and response to the environment. The model is outlined in Figure 10.1. As the figure shows, crowding initially produces *cognitive inconsistency*, which may be defined as the individual's recognition of the inconsistency between the availability of space and his or her own space requirements. The recognized disparity between supply and demand necessitates certain adjustments (Heider, 1958), which may take one of several forms. The individual may alter the environment by leaving it or by withdrawing from social interaction. Since it is unlikely that an individual can change the basic social and psychological attributes of the environment, the individual often changes his or her definition of it. The theory of *cognitive dissonance* (Festinger, 1957) addresses this condition, suggesting that the original dissonance between the discomforts of

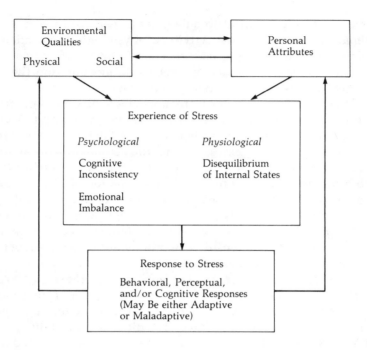

Figure 10.1 *Stokol's Equilibrium Model of Human Response to Crowding* Crowding is not a simple stressor. Therefore, response to the stress of perceived high density varies. Responses may occur at a number of levels, and they may be adaptive or maladaptive. (*Source:* Adapted from D. Stokols, "A Social Psychological Model of Human Phenomena," 1972. Reprinted by permission of the Journal of the American Planning Association, Chicago, IL.)

crowding and the decision to remain in the environment will be reduced by increasing the desirability of remaining and decreasing the desirability of leaving. In essence, human response to crowding is far from simple, and in many cases not pathological.

As complicated as our reaction to the "madding crowd" may be, research on the subject has been further confused by the great variety of methodologies and statistics for assessing the crowding response. Human research has consisted of statistical studies of group responses to neighborhood crowding, individual responses to high neighborhood and household densities and experimental studies of laboratory responses to space limitations. Crowding has been measured in various ways: number of persons per unit of land (gross density), number of households per unit of land (neighborhood density), average number of rooms per person within a household (household density), and the individual's perception of either neighborhood or household density. Given this array of methods and statistics, it is hardly surprising that current research provides contradictory evidence.

Despite these problems we can say certain things about the individual's response to crowding. Studies of household and neighborhood crowding suggest that in many cases high densities have only limited behavioral consequence. Mitchell's (1971) data on Hong Kong provide striking evidence of this fact. The citizens of this area live under extremely crowded conditions. For example, nearly 30 percent of Mitchell's sample reported sleeping three or more to a bed, yet only general measures of strain (unhappiness and worry) show any relationship to density when the socioeconomic status of the family is controlled. That is, more specific measures of stress (psychosomatic symptoms and behavioral impairments like mental illness, depression, and withdrawal) are unaffected by the household's density. Clearly the residents of Hong Kong do not suffer the severe pathologies encountered among Calhoun's caged rats, yet no urban laboratory comes closer to the experimental conditions imposed by Calhoun.

While high densities do not usually produce stress, evidence suggests that those people who do exhibit some degree of mental strain are more affected by objective and subjective density (Booth, 1976). To use Lawton's (1973) phrase, these people are environmentally docile—that is, they cannot adequately adjust to the cognitive inconsistency produced by high density.

Since most people can adapt to crowded conditions, pathological effects are unlikely. Nevertheless, high densities do require adjustments, and thus limited space should have some behavioral impact. Within the home, crowding appears to have its greatest impact on parent-child relationships. In Hong Kong, high densities forced children into the streets and away from the surveillance of their parents, creating a potentially unhealthy street environment (Mitchell, 1971). In an American study (Booth, 1976), household crowding increased the use of physical punishment by parents.

It is noteworthy that density has no effects on marital relationships (Booth, 1976). After class factors are controlled, partners living under crowded conditions are just as likely to be happy in their marriage as those living under low densities. As Milgram and Stokols suggest, individuals can adjust to crowding, in many cases by imposing an already agreed upon social order on a potentially stressful situation. In all societies age stratification is a basic mechanism of social order. Apparently under high-density situations such stratification is exaggerated to maintain order, as is suggested by Booth's finding that crowding increases the frequency of parents' use of punishment.

This intensification of already existing roles and relationships is apparent in several other contexts. High neighborhood densities encourage selective social withdrawal. Given a situation of abundant social relationships (high neighborhood densities), people reduce casual encounters such as neighboring and spend more energy on friendships (Baldassare, 1976). Primary relationships become more primary and secondary ones more secondary.

Under laboratory conditions, subjects tend to intensify their "typical" reaction to the setting. Using a competitive game in both crowded and uncrowded rooms, Freedman (1975) finds that women are less competitive in the smaller

room, while men are more competitive. Similarly, in a simulated jury delibera-
tion, women give less severe sentences while men give more severe ones in the
smaller room. The differences between men and women in these settings is a
function of traditional sex roles—women are supposed to be less aggressive
and competitive than men (Freedman, 1975). Crowded conditions exaggerate
such roles. Freedman refers to this explanation as the *density-intensity hypothesis.*
The findings of Baldassare, Booth, and Mitchell support this thesis. Although
density does not usually produce pathological behavior, it intensifies socially
established role relationships. Under some circumstances this behavior can be
maladaptive for both the individual group and the larger society.

Access to Social Interaction

As we have seen in our discussion of privacy and individual distance requirements, the environment can provide too much stimulation. At the same
time the human species requires a certain amount of social interaction to maintain social and psychological well-being. *Homo sapiens* is by nature gregar-
ious—the human individual is an especially dependent creature. Because of
our tremendous intellectual capacity we are anatomically doomed to a prema-
ture birth. That is, our heads are so large that the birth canal could not serve as
a passageway for a fully developed human being. No other mammal is born so
dependent on others. This dependency, to a degree, fades with the development of spatial mobility and language, but our early encounter with the human
primary group and our socialization into a particular human culture make us
social creatures. Such dependency is perhaps most apparent in modern man
and woman, for the modern social creature is born of a technology and social
structure that promotes minute specialization of task and thus heightened in-
terdependencies. These dependencies, however, are typical of all human societies.

We require contact with others; thus, we can discuss an optimal level of environmental stimulation. While too much stimulation is potentially stressful,
so is too little. There is a U-shaped relation between the social environment
and human behavior. Designers must build environments that minimize over-
stimulation, yet they must at the same time provide opportunities for social interaction.

The design of interior spaces within the household limits the number of
contacts we have with family members. The site plan (the location of buildings
in relation to their own external spaces, to other buildings and the larger community) influences our contacts with other members of the community. We
have already discussed the interior design and its influence on privacy and individual distance. Now let us turn to the site plan and its impact on social relations.

Site planning allows the urban designer to manipulate both the physical
and the functional distance between people in a neighborhood. Festinger et al.

(1950), for instance, show how engineered proximity affects social networks and interaction patterns. The researchers asked students in seventeen low-rise dormitories to identify their friends and to say whom they saw most often socially. The findings of the study were (1) friends were likely to be physically close to one another; rarely did friendship choices include people separated by more than four houses; (2) friendship choices that included people from different floors were more likely between people in apartments closest to the stairways; (3) people at the bottom and top of a stairway were more likely to choose each other as friends than they were to choose others on the same floor. Essentially, the study suggests that physical nearness per se plays less of a role in forming ties than features of building design. This type of engineered proximity is referred to as *functional distance*.

Kuper's (1953) study of a socially heterogeneous Coventry housing estate tries to further distinguish *sociofugal* (spaces that bring people together) from *sociopetal* spaces (those that separate people). In this study, side neighbors were more likely to become friends than front neighbors, because the front of the house was not regarded as living space.

The importance of socially defined living spaces (or interaction spaces) is stressed in a variety of research contexts. There is variation between social areas in the definition of just what constitutes an appropriate space for interaction. In the suburbs the front lawn receives a great deal of attention from homeowners, and thus it serves as an arena for neighborly interaction (Whyte, 1956). This behavior pattern tends to encourage friendships along and across the street rather than the backyard, which is viewed by the American middle class as a private living area. Whyte describes the social structure of the suburb as a filiarchy—that is, children rather than adults form the basic social ties. Children's play groups get translated into mother's kaffeeklatches which in turn may influence father's friendship patterns. Driveways often serve as play areas for young children, especially those capable of riding tricycles, big wheels, and such. These form ideal areas for watching children and for gossiping with other mothers. Therefore, adult friendships are most likely between neighbors with adjoining driveways.

Cooper's (1975) study of a low-income housing project (Easter Hill Village) in Richmond, California finds the sociofugal spaces there to be somewhat different from those of the suburbs. Because homes are not individually owned and because there are common rather than private driveways, neighbor contacts tend to be enhanced by the placement of commonly shared spaces. Here casual neighboring is facilitated if a group of neighbors share a common pedestrian open space that is traversed on the way to parking lots, play areas, laundry facilities, and so forth.

Functional distance is important in forming social interaction. But a great deal of research suggests that a variety of variables intervene in the relationship between engineered distance and friendship patterns (Keller, 1968). Time is one such variable. Gans (1961) suggests that proximity is important in initiating social ties, but that maintaining such ties over an extended period is a function of neighborhood characteristics rather than physical or functional distance. Time wears away at the distance effect.

Planners can manipulate space to guarantee contact. They cannot, however, produce lasting friendships nor an atmosphere of community through such design features. According to Gans, such social networks are a function of neighborhood homogeneity and the ability of the individual to move about in space. Propinquity brings people together, but social similarity makes these contacts positive and worth sustaining. Perceived social distance is more critical than physical distance. In this light Gans (1967) suggests that Festinger's findings hold true only for homogeneous communities (similar in life cycle and class status).

Gans's argument, however, rests solely on observational data from a single community. Athanasiou and Yoshioka (1973) analyze friendship patterns more systematically. Their research contradicts Gans's simple statement that homogeneity is necessary to maintain a relationship between propinquity and friendship. Distance is important in both friendship formation and maintenance, even among those who have nothing else in common but a similar stage in the life cycle. In their study propinquity was more significant than class in predicting friendship patterns. This suggests that socioeconomic homogeneity is not an intervening factor in creating and maintaining social networks. Life cycle similarity, however, appears to be crucial to the distance-friendship pattern.

In addition to life cycle similarity, propinquity influences friendships more often among the spatially impaired. The housewife, the elderly, the poor, the adolescent are more likely to have their social networks engineered by maneuvering functional distance than more spatially mobile groups.

Within certain limitations then, the architect and the planner can wield great influence over our social lives. In one sense this role is somewhat antidemocratic in character. We do not elect our architects, nor do they have very clear-cut constituencies to which they must answer (Gans, 1978). In the right hands, however, these activities can be used to redress injustices that are difficult to change voluntarily. Perhaps the most obvious example of this social engineering capacity revolves around the American government's attempts to modify racial prejudice during the 1960s and 1970s. The government's stress on residential desegregation was greatly influenced by several decades of research on the impact of equal-status interracial contacts on racial tolerance (Deutsch and Collins, 1951; Wilner et al., 1955; Fishman, 1961; Greenfield, 1961). This research has led to the development of the *contact hypothesis*. In simplest terms the thesis suggests that "attitudes shape themselves to behavior" (Ford, 1973:1427). What we think and feel about those of another racial group is a function of how much contact we have had with equal-status members of this group.

Deutsch and Collins's (1951) study of interracial housing was perhaps the first attempt to test this thesis systematically. In the study, two low-rent desegregated housing projects in New York were compared with two biracial but segregated projects in Newark. The authors found that integrated housing produced more social contact between the races and more favorable interracial attitudes.

As the results of studies by Festinger et al. (1950) and Athanasiou and Yoshioka (1973) suggest, proximity serves as a catalyst to the formation of friendship groups. To this extent propinquity ensures contact. Unlike Athanasiou and Yoshioka's findings for intraracial ties, however, interracial contacts are positive only if the parties are of equal socioeconomic status.

Ford (1973) suggests an additional qualification of the propinquity relationship. He found that black housewives reacted to contact differently than their white counterparts. Interracial contact for black women had no bearing on racial attitudes. This difference may be a function of the fact that blacks have learned to suspect any relationships with whites. For this reason racially engineered housing may substantially reduce majority prejudices, but have no bearing on minority attitudes. Changes in these attitudes may come about more slowly and reflect the changing life experiences of generations of black adults. Nevertheless, spatial engineering can, to a degree, change the very fabric of society.

Safe and Defensible Spaces

The home provides a sense of identification and personal security. Maslow (1954) argues that the need for security is basic, ranking just below physiological needs such as hunger and thirst. Since basic needs must be satisfied by the organism, we must feel safe and secure in our home spaces if we are ever to attain higher needs such as affiliation (love, group membership), esteem (personal satisfaction), actualization (achievement), and learning. Without such security we will most likely become socially isolated and lose contact with the institutions capable of satisfying higher goals.

Within societies, systems of stratification control access to the resources necessary to satisfy this hierarchy of needs. As a result, certain individuals at the lower end of the class stratum cannot even satisfy the basic requirements of nourishment, health, and security. Because of this, security is usually defined by the lower classes as a paramount requirement in housing, whereas for the middle and upper classes it is taken for granted (Rainwater, 1966; Suttles, 1968). Unquestionably, the lower-class home space is inherently more dangerous. In many cases housing is structurally unsound and hazardous. Poor neighborhoods are also less safe, with more street traffic, higher crime rates, and dirtier air.

If those in control expect the lower classes to be productive social beings— "hard workers of sound moral character"—Maslow's thesis implies that lower-class residential areas must be made more secure. For those unable to attain security, achieving affiliation, esteem, actualization, and cognitive skills will become even more difficult. This lack of security may produce overwhelming fear or exaggerated aggressive stances.

C. R. Jeffrey (1971) and Oscar Newman (1973) argue that security can be attained through better design of public housing. A *defensible space* is an area that has clearly defined rights of possession. It is secure because it appears to belong to someone. Space can be made defensible by making projects smaller, with low-rise structures; "by grouping dwelling units to reinforce associations of mutual benefit; by delineating paths of movement; by defining areas of activity for particular users through their juxtaposition with internal living areas; and by providing for natural opportunities for visual surveillance, architects can create a clear understanding of the function of a space, and who its users are and ought to be" (Newman, 1973:325).

Pruitt-Igoe, a high-rise public housing project built in St. Louis in the 1950s, represents an example of an indefensible home space. Absent from the design plans of this project is what the economy-minded architect considers wasted space—space within the building that can be used for meeting others and for play.

> In lower- and working-class slums, the littered and often trash-filled alleys, streets, and backyards provide the ecological basis around which informal networks of friends and relatives may develop. Without such semipublic space and facilities, the development of such networks is retarded; the resulting atomization of the community can be seen in the frequent and escalating conflict between neighbors, fears of and vulnerability to the human dangers in the environment, and, finally, withdrawal to the last line of defense—into the single family dwelling unit (Yancey, 1971:17).

Yancey's quotation sounds much like the script of a war correspondent reporting from the front lines. Indeed, areas such as Pruitt-Igoe and the Bronx resemble the battle-scarred cities of Europe during World War II.

In a somewhat similar vein, Newman compares two housing projects in New York and shows how spaces can be designed to be either secure or insecure (see Figure 10.2). The Van Dyke project is composed primarily of fourteen-story structures located around a great deal of open space, whereas Brownsville is comprised of three- and six-story structures that cover a greater percentage of the available land. At Brownsville entrances are directly off the street, whereas at Van Dyke tenants are forced to walk along blind interior pathways to get to their residences. Exterior spaces are thus more easily watched at Brownsville. This ease of surveillance carries over into the interior spaces of the project. Apartment doors are clustered around open stairwells, and each grouping of three apartments shares an open space for play. Such is not the case at the Van Dyke project, where the elevator is located at the middle of the hall and where hallways are small and meant solely for access to the apartment. Although the projects are located next to one another, total reported crimes at the Van Dyke project were 66 percent higher than at Brownsville.

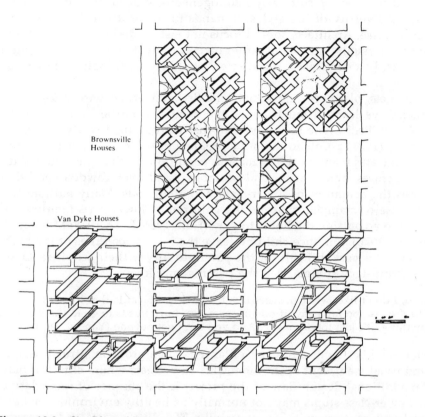

Brownsville
Houses

Van Dyke Houses

Figure 10.2 *Site Plan of Brownsville and Van Dyke Houses*   The high-rise structures and vast amounts of open space at the Van Dyke project made surveillance and defensibility difficult. Brownsville housing, on the other hand was low rise, with moderate amounts of secondary territory. Spaces there were more defensible. The differences in design between the two projects produced great differences in deviance in the two areas. (*Source:* From *Defensible Space* by Oscar Newman. Copyright © 1972 by Oscar Newman. Used with permission of Macmillan Publishing Company, New York, NY.)

In essence, design can encourage contact, both desirable and undesirable. A secure environment enhances surveillance, for surveillance gives its occupants a sense of control over their primary and secondary territories.

Experiential Congruence — Culture's Modification of Universal Requirements

The universal requirements of a population for certain levels of privacy, density, social interaction, and security are modified by culturally defined

goals. Urban society is culturally heterogeneous; indeed, the city is characterized by its diversity of life styles. It stands to reason then that urban design
must be diverse. Architects should focus not just on designing for a set of universal spatial requirements, but rather on culturally defined subsets of these requirements. In many cases, social scientists have yet to define these requirements.

Architects, planners, and social scientists concerned with a user-oriented
approach have learned much about experiential congruence from their mistakes. Again, Pruitt-Igoe has proved an instructive, albeit costly, error.

Yancey (1971) points to the basic problem of the project design. While the
project alleviates many of the hazardous conditions of the slum, such as dilapidated structures, poor wiring and plumbing, and overcrowded conditions, it
also loses the amenities of lower-class neighborhoods. Many authors suggest
that because of cramped quarters the children of lower-class families are encouraged to go outside the home to play (Hall, 1966; Kerr, 1958; Mitchell, 1971;
Michelson, 1976). But once children leave the interior confines of the high-rise
apartment, it is very difficult for the parent to survey their activities. One resident of Pruitt-Igoe summarized the parents' problem:

> Well, I don't like being upstairs like this. The problem is that I can't see the kids.
> They're just too far away. If one of them gets hurt, needs to go to the bathroom or
> anything, it's just too far away. And you can't get outside (Yancey, 1971:12).

In older neighborhoods adult surveillance is not a problem. Structures are low
rise and usually adjacent to the sidewalks and streets where children play.

An additional design flaw of the project is the absence of secondary territories. Lower-class slums may not normally be healthy environments, but they
are vital and bristling with social activity. The dirty streets and littered back
alleys provide space where informal social networks may flourish. Such semi-
private spaces were not available in the high rise, in which hallways were designed for access to the home only. This lack of secondary spaces hindered the
formation of a sense of community. It is no wonder then that the project's most
famous resident was the prize fighter Leon Spinks.

A clear sense of alienation and anomie settled deep into the community's
fiber and created a disorderly environment. Here propinquity had no impact
on neighborhood relationships, for there were no spaces within which to be
neighborly. This design was clearly unsuited for people with families and with
limited spatial mobility. The atomistic nature of the project was further enhanced by its physical removal from the stores and services necessary to sustain
community.

Clare Cooper (1975) provides a series of recommendations to avoid past
mistakes in designing public housing.

1. Primary, secondary, and tertiary territories should be clearly delineated
   so that there is no question of who has access to and control over spaces.

A stronger feeling of community will develop if access to the site by outsiders is discouraged.

2. Families with young children place great emphasis on a safe residential environment (limited traffic flow and reasonable adult control over child's play). Ideally the housing should consist of a low-rise structure that overlooks a common open space for preschool play activities.

3. There must be a balance struck between the need for social interaction and the need for privacy. Dwellings should not be arranged so as to either maximize or minimize contact. Reasonable levels of contact tend to be encouraged by grouping dwellings or apartments around a common pedestrian open space or other shared space.

4. Some degree of homogeneity (especially life cycle similarity) is desirable if a sense of community is to develop.

5. Security is enhanced when entrances to individual dwellings are potentially under continuous surveillance by the area's residents.

6. Where relatively less mobile population groups constitute a large portion of the residential population, on-site community facilities and services should be provided.

7. Every large housing project should provide a variety of dwelling sizes so that families can move within the project as their space needs change.

The findings from social area analysis and factorial ecology should provide a framework for designing experientially congruent environments. Thresholds of residential satisfaction are a function of life cycle, class and ethnic statuses, as well as life style aspirations (Chapter 7). Different combinations of these factors produce different environmental requirements. Much observational and survey research must be done before such requirements can be established. (Michelson, 1976, provides a tentative list of current knowledge in this area.)

If we were to design strictly for mental congruence, ignoring information on behaviors within spaces and concentrating only on what people say they want, a user-oriented system could be established before such research is complete. Yona Freedman (1975) suggests such a program, arguing that users should be allowed to design their own environments. In such a system the responsibility of the architect should be to establish the repertoire of factors the user will eventually work from. Once such a framework is established, the user can choose from a variety of combinations of furniture and equipment, floor plans, and community plans. A particular structure can be arrived at through consultation with a computer that stores all possible solutions and the consequences of each choice. Freedman's proposal is intriguing although the sheer complexities of such a combination of design elements may overwhelm the average user. Also, in a system such as ours in which the ability to pay is a primary determinant of spatial usage, such a revolutionary program is unlikely. It is, for example, extremely doubtful that public housing can be affordable unless user choice is severely constrained.

SUMMARY

Architects have great influence over our everyday lives. This influence, however, is not straightforward. Behavior settings are not simply physical settings; they are governed by social definition. Well-designed environments are spaces that are congruent with the expectations and the behaviors of the actors using these behavioral arenas. Until quite recently architects did not design interior and exterior spaces with these requirements in mind. Historically their role has been client-oriented and esthetic in nature.

Sound planning must address basic questions of human nature and subcultural needs. The environmental psychology literature suggests four basic requirements: the need for privacy, the related demand for personal space, the need for easy access to interaction, and the right to secure spaces. These requirements are complicated and modified by culturally defined goals. Some life styles emphasize certain needs while downplaying others. Research in factorial ecology suggests that designing for these life-style–modified needs is complex. We cannot simply design homes for the middle class or the poor, for within each social class people may hold a variety of values. Housing design is a costly and complex endeavor.

Chapter 11

Inner City, Outer City:
The Results of Segregated Settings

INTRODUCTION

Now we turn to consider what Wirth (1938) termed the urban mosaic. Unlike the built environment, the urban mosaic results from a complex intertwining of decisions originating from a variety of institutional spheres; hence it is an unintentional environment. Despite its unintended character, the urban mosaic structures the city experience in a variety of ways. The social and moral consequences of these segregated social worlds are the subject matter of this chapter. Our concern with the sociology of place leads to an interest in the macrospace at two levels: the neighborhood and the larger metropolitan community of which it is a part.

The chapter is divided into four broad sections. The first addresses the issue of the neighborhood unit as a social reality. While some writers have claimed to witness the demise of the urban neighborhood, this local territory is far from dead. Indeed, neighborhood context has a significant impact on the content of behavior. These segregated local units are social areas with distinctive life styles and rates of social participation.

At the level of the metropolitan community, the significance of neighborhood segregation patterns appears to be further bolstered by an even more clear-cut division between the inner city (or, more properly, the central city) and the outer city (the suburbs). Data from recent censuses indicate significant differences in the demography of these two places. Cities are generally composed of an older population, with fewer children, more minorities, and more blue-collar and clerical workers. As a result the central city has been variously characterized as a "geriatric ghetto" (Clark, 1971), a "chocolate city with vanilla suburbs" (Farley et al., 1976), and an "unheavenly city" in which skills do not adequately match employment opportunities (Banfield, 1974). The consequences of these population differences are addressed in the next two sections. The second section deals with the social implications of suburbanization. Special attention is given to the white flight phenomenon and its effects on socioeconomic achievement and social contact. The third section details the impact of suburbanization on the operation of urban services. As you might expect, the consequences have been anything but positive. The final section of the chapter reviews the governmental policies that have fueled the fires of suburbanization and indicates the inadequacies of past and current urban policies. It details the "hidden agenda" that have been at the base of such efforts and suggests the dangers of simple solutions to the problem of urban housing and social justice.

THE NEIGHBORHOOD AS A SOCIAL REALITY

The city can be described as a mosaic of social worlds, an area of great diversity characterized by an equally intensive pattern of residential segregation. This pattern of segregation by area or neighborhood is the basis for the urban order (see Chapter 3). Segregation allows for Gemeinschaft-like relations in an environment that is diverse and prone to estrangement. In order for space to structure social relations in this manner, however, the neighborhood must be a viable social unit rather than a figment of the social theorist's imagination. Is the neighborhood unit a social reality in the contemporary city? Such a question demands investigation of the neighbor role and the neighborhood in urban-industrial society.

The neighbor in the contemporary city is a proximate stranger—spatially close, but not necessarily socially or psychologically close. The neighbor is usually neither relative nor intimate friend. While friend is a chosen status, neighbor is not. Keller (1968:25) suggests the major differences between these two social roles:

1. While proximity is significant for creating and maintaining the neighbor role, it is much less so for the friend role.

2. The neighbor relation is collectively defined and thus has wider social implications than does friendship, which generally involves more intimate and personal concerns.

3. The degree of intimacy of the partners varies; to be a good neighbor is not to be a good friend.

Through history the neighborhood has functioned as a place for exchange and mutual aid, providing for both psychological and material needs. At the same time it has been a locus for the exercise of reciprocal social control and the quick dissemination of information, and thus has been a major force in creating and maintaining social standards. Industrialization profoundly changed this state of affairs. Neighboring declined in the industrial stage for a variety of reasons (Keller, 1968:58).

1. Most obvious is the increased mobility permitted by transportation improvements. The change in mobility multiplied the activity spaces of community members and permitted social networks to expand spatially beyond the bounds of the neighborhood.

2. With the growth of the mass media and general improvements in communication networks, the sources of information and opinion multiplied. As a result the degree of social control exercised by the neighborhood declined.

3. The increasing division of labor led to more differentiated interests and work rhythms, lowering the inclination to neighbor unselectively.

4. The growth of formally organized social services and the increase in economic security limited the likelihood of unattended social or economic crises.

5. The change from extended to nuclear families produced a family unit whose needs were less localized and more capable of being met by alternative institutions.

The result was a shift from a "neighboring of place to a neighboring of taste" (Keller, 1968:58).

All of this fits well with the social evolution typologies of Tönnies and Durkheim and the urbanism thesis of Wirth (see Chapter 3). This perspective, sometimes labeled the *urbanism tradition*, argues that the changes produced by industrialization caused close community ties to be replaced by more secondary ties in the city. In reaction to this, numerous *community researchers* have provided evidence of the continued viability of such ties within specific local areas (Suttles, 1972; Gans, 1962a; Reiss, 1955). These studies, however, require some clarification. Current work in an area of sociology termed *network analysis* provides such qualification. Instead of focusing on relationships within a bounded local area such as the neighborhood (community research), network analysis focuses on the social linkages themselves. While community research can address such questions as the intensity and extent of neighborhood ties, it can say nothing about the metropoliswide organization of social linkages. Such studies assume, a priori, that a major portion of an urbanite's social relationships are organized by locality (Wellman, 1976). Network analysis allows one to test this assumption.

Barry Wellman's study of social ties in an ethnically diverse suburb of Toronto (1976, 1979) provides the opportunity for such a test. With regard to neighboring he found that, on average:

1. Urbanites maintain at least three neighboring ties.

2. These ties are usually less intimate than other primary relationships, although typically at least one out of six intimate linkages are with neighbors.

3. Most intimate ties are with nonlocal people.

4. Locally based ties are maintained primarily for purposes of nonintimate or easy sociability and for quick access to routine material goods (borrowing) (1976:16).

Neighboring is clearly not a thing of the past (only 18 percent of the sample said that they could not call on neighbors for help in an emergency), but neighboring is usually a weak rather than intimate tie. Weak ties, however, play an important role in the individual urbanite's life (Granovetter, 1973). Intimate links tend to be with socially similar others; as a result, the secondary linkages such intimate friends provide are extremely limited. Such cliques do not yield access to the diverse others present in the urban space. Granovetter (1973), in a reanalysis of Gans's data on the Boston West Ender, argued that the inability of the West Ender to alter urban renewal plans in the area resulted from the ethnic culture's emphasis on cliques. The absence of weak ties left the neighborhood socially and politically fragmented, unable to prevent the bulldozing of their homes. Because one's neighbors are usually more socially diverse than the people with whom one is intimate, neighborhood ties are important in gaining access to a wider range of social circles and situations than are available through strong ties. Neighboring, then, is still of great social significance although it is generally not an intimate tie.

Most intimate links are maintained within the metropolitan area, but are not local. Location, nevertheless, still constrains intimate ties. Strong ties exhibit a gradient effect, with ties falling off as distance increases (Wellman, 1976; Fischer and Jackson, 1976). Also intimate social networks tend to be confined to sectors of the city (Johnston, 1972). The spatial form of these patterns of contacts has been studied under the headings of acquaintance fields and contact fields. The former describe the pattern of acquaintances named by respondents in an interview context. The latter portray the actual social contacts observed during a sample period (Moore and Brown, 1970).

It is apparent that the "community without propinquity" (where distance costs do not significantly affect behavior) envisaged by Melvin Webber (1970) is nonexistent. At the same time it is also apparent that social linkages are less constrained by space than ever before. Intimate linkages are more likely now to be organized into spatially dispersed networks. In turn these intimate linkages have acquired many of the mutual-aid functions formerly localized in the neighborhood. Wellman (1976), for example, finds that the strongest predictor of help in both everyday and emergency situations is the strength of the intimate bond.

THE SOCIAL
IMPLICATIONS OF SPATIAL STRUCTURE

Although intimate relations are less constrained spatially than in the cities of previous civilizations, spatial structures continue to affect the urban experience. The neighborhood still functions as the basic socio-spatial unit of the city. As we have suggested earlier, these homogeneous, miniature social worlds allow order in the presence of diversity and strangeness. In this sense, segrega-

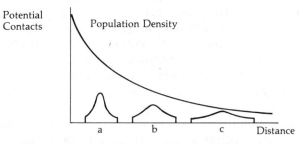

A.   *The Effect of Varying Population Density on the Spatial Form of Acquaintance Fields for Households*

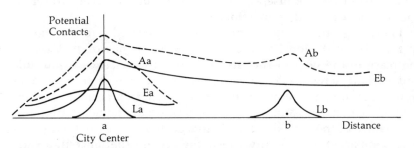

B.   *Local and Extensive Components of Contact Fields*

Figure 11.1   *The Effects of Density Distributions on Contact and Acquaintance Fields*
Geographic studies of the effects of density on potential and actual social ties indicate systematic variation in the opportunities for social contact. In A the fields centered at points a, b, and c in the metropolitan area all contain the same number of social contacts, but social ties are more localized as distance from the center decreases. Since there are class, sex, and age differences in mobility, some of these contact fields are even further localized. In B, the social contact field is broken into neighboring and friendship components, yielding a bimodal form for the general contact field. L stands for local, the neighboring component; E, for extensive, the friendship component; and A, for the aggregate field. A centrally located household is indicated by a, and a suburban household by b. (*Source:* Adapted from ideas in Moore and Brown, 1970:449.)

tion is functional for the urban system. But what are the consequences of the urban mosaic for the urbanite and for specific segments of the urban population?

In Chapter 6, we discussed the implications of spatial structure for human cognition and the creation of urban images. These influences are subtle. There are, however, more obvious social consequences of the unintended environment. Space structures or bounds the social landscape of the city. This structure is significant to the urban experience if spatial boundaries, both real and imagined, are capable of isolating and disrupting the flow of communication and resources between areas.

Studies in factorial ecology clearly suggest that neighborhoods are segregated along a series of life style dimensions. If social groups are spatially bounded in the city, then social networks are, at least to a degree, spatially bounded as well. Socially homogeneous individuals in close proximity to one another are likely to develop social ties (Athanasiou and Yoshioka, 1973; Festinger et al., 1950). At the same time, segregation isolates these individuals from the "world of strangers" and produces a real variation in normative structures and socialization.

Additionally, because neighborhood densities are distributed in an orderly fashion, the opportunities for social contact vary systematically in the city. Geographic work suggests the importance of population density for the territorial scope of social contacts. In areas of low population density the spatial range of contacts are more extensive because an individual needs to travel farther to make the same number of social connections (see Figure 11.1).

From the knowledge that neighborhoods are segregated and that social contacts vary spatially with density, you might expect behavior patterns to vary from one place to the next in the city. The urban experience is multidimensional and variant across social areas. Research to this point has documented spatial variation in a range of behaviors including social participation, deviance and criminality, and educational and occupational attainment. While the exact nature of the spatial determinants of these behaviors has yet to be identified, it is apparent that locality affects the urban experience in a variety of ways.

Social Participation and Neighboring

Perhaps some of the most obvious spatial variations in behavior can be identified by the traditional distinction between the inner city and the outer city. The suburban experience clearly differs from the city experience. Although not all suburbs are identical nor all suburbanites characterized by a stifling sameness (see Kramer, 1972), the suburban community differs basically from the inner-city community in social participation. Social commentators have identified the suburbs as "hotbeds of participation" and "wellsprings of the outgoing life" where the chief feature of life is "compulsive, frenetic, outgoing social life—togetherness, belongingness, Kaffeeklatsches, PTA, back fense gossip confabulations, cocktail parties, carpools, and the 'open door' " (Dobriner, 1963:6). While such stereotypes are clearly exaggerated, a great deal of evidence tends to show that neighboring and other local activities increase with distance from the city center (Fischer and Jackson, 1976).

How can such differences be explained? Gans provides what might be termed an individual explanation: "When one looks at similar populations in the city and suburb, their ways of life are remarkably alike. . . . The crucial difference between cities and suburbs, then, is that they are often home for different kinds of people" (1967:228). While this statement is correct in part, an individual explanation of city-suburb variation is insufficient. Social worlds are the product of each individual's personal associations or networks. These associations are influenced by the individual's social characteristics, as well as the particular social climate of the neighborhood, and the neighborhood's location with regard to potential friendship ties.

A study of localized social networks for a national sample of urbanites and for a sample of Detroit area residents found that when individual characteristics are controlled, social climate and location variables emerge as significant predictors of urban-suburban differences in neighboring (Fischer and Jackson, 1976). Both the extent of neighboring and its intensity (percentage of friends in the neighborhood) are explained in part by the average income of the area, the proportion of young and school-age children, and the distance of the community from the city center. Wealthier, family-centered areas at considerable distance from the center tend to be characterized by a great deal of localized sociability.

Social area analysts have long noted the effects of "social climate" on participation (Bell and Boat, 1957; Bell and Force, 1956; Greer, 1956, 1960; Greer and Kube, 1972; Greer and Orleans, 1962). In his earliest work on this subject, Greer compares the associational patterns of two areas that differ greatly in family status, but that have similar social rank and ethnicity scores. These two areas could not have differed more in their participation styles. Satisfied high-family-status-area residents typically cited the close-knit personal world of the locale as the basis for their satisfaction, while low-family-status residents cited the convenience to downtown and the low profile kept by most neighbors. The commitment to the local social world of the high-family-status area was reflected in the interaction networks of its members. These residents had higher rates of neighboring and more local friendships as well as more secondary local ties (exhibited by extensive participation in locally based voluntary associations and cultural activities). Further comparisons by Bell (1957) of social areas in San Francisco confirm this pattern. These relationships clearly result from social context and not just individual characteristics. While not all the inhabitants of the high-family-status area have sizeable families or women who work primarily as housewives, their participational behavior has more in common with those in the neighborhood than it does with family status equals in other types of neighborhoods (Timms, 1971).

In addition to these social climate effects, location constrains the nature of social relationships (Fischer and Jackson, 1976). In the metropolis portrayed by Clark's Law (see Chapter 5), population densities decrease with increasing distance from the center. Effectively this thesis suggests that the farther away from the center an individual is, the greater also is the distance to other persons in the metropolitan space. Distance limits not only accessibility to the center but also the potential for local interaction. As Figure 11.1 indicates, the suburbanite requires a more extensive contact field than the urbanite to make the same number of contacts. The automobile is crucial for the social travel of the suburbanite. Adolescents, the elderly, ethnic minorities, and housewives are therefore particularly susceptible to suburban ennui or isolation—much more so than their urban counterparts. These persons tend to be members of a captive community, with all its attendant problems of alienation and social isolation. Gans's analysis of the suburb of Levittown suggests that "the smallness and homogeneity of the population made it difficult for the culturally and socially deviant to find companions. Levittown benefited the majority but punished a minority with exclusion . . ." (1967:239).

Deviance and Criminality

Urbanists trained in the traditions of the Chicago School have provided substantial evidence to suggest that the distance gradient can be applied to both the amount and types of deviance found in the metropolitan area. Generally a crime gradient can be observed in the spatial patterns of contemporary industrial cities, with the lowest rates in the suburbs and a peak at the center. The early studies of Chicago juvenile delinquents by Shaw and McKay (1942) found that delinquency and adult criminality showed pronounced spatial variation. Arrest rates tended to concentrate around the central business district and major concentrations of industry. Patterns of delinquency and adult crime were inversely related to distance from the city center. High arrest rates were associated with physical dilapidation, transiency, and population decline. Similar spatial distributions have been found for a variety of cities.

Despite the generality of such findings, criminologists have to this point provided no generally accepted explanation for them. Instead, a series of overlapping hypotheses have been suggested, including the differential association thesis, anomie theory, and the theory of differential opportunity. All of these theses attempt to isolate the organizational conditions of the slum that might produce increased delinquency and adult crime.

The slum represents a way of life as well as a social space. Historically, it has been so successfully hidden from the daily activities of middle-class consumers of the city space as to appear invisible. Indeed, the term *slum* is believed to derive from the word *slumber*, because slums were composed of "unknown, back streets or alleys, wrongly presumed to be sleeping or quiet" (Partridge, 1958). While the contemporary mass media have depicted the slum as anything but quiet, patterns of segregation still permit the great mass of urbanites to avoid such areas on a daily basis. For most, knowledge of the slum is categoric or stereotypic. Nevertheless, the slum is a significant segment of the urban structure. Current estimates suggest that about one-sixth of the urban population resides in slum environments (Clinard, 1974:64). To understand the urban experience it is essential to consider the organization and ways of life in this particular social space.

Much social commentary tends to depict the ghetto as "disorganized" and composed of socially detached peoples, but the ghetto as Whyte (1943), Gans (1962a), Suttles (1968), and Thrasher (1927) all suggest is far from disorganized—its organization is simply of a different type than that found in other communities within the city. While some ghettos may lack unity (see for example Rainwater, 1970, for a description of the Pruitt-Igoe project in St. Louis), this is not a general feature of the slum condition. Indeed, these areas appear to be disorganized only because slum residents may not always subscribe to middle-class standards of conduct (Clinard, 1974).

The slum has a culture all its own. Certain styles of life are typical. Toughness, for example, is considered a virtue, as is tolerance of deviant behavior. Suttles speaks of the Addams area of Chicago:

> First, there is a great deal of concern about illegal activities. . . . Those involved in these activities are few in number, but the residents are anxious to make peace with them or, if possible, to avoid them. . . . The result is a sort of social compact in which respectable residents and those not so respectable are both tolerant and protective of one another.
> A second focus of interest is in each other's trustworthiness, sincerity, or loyalty. . . . They hesitate to reveal too much about themselves, lest they become vulnerable. . . . Trustworthiness, then, is valued far more than some formal appellation that connotes high morals and good character.
> Third, the residents share a number of apprehensions over the exercise of brute force. . . . Leadership, social rank, and associations, however, are partially based on shows of strength which, in turn, lead to some measure of violence and force (1968:232).

The invisible walls of the ghetto that hide it from the "outside" world make its isolation apparent to the insiders. Within the slum this feeling of isolation has led to a generalized suspicion of those who live outside its walls. But the suspicion or uncertainty is directed inward as well. The outsider's stereotypes of the area produce a psychological uncertainty of others sharing the same space. This lack of knowledge of the "ghetto other" requires coping strategies. Several alternatives are available:

1. Individuals may take refuge in ethnic subcultures with which they are already familiar.

2. Individuals may withdraw into a personal world in which linkages are exclusively kin based.

3. Residents may take things into their own hands and establish a personal relationship with previously unknown others.

4. The public stereotypes of the area may afford a certain degree of honor to some. Some may thoroughly embrace one or more of the negative stereotypes and use this role to gain entry into selected social circles (Suttles, 1968:232).

The great variety of social linkages implied in the choice of coping strategies makes for a heterogeneous social milieu. The slum is indeed characterized by its diversity of life styles. Such diversity coupled with the high rates of spatial mobility characteristic of the slum foster normative confusion.

In communities with great normative confusion, many of the standards upheld by children's play groups may be antithetical to those of the parents (Shaw and McKay, 1942). Such normative conflicts make deviance likely. At the same time, delinquency is frequently not so much a function of normative conflict as it is the result of the fact that criminal behavior has become a more or less traditional aspect of social life handed down between generations (Shaw and McKay, 1942). This reasoning summarizes the essential theses of two major schools of thought in deviance theory—anomie theory and differential association theory.

Differential association theory was formulated by Edwin H. Sutherland. Its basic premise is that criminal behavior is learned in intimate personal groups. Crime is a product of socialization. Adolescents become delinquent because of associations with groups that define crime in generally favorable terms. In this theory it is not so much that "birds of a feather flock together," but rather that "birds of a flock become of a feather." Persons become criminal because of an excess of contacts with criminal behavior and also because of isolation from anticriminal patterns. Because communities with high crime rates are spatially separated from those with low rates of deviance, these areas become a fertile training ground for future criminal behavior. Simply put, people become deviant because of contextual factors rather than personal inclinations.

This abstract approach to a sociogenic theory of crime, however, leaves many questions unanswered. Perhaps the most significant of them for a spatial approach to crime is, Just why are certain social spaces conducive to such a climate to begin with? *Anomie theory* addresses this issue. Writing in 1897, Durkheim (1951) felt that anomie, or alienation, is most likely in the industrial urban society, where social disengagement is more possible. A state of normative confusion or normlessness (anomie) may occur, however, in any society where some social disruption such as sudden depression, sudden prosperity, or rapid technological change leads people to aspire to goals that are structurally unattainable.

The contemporary sociologist Robert Merton (1957) sees this situation as potentially criminogenic. Merton distinguishes two basic elements of the social and cultural system: the culturally defined goals we are all expected to strive for, and the social structure that controls the access (or means) to such goals. Contemporary Western civilization produces a situation of conflict between socially structured means and culturally accepted goals—a situation that Merton calls *anomie*. In American society, for example, the school system extols the virtues of success and material achievements, yet the socially acceptable routes to these goals are not accessible to all. Success, as studies of the American stratification system indicate, is a product of educational attainment (Blau and Duncan, 1967). These same studies, however, clearly show that access to the educational system is a function of class position. Poor neighborhoods provide equally poor educational climates.

Merton identifies five strategies of adjustment to this situation of anomie: conformity, innovation, ritualism, retreatism, and rebellion. *Innovation* is of particular interest to the criminologist; it involves a situation in which the individual accepts the culturally defined goals but chooses illegitimate means to achieve them. Highly segregated lower-class communities are likely to have many more of these innovators simply because the legitimate means to achieve such goals are usually out of their members' reach. Thus a criminogenic climate is likely when communities are clearly segregated along class lines (for this will produce a situation with an overbalance of norms favorable to deviance) and when the culture greatly stresses goal attainment while at the same time rigorously restricting legitimate access to such goals.

Cloward and Ohlin (1960) combine anomie theory with the theory of differential association to more precisely explain juvenile delinquency. Their approach is referred to as the *theory of differential opportunities*. Merton's thesis revolves around differential access to legitimate means of achieving cultural goals. Cloward and Ohlin argue that there is also differential access to the illegitimate means as well, and that this differential opportunity plays a large role in the distribution of deviant behavior. The lower-class poor living in slums are by the very nature of their location given greater access to deviant subcultures and institutions such as the fence, the pusher, the adult criminal, the crooked lawyer, and so forth. Depending on the availability of these illegitimate institutions and subcultures, three types of delinquent responses are possible:

1. The *criminal gang* usually involves crimes against property such as theft. This type of delinquent gang occurs in communities in which illegitimate means are easily accessible. In such a community, adult violators act as role models and have close personal ties with juveniles.

2. The *conflict gang* usually centers around violent crime; gang fighting predominates. This form of delinquent behavior is most common in the disorganized, low-status community where land use is changing and populations are highly mobile. In such areas the adolescent is cut off from both legitimate and illegitimate institutions and subcultures, and socialization into deviant roles is not guided by an institutional struc-

ture. Violence is stressed as an avenue of success because it requires no connections with a network of adult criminal institutions.

3. The *retreatist gang* involves juveniles who have failed to attain status in either the criminal or conflict gangs. Faced with failure, they retreat into a drug culture.

This thesis stresses the role of stability in the community space in the genesis of various types of delinquency.

Opportunity theory, however, neglects two significant "opportunity" factors. First, access to opportunities for deviance involves access not only to a deviant subculture but to potential victims as well (Cohen and Felson, 1978). Deviant roles can be analyzed in terms of an illegitimate occupational structure. The location of this illegitimate occupational structure, in turn, can be accounted for in terms of the density-distance relationship in contemporary cities. Victims are most numerous at or near the city center. Thus, a self-selection process operates in which those involved in criminal activity locate toward the center. That is, they tend to concentrate where the opportunity is greatest. Opportunity not only is structured according to density gradients, but also results from the spatial structure of daily activities. Since World War II daily activities have moved away from the home as the employment of women has increased and as leisure has expanded. As a result, the daytime population of many residential areas has decreased, clearly increasing the opportunity for property crimes (Cohen and Felson, 1978).

Additionally, crime involves the interaction between the deviant and some institutionalized authority structure. Essentially, an act is criminal only if those in authority label it as such. Crime in this sense is rooted not so much in the behavior as it is in the social rules and their enforcement. A complete theory of differential opportunity, then, must focus not only on the opportunities for illegitimate activities, but also on the opportunities for their detection by those in authority. Deviance involves two acts: the potentially deviant act itself, and its interpretation as deviant.

Chambliss (1975) suggests that the extensive nature of lower-class crime is the result of a self-fulfilling prophecy. He (1975:167) estimates that as much as 80 percent of the crime effort by law enforcers consists of arresting and processing persons accused of very minor offenses such as drunkenness, vagrancy, streetwalking, and so forth. While no data are available for an accurate comparison, he suggests that the frequency of drunkenness, gambling, and other minor offenses is probably as great in respectable middle-class neighborhoods. The great differences appear to be in spatial usage in the two areas. Most middle-class deviance is privatized, since the middle class is home centered. Privacy, however, is at a premium in the slums, where street activity is intense. Especially in warm weather people move outside and the street becomes everyone's front room. The critical difference, then, is that deviant acts are more visible to law enforcers in the ghetto and thus crime rates are higher.

Clearly the higher rates of deviance found in the inner city result, at least in part, from spatial factors. Because the city is highly segregated by social class, and because social class limits the ability to achieve socially desirable goals, some children are more likely to be exposed to deviant norms and activities than others. At the same time since household crowding is more typical of lower-class residential areas, deviant acts are more likely to be detected in such areas. In this sense the spatial structure of the city makes deviance more probable in certain neighborhoods.

The Implications of Segregation for Attaining Status

The qualities of inner-city and outer-city space differ fundamentally, and these differences have significance for the people living within them. Nowhere is this significance more apparent than in the status attainment process.

A decade ago, the Kerner Commission suggested in no uncertain terms that America was moving toward two separate societies—one black and one white (National Advisory Commission on Civil Disorders, 1969:407). The spatial bounds of these two societies have already become apparent in the urban community—large cities are becoming black, while suburban areas are remaining white (Farley et al., 1976). By 1970, for example, 58 percent of the total black population resided in the central city, while only 28 percent of the white population claimed the central city as its place of residence. This phenomenon is relatively recent. Just prior to World War I, 73 percent of the black population was rural (Taeuber and Taeuber, 1972).

The spatial separation of the urban area into two distinct communities indicates the existence of an ethnic class structure. Systems of ethnic stratification depend on the maintenance of some form of separation between majority and minority groups for their continued existence. Spatial segregation offers one means of separation. Pierre van den Berghe (1967) suggests that the form of this social distance depends on the nature of the stratification system in the society. In what he calls the *paternalistic system*, characteristic of the South until recently, majority and minority intermingle in the same physical spaces because there is never any question of their relative position in the society. In this caste-based system, position is determined by rules of etiquette that define the stations of each group. Although a particular ethnic caste may share the same space with majority members, the groups live in different universes. "The master calls the slaves he has bought by their first names, they call him 'Sir' " (Goodman and Marx, 1978:300).

In the *competitive system*, characteristic of urban industrial society, these caste barriers have diminished (van den Berghe, 1967). Here the relative positions of minority and majority groups are not always clear. As a result, cultural and social assimilation become a real possibility. As society shifts toward emphasizing achievement status, majority status must be bolstered by segregation since the rules of ascription no longer apply. According to van den Berghe, segregation in the era of the southern plantation was both unnecessary and impractical, but as the South industrialized the social position of whites became less secure. As a result, the white majority re-created in physical space what it had lost in social distance. At the heart of this thesis is the assumption that minority group status can be maintained in industrial societies by spatial segregation. How accurate is this assumption?

Hawley (1944), like van den Berghe, maintains that the physical isolation of a group is necessary to preserve minority status. Although this belief is at the very root of our civil rights legislation and current housing policies, until recently only a few empirical studies have dealt with this issue. Perhaps the first effort to examine the social consequences of segregation was Lieberson's (1961) study of ethnic assimilation, which examined the impact of ethnic segregation on citizenship status, intermarriage, the ability to read and speak English, and occupational mobility for ten cities. The results tend to suggest that ethnic segregation does more than merely reflect how assimilated a particular ethnic group is. Apparently the small social worlds eliminate the need and therefore the motivation to acquire citizenship and to speak the host country's tongue. Highly segregated groups were less apt to become citizens or to speak English even after other relevant variables were controlled. Additionally, spatial variables conditioned rates of intermarriage and occupational mobility. The more segregated an ethnic group, the greater its tendency toward endogamy (marriage within the group) and the greater its deviation from the general pattern of occupational mobility.

Nowhere is the impact of segregation on social standing more significant than in the case of the black American. Blacks are clearly the most segregated group in American society. What are the immediate products of this segregated society? In America eventual occupational status is primarily a function of education (Blau and Duncan, 1968). Educational achievement, in turn, is influenced by the degree of racial segregation in the school.

Perhaps the most widely influential piece of sociological research in the 1960s and early 1970s, Coleman's *Equality of Educational Opportunity* (1966) focused on the determinants of educational inequality for nonwhites. Nearly 600,000 students in 4000 grade schools and high schools were questioned along with teachers, principals, and superintendents. The results of the survey sent shock waves through the educational establishment, challenging long-cherished understandings of the school system and its functions. Coleman's analysis essentially suggested five general conclusions:

1. The schools were highly segregated by race and social class. Eighty percent of all white pupils in grades one to twelve attended schools that were ninety to one hundred percent white. Sixty-five percent of all black students in the first grade attended schools ninety to one hundred percent black.

2. The differences in educational inputs between black and white schools were generally small in terms of facilities and teachers' salaries and edu-

cation. While the teachers in black schools were generally less qualified, this mainly resulted from regional factors. Black schools were overrepresented in the South, an area where teachers were typically underqualified.

3. While educational inputs did not vary much, minority pupils scored significantly lower at every level of achievement (reading, verbal, and mathematical) than white pupils. This gap in achievement scores actually increased rather than declined from the first to the twelfth grade. Schools, instead of remedying the initial deficiencies of the minority pupil, actually accelerated them.

4. The only school-related variable that explained any of the variation between whites and nonwhites was the racial and class composition of the school. Racial integration improved the levels of educational achievement for nonwhites, without significantly lowering the achievement of white students. These improvements, however, were not great.

5. The background of the student was what really mattered. Family background, including factors such as family structure (presence of both or only one parent), head of the household's occupational status, and family life style (presence of T.V., telephone, newspapers, encyclopedia, dictionary, etc.), was the major determinant of educational achievement.

Thus, the basic finding of the Coleman report was that after receiving students who were unequally prepared, the schools failed to bring students to educational parity. The school neither slows down those who are initially ahead nor does it speed up those who are behind.

In one sense this finding is distressing. It suggests that schools can do little to transform the inequities of the existing class structure. Short of removing children from their families at a very early age, educational opportunities cannot be equalized—with some qualification. One spatial factor, the level of segregation in the school, has a significant, though small effect on achievement differences. The size of the effect really does not matter, however. What matters is that changes in the racial composition of the schools are more easily attainable than basic changes in family structure.

This is the real significance of spatial variables for social policy. Although time and time again research has shown significant spatial consequences for a variety of behaviors, these consequences are sometimes small. For social policy, however, the size of the effect is less significant than how subject the variable is to change. Generally, space is readily manipulable.

Space then, has significance for the educational process. By placing students from a lower-class or ethnic-family background into schools with predominantly middle-class values, these children's aspirations and values are likely to change. In turn, this transformation of values is likely to be expressed in higher achievement test scores and educational attainment (Duncan et al., 1972).

Segregation, however, has additional consequences for status attainment. A second aspect of the segregation phenomenon is its impact on the choice of occupation. The physical separation of blacks from whites expressed in the city-suburb statistics produces racial differences in accessibility to employment and information about employment opportunities (Kain, 1968; Newman, 1967). Although the evidence is not clear-cut (Harrison, 1974), Kain (1968) suggests that the underemployment of inner-city residents results from a mismatch of opportunities and skills (the so-called *mismatch hypothesis*). In short, the low skill levels of the central-city labor force contrast with the high skill characteristics of those few job categories still growing in central cities. In support of this contention Kain provides evidence for the suburbanization of jobs between 1948 and 1963. During this period suburban areas gained heavily in manufacturing. Between 1954 and 1963 the forty central cities in his sample sustained a net manufacturing job loss of well over 1 million, while the suburban areas gained nearly the same number of jobs. Although more recent statistics suggest that since 1963 jobs have increased substantially in the central city, the growth of suburban jobs continues to outstrip that of the central city (Cohen, 1971). Also, the greatest increases in central-city jobs have come in the service sectors, where skill level requirements are generally higher.

The decentralization of employment results from several factors:

1. The movement of economic activity tends to follow the movement of populations. Population increases in suburban areas attract market-oriented activities to locations at increasing distances from the city center (Alonso, 1964b).

2. Residential land use competes with industrial and commercial uses and pushes commerce outward from the core by bidding up land values (Alonso, 1964b).

3. The high-density development of the urban core constrains potential investments in the city. The development of mass-production methods places a high value on horizontal space, which is rarely attainable in the urban core. The incredible durability of buildings and the difficulty of assembling large parcels of land in the city hinders the growth of employment (Noll, 1970).

Given these forces and the evidence for the suburbanization of jobs Kain argues:

The most central parts of metropolitan areas are losing employment to outlying areas and . . . this process is, if anything, accelerating. Slow growth and not infrequent decline of central city areas have accumulated to the point where absolute declines in central city employment are now commonplace (1968:27).

To a certain extent this overstates the case for the decline of central-city employment. Evidence, for example, suggests that population is still moving to the suburbs at a faster pace than employment (Lewis, 1969). Nevertheless, the jobs are increasing in the suburbs.

Among urban economists a serious debate has developed over the mismatch hypothesis. This debate is as yet unresolved because of the difficulty over assembling statistics on employment. On the one hand, it can be argued that the trend toward the decentralization of jobs has created a serious problem of underemployment for the inner-city resident (Kain, 1968). Those least able to bear the costs of transportation to work find themselves most distant from available jobs. Many policy analysts support this position (Moynihan, 1968; Advisory Commission on Intergovernmental Relations, 1968). At the same time the situation is considerably more complex than the mismatch hypothesis indicates. "Measured by job growth, the central cities are not stagnating economically. They have experienced slower growth than have the suburbs, but jobs there have grown, and at an increasing rate" (Fremon, 1970:1). The central problem according to Fremon is not one of geography, but rather of discrimination. Most of the job increase experienced by central cities is being absorbed by suburban commuters, rather than inner-city residents.

The dimensions of this argument are familiar. The effects of discrimination are evident, but does this mean that spatial structuring of jobs and population skills has no effect? Once again it seems we are faced with the debate over small effects. Certainly a mismatch hypothesis provides a partial explanation for inner-city unemployment. The spatial effects, however, may be smaller than the effects of pervasive and persistent discrimination. While a spatial solution to the problem of urban unemployment is not the sole answer to ghetto unemployment, it represents at the very least a partial solution.

To this point we have seen the variety of ways in which space structures urban behavior. It should be apparent by now that spatial constraints are most crucial to those populations with limited spatial mobility—the poor, the young, the old, and the housewife. Some, though not all, of these spatial effects have been shown to have negative consequences to the individuals involved. We argued in Chapter 3 that spatial structures are conducive to the operation of the city. To what extent is this functional view of the urban space accurate?

It is undeniable that for the aggregate, segregation contributes to the urban order. Since intimate interactions are to a degree conditioned by distance, and since the urban space consists of a mosaic of small social worlds, spatial structures ensure a certain harmony in social relations that might not otherwise exist. Simply put, people generally find themselves living with others whom they feel comfortable with.

To answer the functional question, however, we must delve deeper into the mechanisms that create the structure. Alonso (1960) describes the land use market as a system that maximizes efficiency. A lot generally is occupied by the type of use that yields the highest return. This produces an efficient, but not necessarily a just system (Harvey, 1972b, 1973). Since land is scarce, no one individual unit can move without the advantages being offset by some loss to another unit. A good example of this profit-loss relationship can be found in the urban renewal of a great many United States cities during the 1960s. The bull-dozing of lower-class inner-city ghettos led to a more "efficient" allocation of space, with more intensive consumers of land (commercial activities) replacing lower-class residents. The costs to the ghetto resident, however, were high. Their old neighborhoods were replaced by more cost-efficient, high-rise ghet-tos without community structures. Some structually adequate housing was eliminated because of the spatial needs of the more efficient users.

In any system where the "ability to pay" is a major mechanism for allocat-ing space, some people will find themselves occupying relatively undesirable spaces. These places will be all the more undesirable when space is extremely scarce. Under certain conditions then, this "efficient" system produces injus-tices.

A system without justice, however, is by its very nature inefficient. If we pursue efficiency and ignore its social costs, then those individuals who must bear the costs are likely in the long run to be a source of inefficiency (Harvey, 1972b). They simply no longer have the motivation to cooperate. This lack of motivation may itself produce unemployment, limited productivity, or deviant behavior.

The benefits of the spatial structure are, then, not without their social costs both to certain individuals and to the larger society. Segregation is perhaps most costly to the lower classes. Because of the nature of the cityscape the low-er class is more likely to become deviant or to be labeled as such by law en-forcement agencies. At the same time, their life chances are sufficiently nar-rowed by the spatial structure. Education and jobs are less attainable commodities.

THE IMPACT OF SEGREGATION
ON THE DELIVERY OF SERVICES

It is useful to view the city "as a gigantic man-made resource system which contains an abundance of resources for individuals and families to exploit for their own benefit" (Harvey, 1972b:3). This resource system, however, has a spa-tial structure. That is, resources occur in fixed locations and thus are more ac-cessible to some than others. As we have seen, the friction of distance is ever present in the territorial system. This distance constraint is a function of in-come—those most able to bear the costs of distance profit, while others lose. In such a system the poor pay more (Caplovitz, 1963), for the location of services favors those whose demands are greatest and handicaps those whose ability to pay is limited.

You can view the location of services as an element in the distribution of income.

Changes in location of services and facilities have the potential to add or subtract use value to a place of residence and thereby may have progressive or regressive effects upon the real income of different individuals and groups (Harvey, 1972a:25).

Thus spatial structure provides one means whereby certain groups may acquire more than their fair share of a socially produced set of services and commodities. Since demand, under a capitalist system, is related to income, the location of economic activities in general favors the upper- and middle-income groups. This favored status may be seen in a variety of market-related activities. Perhaps the most often cited case is urban retailing activities. The Kerner Commission summarized the problem for the black ghetto population:

> Residents of low-income Negro neighborhoods frequently claim that they pay higher prices for food in local markets than wealthier white suburbanites and receive inferior quality meat and produce. . . . There are significant reasons to believe that poor households generally pay higher prices for the food they buy and receive lower quality food. Low-income consumers buy more food at local groceries because they are less mobile. Prices in these small stores are significantly higher than in major supermarkets because they cannot achieve economies of scale, and because real operating costs are higher in low-income Negro areas than in outlying suburbs. For instance, inventory "shrinkage" from pilfering and other causes . . . can run twice as much in high crime areas. Managers seek to make up for these added costs by charging higher prices or substituting lower grades. . . . These practices do not necessarily involve exploitation, but they are often perceived as exploitative and unfair by those who are aware of the price and quality differences involved, but unaware of operating costs. In addition, it is probable that genuinely exploitative pricing practices exist in some areas (National Advisory Commission on Civil Disorders, 1969:274–277).

The end result of all this is that the suburbanite profits from segregation, while the inner-city ghetto resident loses.

Much the same situation holds for the delivery of medical care. Primary care (as opposed to hospital services, nursing homes, etc.) is still located on the basis of private decisions, and thus subject to the market mechanisms governing location. As a result, primary-care physicians are heavily located around middle- and upper-income areas. Harvey (1972a:26) cites the example of Baltimore. In the low-income areas of the western side of the inner city there were 53 primary-care physicians for every 142,500 people, whereas in the northern portion of Baltimore, an affluent area, there were 115 primary-care physicians for 71,800 people—about twice as many doctors for half as many people. This problem was exacerbated by the accessibility of hospital care in the pre-Medicare era. The poor were forced to seek charity care directly from hospitals, but not all hospitals could afford such care. As a result, most charity care was usually given in one hospital. Typically this meant that many poor patients traveled great distances, often beyond closer hospitals, to receive treatment (Morrill and Earickson, 1969).

While segregation is, then, functional for the vast majority of urban dwellers, some must pay tremendous costs for its usefulness to the urban order. As seems to be the case in such efficiency-oriented market systems, those least able to bear these costs pay the most.

To this point we have spoken only of the impact of segregation on the delivery of private sector services, but the quality of public services is also conditioned by the land market. Again, we must view the urban area as a gigantic man-made resource system. It is apparent that as urban populations have decentralized, the boundaries of this resource system have grown considerably beyond the political boundaries of the central city. The true resource system is metropolitan in character (that is, it tends to coincide with what the Census Bureau calls the standard metropolitan statistical area, or SMSA—an economically integrated territory consisting of one or more central cities and its outlying suburbs and rural-urban fringe). This resource system, however, has been broken up politically into a multitude of smaller governmental units. While the metropolitan community is an integrated economic and social unit, it is not by any means politically integrated. On the contrary, local government has become highly decentralized. Local government units may now include municipal governments, villages, towns, counties, and school boards, as well as health districts, housing, transportation, and renewal authorities, and water and sewage districts. As a result each locale is governed by a variety of separate units, some of which coincide with local community boundaries and others of which do not (Smith and Weller, 1977). The chaos of local government may be seen in the census figures on the average number of governmental units for each SMSA in Table 11.1.

The result of this proliferation of governments is twofold. First, the task of governing metropolitan areas has become increasingly difficult, and second, the territorial resources have been unevenly divided, so that services no longer correspond to need. In effect, decentralization has led to both problems of inefficiency and injustice. The great brunt of these burdens has been shouldered by

Table 11.1   Total and Average Number of Local Governments by Size Class of SMSA, 1967

SMSA Population	Number of SMSAs	Number of Local Governments	Average Number of Local Governments
All SMSAs	227	20,703	91.2
1,000,000+	24	7367	307.0
500,000–1,000,000	32	3878	121.2
300,000–500,000	30	2734	91.1
200,000–300,000	40	2919	73.0
100,000–200,000	74	3123	42.2
50,000–100,000	27	682	25.3

Source: Data from United States Census Bureau, 1969 cited in Smith and Weller, 1977:134.

Each metropolitan area contains a large number and variety of local political units. This characteristic decentralization of government makes coordinating management and planning efforts very difficult.

the central city. The result has been immense economic, political, and social problems.

It should be obvious, given the great spatial changes in twentieth-century cities, that local jurisdictional concepts developed in the nineteenth century and before can no longer be effective in the modern urban community (Hawley, 1971). Yet that is the current basis of metropolitan governments. Problems such as health, transportation, water delivery, pollution, public welfare, recreation, and so forth do not stop at artificial political boundaries. While the federal government now requires regionwide planning in many of these areas, the difficulties of coordinating and implementing such plans are immense. The regional planner must cut through this tangled political web and provide proposals that are acceptable to leaders of quite different constituencies, a frustrating task. The general lack of coordination characteristic of metropolitan government wastes resources, duplicates efforts, and leaves the complex problems of the metropolis unsolved.

Governmental inefficiency is only one side of the metropolitan problem generated by the political slicing of the territorial pie. At the root of the central-city–suburban dichotomy lie certain basic social injustices. Generally these injustices have been tied to the fiscal plight of the central city. Cities are in a double bind. Expenditures keep going up, while revenues are sagging (Pettengill and Uppal, 1974). A former mayor of New York, John Lindsay, summarizes well the "expenditure problem" faced by central cities:

> Over the last couple of decades, our cities have become the guardian of the country's unwanted stepchildren. We have inherited the Nation's problems of poverty, race, and class conflict, physical deterioration, drug addiction, archaic public educational systems, pollution. Over the last two decades, the chief problems of the country have grown and festered in these cities, and we are the ones who have been asked to find the solutions.
>
> After fixed costs of pensions and debt service, almost 90 percent of our city tax levy goes into six basic areas: welfare, education, health services, police, fire and sanitation (cited in Pettengill and Uppal, 1974:7).

The great concentration of low-income peoples in the central city is further exacerbated by generally higher population density, heavy concentrations of property and business, and large numbers of daily commuters. The expense of basic services, such as police and fire protection, appears to be extremely sensitive to population density, as Table 11.2 shows.

Somewhat surprisingly, the expenditures of cities, however, are less sensitive to the size of their own population than to the size of the population in the surrounding suburbs (Hawley, 1956; Kasarda, 1972). Hawley claims that this indicates that the suburbs represent a basic cost to residents of the city.

> The latter are carrying the financial burden of an elaborate and costly service installation, i.e., the central city is used daily by a noncontributing population that in some instances is more than twice the size of the contributing population (1956:781–782).

Table 11.2   The Variation of Per Capita Police Expenditures with Population Density

Population Density Per Square Mile, 1950	Police Expenditures, Adjusted Deviations from Mean, 1957
433–598	−.105
599–930	+.191
931–1760	+1.378
1761–3420	+1.964
3421–5080	+4.697
5081+	+6.492

Source: Robert Adams, "On the Variation in the Consumption of Public Services," in Harvey Brazer, ed., *Essays in State and Local Finance*, p. 18. Reprinted by permission.

Expenditures for basic services are extremely sensitive to the population density in the community. The cost per capita for police services, for example, rises in a more than linear fashion with increased population density.

Weicher (1972) suggests that this thesis requires modification. Hawley and Kasarda find a strong relationship between suburban population size and central city expenditures. Cities, however, are generally required to balance their budgets, at least for current operating expenses. This means that revenues must approximately equal expenditures. Therefore, any factor highly correlated with expenditures also correlates highly with revenues unless the city borrows extensively. This means that while suburbanites may use central-city facilities heavily, they also pay for them through sales taxes and income taxes.

Suburbanites are not robbing central cities, but they are contributing to the cities' fiscal problems. In a "just" territorial distribution system a city would receive more in taxes from business and the well-to-do than it spends in providing services to them. In turn, it would spend more in serving poor residents than it would receive from them. This income redistribution system, however, has been fragmented by suburbanization (Weicher, 1972). With the growth of the suburbs, industry has moved out, along with significant portions of the well-to-do. As a result, the excess wealth has concentrated in such a manner that the poor experience declining welfare benefits and the working classes shoulder a greater burden than previously. These "costs" can best be seen by considering the revenue of cities and suburbs. Data for the Milwaukee urbanized area shows the revenue problems of the central city (Riew, 1970). In the urbanized area the per capita property values of the central city are only 58 percent of the average suburb's values. Given this differential, the city has been forced to greatly increase tax rates. The city of Milwaukee's tax rates are over 50 percent higher than the suburbs' and are increasing much faster (Riew, 1970). Despite the higher taxes, however, central cities have low per capita revenues compared to suburbs. As a result the urbanite pays more for less, while the suburban resident pays less for more. That is, of course, only the tip of the inequity iceberg. Owing to the current metropolitan distribution, the average central-city resident can afford less than the average suburbanite. The costs to those below the poverty line are also high, for the fragmentation of the metropolitan space simply leaves less income to distribute.

The injustices and inefficiencies of this system are apparent, but what can be done about it? Metropolitan government has been touted as one answer (Greer, 1962b; Soffen, 1963), yet government in metropolitan areas is unlikely to be consolidated in the near future. Only two areas have achieved such a merger: Miami and Toronto. Strong resistance to such efforts has come from two strange bedfellows: the suburbs, and central-city blacks. Suburbanites, of course, have much to lose financially. Consolidation would inevitably increase their taxes and provide few tangible returns. Central-city blacks, on the other hand, stand to lose political clout from consolidation just as they are beginning to acquire substantial influence. Metropolitan government, therefore, is unlikely in a society where local political autonomy is a cornerstone of government philosophy. Short of a basic reordering of the American political system, however, the urban crisis will remain in one form or another.

One institution that can intervene across the boundaries of local jurisdictions is the federal government. Federal funds play a crucial role, for example, in developing urban transportation facilities such as expressways, which weld together metropolitan social and economic structure and which would be beyond the means of any one local authority. One particular class of goals has been consistently pursued by the federal government over the past forty years: policy on housing. These policies have had enormous (and partly unintended) impact on the polarization of city and suburb.

THE IMPACT OF GOVERNMENT HOUSING POLICY

In the United States, governments at all levels have come to play a dominant role in molding residential space. This intervention dates principally from the time of the Great Depression and the New Deal, though it has rapidly accelerated in the past two decades.

Because of the United States' political commitment to free choice and to market mechanisms, government intervention has been indirect and less overt than in planned urban systems such as those of the Communist blocs. Nonetheless, forty years of intervention has decisively reinforced the polarization and segregation forces at work in the city. Broadly speaking, government policy has had two aims. The first, and largely successful effort, has been to encourage homeownership. Policy to accomplish this goal has been directed primarily at the upper one-half of income groups. This has fostered suburban sprawl and outward movement of successively lower income classes. The homes left behind by the exodus have eventually filtered down to yet lower-income groups in the inner city. This process "has the same effect as an explicit law that segregates families geographically by income" (Kohler, 1973:272).

The second and far less successful component of policy has been directed at improving living conditions for low-income groups (who are predominately renters). Rent control, public housing, rent supplements, and, above all, urban renewal, have been conspicuously unsuccessful in achieving this goal. Many indictments of these policies may be found in the social science, planning, and popular literatures. For example, Muth (1975) indicates that between 1937 and 1968, government programs demolished more lower-income housing than they built! A number of more recent policies hold out some hope of changing this record of failure.

We shall review the major policy goals in turn, commenting upon their spatial implications and their impact on residential structure.

Incentives to Homeownership for Upper- and Middle-Income Groups

According to the National Commission on Urban Problems (1969:66), during the 1950s and 1960s the nation made phenomenal progress in providing owner-occupied housing for families in the upper 50 percent of income levels. Overt and hidden subsidies have taken several forms.

Federal support of homeownership began in the early 1930s, at the time of the Great Depression. Mortgage defaults and a decline in construction prompted the Federal Home Loan Bank Act (1932) and formation of the Federal Housing Administration (1934). Before this time, down payments had been as high as 50 percent and the repayment period averaged about five years. The federal intervention insured mortgages, inaugurating an era that was to last until 1973–1974 and that made homeownership cheaper and easier than pure market considerations warranted. During this period, down payments averaged 10 to 20 percent and repayment periods were very long (up to thirty years). Economic studies (e.g., Gelfand, 1966) show that housing demand is very sensitive to the size of down payment and much less sensitive to interest rates. This suggests that the low down payments were the decisive factor in government-subsidized homeownership.

At the end of World War II a variety of GI bills facilitated home acquisition for ex-servicemen. The Veterans Administration guaranteed mortgages and lowered mortgage down payments (sometimes to zero). Individual states such as California and Connecticut also facilitated home purchases by veterans (Clawson, 1971:35). Between 1967 and 1971 almost one-quarter of new private housing units involved assistance from the Veterans or Federal Housing Administration (Kohler, 1973). Together, these schemes were decisive in making homeownership feasible for families above the median income level. Such schemes were discriminatory because they were predicated on the long-standing rule of thumb that a household should not spend more than 25 percent of its income on housing. Generally the cutoff point for these programs has corresponded almost precisely with the median income (Kohler, 1973). Households with a lower income were, in practice, ineligible.

Another pervasive method by which the federal government has fostered homeownership is tax breaks for owners. Real estate taxes and mortgage interest are both tax deductible. Thus homeownership incurs property tax, but it leads to significant reductions in federal income tax. Although landlords of tenants enjoy these privileges, there is little evidence that the savings are passed on to tenants. Thus the net effect of tax law is to foster and, in effect, subsidize homeownership (Struyk, 1976).

Several other policy instruments less direct than intervention in the mortgage market and tax breaks have also been employed to foster homeownership. For example, governments can raise money at far lower interest rates than individuals can. The Federal National Mortgage Association, has, for forty years, raised money on the capital market and bought up FHA-insured mortgages. In 1970 the FNMA also began to buy up non-FHA-insured mortgages. The criteria for purchasing such properties were extremely discriminatory: "The mortgaged property must be located in a well-maintained neighborhood, not in certain central city areas; borrowers may not spend more than 25 percent of income on housing and must have excellent credit ratings . . ." (Kohler, 1973:276). Direct cash subsidies on interest rates are also available to households under Section 235 of the 1968 Housing Act. For households that satisfy certain conditions, mortgage interest rates are effectively 1 percent. Kohler suggests that this program aided "families *near* the poverty level, most of them blue-collar whites. It has not reduced housing costs sufficiently to aid poor families" (1973:277). He indicates that the 1968 program has not been administered on a racially neutral basis. Whites have been encouraged to move to the suburbs while blacks have used the funds mainly to rehabilitate old housing in central cities.

The phenomenon of postwar white middle-class suburbanization has been studied extensively. That research produces substantial consensus on several points:

1. Although the social desirability of suburban housing is an historical fact that predates federal housing policy, these policies have been primarily responsible for the magnitude of the exodus. Universal ownership of automobiles provided the physical means of suburbanization, but federal mortgage and tax policies have provided the financial means.

2. Government policy has not necessarily been discriminatory in intent. On the contrary, the extension of home ownership to wider segments of the population has been a principal goal. But in practice, policies on homeownership have benefited those with a higher than median income and select groups such as military veterans. Young, white, upper-income families have reaped the primary benefits.

3. The net effect of policies to encourage homeownership among upper-income groups has been judged successful. David Harvey provides a Marxist analysis of the groups who benefit from housing finances. Although he is highly critical of inner-city rental housing policy, he concedes that:

> The white ethnic areas [of Baltimore] are dominated by homeownership which is financed mainly by small community-based, savings and loan institutions which operate without a strong profit orientation and which really do offer a service. As a consequence little class-monopoly rent is realized in this submarket and reasonably good housing is obtained at fairly low purchase price, considering the fairly low incomes of the residents (1974:246).

It should be noted that only the security of government mortgage insurance permits local savings institutions to offer this service.

Policy Designed to Improve Housing for Low-Income Groups

Policy aimed at improving the quality of housing for the poor and for disadvantaged groups has been far less successful than attempts to foster homeownership. The Report of the National Commission on Urban Problems states:

> In contrast to its truly amazing record in housing construction for the upper half of America's income groups, the nation has made an inexcusably inadequate record in building or upgrading housing for the poor to provide them with decent standard housing at rents and prices they can afford (1969:67).

Concern with low-income housing began in the 1930s. The Low Rent Public Housing program was established in 1937, and the Housing Act of 1949 enunciated a general "national housing goal" to provide a "decent home" and a "suitable living environment" for every family (Mercer and Hultquist, 1967:102).

Rent Control   A number of direct measures have been taken to aid low-income renters. *Rent controls* (discussed in Chapter 8) represent one such attempt. They have been severely criticized, even from diametrically opposite economic perspectives. Rent controls impede market mechanisms and discourage landlords from keeping buildings in repair (Muth, 1975; Kohler, 1973). Harvey (1974) argues that if inner-city landlords cannot realize an annual return of around 15 percent, they will "disinvest" and put their money to work in the capital market rather than in housing. This disinvestment process entails poor building maintenance and an actual decrease in the supply of rental housing, until the annual rate of return (rent) is driven to a sufficiently high level. In either case, the resident loses.

To counter such problems a program of *rent supplements* was initiated in

1965. Families with a sufficiently low income pay only 25 percent of their income in rent; the federal government makes up the difference. This program directly attacks segregation by income (Kohler, 1973). The supplements are tied to families rather than to specific dwelling units. As a result, they do not hinder spatial mobility within areas of rental housing. Additionally, each household pays only 25 percent no matter what its income. Thus families with different incomes can live side by side, with the income difference being absorbed by the government. Unfortunately, this program is not widespread because it is considered excessively expensive and because it is politically unpopular.

Public Housing   Public Housing has been politically embattled from its inception, especially by the real estate lobby (Gans, 1965). Public housing began in 1937 with the creation of local public housing authorities. The program was bolstered by the Housing Act of 1949. Developments (and operating costs) undertaken by local authorities were financed by the federal government. This conventional approach can be distinguished from two variants (Mercer and Hultquist, 1976). Under *leased public housing,* local authorities lease units from private owners and rent them at reduced rates; the cost difference is absorbed by local and federal authorities. A more radical variant is *turnkey housing,* in which the agencies purchase units in the private market and rent them to low-income families, who maintain the buildings and, after eighteen years, obtain title (Kohler, 1973:283). Leased public housing began in 1965, while Project Turnkey was inaugurated by the Housing and Urban Development Act of 1968.

The overall record of the public housing program is poor. For example, the 1949 Housing Act authorized 810,000 units to be built by 1955, yet by 1969 only 740,580 units existed (Mercer and Hultquist, 1976:105). Despite this fact, the demolition of low-cost units was proceeding rapidly during the same period! The 1968 Housing and Urban Development Act set an extremely ambitious goal of 26 million units between 1968 and 1978. Even though mobile homes were counted in to boost totals, this goal could not be reached (Kohler, 1973).

In social terms, public housing has been a failure (Gans, 1965; Suttles, 1972). Social structures have disintegrated in the desolate high-rise settings, and vacancy rates are, in some cases, astonishingly high. Many projects are ripe for demolition. One of the most notorious demolitions was the Pruitt-Igoe project in St. Louis. When built, it won an architectural prize, but as we saw in Chapter 10, it epitomized the ills of public housing.

Spatially, most conventional and leased public housing is segregationist. It explicitly implements segregation by income, since the occupants must not exceed a low-income threshold. (The turnkey program is an exception, since it does attempt to disperse low-income households and to facilitate the transition from renter to owner.)

The failings of public housing have not gone unheeded. For example, the General Accounting Office has criticized the Department of Housing and Urban Development for its inability even to identify the housing needs of the families it aims to serve. The economist Muth, too, is critical. He offers evidence that the private sector has consistently outperformed the government in providing low-income housing. He writes, sarcastically, "The failure of Congress to make larger appropriations may indeed have been a blessing in disguise, for until recently, government programs have almost certainly destroyed more lower income housing than they have built" (1975:112).

The bulk of the criticism, however, has been directed at the most controversial component of low-income housing policy: urban renewal.

Urban Renewal   The fundamental philosophy of urban renewal was formulated in the Housing Act of 1949. Local governments were subsidized by the federal government to acquire, consolidate, and clear slums, selling the land to private or public developers.

The program was conceived as an attack on blighted, inner-city residential areas. It aimed primarily to improve the quality of neighborhoods, but did not explicitly address the problem of rehousing the poor who were displaced in the process. Public housing was only one—and a relatively minor—component in the development. Quite often residences for higher-income groups, or even nonresidential uses, were built on the cleared land. One notorious example was the Yerba Buena project in San Francisco. The intent was to demolish a twelve-block area of private residences, cheap residential hotels, and other dilapidated structures. The area was to be built over with "a convention center, a sports arena, a high-rise luxury hotel, six office towers, a 4000-car garage, an Italian cultural center, and an airline terminal" (Kohler, 1973:285). Overall, 4000 dwelling units were destroyed and fewer than 300 were to be built.

A very large number of cities joined the urban renewal program, which was very lucrative for local governments since low-revenue sources were often replaced with high revenue ones. Criticism grew, and the program was halted in mid-1973. Muth succinctly summarizes one theme of critics: "It is very difficult to understand why anyone should think that tearing down their homes would improve the lot of the poor" (1975:113).

Legally, inhabitants of renewal areas have to be relocated before demolition begins. But because of strong political pressures to get projects under way, tenants were relocated capriciously if not ruthlessly (Gans, 1965). Cynics have gone so far as to term urban renewal "Negro clearance." Quite often those relocated have simply gone into other slums.

> Indeed, urban renewal projects have had the tendency to force the poor into playing a game of "musical houses." The highest density slum area is typically selected for urban renewal; the poor are "bulldozed" out of the area and spill over into surrounding territory. They are turned into a kind of urban gypsy, raising densities elsewhere, making other areas, in turn, prime targets for urban renewal (Gans, 1965:29).

Even more damaging is evidence that urban renewal has been used to develop pet projects of municipalities, and that unnecessary demolitions have occurred. In a study of clearance in Boston's West End, Hartman (1964) found that 41 percent of West Enders lived in adequate housing that should not have been demolished. These households were moved from adequate housing to adequate housing; their net "gain" was an increase in median rent from $41 to $71 per month (Gans, 1965).

Thus even in the simplest terms of supply, demand, and price, urban renewal in the traditional sense seems to have been a questionable solution to the housing problems of the poor. The social impact of renewal—the destruction of the intimate and long-standing social networks of the slum—has been described by Gans (1962), Suttles (1968), Jacobs (1961), and others. The slum space provides an intimate home area and fosters social networks that are in many ways closer knit than those of suburbanites (recall the discussion of the Boston West End in Chapter 8). Nearness is an essential component of these communities (Fried and Gleicher, 1961) in contrast to the "community without propinquity" of far-flung suburbs. Communities such as these are far more fragile and far more inextricably related to the physical neighborhood of streets, corners, stores, areas of play and meeting than are suburban communities. Wholesale demolition completely destroys them.

The Present State of Government Intervention in Housing

Since the housing-market crisis of 1974 and the growing criticism of traditional public housing and urban renewal programs, government housing policy has been going through a period of reappraisal. Several new concepts have proved successful in small-scale experimental settings, such as turnkey housing, housing allowances, and urban homesteading. Despite these changes even our goals (much less our techniques) are still poorly formulated. Three basic problems are those of policy, data, and administrative units.

First, urban policies have been formulated intermittently, and in a piecemeal and sometimes mutually contradictory way. Second, data on housing quality are astonishingly sparse, particularly since assessment of structural quality was dropped from the 1970 census. Nor can "decent housing" be defined in purely structural terms. Virtually no housing proposals have seriously addressed all the social, economic, and psychological dimensions discussed in Chapter 10. Emphasis on the visible physical components of slums led, in a very logical way, to the urban renewal solution. Finally, housing policies emanate from many different administrative levels, ranging from federal intervention through HUD to local planning boards and building codes. The federal government has been the prime mover to date, though, as we have seen, most components of urban social space can be adequately viewed only in the local context. The emergence of metropolitan authorities, with sufficient powers to impose solutions on disparate local authorities, has been seen as a potential political solution to problems of fragmentation and conflict between authorities with jurisdiction over housing (Berry, 1973b; Yeates and Garner, 1976).

Many economists question whether the housing problem should be considered in isolation. For example, many federal programs are predicated on two assumptions: first, that a household should not spend more than about 25 percent of its income on housing, and second, that the price of housing should be lowered by allowances, loans, and cheap mortgages until the poor can afford it. Muth (1975), Kohler (1973), and others claim that a more desirable solution would be to raise the incomes of the disadvantaged rather than artificially lower housing prices. This line of argument suggests that the housing problem may be alleviated by income policy instead of housing policy as such.

We have shown here that government intervention in the housing market has had profound impact on the social structure of the city. Its unintended but actual effect has been twofold. Subsidized home-ownership for upper income groups has fostered segregation. Ill-conceived public housing and renewal policies have destroyed the homes and the social networks of the poor without substituting adequate alternatives. To some extent the poor have been dispersed (for example, by renewal projects). But large-scale public-housing projects have concentrated (and segregated) the poor to an unprecedented degree. It has been belatedly recognized that potential housing policies must be evaluated in the spatial and social terms of these segregation processes, rather than by facile economic and physical criteria such as income and housing structure.

It is easy to criticize the administrators and bureaucrats who have grappled with the housing problem over the past decade. Gans (1965) argues that such criticisms are rather unjust:

> Many of these officials are as unhappy with what urban renewal has wrought as their armchair critics and would change the program if they could—that is, if they received encouragement from the White House, effective support in getting new legislation through Congress, and, equally important, political help at city halls to incorporate these innovations into local programs (1965:37).

Table 11.3   Components of President Carter's Urban Policy

1. Encourage and support efforts to improve local planning and management capacity and the effectiveness of existing Federal programs by coordinating these programs, simplifying planning requirements, reorienting resources, and reducing paperwork.

2. Encourage states to become partners in assisting urban areas.

3. Stimulate greater involvement by neighborhood organizations and voluntary associations.

4. Provide fiscal relief to the hardest pressed communities.

5. Provide strong incentives to attract private investment to distressed communities.

6. Provide employment opportunities, primarily in the private sector, to the long-term unemployed and disadvantaged in urban areas.

7. Increase access to opportunity for those disadvantaged by a history of discrimination.

8. Expand and improve social and health services to disadvantaged people in cities, counties, and other communities.

9. Improve the urban physical environment and the cultural and aesthetic aspects of urban life.

Source: The White House, 1978.

In mid-1978 the newest concerted attack on these problems was announced in a status report on President Carter's urban policy. The main points of the policy are listed in Table 11.3. One major focus of this policy was the New Partnership, which attempted to coordinate and support the various public and private sectors concerned with housing. For example, the states have usually been silent partners, while federal and city governments have addressed the housing problem. Attempts were made to encourage states, through federal grants, to assist in implementing development strategies. A particularly appropriate aspect of the policy was the way in which it set the housing problem in the more general context of urban policy; for example, urban sprawl and urban transportation are explicitly addressed under point 9 of Table 11.3. Although this program is still in its infancy (and may be dismantled in the Reagan administration), it is instructive to note that housing issues were not directly or specifically addressed. At this point it is still too early to critically evaluate this approach. But given the current political climate, it seems doubtful that a radical restructuring of housing policy is on the horizon.

SUMMARY

Federal housing policy has, at least indirectly, enhanced the development of spatial structures that undermine the fiscal integrity of cities and maintain the poverty of ghetto residents. Policies designed to encourage homeownership fostered suburban growth and the migration of middle-class populations out of the central city. At the same time urban renewal programs, ostensibly developed to improve housing for the lower classes, have in practice disrupted existing social networks in lower-class neighborhoods. In essence, the government has engineered an urban spatial structure that promotes social injustice.

Spatial structures, and changes in spatial structure, then, do have social consequences. Location modifies the urban experience by bounding social groups and resources, thereby preventing easy movement between groups and concentrations of services.

Since neighborhoods are segregated along various status dimensions, social networks are to a degree spatially bounded as well. People in close proximity to one another, who share similar social characteristics, will be likely to become friends and maintain this friendship over time. At the same time segregation isolates the members of this community from the experiences and expectations of the larger community. As a result cultural differentiation is both fostered and maintained in the city. Segregated communities may produce normative structures that vary from those of the larger community. Deviance will thus be more likely in some areas than others. Deviance rates, like density, appear to be a function of distance from the center.

Socioeconomic status also varies directly with central distance (see Chapter 5). This variation is most obvious in the distinctions between inner city and outer city. With the loss of substantial portions of the middle and upper classes to the suburbs, the central city subsequently lost vast amounts of revenues and services. These losses have exacerbated the traditional problems of inner-city residents. Access to unskilled jobs and to racially integrated schools is no longer a simple function of discrimination. The loss of unskilled jobs and young white families to the suburbs makes both ghetto employment and school integration more difficult to achieve. At the same time, as services continue to cluster in the suburbs, the poor are likely to pay more for inferior services. The consequences to the poor of the "unintended" environment indicate the need for greater attention to social justice concerns in a spatial market that has in the past been the product of norms of efficiency.

Chapter 12

Urban Planning:
How It Has Been Done,
How It Might Be Done

INTRODUCTION

The activities and the well-being of all urbanites are intimately bound to the structure of the urban space. It follows that planners and officials charged with engineering and manipulating the urban fabric inevitably affect social structures and behavior, for either good or ill. The idea that planning can be a value-free enterprise is dead. American planning has recognized more and more the urban planner's role as an architect of social change. Yet the effects of planning on social structures are poorly understood. All the preceding material of this book points to the complexity of urban social space. Social sciences' findings are needed to inform the planning process.

This book has provided a range of findings on urban social space that are clearly important for planning practice. Nevertheless, a variety of problems has traditionally impeded the interpretation and application of such findings by planners. These problems include a communication problem inherent in the diverse languages and frames of references of social scientists and planners, and an orientation problem inherent in the different audiences to which social scientists and planners must respond. Social scientists can develop elaborate theoretical structures and normative models, while practitioners are almost always constrained to act within rigid and sometimes arbitrary physical and legal restrictions. This book has dealt with only one component of the spatial organization of the city—its social dimension. Though we have repeatedly emphasized the importance of this perspective, the artificial separation of the social component is a luxury that practitioners cannot afford in dealing with multidimensional problems. In effect, social scientists can deal with the abstract and theoretically simple; practitioners cannot.

This chapter is organized into two parts, as its title suggests. The first portion describes urban planning practice: its historical context, some ideals of urban control, and planning in the United States, the United Kingdom, and the Soviet Union. The second half considers the issue of the ideal urban form.

After discussing past statements on the urban ideal, we attempt to describe some of the requirements and possibilities for planning cities that arise from the preceding chapters.

HOW IT HAS BEEN DONE

The Historical Roots of Modern Urban Planning

The industrial city, particularly in North America, grew up under weak institutional constraints. During the nineteenth and the first half of the twentieth centuries, spatial decision making by individuals and businesses had a freer rein than it is ever likely to have again. In a sense, contemporary planning represents a reversion to preindustrial practice, for the principle of manipulating urban structure toward civil, religious, political, or social goals is very ancient. Recent decades have witnessed increasing government intervention on a worldwide scale. In the United States this intervention, originating with the New Deal era of the 1930s, includes a wide range of legislation that regulates urban development in a relatively permissive and piecemeal way. In some European democracies far stronger government roles are politically acceptable, while in most socialist urban systems regulation is highly centralized and very far reaching.

Modern urban planning philosophies, however much their political and economic premises may diverge, share the abstract goal of maximizing the good of the greatest number of urbanites. This was not so during most of urban history (Porteous, 1971, 1977). The evolution of Western urban planning can be characterized as a transition from *autocratic planning* by and for political elites to a mode of planning by *enlightened elites* (a specialized planning class supposedly working for the public good) (Porteous, 1971, 1977). This change occurred in the nineteenth century, as social thinkers such as Marx, Durkheim, and others began to recognize the evils of the industrial city. A third and still largely hypothetical stage in this evolution is *popular planning,* in which the needs and concerns of users and local residents are articulated through dialogues between planner and user. Modern *advocacy planning*—in which planners work as advocates for disadvantaged and underrepresented communities—represents a step in this direction, though the ideal of popular planning remains unrealized and the role to be played by "experts" and "laymen" is still debated. Most modern planning remains client oriented rather than user oriented, addressing problems defined by local government rather than by local communities.

In the earliest cities this comparison of elitist with popular needs would have been almost unthinkable. In the city-states of Mesopotamia and in Egypt, unchanging religious tradition and political fiat stipulated the form and function of the city as well as the social, political, and economic roles of citizens. In

India and China the very form of the city itself was determined by religious symbolism (Morris, 1972; Tuan, 1974). Religious writings provided ideal forms of the Indian city, for example, as mandalas, or repetitive geometric forms based on the circle and the square. In Egypt and Mesopotamia the principal planned items in the urban space were the monumental buildings associated with royal government: the temple, the palace, the centralized granaries, and the royal tombs. In the Harappan Bronze Age civilization these monumental buildings were coupled with a rigid organization of the whole urban space on a grid plan. The religious and political significance of this plan is unknown (Morris, 1972), but this early example of integrated planning (i.e. planning of the whole urban space) undoubtedly derived from autocratic and religious control.

The city-states of Greece established planning norms adopted throughout the ancient Mediterranean world. These plans were highly prized in the European Renaissance. The conspicuous features of this ideal were lavishly decorated and artistically impeccable public buildings and spaces and the grid plan, or rectilinear arrangement, of streets. Greek architectural theorists such as Hippodamus codified the grid plan form, which the Romans adopted with little modification and diffused throughout the Mediterranean world. Numerous European, Asian, and African cities still bear the Roman imprint in their layout.

The role of religious tradition in classical urban design was emphasized in Chapter 4. So far as can be determined, functional concerns (structuring the urban form to achieve social or economic goals) were largely absent from classical urban planning, except perhaps for the military need for defensibility and easy troop movements. Most Roman colonial cities were planned by military surveyors who laid out the rectilinear plan of the site according to traditional forms with appropriate religious ritual. However, in the case of metropolitan Rome with its unprecedented size (exceeding 1 million people), distinctive problems arose that were quite closely analogous to those in the laissez-faire industrial city of nineteenth-century Europe (Mumford, 1961; Morris, 1972). For example, the problems of jerry-built tenements, fires, and traffic congestion were addressed, respectively, by legislation on building heights, building spacing (density), and vehicular traffic movements (Morris, 1972). These planning problems were approached in a pragmatic and piecemeal way uninformed by the social conscience motivating the evolution of modern urban planning. Except in the case of Rome itself, classical planning occurred in the context of small, ethnically homogeneous cities with a rigid and immobile stratification system and a stable (nonevolving) technology. The only legacy of classical planning that has any real relevance today are some of its aesthetic tenets, especially the highly prized architectural forms of ancient Greece. The social, economic, and political context of ancient planning is completely alien to contemporary situations. Even its main formal device, the grid plan, has been severely criticized by modern planners.

The medieval city as it emerged after the European Dark Ages was largely unplanned. Within the city wall a haphazard street plan surrounded the symbolic foci of the urban space: the marketplace, the cathedral, and the town- or guildhall. Where unified planning of medieval cities did occur—for example, in the royal bastide towns of Wales and southern France—a rectangular street plan within the defensive wall was usually employed. The medieval period was influential in defining the role of municipal governments in planning. During this period municipal government structures emerged (such as city councils). Rules concerning building construction, access to the urban public space, and welfare services that laid the foundation for current local urban government action were developed (Berry, 1973a:123).

The Renaissance and baroque periods witnessed the revival of classical formal principles for adorning individual buildings and closed spaces and, later, for manipulating open space. The geometric tenets and the autocratic political implications of this planning mode were discussed in Chapter 4. Here we need only repeat that these planning modes emphasized geometric forms and physical rather than social planning. They were nonfunctional for the most part, and took no account of the social and economic configuration of the city.

The industrialization of the city profoundly changed the form and function of urban space. These changes included a pluralistic definition of citizenship, continuing immigration and associated assimilation, social repolarization involving reversal of the center-periphery gradient of prestige, separation of home and work, and a profound reorganization of urban economic activity under the impact of scale and agglomeration economies. In Europe and North America, this period was one of unprecedented laissez faire. Dissatisfaction with the results of industrial urbanization forms a common theme in late nineteenth-century literature and social writing. Engels and Marx scathingly criticized the oppressive industrial city and the political and economic conditions that produced it. Adna Weber (1958), Durkheim (1947), and their successors documented and discussed these effects in specifically social terms.

The dissatisfaction generated the foundations of modern urban planning. Within the industrial system "enlightened entrepreneurs" such as Owen (1813) and Buckingham (1849) developed proposals for idealized industrial settlements. Owen emphasized the merits of low densities and of physically separating dwellings from factories and workshops. Buckingham proposed a more detailed scheme that included neighborhoods designed for a variety of social classes (see Gallion and Eisner, 1963). Out of this tradition emerged the company town, exemplified by Port Sunlight and Saltaire in Britain and Pullman, Illinois. This tradition continues in areas of the developing world, for example, in Latin America (Porteous, 1970). Similar ideas were also to be found in the work of pragmatic social thinkers such as Ebenezer Howard (1965). During the industrial period, and particularly the early twentieth century, the middle class expanded and the enlarged urban proletariat gained considerable political strength. Such conditions made these ideas politically desirable, establishing the foundation for the ideals and practice of the modern planning profession.

Ideals and Practice of Political Control

The history of urban planning suggests a growing appreciation of the role of spatial structure in shaping the everyday activities and experiences of urban populations. Planners have come to define their task as one of controlling physical and social changes in the city in order to meet the requirements of the entire population. Although this service-oriented approach to planning is widely accepted in modern planning, the means for realizing such goals vary significantly in different societies and political systems. The issue of how control over the urban form should be exercised has been solved in a number of ways. Today political strategies range from laissez faire in the United States, Canada, and Australia through moderate degrees of control in the European welfare states to controls that, in theory, are absolute, in the countries of the Communist blocs and other socialist regimes.

Since the theory of competitive mechanisms was conceived by Adam Smith in the eighteenth century, free enterprise in the marketplace has come to be associated with other political freedoms in Western democracies. In practice, however, government intervention, direct and indirect, pervades every aspect of urban structure in the form of zoning controls, building codes, intervention in the housing market, and other actions. Moreover, government interference in the United States has been growing rapidly in recent years, with the establishment of centralized agencies such as the Department of Housing and Urban Development and with large-scale government programs to regulate welfare, housing, business, transportation, commerce, and virtually all other forms of activity. This government intervention can be viewed in two radically different ways, depending on your philosophy.

To proponents of free competition, government activity should be confined to a relatively passive role aimed at facilitating the competitive process. The model of this kind of legislation would be the antitrust laws, which protect trade and commerce from unlawful restraint and unfair business practices. Many urban economists argue that free-market mechanisms are being stifled by government activities that go beyond this passive role (Muth, 1975; Kohler, 1973).

By and large this belief in the passive or catalytic role of government is the dominant political and economic philosophy in the United States today, although government intervention in urban affairs has gone much farther. This conservative philosophy seems to have received a new lease on life in recent political events including the concern for balancing the federal budget, the victory of Proposition 13 in California in 1978, and the general reaction against big government. The ideal of competitive free enterprise has left a very distinct imprint on the American urban planning process, as we will soon show.

The ability of market mechanisms to regulate urban form has been questioned from a variety of political and philosophical positions, not all of them socialistic. Within fairly conservative economic terms, it is possible to point out peculiarities in the urban context that make the application of classical economic theory debatable. Land itself does not behave as an ordinary economic commodity. Unless a town annexes new land, its supply function is fixed; new land cannot be coaxed into the marketplace by an increase in its price. Also, investments in the urban space are extremely long lived. Highways, once built, mold urban form for centuries, long after economic conditions may have changed. The supply function for housing also is peculiar. Since housing survives over generations, much of it is supplied indirectly by the filtering mechanism (see Chapter 8)—it is impossible to build old houses! Market mechanisms in the urban land economy are extremely sluggish in comparison with the supply-demand relationships for normal consumer goods.

It seems significant that most proponents of market mechanisms focus on the ability of market forces to allocate resources, housing, incomes and the like. These concerns have produced no comprehensive or coherent ideals of urban form and structure. It is true that the normative literature on location theory in economic geography and regional science contains many techniques for optimizing the location of facilities such as stores, industrial plants, day-care centers, schools, firehouses, and the like, under specified objectives such as minimum aggregate travel, minimum cost, maximum welfare, maximum profit, and so on. But these piecemeal solutions shed little light on the whole socioeconomic complex. The concentric model of urban rent theory is virtually the only normative statement on aggregate form that attempts to spell out the implications of the competitive assumptions in a comprehensive way (see Chapter 8).

Clearly the economic ramifications of the competitive ideal are imperfectly understood. And its social implications, its implications for the ideal social and spatial form of the city, are very hard to discern. Monetary wealth or profit is an oversimplified measure of social well-being. This conceptual problem is compounded by the fact that in Western society economic competition is viewed in a far broader context of highly prized social and political liberties involving freedom of individual choice.

It is perhaps this perspective of choice that provides the link between the debate on economic competition and the issue of urban social well-being. The social revolutions that accompanied industrialization freed the individual from socially ascribed roles and produced a freedom of both social and spatial mobility. This freedom bears costs and potential dangers such as loneliness, alienation, and anomie. But it offers opportunities that should not be constrained.

The power of economic competitive mechanisms has been criticized far more radically. A school of radical geographers has emphasized the intrinsic spatial disparities and inequities of the current urban system. Harvey (1973, 1974) and Bunge (1971) both argue that operation of the traditionally conceived rent model leads to a structured inequality between the welfare of disadvantaged inner-city residents and suburban landowners and to a continuing flow of wealth away from the city center.

Recognition of the costs of the free-market philosophy has led to political change ranging from modifications of the free-enterprise system in the welfare states of Western Europe to a radical reorganization of economic production in the socialist states. The actions taken in Western Europe were designed to guarantee minimum standards for health care, housing, employment, and other material benefits. To achieve these goals a stringent system of differential taxation was developed along with an increasing centralization of control over the marketplace. The delicately designed power relations between business corporations on the one hand and government on the other allow for political control to be exercised in two ways. As in the American system, much of the power is exercised negatively by constraining individual and corporate interests. At the same time, however, this system allows for developmental leadership that cannot be exercised in America. A substantial public sector devoted to meeting the welfare requirements of the populace exists alongside the private economic system. This public sector is intended to lead as well as control (Berry, 1976). Directing the society towards goals of social justice and material redistribution reorients economic competition to meet the needs of the whole population. At the same time, the government sectors in these countries have constructed a large share of all the available housing and have also built a number of new towns and cities. As a result, they have had a direct hand in developing their own urban futures.

While the welfare state can directly control urbanization, far greater controls are used in the socialist states. Here the state machinery is highly centralized, and far-reaching influence over the urban form is possible. Government is dominated by a single party and industry controlled by the state. Thus the direction of economic and population growth is easily channeled.

Socialist philosophy invests great faith in the power of the government to transform society and provide for the benefit of mankind. The Communist Revolution of 1917, unlike the earlier American Revolution, intended to seize the reins of government in order to increase state control over the society's direction rather than to restrict its control. Following Marx and Engel's call in 1848 to revolution in *The Communist Manifesto* (1969), the state acquired control over the production of goods, the means of communication, the redistribution of population, and the provision of services. Dissolving the free market abolished capitalists' control over the means of production and the livelihood of the workers. Such a step was necessary, according to Marx, because the capitalist economy was at the root of social inequality in urban society.

Although Marxist-Leninist social thought underlies most communist urban systems, the philosophy of urbanism varies substantially. This variation depends, in part, on differences in economic development. In several East European nations, socialism was imposed when industrial urbanization was well under way. In Russia, however, urbanization has been accomplished by the Communist Revolution itself.

This implied spectrum of political controls ranging between the extremes of free market mechanisms and the socialist state is, of course, an oversimplification. Neither can be found in a pure form in any urban system. Modernization appears to carry with it a requirement for more explicit controls. This is exemplified by the increasing intervention in the American urban system since Roosevelt's New Deal. Rodwin writes:

> Before World War II almost no one wanted the central government to determine how cities should grow. Today, only a generation later, national governments throughout the world are adopting or being implored to adopt urban growth strategies (Cited in Berry, 1973:165).

Types of Planning Practice

The philosophy of political control espoused by a society suggests the ideal organizational structure for achieving planning goals. Although these organizational ideals are probably never fully realized in practice, they clearly influence the machinery of planning. Political ideology also influences the planners' time reference (present or future orientation) as well as their ability to achieve consensus over particular urban goals (Berry, 1973a, 1976). Berry identifies a fourfold taxonomy of planning styles that roughly follows the continuum from minimum to maximum degrees of government intervention. These four planning styles are compared in Table 12.1.

Although components of the four modes are to be found in most planning systems, the dominant mode in a given country depends upon local value systems and traditions.

Reactive or Ameliorative Problem Solving This is a conservative and pragmatic planning style that is present oriented. This approach does nothing until problems significant enough to demand correction arise. The focus is on present problems. Thus this approach involves "continually reacting to processes that have already worked themselves out in the past" (Berry, 1973a:178). The implicit goal in such a strategy is preserving the mainstream values of the past. American local authorities run by elective officials with short terms of office, restricted budgets, and limited legal jurisdiction are often forced to act in this mode. The enormous cumulative inertia of the existing urban structure and the small time and space framework of intervention make such government actions seem piecemeal and even futile on occasion. The reactive mode of traditional transportation planning falls into this category: Local engineering solutions are sought to local problems of congestion.

Allocative Trend Modifying This is a future-oriented version of reactive problem solving. It involves identifying current trends in the urban system, projecting these trends into the future, and allocating available resources to promote the most desirable outcomes. This procedure devises regulatory mechanisms to modify trends and preserve existing values. One important way of exercising control over urban form at the local level is the master plan,

Table 12.1   Modes of Planning Control   277

Planning for Present Concerns	Planning for the Future		
Reacting to past problems	Responding to predicted futures		Creating desired future
AMELIORATIVE PROBLEM-SOLVING	ALLOCATIVE TREND-MODIFYING	EXPLOITIVE OPPORTUNITY-SEEKING	NORMATIVE GOAL-ORIENTED
Planning for the present	Planning toward the future	Planning with the future	Planning from the future
PLANNING MODE — Analyse problems, design interventions, allocate resources accordingly.	Determine and make the best of trends and allocate resources in accordance with desires to promote or alter them.	Determine and make the most of trends and allocate resources so as to take advantage of what is to come.	Decide on the future desired and allocate resources so that trends are changed or created accordingly. Desired future may be based on present, predicted or new values.
PRESENT OR SHORT-RANGE RESULTS OF ACTIONS — Ameliorate present problems	A sense of hope New allocations shift activities	A sense of triumphing over fate New allocations shift activities	A sense of creating destiny New allocations shift activities
FUTURE OR LONG-RANGE RESULTS OF ACTIONS — Haphazardly modify the future by reducing the future burden and sequelae of present problems.	Gently balance and modify the future by avoiding predicted problems and achieving a 'balanced' progress to avoid creating major bottlenecks and new problems.	Unbalance and modify the future by taking advantage of predicted happenings, avoiding some problems and cashing in on others without major concern for emergence of new problems.	Extensively modify the future by aiming for what could be. 'Change the predictions' by changing values or goals, match outcomes to desires, avoid or change problems to ones easier to handle or tolerate.

Source: From *The Human Consequences of Urbanization* by Brian J. L. Berry, 1973. Reprinted by permission of St. Martin's Press, Inc., New York, NY.

which uses zoning as its basic regulatory tool. New zoning schemes, or comprehensive rezonings, are frequently predicated on comprehensive and projective planning, but the mechanisms of variance and appeal that form the basis of day-to-day zoning practice are unquestionably reactive.

Most urban planning, particularly in the United States, uses some variant of allocative trend modifying. One of the clearest examples is the elaborate forecasting methodology currently used to estimate future travel demand (e.g., Stopher and Meyburg, 1976). Ideally, the physical organization of urban transportation may be planned to meet, and in some ways to mold, future travel patterns. Federal financial activity often provides a powerful tool for modifying projected trends. It is well known, for example, that by manipulating interest rates, subsidies, grants, and taxes, the government attempts to intervene indirectly in the housing market (see Chapter 11), the transportation system, and the labor market. Interventions such as government job programs, public housing, or gas mileage standards for new cars represent more direct attacks on problems perceived to be particularly acute.

Exploitive Opportunity Seeking   This planning mode is not oriented toward problem solving, either in the present or the future. Rather it involves actively searching for new growth opportunities identified by one or a few imaginative leaders. This is the ideal mode for the corporate manager, the real estate developer, the industrialist, and the private risk taker, as well as the national leader concerned with encouraging economic development. It involves identifying the planning goals themselves as well as the strategies for achieving these goals. As a mode of operation, it is relatively rare in most modern public sector planning, although the Brazilians have adopted this style in planning for the huge interior of Brazil. Generally this approach is most suitable to the corporate world, which emphasizes growth and profit seeking. It often produces unsettling changes and attendant social problems.

The American system, with its publicly supported private developmental style, represents a unique mix of the three planning modes. Private entrepreneurial interests are protected by reactive or regulatory planning. At the same time, these same planning strategies are used to control the social problems that attend such growth. This balancing of interests incorporated into American planning practice has led to severe criticisms by those more accustomed to the liberal and socialist traditions of Western Europe.

Normative Goal-Oriented Planning   This planning mode is oriented toward creating an ideal urban future. It is substantially harder to implement than the other modes, partly because it requires wholesale marshaling of resources, but mainly because it requires goals to be clearly identified in advance. Most visionary architects of the urban form, the major spokesmen for the new town movement—which we will soon discuss—assume that this is the most desirable planning style. Their ideals of the urban form, however, tend to oversimplify urban processes and structures. Typically, they provide unidimensional portraits of what is in reality a complex urban form. Planning whole cities based on such visionary forms is probably unwise.

Normative goal-oriented planning is most likely to be found in national or local systems with adequate centralized coercive power. Urban systems that stress the virtues of free enterprise and private ownership of property are less capable of garnering the land and resources necessary for implementing the visionary's plans. In particular, this mode of planning toward idealized ends is alien to the American political tradition, as Berry indicates:

> The publicly supported private developmental style that characterizes the American scene, incorporating bargaining among major interest groups, serves mainly to protect developmental interests by reactive or regulatory planning. . . . On the other hand, hierarchical social and political systems, where the governing class is accustomed to govern, where other classes are accustomed to acquiesce, and where private interests have relatively less power, can more readily evolve urban and regional growth policies at the national level. . . . This is one reason urban growth policies burgeoned earlier in Britain than in the United States (1973a:180).

American Urban Planning Practice

American urban planning, or the lack of it, has long puzzled foreign observers, particularly those familiar with the European tradition of centralized regulation. These critics have been struck by the anomalies in the American city—a remarkably high and diffuse level of material wealth contrasted with minorities living in poverty; tremendous construction achievements in the suburbs such as low-density tract housing and new highways coexisting with inner city decay (Hall, 1975:267). Gould has been especially critical of the American style of planning with its seemingly structured incapacity to solve fundamental problems of public welfare.

> A paucity of fair and equitable solutions characterizes many of America's urban centers today. What few and halting steps we are taking are basically directed at alleviating social injustices that have exploded with the very cities in which they are embedded. . . . The causes are wearyingly familiar: archaic political forms that divide a metropolitan region such as New York into over 1000 often antagonistic decision-making units; rapacious commercial values that drive all nonmonetary considerations out of court; gross inequities in schooling, educational opportunities, and medical care, and so on. We must recognize that we have lost our ability to lead in this crucial area of human social organization. Indeed, the situation is even worse than this: We are being monitored by others to give them sufficient lead time to avoid our mistakes (1973:38).

During the late nineteenth and early twentieth centuries, the principal theme in American urban growth was speculative development of land for private profit. This development kept pace with the expansion of cities because of heavy immigration, and its morphology was guided by transportation innovations such as the streetcar and the private automobile. This period was by no means devoid of statements and practical examples of urban (or, more strictly, suburban) design. These ideals did not emanate from government or from any coherent physical or social theory of urban form. They were instituted by large- and small-scale builders, subdividers, corporations, and other investors in large areas of real estate. As Gallion and Eisner put it:

> Although the history of speculation in land has not been of the most savory variety, there were those who chose this medium as an instrument for the improvement of land development. This choice was not motivated by the high purpose of the Garden City movement in England, for instance, nor was it prompted by deep concern for the nature of the city or its social and economic welfare. It was rather the natural result of competitive necessity. . . (1963:117).

Yet it is a gross oversimplification to regard the American city as an unregulated arena where private interests are pursued regardless of their impact on the whole system. On the contrary, the urban fabric is regulated by numerous agencies ranging from local school, sewer, and water districts to townships, cities, counties, and states, while the Federal government exerts substantial indirect control. Paralleling this elaborate regulatory machinery is a system explicitly designed to ensure democratic control by interested parties (lobbying, public hearings) and by the electorate as a whole (the election and recall of officials). In addition, numerous public and private planning agencies play a consultative role at all levels, while the academic planning professions are growing rapidly. How can such a formidable and democratically conceived apparatus be said to have failed? Not only have certain conspicuous urban problems resisted any solution, but also even those planning precepts that have been implemented have been scathingly criticized (Alexander, 1966; Jacobs, 1961).

The earliest attempts to articulate planning principles for industrialized America were made against the background of nineteenth century laissez faire. They included the City Beautiful movement and the elaboration of the concept of the planned neighborhood. The former, led by Daniel Burnham in the 1890s, represented a baroque approach to large-scale integrated urban planning—organized around plazas, avenues, and radial and grid street plans. One of Burnham's precepts was "make no little plans" (Gallion and Eisner, 1963:81).

The *planned neighborhood* concept has had a far more significant impact on modern planning. The ideal of a neighborhood which is socially workable, reasonably self-sufficient economically, and developed at quite low physical densities was originally propounded by Ebenezer Howard in 1902 in *Garden Cities of Tomorrow* (1965) and discussed in American planning circles by Clarence Perry (1929). Perry organized neighborhood space around walking distance to such local services as shopping facilities, churches, and libraries. Street systems were to be designed to discourage through traffic—the neighborhood clearly was to be a walking community. The population was not to exceed 5000, and its nucleus would be the elementary school with facilities for community meetings. Perhaps the best known example of this garden suburb approach is Radburn, New Jersey, planned by Henry Wright and Clarence Stein in 1928.

Although a variety of indigenous and European concepts were adopted by builder-developers and theorists, particularly in the 1920s and 1930s, no new town policy has ever been implemented on a large scale in this country. This remains true today even though, as Alonso puts it, "just about everyone in the United States seems to be advocating the development of new towns" (1970:37). Alonso suggests that such a policy of distinct and small towns may be quite inappropriate for economic, demographic, and social reasons. More to the point, however, new towns are politically impractical. The usual American stance has been to foster privatism and to redevelop and expand existing centers.

The political acceptability of a government role in planning cities grew from large-scale government intervention in the 1930s. The 1937 government document *Our Cities: Their Role in the National Economy* suggested "judicious reshaping of the urban community and region. . . . with forward-looking and intelligent plans" (cited in Berry, 1973a:30), and acknowledged problems that dominate social thought on the city today, including transportation, health, delinquency, and the fragmentation of government control (Berry, 1973a:28–30). The New Deal witnessed the realization of three new towns that broadly accepted the garden city concept of Howard (discussed further below) and the more explicit neighborhood concepts of Stein and Perry. These towns were imaginatively named Greenbelt, Greenhills, and Greendale, and they represent exceptions to political and economic aversion to de novo urban planning.

In the past forty years agencies responsible for aspects of the urban space have steadily proliferated. For example, at the federal level agencies such as the FHA, the departments of Energy, Transportation, and Housing and Urban Development, and the Environmental Protection Agency have been established. It is highly significant that no national agency has ever been founded to promote urban planning per se. The guiding decisions on local growth are still exercised in the cumbersome but democratically conceived mosaic of local city governments, development agencies, zoning boards, planning commissions, and the like in a mode that has most in common with Berry's category of ameliorative problem-solving.

Planning powers are exercised by a variety of agencies. Although areawide regional planning boards and commissions have recently begun to form, planning at the city level remains most prominent. While some cities retain more or less autonomous planning commissions, more often planners serve in agencies in a consultative and staff role for legislatures or executives. These bodies are made up equally of political appointees and professionals who are frequently trained in the academic planning disciplines. This institutional arrangement ensures legislative or executive control over specific technical decisions, but it also insulates planners from their constituency and fosters a perceived role as form givers and a peer orientation in the planning profession. As the methodology of planning develops (e.g., the elaborate mathematical models for fore-casting travel demand discussed in Domencich and MacFadden, 1975), the per-ceived inaccessibility of planning decision makers is increasing.

Strong pressures have grown for a citizen role in the decision process more explicit than that provided by traditional mechanisms of voting and public hearing. One proposed solution is the concept of advocacy planning, in which planning professionals adopt a partisan role for specific citizen interest groups. A more radical solution by which communities could control change in their neighborhoods is proposed by Wolpert et al. (1973). They suggest the forma-tion of a new institution: the community technical services unit. This agency would be locally based and would specialize in eliciting (e.g., by survey) public reaction to proposed planning decisions.

Although a variety of planning documents is mandated in most cities, ranging from the general and comprehensive plans to specific environmental impact statements, the legal heart of everyday planning in the United States is zoning. A variety of zoning devices exist (Babcock, 1966; Natoli, 1971), but the fundamental concept is conservative. Most often the intent of zoning is to pre-serve the values and returns inherent in existing developed land (e.g., preserv-ing residential property values). A variety of mechanisms including zoning amendments, zoning variances, and conditional use permits balance communi-ty welfare and hardships to specific users of land. Zoning regulations (and also building codes) are quite specific on the density and physical structure of de-velopments in residential areas. Such strictly physical specifications can exert substantial control over housing prices and the general attractiveness of devel-opments to various social groups. In practice, zoning in middle-class suburbs has been a strong force for social segregation. Because zoning regulations are usually conceived to protect the value of developed rather than agricultural land, a paradoxical situation arises. Regulation has been extremely permissive in allowing extensive, wasteful speculative private development of the subur-ban fringe. The shape of these developments is determined by market forces. However, once land is developed, zoning represents an extremely conservative force for socioeconomic uniformity.

For the most part, American planning has been conservative and ameliora-tive. At the same time the urban social sciences are perhaps more developed in the United States than anywhere else in the world. This level of sophistication has led to a wealth of imaginative urban ideals, few of which are likely to be implemented in the conservative American political system. This tension be-tween the ideals of form and control and the reality of the current capitalist system is unlikely to be resolved in the near future.

The British New Towns Program

To better understand the problems of American urban planning, we should look at the earliest and most far-reaching experiment in the postindustrial western world: the new towns program of the United Kingdom. The foundations of the new towns movement were laid in the nineteenth and early twentieth centuries by visionary writers such as Owen, Buckingham, and, especially, Ebenezer Howard. The immediate causes of the program's implementation in the mid-1940s were the perceived overdevelopment and overpopulation of London, the critical housing shortage posed by wartime bombing and the postwar surge in family formation, and more general national problems of economic depression.

These problems were addressed in a series of laws by the wartime coalition government and by the postwar socialist government. Far-reaching government intervention in the land market and the whole private sector was required to implement the programs. First, the future locations of all industries above a certain size were controlled by a certification system. This system of location certificates was used to encourage industries to locate away from London in less-developed regions. The New Towns Act of 1945 and, particularly, the comprehensive Town and Country Planning Act of 1947 established the right of government to control all land development throughout the country. Legal principles of compensation were developed (Gallion and Eisner, 1963:334). Powers of compulsory purchase (eminent domain) in Britain were traditionally stronger than those in the United States. The British equivalent of zoning by local authorities has also been far stronger than would be politically acceptable in America; in particular, it allows the protection of entirely undeveloped land. American zoning procedures are phrased only in terms of alternative means of development and are relatively powerless to prevent speculative development of new land. This is one reason why the boundaries between town and country are far more clear-cut in Britain (and in other European countries) than they are in the United States.

Against this background of traditional government powers plus new enabling legislation, urban problems broadly comparable to those of the United States were attacked in a coherent and large-scale fashion. It is necessary to emphasize that the construction of New Towns represents a minor part of the total strategy on housing and the solution of urban problems. There is a long tradition of public (local authority) housing in the United Kingdom, particularly for lower-income groups. Local authority public housing accounts for one-half of all new housing in Britain (Berry, 1973a:134). Most of this development occurs in and around existing centers. However, the new towns are of particular interest, for they represent a social experiment that at the time was almost unique in the Western world: an attempt to grapple practically with the ideal physical and social forms for the city. In the thirty-year history of British new towns a variety of social and spatial structures have been attempted. A central theme has been the issue of the appropriate level of social diversity at the neighborhood level. In one sense the series of new towns may be viewed as experiments in the social structure of neighborhoods.

The physical and social premises of the first generation of new towns were established in a series of government reports culminating in the work of the

Reith Committee on New Towns (1946) and the Greater London Plan developed by Abercrombie (1945) (see Hall 1966, 1975 and Schaffer, 1972). The extension of London was halted, and further development was excluded by a green belt. A total of fifteen new towns were projected throughout the country, of which eight formed a ring within thirty or forty miles of London (e.g., Crawley, Harlow, Hemel Hempstead). Originally the populations of these towns were projected in the tens of thousands, with none exceeding 60,000. Many of these projections have since been revised upward. The towns were built by quasi-independent development corporations constituted and financed by the government but operating independently.

The new towns achieved a reasonable degree of economic self-sufficiency. Low development densities were axiomatic in the earliest new towns. Social diversity was an explicit goal. The principal tool to achieve such diversity was a mixture of alternative dwelling types in neighborhoods, including owned, leased and rented, detached, semidetached, one-, two- and three-story, with about 15 percent of all dwelling units designed to be physically suitable for the elderly (Schaffer, 1972:111). The kinds of planned neighborhood structures in early British new towns are illustrated in Figure 12.1. Neighborhoods were designed as cohesive physical entities with schools, churches, parks, shopping and other facilities, and with populations on the order of 3000 to 7000.

Opinions differ on whether the new towns succeeded in achieving the desired social integration. Statistics on the social and economic structures of some new towns are given in Table 12.2. The employment structures of the new towns are quite varied; certain employed categories are consistently underrepresented in all early new towns. Foremen and supervisory manual workers appear in higher proportions than in England and Wales as a whole, the Southeast region, or the Greater London Area. Most other employment percentages vary on either side from the national and regional means, suggesting that qualitatively the economic structure of the new towns does not differ significantly from other cities in the country. The age structure of the new towns suggests a relative deficiency of elderly and teenagers and a relative excess of children.

Attempts to socially integrate neighborhoods by juxtaposing various types of accommodation have been unsuccessful (Porteous, 1977). Selective migration has, on the whole, increased social and age segregation. As Porteous puts it, and as preceding chapters imply, "Most people prefer homogeneity, to live near people like themselves, the ideal of the socially balanced neighborhood is virtually unattainable" (1977:76).

The first-generation new towns have been criticized for their relatively small size and, in the case of the towns of the Southeast, for their close proximity to London. Structurally, the two main points of criticism have been a commitment to excessively low densities and to an oversimplified social and physical neighborhood concept. Cullen (cited in Schaffer, 1972:105) terms low densities "prairie planning," and indicates their high social and economic costs in terms of unnecessary movement, especially pedestrian trips. In the second

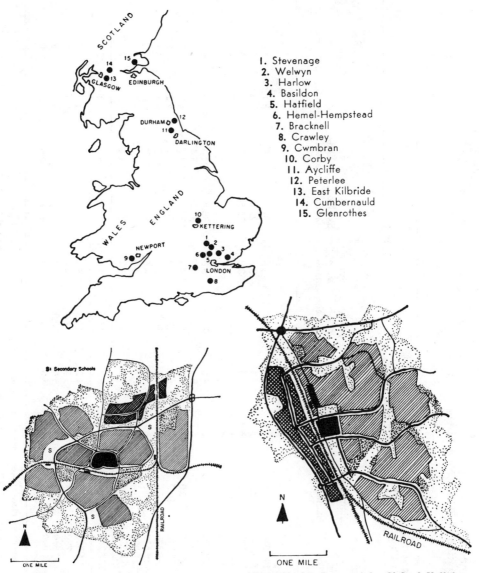

1. Stevenage
2. Welwyn
3. Harlow
4. Basildon
5. Hatfield
6. Hemel-Hempstead
7. Bracknell
8. Crawley
9. Cwmbran
10. Corby
11. Aycliffe
12. Peterlee
13. East Kilbride
14. Cumbernauld
15. Glenrothes

CRAWLEY *Designed by Anthony Minoprio*   STEVENAGE *Designed by Clifford Holliday*

Figure 12.1 *British New Towns* Fifteen sites comprised the first generation of New Towns. Their original populations were planned in the range of fifty thousand to sixty thousand, but these sizes have since been exceeded. Plans were organized around functionally integrated neighborhoods with populations of about three thousand to six thousand. The neighborhoods incorporated small shopping centers, primary schools, and social facilities, and they were geared to pedestrian movement. (*Source:* From *The Urban Pattern*, 3rd ed., by Arthur Gallion and Simon Eisner. © 1975 by Litton Educational Publishing, Inc. Reprinted by permission of D. Van Nostrand Company.)

Table 12.2 Employment and Age Structure of the First Generation of British New Towns

Area	Total	Social structure of new towns (Comparison with national and regional averages)									
		Employers and managers, %	Pro-fessional workers, %	Inter-mediate non-manual, %	Junior non-manual, %	Foremen and Super-visory manual, %	Skilled manual, %	Semi-skilled manual, %	Un-skilled manual, %	Personal service and own account, %	Farmers forces, and indefinite, %
Averages											
England and Wales	14,490,540	10.1	4.6	4.5	12.7	3.6	31.3	14.9	8.1	4.6	5.6
Greater London	2,468,300	12.0	5.6	5.4	18.1	3.3	27.6	12.7	8.0	5.9	1.4
South East Region	5,157,197	12.3	5.9	5.4	15.7	3.3	27.8	12.5	7.2	5.5	4.4
New Towns											
Basildon	19,950	6.0	3.4	4.8	12.4	5.3	33.8	22.3	7.1	4.2	0.7
Bracknell	7,450	9.0	8.7	5.6	13.7	4.3	32.9	15.4	5.2	2.1	3.1
Crawley	19,120	10.0	7.7	6.2	15.4	3.8	33.6	13.4	4.9	4.2	0.8
Harlow	19,740	10.3	6.8	6.2	12.3	4.9	34.9	14.9	4.2	4.8	0.7
Hatfield	7,330	7.6	6.7	4.6	14.7	5.0	37.2	13.8	6.4	3.3	0.7
Hemel Hempstead	19,610	10.1	6.7	5.5	11.6	4.6	34.1	17.1	5.6	4.2	0.5
Stevenage	17,030	8.4	7.5	7.8	14.4	4.0	33.5	16.3	4.6	2.8	0.7
Welwyn Garden City	11,970	11.4	10.9	9.0	14.5	4.2	27.9	14.4	4.3	2.7	0.7
Total, London new towns	122,200	9.1	7.0	6.2	13.5	4.5	33.5	16.3	5.3	3.8	0.8
Aycliffe	4,530	5.7	4.2	4.2	14.6	8.4	37.8	18.5	4.2	1.5	0.9
Corby	13,780	4.4	2.6	3.8	7.6	4.1	42.7	17.7	15.5	1.2	0.4
Cwmbran	10,910	7.3	5.1	5.0	10.0	6.9	30.6	21.7	9.3	3.5	0.6
Peterlee	4,990	5.8	3.0	4.0	9.2	5.4	40.4	20.6	8.2	1.0	2.4

Note: Classification is by area of residence, not place of work. Retired people are excluded.

Source: Schaffer, 1972:186. Copyright British Crown. Reprinted by permission of the Controller of Her Majesty's Stationery Office.

(Percentages)

Age Groups (years)	Bracknell	Crawley	Harlow	Hemel-Hempstead	Corby	Aycliffe	Peterlee	Skelmers-dale	England & Wales
0–4	10.3	10.1	12.9	9.5	13.5	12.9	15.1	11.8	8.5
5–9	11.4	11.3	12.6	10.2	11.2	11.3	13.7	8.2	7.6
10–14	9.2	10.6	10.2	9.4	9.2	9.1	8.6	5.7	6.9
15–19	8.2	8.4	7.3	8.2	8.0	6.4	6.8	8.4	7.8
20–24	5.9	4.7	6.0	5.7	7.2	6.1	8.6	5.6	6.7
25–29	6.9	5.6	7.2	5.5	7.9	8.2	9.3	8.4	6.0
30–34	7.8	7.9	8.6	7.2	7.0	8.0	8.4	6.8	5.9
35–39	9.0	9.1	9.0	8.9	7.1	9.3	7.2	5.1	6.2
40–44	7.3	9.3	7.7	8.2	6.4	8.6	6.5	6.4	6.7
45–49	6.5	6.8	6.0	6.5	6.3	5.6	3.7	7.4	6.3
50–54	5.4	5.0	4.0	6.1	4.9	3.5	3.1	6.1	6.6
55–59	3.7	3.6	2.9	4.3	4.5	2.9	2.1	6.0	6.5
60–64	2.9	2.6	1.6	3.2	3.1	3.0	2.3	3.9	5.7
65–69	2.0	1.8	1.5	2.6	1.8	1.8	2.1	4.1	4.6
70–74	1.6	1.2	1.2	2.3	0.9	2.0	1.1	2.4	3.4
75+	1.9	2.0	1.3	2.2	1.0	1.3	1.3	3.7	4.6
All %	100.0	100.0	100.0	100.0	100.0	100.0	100.0	100.0	100.0
Ages No.	23,710	62,680	67,920	64,130	43,850	15,850	18,330	12,040	

Note: Percentage figures have been rounded and do not therefore always add to 100 per cent.

Source: Schaffer, 1972:189. Copyright British Crown. Reprinted by permission of the Controller of Her Majesty's Stationery Office.

generation of British new towns, higher densities have been encouraged, with populations in the hundreds of thousands.

Soviet Urban Planning

A recurring theme in this book has been the role of subtle social distinctions as both products and determinants of segregation in the urban space. Considering the Marxist aim of destroying all such distinctions, the ideal socialist city should be quite different from that of the industrialized West. Judged by idealist statements on the socialist city in the classical writings of Marx, Engels, and Lenin or in more modern Soviet writings (e.g., Khodzhaev and Khorev, 1973), the concrete accomplishments of Russian urbanism appear meager. Yet, considering the state of Russia in 1917, Soviet urban and industrial growth has been phenomenal. According to Berry (1973a:156) the Soviet population was 18 percent urban in 1926 but 56 percent urban in 1969.

Because of Russia's very recent industrialization and modernization it is difficult to compare Western and Soviet urbanism. It is impossible to tell which differences are due to disparities in relative economic growth and which are products of planning ideology itself. For example, levels of private automobile ownership are far lower in the Soviet Union than in the United States. This fact alone could account for the compact centralized form of the Soviet city and for the lack of sprawling, socially segregated suburbs, quite aside from the fact that such segregation is unacceptable ideologically.

Khodzhaev and Khorev (1973) summarize some of the main premises of Soviet planning. They strongly emphasize structural economic planning for the entire urban system and for integrating the rural and urban economies. They say little about the internal structure of cities beyond implying that socioeconomic segregation should not exist. Both Marx and Engels argued for the erosion of the historic class distinction between town and country, which they viewed as a product of the ancient parasitical relationship between town and country. Khodzhaev and Khorev's main prescriptions to accomplish this goal are unified planning of the rural and urban economy, developing of functional and communications links between town and country, and "overcoming" (presumably dispersing) excessively large urban concentrations. The third goal has recently been pursued in attempts to limit the growth and dominance of Moscow. Although a British-style green belt solution has been adopted, and although substantial controls are exerted over all individuals' rights to work and reside in specific localities, Moscow has continued to grow. While traditional Soviet planning has maintained that the ideal city size is around 250,000 (Blumenfeld, 1964:195), it has been argued recently that larger sizes may lead to appreciable scale economies and that even Moscow may not be too large (Perevedentsev, 1972).

The internal configuration of urban space is planned in neighborhood units (*microrayons*) ranging in size from 6000 to 12,000 people with integrated service facilities, again predicated on the dogma that no class distinctions in residential space or in access to services should exist. Smith (1976), though, suggests that an elite exurban *dacha* (villa) culture, disparities in access to housing opportunity, and alternative economies including an elite market in luxury goods exist and are officially tolerated. Apartment living is the principal form of urban occupancy, and a high degree of physical uniformity is imposed in standardized and apparently ill designed high-rises. Chronic housing shortages before and after World War II led to an emphasis on mass production. Berry characterizes the form of the Soviet city as follows:

> Since quantity was so important, quality was sacrificed, and nowhere does one find more drab and monotonous modern cities, and buildings with poorer internal design, than in the U.S.S.R., although there are attempts today to provide a greater range of building styles, apartment sizes, and qualities of development. The industrialized methods produce standard apartment blocks almost exclusively. Movement in the cities is by public transportation. Services and facilities are the minimum necessary. An elaborate, often monumental, political-cultural administrative core is provided for the city, surrounded by a succession of self-contained neighborhood units, undifferentiated socially (1973a:157).

Soviet urban planning has achieved its goal of providing sufficient housing in the face of rapid urbanization. It seems also to have achieved its principal socio-spatial goal of avoiding the kind of class segregation and urban sprawl that attended Western urbanization. Soviet cities have avoided the chronic problems of slums, crime, and poverty that are favorite targets of Russian critics of the American urban system. However, total and centralized controls over the urban space have produced disappointingly few innovations in either the physical or social form of urban space. Viewed as systems to provide access to choice opportunities and a high material level of living, Soviet cities have yet to attain the standards of the industrialized West, still less those of the Marxist ideal.

PLANNING THE URBAN FUTURE

Some Ideals of Urban Form

Urban planning, whatever style it may take, represents a conscious attempt to influence the form and content of future cities. It is goal-oriented activity, and, as such, its success or failure depends on the clarity of its urban vision. An efficient and just urban plan is one whose goals are rooted in a firm grasp of city structure and dynamics, a balanced appreciation of the welfare requirements of the city's varied subpopulations, and a practical concern for the political and economic feasibility of the goals themselves. Good urban practice, then, requires visions that are achievable, democratic, and functional.

Since ancient times much has been written concerning the ideal city. Classical philosophers, including Plato and Aristotle, made many statements on the optimal urban form. They were concerned with the ideal size and social composition of the city necessary for subsistence, defense, and efficient government. Generally, recent commentators on the urban form have either been practical social thinkers (such as Ebenezer Howard) or architects (such as Frank Lloyd Wright or Le Corbusier). Typically such writers have prescribed an urban form without considering practical problems such as its implementation and cost effectiveness.

Ebenezer Howard and the Garden City Movement   One of the most influential concepts of the ideal city, particularly in Great Britain, has been the notion of the garden city published by Howard in 1902 in his *Garden Cities of Tomorrow* (1965). Howard's work belonged to the tradition of nineteenth-century social concern with the plight of the industrial city. It combined a utopian idealism with a practical concern for detail that actually led to the construction of two cities and directly influenced dozens more.

Howard based his argument on a comparison of the problems of rural and industrial urban living. He argued for a synthesis of town and country that would combine the best features of each (e.g., the social diversity and economic opportunity of the city and the light, clean air, and recreational opportunity of the country). He termed the result a garden city. Unlike previous theorists, particularly those with an architectural orientation, Howard was not obsessed with physical layout; rather, he recognized the central importance of a socially and economically balanced settlement. Lewis Mumford argues that Howard's "prime contribution was to outline the nature of a balanced community and to show what steps were necessary, in an ill-organized and disoriented society, to bring it into existence"(in a foreword to Howard, 1965:33).

Howard's ideal is portrayed in Figure 12.2. His design for urban form is predicated on the belief that urban growth must be limited to ensure a healthy social and physical environment. This Wirth-like view of the urban experience led to a number of specific proposals. He emphasized the need for the city to be quite small (around 30,000) with reasonably low densities. The city itself should contain approximately 1000 acres—the central five acres of which would include community-oriented and commercial activity. Beyond this area would be a residential ring and an industrial ring. To prevent further growth and to establish a healthy physical milieu, a green belt of 5000 acres should surround the industrial area.

Though he wrote before the automobile had its major influence on urban form, Howard proposed development densities that were quite low for the time. Even more remarkably, he anticipated the growth of *regional systems of cities* (closely spaced cities with a great deal of economic interchange). He argued the virtue of *balanced suburbs* with a mixture of residential and industrial usage, and he believed that such new towns should be built reasonably close to each other. Such proposals are very modern in outlook (Schaffer, 1972). The

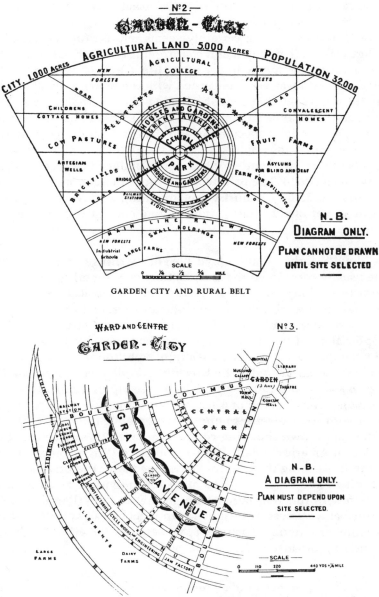

Figure 12.2 *Ebenezer Howard's Garden City*   Howard's urban design attempted to combine the virtues of rural and urban living. The projected size was small (approximately thirty thousand people), and ready access to the country was guaranteed by the design. Howard emphasized the need to adapt his ideal scheme to the requirements of particular sites. (*Source:* Reprinted from *Garden Cities of Tomorrow* by Ebenezer Howard, by permission of The MIT Press, Cambridge, MA.)

same can be said for Howard's concerns for social diversity and the maintenance of environmental quality.

Some of Howard's writing certainly seems impractical and idealistic. He
suggests, for example, that "town and country must be married, and out of this
joyous union will spring a new hope, a new life, a new civilization" (1965:48).
Nevertheless, Howard was very concerned with the practical fiscal needs of his
proposals. He suggested that land be owned not by individuals, but by a
limited dividend company. This mechanism would alter the competitive process since it eliminates land speculation and the competition between industrial and residential units. In conjunction with the architect Unwin, Howard realized his proposals in two garden cities near London: Letchworth (begun in
1903) and Welwyn (1920). The private financing of these projects, however, encountered serious difficulty. Industry was unwilling to move its base from London, and thus government intervention became necessary to complete the effort.

Frank Lloyd Wright   Frank Lloyd Wright's writings on the ideal form of
the city are usually considered the most distinctively American contribution to
this concern (e.g., Hall, 1975:67). In *When Democracy Builds* (1945), *The Living
City* (1958), and other works, Wright spelled out an urban form that combined a
desire to preserve essentially rural life styles and social structures with a far-
sighted appreciation of the spatial dispersion made possible by universal automobile ownership. The central idea in Wright's philosophy is the value of low
density—a concept he shared with Howard. He planned a hypothetical city
embodying this ideal and called it Broadacre (see Figure 12.3).

The result is a combination of a semiagrarian life style (an acre of farmland
is associated with each dwelling) and an automobile-oriented economy that
foretold "the out-of-town shopping centre some twenty years before it actually
arrived in North America" (Hall, 1975:70). Some of Wright's ideas anticipated
other American planning thought that developed after the private automobile
had had its dispersive effect. Wright's plans for individual dwelling units display a concern with function rather than geometric form (Porteous, 1977).

The principal weakness of Wright's plan is its lack of concern for the spatial organization of individual activity spaces and for the economic base of the
design. Criticizing Broadacre, Eliot-Hurst writes:

> It is not an urban plan but a rurban continuum; Broadacre City is everywhere and
> nowhere. Industry is decentralized to a series of scattered nodes among the one-,
> two-, and three-acre lots. Wright provided no plan for decentralization: It simply
> happens. The automobile connects large tracts of "agricultural residences" with
> workplaces. The individual lots are not intended to provide full-time work, but to
> establish the organic home base of life. Away from home, the comprehensiveness
> of Broadacre is less clear—the semiagrarian vision—must obviously be supported
> by a full-scale business economy. The corporate locale is not really identified, how-
> ever, and the stress remains on integrating rural topography and architecture; to be
> plain, Wright's socioeconomy is confused (1975:299).

Area of Plan is
Two Square Miles

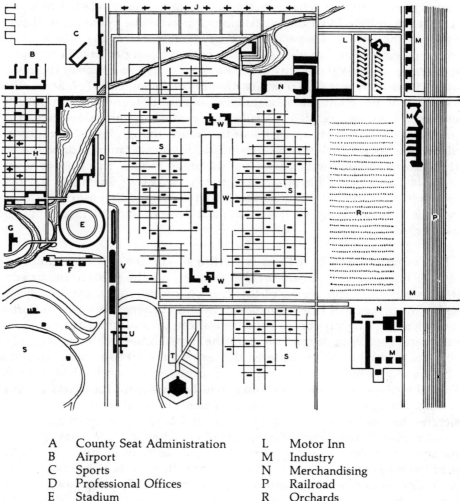

A	County Seat Administration	L	Motor Inn
B	Airport	M	Industry
C	Sports	N	Merchandising
D	Professional Offices	P	Railroad
E	Stadium	R	Orchards
F	Hotel	S	Homes and Apartments
G	Sanitarium	T	Temple and Cemetery
H	Small Industry	U	Research
J	Small Farms	V	Zoo
K	Park	W	Schools

Figure 12.3 *Frank Lloyd Wright's Broadacre* Wright's design was highly dispersed, emphasizing the role of highways in providing access to commercial, industrial, and social activities distributed over extensive areas. In an attempt to conserve aspects of rural living which Wright valued highly, homes are located in lots of about one acre, providing for some agricultural activity. (*Source:* From *The Urban Pattern*, 3rd ed., by Arthur Gallion and Simon Eisner. ©1975 by Litton Educational Publishing, Inc. Reprinted by permission of D. Van Nostrand Company.)

The notion of a dissolving urban form has also been elaborated in Jean Gottmann's discussion of Megalopolis (1961). Geographic research on travel patterns, interaction and activity fields, and distance-decay relationships suggests that a landscape free from the friction of distance has yet to occur, though the attenuating effects of separation are measurably decreasing. The intrinsic merits and demerits of dispersed sub- or nonurban life styles have been repeatedly referred to throughout this book. Riesman (1957) emphasizes the disadvantages, as does Whyte (1962), while Kramer (1972) and Gans (1962) question the traditional arguments on suburban homogenization and cultural poverty. These social consequences of a spatially dispersed community were implicit in Frank Lloyd Wright's physical vision of the future, though he did not fully articulate them. As with other formal proposals, his ideals fail to address the underlying social and political dynamics of the urban system. This naiveté has serious costs. For example, his proposals ignore problems of financing. His ideal form would be exorbitantly expensive. Given the current dimensions of the energy crisis, it is extremely unlikely that such decentralized plans can ever be implemented.

Le Corbusier and High-Density Settings   The Swiss-born architect Le Corbusier has dominated European architecture from the 1920s to the present. His ideas are often considered distinctively European and diametrically opposed to the precepts of Frank Lloyd Wright and Ebenezer Howard. Le Corbusier emphasized a tightly focused and centralized urban form. His central concerns were geometric formalism and the possibilities of extremely high density, high-rise buildings scattered through open, parklike spaces. His view of social and economic organization was functional and mechanistic. He considered the city a "machine for living," and his dominant focus was physical planning. Though he made numerous statements on ideal social and economic structures, he was first and last a physically and formally oriented architect.

Le Corbusier's two most influential books, written in a rhetorical and dogmatic style, were *The City of Tomorrow* (1929) and *The Radiant City* (1933). He designed buildings and portions of cities as far afield as France, Sweden, and India. His Contemporary City is portrayed in Figure 12.4. The downtown focus of business activity is preserved in sixty-story office buildings in the center, where densities attain 1200 persons per acre. The bulk of the residential space is in surrounding eight-floor apartment buildings (120 persons per acre). In the parklike surroundings is a garden city of single-family housing. Transportation activity focuses at the center with a hub of motor, rail, and air termini. The total proposed population of the city is 3 million.

Despite Le Corbusier's engineering and architectural expertise, his attitude toward financing was casual. *The City of Tomorrow* contains a chapter on "Finance and Realization," which begins, "When I began to write this book, I thought I would entrust some well-known economist with this chapter on the financial aspect. . . . Finally, it was too late, so this chapter on figures must be without them" (1929:293).

Le Corbusier's writings express a concern for functionality (for example,

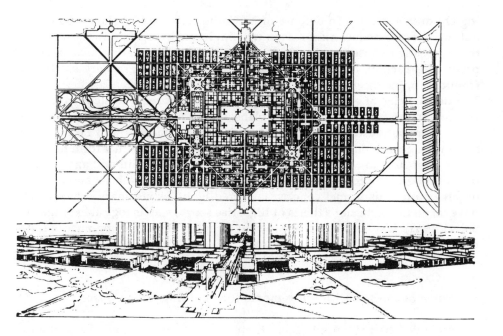

Figure 12.4   *Le Corbusier's Contemporary City*   This city, designed in 1922, would accommodate 3 million people. Le Corbusier combined high population densities with parklike surroundings by means of high-rise dwellings. Eight-story apartment buildings and sixty-story office buildings are surrounded by a "garden city" of single family units. (*Source:* From *The Urban Pattern*, 3rd ed., by Arthur Gallion and Simon Eisner. © 1975 by Litton Educational Publishing, Inc. Reprinted by permission of D. Van Nostrand Company.)

proximity to recreational opportunities and shopping activities) that compare favorably with recent statements on the inadvisability of low spatial densities in the British new towns (e.g., Schaffer, 1972). His concerns for light, air, and a livable (cellular) arrangement of living quarters have also been admired (e.g., Mumford, 1961). But his most influential ideal was the use of high-rise architecture to attain the paradoxical union of high densities with a landscape that emphasized open space. Indeed, a whole generation of architects and planners in the 1930s and 1940s came to revere these ideals (Hall, 1975:75). His impact can be seen in numerous multistory projects in England and elsewhere.

> All over Britain the remarkable change in the urban landscape during the late 1950s and the 1960s—as slum clearance and urban renewal produced a sudden unprecedented crop of skyscrapers—is a mute tribute to Le Corbusier's influence (Hall, 1975:76).

As we outlined in Chapter 10, high-rise residential developments have been criticized by social scientists for many reasons. For example, high-rise public housing projects have been shown to inhibit neighboring and supervising children's activity. In defense of Le Corbusier's ideas, it should be pointed out that there is no technical reason why high-rise living conditions must have these negative consequences. Supervised play areas, meeting spaces, sound-proof construction, and even off-the-ground parks and greenery are feasible from an engineering viewpoint, as many of Le Corbusier's sketches indicate. The deficiencies of existing high-rise developments seem to stem from financial constraints and unimaginative plans.

A more serious deficiency in Le Corbusier's ideals seem to be his infatuation with geometric form, and his general design premise that form has precedence over function. Le Corbusier's writings confirm again and again that he put form before function, despite his frequent remarks on social and economic organization. This formal concern is shared by other visionary urbanists who have taken Le Corbusier's thesis of high-rise settings to its logical extreme (e.g., Soleri, 1969). It should be apparent from Chapter 10 that this premise is fundamentally wrong.

Some Socio-Spatial Requirements for Planning Urban Space

Now we shall attempt to focus the material from previous chapters and to outline several specific ways in which knowledge of urban social space can inform the planning process.

As we have seen, ideals of urban form and actual planning practice diverge. Howard, Le Corbusier, and Frank Lloyd Wright, as well as many more recent theorists of urban form, imply that the best strategy in solving urban problems is to start over again in newly planned cities. They paint an ideal urban future in broad strokes, without any detailed concern for solving immediate problems in existing cities. These ideals have tremendously influenced urban form. Howard was the conceptual father of a whole generation of British New Towns, while Le Corbusier's influence is evident in the architecture of almost all modern cities. In a handful of new towns in Europe and North America, visionary ideals have been realized: The urban future has come to the few million inhabitants of such places. However, the problems of most cities and most urbanites are more local and more immediate. In the aftermath of the urban renewal programs of the 1960s and in the present economic climate, sweeping and large-scale solutions are politically undesirable and economically infeasible. In the 1960s the problems of cities were seen as analogous to the problems of traveling to the moon. They could be solved, it was felt, by careful technological planning and by an unlimited infusion of money. In the 1970s this confidence waned.

> We are on the whole more somber, less confident, more apprehensive about the future—less trusting of government to solve the critical problems of our collective life, our life in community. It is a time for reflection, stock taking, reappraisal of our strengths and weaknesses (Reilly, 1976:202).

These times of political suspicion and fiscal uncertainty require less bold goals of form, goals that accept the past accomplishments of cities and attempt to solve the inequities that have evolved over time. We shall never lack idealistic prescriptions for the city. Indeed, it is easy to articulate general urban goals and an idealized form. The practical problems of realizing such forms, however, are monumental. They include the political fragmentation that pits agency against agency and the trillions of dollars of capital inertia in existing spatial structures that condemn most practical planning efforts to be partial, piecemeal, and incremental.

Perhaps our most fundamental and chronic need is for detailed knowledge of how the urban system works. It is unnecessary to belabor the point of our ignorance. Public housing projects win architectural prizes and are demolished a few years later as hopelessly ill conceived. Socialist planners, enjoying absolute and centralized powers of control, have not equaled, much less improved upon, the Western systems they have criticized for fifty years. British planners, who set out neighborhoods according to the best available social knowledge, failed to engineer the social diversity they aimed for. In brief, almost all urban problems manifestly resist solution. No single perspective can provide the required knowledge, but this book has attempted to outline one crucially important area of our ignorance: the relationship between social and spatial structures in the city.

The required knowledge cannot be provided merely by gathering data, though it is true that we are almost completely ignorant of many facets of urban structure and that traditional data bases such as the publications of the Census Bureau are inadequate for ecological studies. A data explosion is in progress concerning some aspects of the urban space, including, for example, the deluge of continually updated land use data provided by LANDSAT and other remote-sensing satellite systems.

The inadequacy of data collection stems from the fact that conceptualization (the definition of what is relevant and how it is to be measured) precedes, not follows, determination of facts. Turner (1967), discussing the distinction between "facts" and "data," shows how the latter depends upon the conceptual and theoretical predisposition of the researcher. Kemeny states, "I doubt that we can state a fact entirely divorced from its theoretical interpretation" (1959:89). The precedence of theory construction over data collection is clearly seen in Harvey's (1972b) critique of classical economic models of the urban space (see Chapter 11). Although the economic processes of the urban land market have been studied in detail, few authors have viewed the metropolis as a spatial system for redistributing income. Radical geographers such as Harvey and Bunge imply that the dominance of the classical economic perspective has led to solutions that are doomed to failure. This perspective, by its very nature, produces knowledge directed to concerns for efficiency rather than social justice.

Conceptual developments, theory construction, and data collection proceed hand in hand. Our crisis of knowledge is a crisis of terminology and theory. If we construe the term *theory* to embrace the conceptual and operational specification of data, Sherlock Holmes seems to have been wrong in repeatedly telling Dr. Watson, "It is capital error to theorize in advance of the facts." This point is also argued in a widely accepted model of the evolution of science by Thomas Kuhn (1962), who argues that sciences establish general conceptual frameworks, or *paradigms*. One of the first symptoms of a paradigm change is a data shortage. This is not a shortage of "facts" but rather a shortage of data specified according to the new theoretical conceptual framework.

The approach to urban society advocated in this book—an amalgam of ideas from ecology, social geography, and ethology—represents an apparent paradigm change in urban sociology, urban and behavioral geography, environmental psychology, urban planning, and architecture. We shall attempt now to summarize some of the main findings of preceding chapters that appear to be relevant to urban policy and, more specifically, to the design of urban residential space.

The Diversity of Spatial Experience   The question of how space influences behavior is extremely difficult to answer because spatial structure exerts its effects in such an enormous variety of ways. Space is objective and cognitive, absolute and relative; it has both metric and topological attributes; spatial structures both cause and indicate social structure.

There are many ways in which spatial structures can be characterized and measured, but human reactions to space are even more diverse. The issue of how much (if any) human spatial behavior is intrinsic and how much is acquired is controversial. Proponents of the territorial imperative and sociobiology argue that the instinctive component may be substantial. Experimental and observational research has confirmed the importance of various spatial behaviors in humans, including territorial attachment to the home base, cognition of local neighborhood, habitual travel behaviors in the whole urban space, and the maintenance of individual distance in social interactions of various degrees of intimacy (see Chapter 2). Although we know little about these behaviors, it is clear that there is not only cross-cultural variation (revealed, for example, in Hall's (1966) work on individual distance), but also variation by age, sex, and social class within a given society. This constitutes strong evidence that these spatial behaviors are learned and culturally transmitted. In fact, as Chapter 6 argues, the impact of space on behavior must be understood mainly in cognitive terms: we react to all aspects of space symbolically by means of our concepts, language, images, and stereotypes. People react to cognitive image, not to reality. In their role as manipulators of physical space, planners can also influence urban imagery and mental maps. This role of information manager is critical, for by improving the public's mental maps planners can further reduce the constraints on residential choice and access to services. Designing legible and functional spaces can foster more efficient spatial behavior and demolish the spatial boundaries that are more imaginary than real. Future planning must emphasize the crucial role of planners in facilitating more accurate, less constrained cognitive imagery.

Human Adaptability and Permissive versus Coercive Design   The directions of causal relationships between spatial arrangements and social structure are hard to establish. By comparison with all other animals, humans are uniquely active toward spatial arrangements. We live in environments that are predominantly or exclusively artificial. Yet we have clearly shown that settings control behavior in numerous obvious and subtle ways. This is true of microspace, in which furniture arrangements and engineered arrangements of the participants may determine the roles in social interaction, and of the entire urban space, in which the arrangement of facilities, stores, workplaces, and schools partially determines the whole activity pattern of households.

The distinguishing characteristic of human spatial behavior is its flexibility and adaptability. Cross-cultural comparisons of urban form, living densities, neighborhood structures, individual distance, travel patterns, and the like indicate the variety of behaviors that individuals cannot only tolerate, but actually come to regard as normal. This flexibility has often, in practice, absolved architects and planners from the need to seek any optima. The poor, the elderly, the adolescent, the handicapped, ethnically or culturally segregated groups have often lived and sometimes flourished under conditions significantly less than ideal.

This flexibility suggests several implications for the design of urban spatial arrangements. First, it is perhaps futile to assume that any single ideal may be defined at any scale. A more reasonable strategy than searching for the ideal is surely using spatial arrangements *permissively* rather than *coercively*. Although we may be unable to specify a comprehensive ideal, we know well that some arrangements inhibit social activity while others facilitate choice. Another implication of cross-cultural diversity of spatial behavior is that human spatial and social arrangements are emergent or evolving. This is plainly true of our genetic heritage; we are ground-dwelling primates who have lived in cities for a moment of evolutionary time. But it is also true of our cultural and technological heritage. A single invention, the internal combustion engine, in a period of about fifty years utterly changed the physical and social structure of the city. It is surely naive to believe that the future, perhaps the immediate future, holds no similar transformations. It would be dangerous to suppose that future developments will be any more predictable or controllable than the private automobile, which almost no social commentators of the nineteenth century foresaw. Here, too, is reason for a permissive stance rather than one centered on any specific and predefined ideal of social and spatial arrangements. The social and political mechanisms to provide this permissive framework are somewhat uncertain. The preceding discussion of ideals of political control hints at the debate that has surrounded the efficacy of free-market mechanisms. Community discretion and involvement are frequently advocated as one mechanism for permissive change.

For certain classes of problems, however, it is folly to adopt a permissive stance. Practical planning in our system is local, incremental, and problem oriented. We know very well the evils of slums, ethnic ghettoes, and traffic congestion, and we have a variety of theories that enable us to attack them normatively rather than permissively. On the other hand, it is easy to specify harder problems, ones in which existing theory is fragmentary and ambiguous. How, for example, in light of Chapter 11, can we design to reduce crime rates? Crime is spatially structured in the city. Its structure is at least in part a function of density and segregation patterns. High-density patterns invite high crime rates. At least superficially, then, you might expect crime rates to respond to the spatial dispersion of the urban population. Such a solution conflicts with current knowledge about the diversity of spatial preference. Certain life-style choices make accessibility desirable—accessibility is achieved by trading less residential space for more access. Also, a community-oriented life style appears to require at least minimum densities. Under a problem-oriented solution, with stringent government controls, the planner is faced with a serious dilemma: If crime is to be controlled, densities must be reduced; if densities are reduced, mental and experiential congruence with the environment is also reduced for certain groups. Spatial engineering is complex and difficult. It is all the more difficult given the paucity of scientific evidence and sound social science theory.

The Cognitive and Social Functions of Boundaries   A spatial structure is functional. Its topological features, especially objectively and subjectively perceived boundaries, serve a variety of social and cognitive purposes. In the narrow context of the ethnic ghetto, the term *segregation* has a negative connotation. In the more general sociological sense of real and perceived separation, segregation is a dominant feature of spatial organization, and a central means of cognizing or organizing our personal knowledge of the city. One of the clearest criticisms of current planning practice that flows from this whole text is that we have failed to understand and to exploit social and cognitive segregation processes.

Cognitively, we characterize or stereotype the city into regions and neighborhoods. The topological foundations of this process of knowing were discussed in Chapters 6 and 7. This may be viewed as part of the more general process of cognitive stereotyping (or concept formation) that seems to underlie all thought (Price, 1969:313). Semantic categories underlie ordinary language; so, too, spatially defined categories (regions, neighborhoods, boundaries, nodes) seem to provide the language which "space speaks." As with any other language, this process of stereotyping leads to error; it attributes an internal homogeneity and an external variance to neighborhoods that may not exist. Compared to everyday speech, the conceptual language we use to understand the city is very crude and its vocabulary very small. Lynch (1960), for example, was able to describe the main features of cognitive maps in terms of a simple vocabulary of lines, nodes, edges, areas, and landmarks. Subsequent work on mental maps in behavioral geography and environmental psychology has refined our knowledge of perceived spatial structure, but only reinforced the premise that boundaries are central to all spatial knowledge and understanding.

The cognitive functions of segregation are inseparable from its social uses. Social change theories describe the transition from societies predicated on personal knowing to those based on functional or categorical knowing. Lofland (1973) (see Chapter 3) argues that modern societies have evolved further in the framework of categorical knowing and shifted from an appearential order to one in which spatial or locational cues predominate: We know what people are by where they are. This is a distinctively spatial component of the more general cognitive process by which we ascribe roles and statuses to others.

Just as general social roles are complex and multidimensional, we have suggested that the socially perceived segregation of space is complex, hierarchic, and functional. We maintain and jealously guard our personal space, but individual distances vary depending on the scope and the recipient of the interaction. We move confidently in public spaces populated by depersonalized others. If strangers ask us the time or perhaps make an innocuous comment about the weather we do not feel threatened, but if they initiate a more personal conversation, becoming a real person for us in the process, we experience dissonance and perhaps anger. We have a home neighborhood surrounded by a defensible space over which we wish to exert certain kinds of control, including the exclusion of others. Yet the primary territory of the apartment dweller with anonymous neighbors may extend no farther than his or her door, while the suburbanite may feel threatened by a noisy disturbance several blocks away. In brief, there is immense variability in the scope and nature of socially perceived segregation. Effective planning must surely take this variability into account.

Diversity, Spatial Boundaries, and Scale   The title of a recent ethological study of planning, *Design for Diversity* (Greenbie, 1976) has the ring of a cliché, but it suggests a basic requirement in planning spatial arrangements. The urban revolution diversified society, generating new roles and functions. Industrial urbanization amplified this tendency. Status continua, economic roles, life style options have continued to proliferate throughout the nineteenth and twentieth centuries. Superimposed on such social differentiations are the more fundamental, demographic distinctions of age and family-cycle stage. Traditionally, sociology has been preoccupied with describing this diversity in aspatial terms. This diversity, however, exists in a spatial context. Urban space reflects the multidimensionality of the community, but, at the same time, space itself is multifunctional. The manifold uses of urban public space are determined by location, by occupants, and by time of day (e.g., Central Park as a place to walk at noon and at midnight).

Diversity is plainly inseparable from the issue of scale. Diversity acceptable at one scale (e.g., the city) is perceived as a threat at another scale (e.g., the home neighborhood). This suggests a useful hierarchy for describing scale in spatial arrangements: the home space, the neighborhood, and the whole activity space of a household or group.

The whole activity space is conceptualized in symbolic terms using verbal and pictorial memory. We know where to satisfy various needs, we have well-developed path habits, and we have a well-defined daily activity pattern, which probably encompasses many miles of the urban area. We tolerate and even require a high degree of diversity in the city as a whole. The mechanisms of stereotyping, the formation of spatial habits, and the depersonalization of strangers enable us to cope with this diversity. The traditional literature of human ecology and urban geography provides an appropriate frame of reference to understand the city at this level (e.g., social area analysis, factorial ecology, and descriptions of daily activity patterns). Many of the most pressing planning problems at this level are not social. The most pressing of all may be the urban transportation problem (Meyer et al., 1965). Taking advantage of this diversity requires efficient access to the larger metropolitan community. Design solutions to such ostensibly nonsocial problems have strong social implications. For example, the construction of an extensive network of interstate highways directly influenced the development of suburban land. In turn this development and the subsequent shifts in employment had serious negative consequences for inner-city residents.

Intermediate between the home space and the activity space is the neighborhood. This space is perceived as partly defensible. It is known in personal rather than categorical terms, and at least some group control is exerted over the activity of strangers. We tolerate certain kinds of diversity in the neighborhood but not others. As we have suggested earlier in this chapter, the neighborhood is frequently seen as a natural unit for planning purposes. Planners' view of the neighborhood has evolved from a purely physical concept to a cognitive and social one.

Perhaps the most important issue concerning neighborhoods in planning and social science is, what level of socioeconomic diversity is suitable? This amounts, of course, to a debate on the pros and cons of segregation conceived in its most general sense. A very delicate balance exists between acceptable levels of homogeneity and heterogeneity in neighborhood design, and it depends upon perceived defensibility and the control we are able to exert over strangers (Greenbie, 1976). Simple-minded attempts to foster diversity at the neighborhood level sometimes fail, as selective migrations increase homogeneity. This seems to have been the result of attempts to engineer social diversity in some planned neighborhoods in the first generation of British new towns (Schaffer, 1972; Porteous, 1977).

Strong arguments for diversity in neighborhoods have been advanced, for example, by Jane Jacobs (1961) and by critics of American middle-class suburbanization (Whyte, 1956). It is clear that a certain degree of diversity in age, family-cycle stage, and occupation is desirable in neighborhoods to foster opportunities for choice in life style and social interaction. It is easy to point to examples of segregation that amount to economic and social oppression and that may be categorically condemned. The ethnic ghetto is the clearest example. However, forcible dispersal of the disadvantaged group is no longer viewed as an acceptable solution. For example, many black community leaders argue for neighborhood and community development designed to foster economic equality and equality of opportunity while retaining the ethnic and cultural identity of neighborhoods.

Persuasive arguments for a degree of neighborhood homogeneity (i.e., for segregation) can be advanced. Lofland (1973) indicates the cognitive advantages of such separation. Greenbie (1976), far from criticizing the homogeneous suburbs, claims that they represent the most effective "community of limited liability" yet achieved. (A community of limited liability is a community whose residents can benefit from its coherence and identity without participating in its affairs.) The most compelling evidence for a reasonable degree of socioeconomic homogeneity comes from factorial ecology. Evidence from the cities studied shows that spontaneous (noncoerced) separation of communities follows various ecological dimensions. In North America, these dimensions are the familiar trio of economic status, familism, and ethnicity.

The central problem of planning at the neighborhood and community level may be phrased very simply: What is an appropriate degree of socioeconomic diversity? In some neighborhoods of the English new towns a variety of physical units have been closely juxtaposed; for example, small apartments designed for the elderly were mixed with larger single-family units. After these neighborhoods were occupied, however, selective migration has tended to homogenize them, leading to a mismatch between occupant requirements and dwelling units. Planners must begin to understand the sociological basis for this filtering process.

If spatial barriers are to be reduced, they must be reduced by choice rather than by coercion. As Ford's (1973) study of interracial housing suggests, imposed integration cannot fully resolve racial communication barriers. Under less controlled situations (the housing market), attempts to increase neighborhood diversity may simply result in succession (as with mismatch filtering). This argues for a permissive stance fostering rather than constraining choice. To achieve this, the cognitive image of the city must be broadened. As Johnston (1972) suggests, people tend to view housing choices sectorally. That is, potential migrants are spatially unaware of vast portions of the cityscape because their social networks do not reach beyond their sector. To flesh out cognitive images and perceived housing opportunities, relocation services for all classes must be made available. Such services can reduce cognitive barriers to choice. Real constraints on neighborhood choice, such as income and race, can be alleviated only by government intervention, such as civil rights laws and Operation Turnkey programs.

The neighborhood level of design shades off, abruptly or imperceptibly, into the primary space of the home. The design of this interface is particularly important in fostering neighborhood cohesion. For example, one of the basic design flaws of high-rise public housing seems to be that the dwelling space is conceived to end, abruptly, at the apartment doorway. Beyond lies a no man's land—an indefensible space of anonymous corridors, halls, and stairwells. The problem is aggravated by the fact that the home-neighborhood interface does not fall clearly into the jurisdiction of either planner or architect. Regional, urban, or local planners rarely stipulate the detailed physical configuration of the dwelling space. Zoning ordinances, building codes, fire regulations, and the like usually provide only general parameters for construction. For example, they specify whether development is to be for single- or multiple-family occupancy, and then mandate certain requirements of density, access, and structure. Within these specifications, the design of the fixed feature space of the home is decided by the developers and the architects they employ.

The central sociological issue concerning the interface between home space and neighborhood space is perceived control over the activities of strangers: defensibility. In high-rise public-housing projects an ironic situation arises. Neighborhood structure could be engineered; the home space and neighboring spaces (e.g., play areas, and meeting places) could be developed as an integral part of the architectural design. The architect could, in short, design neighborhoods as a whole, something seldom possible in the suburbs. Yet it is precisely in these settings that the interface between home space and neighborhood has been designed most ineptly.

Finally, regarding the home space itself, if we accept the axiom that form should facilitate function, the program for domestic architecture seems clear. Proxemic and microgeographic research suggests how sensitive fundamental behaviors and need satisfaction are to spatial arrangements. The role of the domestic architect, surely, is to design to provide for these needs. Yet, as Chapter 10 indicates, the architect has normally adopted a client- and esthetic-oriented role (Porteous, 1977). Recently the trend has been toward user-oriented design, and various prescriptions on user requirements have been developed (Bennett, 1977; Cooper, 1975). The problems the design professions face in implementing this program are obvious. Financial constraints and physical constraints inhibit design. Classically, this point has been true of cost-conscious public housing projects. However, these constraints are becoming more acute in the design of single-family units as well.

A more serious design problem, though, is identifying how physical dwelling structures actually affect need satisfaction. Enormous differences in the use of dwelling space and in norms of privacy have been shown across cultures. Within North American society, family cycle, life stage and the dimensions of careerism, familism, and consumerism generate wide-ranging individual requirements for the home space. For some the household is merely a dormitory; for others it is the very heart of their action space.

The Issue of Density Although in many ways the question of design density is inseparable from questions of diversity and scale, it is sufficiently prominent in urban planning to merit separate discussion. Some of the most pervasive empirical regularities of the urban mosaic involve residential population density (see Chapter 5). The main tool used by planners in regulating residential space is development density as specified in zoning ordinances. Although density is an emotional issue for some, no consensus exists on optimal density. Idealistic statements on density range from the extremely low densities advocated by Frank Lloyd Wright and condoned as inevitable by Webber (1964, 1970) to the extremely high densities advocated by Le Corbusier and by Dantzig and Saaty (1973). The traditional model of the planning neighborhood emphasizes very low physical densities, but more recently "prairie" planning has been widely criticized. One obvious drawback of dispersal is an increase in the overall monetary and psychic costs of travel in the individual activity space. In the context of increasing energy prices this is undesirable in itself. But low-density settings have been criticized for social reasons also. Jane Jacobs (1961), for example, specifically advocates relatively high densities.

Social science findings on urban densities are complex and even somewhat contradictory. The preindustrial city, constrained by pedestrian movement, was very compact. The first stages of industrialization, before automobile use became widespread, seemed to increase density. These high densities were indispensable in generating the range of social and economic alternatives that made the city a locus of emancipation and opportunity, as well as the center for economic and cultural production (Chapter 4). Yet Wirth (1938) saw density as a factor in promoting urban ills (Chapters 3 and 10).

A decade ago, research on animal behavior seemed to suggest that Wirth was right and that density-induced pathologies could be identified in humans. Subsequent research (e.g. Freedman, 1975) has failed to substantiate this argument, and a crucial distinction has been drawn between physical and socially perceived density. The effects of scale and design are probably far more important than gross physical density. For example, perceived privacy depends more on domestic architecture than on the number of people per acre. Proxemic mechanisms of depersonalization enable us to tolerate extreme crowding in elevators and subways. Social context obviously mediates the effects of density.

On a larger scale level, proponents of low densities must address the inescapable fact that, as the pervasiveness of the Clark-Newling density regularities (Chapter 5) indicates, high densities arise by choice in some parts of the urban space and for certain groups. It is clearly an oversimplification to regard simple density as a primary design variable at any scale. Socially and cognitively acceptable levels of density may be attained at high or low absolute physical density contingent upon the design of living space and neighborhood. The criteria for acceptable levels of density appear to revolve around a cognitive balance between proximity and social opportunity on the one hand and privacy and defensibility on the other. This balance is subtle and varies from one life style orientation to the next.

Efficiency versus Social Justice   Many of the planning prescriptions in social science and in the planning professions themselves are dominated by ideals of efficiency. Efficiency may be specified in various ways, for example, by minimum-cost travel patterns or by cost efficiency in housing design, but very often the final yardstick is profit and loss. This predilection toward efficiency solutions is perhaps natural in the American economic system. But much recent commentary and analysis indicates the need for solutions that address social justice rather than fiscal efficiency. We need to modify our concept of efficiency to embrace individual and social well-being.

Engineered change conceived in terms of efficiency led to a disastrous chapter in urban planning history—urban renewal. Most ill-fated urban renewal projects were not conceived callously, with reference only to profit and loss, but they were informed by overriding concerns with speedy construction, economy of materials, and by an infatuation with compact high-rise engineering forms in the style of Le Corbusier. The supreme paradox of such efforts was that they were not cost effective, even in simple-minded economic terms. Many renewal projects of the 1950s and 1960s either stand almost empty today or have already fallen to the wrecking ball. Such failures represent enormous monetary losses. We cannot make efficiency a priority without concern for distributive justice.

Also, public housing efforts will continue to fail as long as public housing is designed unidimensionally. If anything is to be learned from this text, it is that housing cannot be designed for the poor as a single group. Berry's (1965) description of the internal structure of the city and the general work of factorial ecologists suggest that spatial design for the disadvantaged must address the diversity of life styles within a single social class. Such a proposal may mean greater short-run costs, but in the long run efficiency will gain. To distribute the population justly, it is not enough to move the disadvantaged to structurally sounder housing. Imposed mobility can only succeed if the issues of mental and experiential congruence between environment and life style are considered (Michelson, 1976).

Many modern discussions of social justice in the city focus on public housing and territorial systems for income redistribution. The urban system cannot be made either more efficient or more just without some attempt to eradicate the dichotomy between cities and suburbs. In the preindustrial system cities siphoned resources from their hinterlands. A reversed flow in the contemporary Western system has allowed suburban areas to drain the cities of their wealth. Until the invidious distinctions between inner and outer city are dissolved, urban problems will be insoluble. One potential solution, which is self-evident in its simplicity but which has proved extremely hard to bring about, is the notion of extending the political jurisdiction of metropolitan governments to embrace the total commuting zone—what Friedmann (1973) termed the *urban field* and what Berry (1973b) defined as the *daily urban system*. A few cities have moved in this direction, but political polarization of city and suburb is still the American norm.

If such major political reorganization cannot be accomplished, then federal, state, and local government should concentrate on revitalizing the central business district. Such efforts can create the jobs and population necessary for the growth of the city's tax base. Also, if this central renewal is carried out with both social justice and efficiency in mind, it can create real spatial choices for a range of social classes. In the past few years the energy crisis has created one specific incentive for capital to trickle back to the central cities. This revitalization process, however, cannot succeed if it is left to unconstrained market forces. Governments should set development goals and limits that maximize choice for a range of populations.

The institutional interaction perspective outlined in Chapter 8 shows that, at the very minimum, certain aspects of the local ecology of games must change. If housing is to continue to be provided by the marketplace, the overseer's role in such a game must change. Currently local government plays such a role, but that role is necessarily weak. Politicians, in order to get reelected, must balance concerns for efficiency with an interest in implementing ideals of justice. This balance of conflicting concerns seems, on the surface, to be desirable. However, the time frame in which such decisions are made is short, and politicians measure their successes in terms of the few years from election to election. Because of this truncated decision-making period, values of efficiency are of greater concern than values of social justice. A just administration is measured in terms of the amount of low-cost housing it produces. Symbols get votes. However, symbols of sincerity do not solve the spatial problems of the poor.

Overall improvement of the social condition of the city, then, faces two classes of problems. First, existing political pressures and economic processes often act counter to individual and social interests. In part, this problem may be solved by political means. For example, planning boards can be made more representative by encouraging citizen and community involvement in planning processes. We can, in short, amend the rules of the ecological game. The second problem is simply ignorance. Cities are the most complex of human creations. The construction of theory and the accumulation of empirical findings on behavior in such settings is a very young and recent preoccupation.

Ultimately, planning practice can only be as good as the knowledge that informs it. Planning ideals should be based on goals that recognize the spatial dimension of social well-being and the design tools that may be used to achieve it.

Some Realistic Expectations for the Urban Future

Although the socio-spatial perspective on the city has a long history, its utility for urban planning has expanded as micro level research in environmental psychology and behavioral geography has begun to be synthesized with traditional macro level research in human ecology and urban geography. It is ironic that knowledge has accelerated and converged just as large-scale government intervention in cities has become unpopular and unlikely. The political and economic climate of the United States and many Western European nations suggests that at least in the near future, few dramatic or costly steps will be taken to alleviate the urban crisis. The rising cost of resources, especially those from Third World nations, have altered the life styles and expectations of Americans. This fact, coupled with the well-documented failings of huge federal aid programs to cities in the 1960s and 1970s, indicates that future planning efforts will be piecemeal and conservative.

However, there are several reasons for optimism about the American urban future. One reason lies in the possibility of more informed policies, as social science findings are assimilated by the policy makers. The main reason, though, stems from changes in the city itself. In the past, explicit planning has played a very small part in dramatic changes in urban living. Historically the urban mosaic has evolved because of social and technological changes beyond the sphere of political control. Successive revolutions in transportation radically altered the urban mosaic. As the automobile became the principal means of transportation for the urban population, suburban areas grew disproportionately, resulting in the loss of urban employment and the decline of the central city's tax base. The welfare implications of the central-city–suburban dichotomy have been extremely serious. The continued impoverishment of the central city and its populations, however, is unlikely.

At present several societal trends suggest the resurgence rather than demise of the city. They are the energy crisis, the decline in the proportion of the married population, the general reduction in median family size, and the growth of the female labor force at all stages of the family cycle. These phenomena signal basic life style changes in the American population—life styles that the city is better able to accommodate than the suburbs. The accessibility benefits of central-city residence has already begun to stimulate neighborhood revitalization efforts in medium and large older cities in all regions of the United States (Williams, 1979). In many such places community conservation programs have encouraged a trend of "regentrification," as middle-class, career-oriented households have purchased and rehabilitated deteriorating housing in older sections of the city and as concerns for neighborhood quality and renovation have grown among inner-city residents. If these trends of regentrification and revitalization continue, cities will benefit in many ways. One notable benefit may be expansion of the tax base. The benefits to the urban poor and the underemployed that may accrue from such a process are twofold. If the tax base begins to expand, vital urban services can be improved, reducing the gap between city and suburban service delivery systems. At the same time, as suburban housing becomes less desirable for certain segments of the middle class (because of the increase in gasoline and heating oil prices, and the growth of the career-oriented, middle-class household), housing in the periphery will become available to the lower classes through the filtering process. If this outmigration is substantial, the employment-residence mismatch will decline. Employment in manufacturing will continue to grow in suburbs because of the spatial requirements of most manufacturing processes. As a result, the underemployed may gain access to employment opportunities in the foreseeable future.

At present little evidence has accumulated on the extent of regentrification. It is speculation to assume that it will continue and that it will benefit other groups in the city. This example, though, provides an extremely important implication for urban planning. Planning efforts are much more likely to succeed, and to be cost effective, if they recognize and reinforce existing favorable trends. The government outlays that could encourage neighborhood revitalization, urban homesteading, and renovation are tiny compared with the expenditures involved in wholesale urban renewal. The best hope for politically acceptable and affordable urban policies is the judicious monitoring and reinforcement of the favorable changes in urban living that began to emerge in the late 1970s. In terms both of social trends and of government policy, the present period may mark a watershed in American urban history. At a minimum the opportunities for judicious government intervention are tremendous. These opportunities must be guided by more detailed monitoring of social changes, and they must be informed by the findings of the social and policy sciences. If current trends continue and if these steps are followed by policy makers, cities, like a multitude of Lazaruses, may be given new life.

SUMMARY

Planning urban space to achieve political and social objectives began in ancient times. The autocratic, geometric designs of the baroque age gave way to the laissez faire policy of the nineteenth and early twentieth centuries. Today a renewed concern for planning and control is evident in varying degrees in all urban societies. United States planning practice is regulative rather than normative. It is characterized by multiple levels of political control designed to mediate private interests. The main tool of everyday planning is zoning. Free market advocates argue that existing controls are inappropriate, hampering optimal allocation of urban resources. Radical critics claim that existing controls institutionalize inequalities. In the United Kingdom stronger government intervention has produced two generations of new towns, incorporating a variety of experiments in physical and social design. The neighborhood is considered an appropriate level for physical and social planning. In the Soviet Union severe housing problems have been addressed in designs for compact monocentric cities emphasizing standardized apartment housing, public transportation, and an ideological bias against all socioeconomic segregation.

Many visionary statements on ideal urban forms have been made by architects and others. Ebenezer Howard coined the term *garden city* and advocated quite small scale designs incorporating the best features of town and country. Frank Lloyd Wright took the dispersal implied by modern transportation to its logical extreme, predicting an amorphous and decentralized settlement pattern preserving some of the virtues of agrarian living. The European Le Corbusier proposed urban forms that combine high population densities with parklike open spaces by means of high-rise living structures.

A number of socio-spatial requirements for planning have been discussed.

Although increasingly recognized by planners, these needs have not been fully incorporated into planning practice. They include needs to recognize the diversity of human cognition of space, to achieve permissive rather than coercive design, to recognize the social complexity of density, to recognize the positive and negative as well as the social and cognitive functions of boundaries and segregation, and to recognize the irreducibly spatial nature of efficiency and equity in urban systems.

Glossary

achieved status   a social position based on characteristics over which the individual has some control, such as an educational or occupational status.

acquaintance field   the spatial pattern of an individual's primary and secondary group contacts. Also termed contact field.

action space   the set of places within an urban area about which the individual has information.

activity space   the set of places that the individual encounters directly in the course of everyday travel and activities.

advocacy planning   a form of planning in which practitioners advocate directly the aspirations of disadvantaged groups (in the manner of lawyers), rather than attempting to remain neutral and value free.

agglomeration economy   a savings that accrues to a firm by virtue of location close to similar or complementary activities. A trained labor pool and well-developed transportation access are examples of factors leading to agglomeration economies.

agora   a combined market and meeting place located near the center of the Greek city.

anomie   the state of normlessness or normative confusion resulting from unclear social standards and conflicting values and norms.

ascribed status   a social position based on characteristics over which the individual has no control, such as age, race, sex, and family background.

assimilation   a process whereby members of a minority culture adopt the life styles, attitudes, and behaviors of a dominant group, eventually leading to the disappearance of the minority's clear-cut independence and identity.

axiom of cumulative inertia   the likelihood of a residential move decreases the longer a household remains in a given location.

bastide   a fortified medieval town built as a strong point on a military frontier.

behavior setting   spaces with socially defined uses structured so that their physical, social, and cultural properties interact to produce regularized forms of behavior.

behavioral geography   a recently developed branch of geography emphasizing psychological and cognitive study of human spatial behavior.

behavioral sink   a condition in which a group's social organization declines, leading to pathological forms of behavior.

bid rent   the profile of land value or potential profitability as a function of distance from the city center.

bounded rationality   a model of human decision making that assumes individuals attempt to maximize utility but have only imperfect or limited knowledge of the alternatives available.

caste system   a rigid system of stratification in which kinship determines social standing and in which virtually no social mobility is possible.

categorical knowing   stereotyping of other persons based on appearance and spatial information about their roles and statuses.

central business district   the center or core commercial area of the metropolis; sometimes referred to as the downtown area.

central place theory   a geographic theory developed by Christaller and Lösch that describes the spatial pattern and economic structure of the settlement hierarchy.

Clark's Law   the negative exponential relationship between population density and distance from the city.

cognition   the process of knowing that involves labeling and understanding aspects of the environment. Individuals' cognitions include all of their beliefs and attitudes concerning the nature of the world, society, groups they belong to, other people, themselves, and their actions.

cognitive dissonance   an experience of internal conflict in an individual produced by several incompatible beliefs and/or experiences.

cognitive map   a person's organized representation of some part of the spatial environment.

cognitive mapping   the ability that allows us to collect, organize, store, recall, and manipulate information about the spatial environment.

community   a group of people living in the same area, within which many of their social, psychological, and physical needs may be satisfied.

competitive interaction model   a form of gravity model that describes spatial competition between retail stores or other spatial choice alternatives.

contact field   see *acquaintance field.*

conurbation   a clustering of interrelated industrial activities usually involving the growing together of several metropolises.

crowding   the psychological experience of high densities.

cultural area   a geographic region whose inhabitants share a common culture.

cultural pluralism   a concept describing a society made up of distinct and diverse ethnic groups.

defended community   a community whose identity and cohesion is not the result of the shared backgrounds or statuses of its members, but rather of outside forces that challenge the community's integrity and threaten its survival.

density-induced pathology   hypothetical social pathologies induced by high physical densities. Confirmed experimentally for some animal populations, but unconfirmed for humans.

descriptive models   models that seek to describe empirical data as accurately as possible.

distance-decay   the decline of most types of interaction, such as social interaction, migration, and travel, with increasing distance. Distance-decay exhibits a characteristic downward curve as a function of distance.

division of labor   separation of the work process so that groups or individuals are charged with carrying out different specific tasks.

domus   a Roman elite dwelling place, usually a large single-story structure with an inner courtyard.

ecological complex model   a theory of human ecology that describes social adaptation and change as the result of interactions between four subsystems: environment, technology, population, and social and economic organization.

ecological succession   the process by which an invading group occupies a community and eventually establishes dominance.

environmental determinism   the discredited theory that cultural patterns in the landscape may be explained by predominantly physical factors such as climate and physiography.

environmental docility hypothesis   the thesis that the more competent the person, both cognitively and physically, the less dependent on environmental conditions that person is.

equilibrium   a steady state or state of balance between the elements in an interacting system.

ethology   the biological study of animal behavior.

extended family   two or more nuclear families tied together by the parent-child relationship and living together.

externality   the effect that features of a particular land parcel have on the value or utility of adjacent parcels.

exurb   settlements on the outermost edges of the metropolis that are not contiguous with the suburban ring.

factorial ecology   the inductive study of urban structure by multivariate techniques such as factor analysis in an attempt to distinguish major dimensions such as familism and ethnicity.

faubourg   a settlement on the outskirts or beyond the wall of a medieval town, later incorporated as a suburb.

field theory   a theory developed by Lewin that describes human behavior as the product of the interaction between psychological states, cognitive images, and values associated with the external environment.

filtering   the occupation of a dwelling unit by a succession of socioeconomic groups. If the groups decrease in status, the process is termed downward filtering. The reverse process, by which high-status groups return to dilapidated units, is termed upward filtering or regentrification.

foreign stock   all foreign-born persons plus those natives who have one or both parents foreign born.

forum   the Roman equivalent of the Greek agora.

Gemeinschaft   term used by Ferdinand Tönnies to describe a community or society organized on the basis of shared values, norms, and sentiments.

Gesellschaft   term used by Tönnies to describe a community or society characterized by a lack of consensus over norms and values and a predominance of individual self-interest.

gravity model   a model of spatial interaction that predicts many activities, such as migration, shopping behavior, and marriage distances. Interaction is assumed to be directly proportional to population or some other measure of size and inversely proportional to some measure of distance such as travel time.

ideal type   a mental construct that exaggerates an actual condition. It generates hypotheses and directs empirical research not by reflecting reality, but by providing an abstract concept against which reality can be compared.

individual distance   the normal distance for a given type of social interaction. This distance varies for intimate, personal, social, and public interactions.

insula   a Roman "city block" containing tenements.

intimate distance   see *individual distance.*

kinship system   a set of durable interpersonal ties derived from descent and marriage.

life cycle   the successive stages through which individuals pass during the life course, each stage involving special demands and expectations. Stages include infant, child, adolescent, young single adult, married adult without children, married adult with children, grandparent, and elderly adult.

linguistic relativity hypothesis   the theory that different languages dissect and encode the universe in different ways, with the result that different languages provide somewhat different ways of understanding the environment.

mechanical solidarity   term used by Emile Durkheim to describe the organization of simple societies that are cohesive and culturally integrated.

metric   the properties of space that depend on distance measurement.

microgeography   the study of the impact of microenvironments such as room design and furniture layout on human behavior and interaction.

natural area   the Chicago School's concept of the local community or neighborhood. These areas had distinctive geographical traits that made them identifiable and that eventually led to distinctive social and cultural communities.

niche   a habitat supplying the basic needs of an organism or species.

normative model   a type of model that specifies the consequences of certain idealized or simplified assumptions (e.g., the rent model of land use).

organic solidarity   term used by Emile Durkheim to describe complex societies that are organized by the division of labor and that cohere because of the economic dependence of their members.

overurbanization   a condition in which the cities of a society are growing faster than the economy's ability to employ the new urbanites.

perception   selective awareness of elements in the environment through physical sensation.

personal distance   see *individual distance.*

personal knowledge   understanding of others based on direct information about their history and beliefs.

primogeniture   an exclusive right of inheritance belonging to the eldest son.

proxemics   the study of individual distance and its effect on social interactions.

psychophysics   the study of the relationship between physical stimulus and subjective sensation. In cognitive geography, one physical stimulus studied is distance.

public distance   see *individual distance.*

redlining   designating an area as deteriorating and ineligible for mortgage loans by lending institutions. Such actions produce a self-fulfilling prophecy accelerating deterioration.

rent model   a model of urban land use developed by urban economists. The use of each parcel is assumed to be the one that yields the highest potential profit or utility. Potential profits vary in a systematic way with accessibility to the central business district.

role   group expectations concerning the rights and responsibilities of an individual with a particular status within the group.

satisficing behavior   a model of human decision making that assumes individuals do not seek the very best or utility-maximizing alternative. Instead, they seek only an adequate or satisfactory alternative, as determined by a threshold of utility. This model describes residential search.

scale economies   a savings in unit or average production cost resulting from an increase in the output or business volume of an enterprise.

segregation   a general term for the ecological process by which areas of a community become more uniform internally and more differentiated from one another according to status, ethnicity, familism, land use, or similar criteria.

SMSA   as defined by the Bureau of the Census, "a county or group of contiguous counties that contains at least one city of 50,000 inhabitants or more or 'twin cities' with a combined population of at least 50,000. In addition to the county or counties containing such a city or cities, contiguous counties are included in an SMSA if, according to certain criteria, they are essentially metropolitan in character and are socially and economically integrated with the central city."

social area analysis   a body of deductive theory developed by Shevky, Bell, and others predicting differentiation of urban space along the dimensions of social status, familism, and ethnicity.

social class   an aggregate of persons who share more or less the same economic privileges in a society.

social distance   the degree of felt separation between an individual and some other social grouping. See also individual distance.

social stratification   the ranking of individuals into levels or strata that share unequally in the distribution of prestige, power, and economic privilege.

society   a large social group that meets most of its own needs, maintains a system of social interaction across generations, and has a discernible social structure.

status   an individual's position in relation to others in the prestige hierarchy of a group.

stimulus overload   an inability to process environmental inputs because either there are too many or they come too fast.

structural differentiation   the process whereby a social structure develops into one characterized by many specialized parts.

substitution   the trade-off process by which a household elects to consume certain amounts of commodities that can possibly be used in place of one another.

suburb   derived from the Latin *sub urbe*, "under the city," to denote the small settlements of the poor located under the city walls in ancient times. In the modern metropolis suburbs are those settlements within the urbanized area but outside the central city or cities.

sumptuary code   regulation of consumption habits by law or custom, particularly regulation of dress to make appearance reflect social status. Common in preindustrial societies.

territoriality   the occupation, habitual use, and defense of a particular area by an animal or group of animals, either seasonally or permanently.

topological   the properties of space that do not depend on distance or distance measurement; for example, adjacency, connection, and containment.

tract   the smallest area for which a great deal of information is generally available from the census; the population of the tract is usually between 3000 and 6000 and is defined according to both physical and social boundaries.

urbanization   the movement of people from rural to urban areas, which results in an increased proportion of the population living in cities.

urbanized area   an area consisting of at least one city of 50,000 or more people and the closely settled territory around it.

urban renewal   an urban development strategy initiated by the Federal Housing Act of 1954. It stressed three basic goals: prevention of the spread of blight, rehabilitation and conservation of renewable areas, and clearance and redevelopment of nonrenewable areas.

urban revolution   the complex of cultural, economic, and political events resulting in the earliest cities. Currently believed to have occurred in Mesopotamia about 4000–3500 B.C.

Bibliography

Aangenberg, R. T.
  1968   "Regional perception and its effects on industrial location." Kansas Business
          Review 21:3–6.

Abercrombie, P.
  1945   Greater London Plan. London: H. M. S. O.

Abrahamson, M.
  1976   Urban Sociology. Englewood Cliffs, N.J.: Prentice-Hall.

Abrams, M.
  1968   "Consumption in the year 2000." In M. Young (ed.), Forecasting and the
          Social Sciences. London.

Abu-Lughod, J.
  1968   "Testing the theory of social area analysis: the ecology of Cairo, Egypt."
          American Sociological Review 34:198–212.

Advisory Commission on Intergovernmental Relations
  1968   Urban and Rural America: Policies for Future Growth. Washington, D.C.:
          U.S. Government Printing Office.

Aldrich, H.
  1975   "Ecological succession in racially changing neighborhoods: a review of the
          literature." Urban Affairs Quarterly 10:327–352.

Alexander, C.
  1966   "A city is not a tree." Architectural Forum 112:58–62.

Allport, G., and T. Pettigrew
  1957   "Cultural influence on the perception of movement: the trapezoidal illusion
          among the Zulus." Journal of Abnormal and Social Psychology 55:104–113.

Alonso, W.
  1960   "A theory of the urban landmarket." Regional Science Association, Papers
          and Proceedings 6:149–157.
  1964a   "The historic and structural theories of urban form: their implications for
          urban renewal." Land Economics 40:227–231.
  1964b   Location and Landuse. Cambridge, Mass.: Harvard University Press.
  1970   "What are new towns for?" Urban Studies 7:37–45.

Altman, I.
1975   The Environment and Social Behavior: Privacy, Personal Space, Territory, and Crowding. Monterey, Calif.: Brooks/Cole.

Altman, I., and Haythorn, W.
1967   "The ecology of isolated groups." Behavioral Science 12:169–181.

Amato, P.
1970   "A comparison: population densities, land values and socioeconomic class in four Latin American cities." Land Economics 41:447–455.

Appleyard, D.
1970   "Styles and methods of structuring a city." Environment and Behavior 2:100–118.

Ardrey, R.
1966   The Territorial Imperative. New York: Atheneum.

Athanasiou, R., and G. Yoshioka
1973   "The spatial character of friendship formation." Environment and Behavior 5:43–65.

Babcock, R.
1966   The Zoning Game. Madison: University of Wisconsin Press.

Bach, R., and J. Smith
1977   "Community satisfaction, expectations of moving, and migration." Demography 14:147–168.

Baldassare, M.
1976   "Residential density, household crowding, and social networks." Paper read at the annual meetings of the American Sociological Association.

Ball, D.
1973   Microecology: Social Situations and Intimate Space. Indianapolis: Bobbs-Merrill.

Banfield, E.
1974   The Unheavenly City Revisited. Boston: Little, Brown.

Barber, B.
1957   Social Stratification. New York: Harcourt, Brace and World.

Barker, R.
1968   Ecological Psychology. Stanford, Calif.: Stanford University Press.

Barrows, H. H.
1923   "Geography as human ecology." Annals of the Association of American Geographers 13:1–14.

Bavelas, A.
1968   "Communication patterns in task oriented groups." Pp. 503–511 in D. Cartwright and A. Zander (eds.), Group Dynamics: Research and Theory. New York: Harper & Row.

Bell, W.
1958   "Social choice, life styles and suburban residence." Pp. 225–247 in W. M. Dobriner (ed.), The Suburban Community. New York: Putnam.

Bell, W., and M. Boat
  1957   "Urban neighborhoods and informal social relations." American Journal of
          Sociology 62:391–398.

Bell, W., and M. T. Force
  1956   "Urban neighborhood types and participation in formal associations."
          American Sociological Review 21:25–34.

Ben-Akiva, M.
  1972   "Structure of travel demand models." Unpublished paper, Department of
          Civil Engineering, M.I.T.

Bennett, C.
  1977   Spaces for People: Human Factors in Design. Englewood Cliffs, N.J.: Pren-
          tice-Hall.

Berger, A.
  1978   The City: Urban Communities and Their Problems. Dubuque, Iowa: Brown.

Bernstein, B.
  1968   "Some sociological determinants of perception, an inquiry into subcultural
          difference." Pp. 126–149 in J. A. Fishman (ed.), Readings in the Sociology of
          Language. The Hague: Mouton.

Berry, B. J. L.
  1965   "Internal structure of the city." Law and Contemporary Problems 30:111–
          119.
  1967   Geography of Market Centers and Retail Distribution. Englewood Cliffs,
          N.J.: Prentice-Hall.
  1973a   The Human Consequences of Urbanization. New York: St. Martin's Press.
  1973b   "Contemporary urbanization processes." Pp. 94–107 in Geographic Perspec-
          tives and Urban Problems, a Symposium. Washington D.C.: National Acade-
          my of Sciences.
  1976   "Comparative urbanization strategies." Pp. 66–79 in H. Swain and R. Mac-
          Kinnon (eds.), Managing Urban Systems. Laxenberg, Austria: IIASA.

Berry, B., and F. Horton
  1970   Geographic Perspectives on Urban Systems. Englewood Cliffs, N.J.: Pren-
          tice-Hall.

Berry, B., J. Simmons, and R. Tennant
  1963   "Urban population densities: structure and change." Geographical Review
          53:389–405.

Birch, D.
  1971   "Toward a stage theory of urban growth." Journal of the American Institute
          of Planners 37:78–87.

Blau, P., and O. D. Duncan
  1967   The American Occupational Structure. New York: Wiley.

Blaut, J. and D. Stea
  1971   "Studies of geographical learning." Annals of the Association of American
          Geographers 61:387–393.

Blumenfeld, H.
    1964   "The urban pattern." Annals of the Academy of Social and Political Science
            352:74–83.

Boal, F.
    1970   "Social space in the Belfast urban area." Pp. 373–393 in N. Stephens and R.
            Glasscock (eds.), Irish Geographical Studies. Belfast: Queens University.

Bogardus, E.
    1925   "Measuring social distances." Journal of Applied Sociology 9:299–308.
    1966   "Comparing racial distance in Ethiopia, South Africa and the United States."
            Sociology and Social Research 52:149–156.

Booth, A., and J. Edwards
    1976   "Crowding and family relations." American Sociological Review 41:308–
            321.

Bossard, J.
    1932   "Residential propinquity as a factor in marriage selection." American Jour-
            nal of Sociology 38:219–224.

Boulding, K.
    1956   The Image. Ann Arbor: University of Michigan Press.

Bourne, L., B. R. Ekstrand, and R. L. Dominowski
    1971   The Psychology of Thinking. Englewood Cliffs, N.J.: Prentice-Hall.

Brand, D.
    1972   "Travel demand forecasting." Reported in Background Papers for the Con-
            ference on Travel Demand Forecasts. Williamsburg, Va.

Braudel, F.
    1976   "Pre-modern towns." Pp. 53–90 in P. Clark (ed.), The Early Modern Town.
            New York: Longman.

Brazer, H.
    1967   Essays in State and Local Finance. Ann Arbor, Mich.: Institute of Public Ad-
            ministration, University of Michigan.

Brennan, T.
    1948   Midland City. London: Dobson.

Briggs, R.
    1973   "Urban cognitive distance." Pp. 361–388 in R. M. Downs and D. Stea (eds.),
            Image and Environment. Chicago: Aldine.

Bronfenbrenner, U.
    1958   "Socialization and social class through time and space." Pp. 400–424 in E.
            Maccoby, T. Newcomb, and E. Hartley (eds.), Readings in Social Psychology.
            New York: Holt, Rinehart and Winston.

Brower, S.
    1965   "The signs we learn to read." Landscape 15:9–12.

Brown, J. L.
    1964   "The evolution of diversity in aviaran territorial systems." Wilson Bulletin
            76:160–169.

Brown, L., and E. Moore
  1970   "The intraurban migration process." Geografiska Annaler 52 B:1–13.

Buckingham, J. S.
  1849   National Evils and Practical Remedies. London.

Bucklin, L. P.
  1967   Shopping Patterns in Urban Areas. Berkeley, Calif.: University of California, Institute of Business and Economic Research.

Buettner-Janusch, J.
  1973   Physical Anthropology: A Perspective. New York: Wiley.

Bunge, W.
  1962   Theoretical Geography. Lund Studies in Geography, Series C General and Mathematical Geography. Lund, Sweden: Lund University.
  1971   Fitzgerald: Geography of Revolution. New York: Schenkman.

Burgess, E. W.
  1923   "The growth of the city: an introduction to a research project." Proceedings of the American Sociological Society 18:85–89.

Burnett, P.
  1973   "The dimensions of alternatives in spatial choice processes." Geographical Analysis 5:181–204.

Burnley, I. H.
  1972   "European immigration and settlement patterns in Metropolitan Sydney, 1947–66." Australian Geographical Studies 10:61–78.

Butler, E. W.
  1976   Urban Sociology: A Systematic Perspective. New York: Harper & Row.

Butler, E., F. S. Chapin, G. C. Hemmens, E. J. Kaiser, M. A. Stegman, and S. F. Weiss
  1969   Moving Behavior and Residential Choice: A National Survey. National Cooperative Highway Research Program Report No. 81, Highway Research Board, Washington, D.C.

Buttimer, A.
  1974   Values in Geography. Washington, D.C.: Commission on College Geography, Resource Paper No. 24.

Calhoun, J. B.
  1962   "Population density and social pathology." Scientific American 206:139–148.
  1966   "The role of space in animal sociology." Journal of Social Issues 22:46–58.

Canter, D., and S. Tagg
  1975   "Distance estimation in cities." Environment and Behavior 7:59–80.

Caplovitz, D.
  1963   The Poor Pay More. New York: Free Press.

Carnahan, D., W. Gove, and O. Galle
  1974   "Urbanization, population density and overcrowding." Social Forces 53:62–72.

Carroll, J. D.
  1950   Home-Work Relationships of Industrial Employees. Ph.D dissertation, Har-
            vard University.

Carroll, J. D., and H. Bevis
  1957   "Predicting local travel in urban regions." Papers and Proceedings of the
            Regional Science Association 3:183–197.

Casetti, E.
  1967   "Urban population densities: an alternative explanation." Canadian Geogra-
            pher 11:96–100.

Cassel, J.
  1971   "Health consequences of population density and crowding." Pp. 462–478 in
            National Academy of Sciences, Rapid Population Growth. Baltimore: Johns
            Hopkins Press.

Catton, W., and R. J. Smircich
  1964   "A comparison of mathematical models for the effects of residential propin-
            quity on mate selection." American Sociological Review 29:522–529.

Chambliss, W.
  1975   Criminal Law in Action. Santa Barbara: Wiley.

Charles River Associates
  1976   Disaggregate Travel Demand Models Project 8-13: Phase 1 Report, Vol. II.
            Cambridge, Mass.: Charles River Associates.

Childe, V. G.
  1950   "The urban revolution." Town Planning Review 21:9–16.
  1966   What Happened in History. London: Penguin Books.

Chombard de Lauwe, P., and M. Chombard de Lauwe
  1959   Familie et Habitation. Paris: Centre National de la Researche Scientifique.

Clark, C.
  1951   "Urban population densities." Journal of the Royal Statistical Society Series
            A 114:490–496.

Clark, M.
  1971   "Patterns of aging among the elderly poor of the inner city." The Geron-
            tologist 11:58–66.

Clark, T.
  1968   Community Power and Decision Making. San Francisco: Chandler.

Clark, W. A. V.
  1968   "Consumer travel patterns and the concept of range." Annals of the Associa-
            tion of American Geographers 58:386–396.

Clawson, M.
  1971   Suburban Land Conversion in the United States: An Economic and Govern-
            mental Process. Baltimore: Johns Hopkins University Press.

Clements, F.
  1916   Plant Succession: An Analysis of the Development of Vegetation. Washing-
            ton, D.C.: U.S. Department of Agriculture.

Cliff, A. D., P. Haggett, J. K. Ord, K. Bassett, and R. Davies
   1975   Elements of Spatial Structure. Cambridge: Cambridge University Press.

Clinard, M.
   1974   Sociology of Deviant Behavior. New York: Holt, Rinehart and Winston.

Cloward, R., and L. Ohlin
   1960   Delinquency and Opportunity. New York: Free Press.

Cohen, B.
   1971   "Trends in Negro employment in large metropolitan areas." Public Policy
             19:611–622.

Cohen, L., and M. Felson
   1978   "Social change and crime rate trends: a routine activity approach." Working
             Papers in Applied Social Statistics. Urbana, Illinois: University of Illinois.

Coleman, J.
   1966   Equality of Educational Opportunity. Washington, D.C.: U.S. Government
             Printing Office.

Cooper, C.
   1975   Easter Hill Village. New York: Free Press.

Cowgill, D.
   1978   "Residential segregation by age in American metropolitan areas." Journal of
             Gerontology 33:446–453.

Cox, K. and R. Golledge
   1969   "Behavioral problems in geography: a symposium." Evanston, Ill.: North-
             western University Studies in Geography, No. 17.

Cressy, P.
   1938   "Population succession in Chicago." American Journal of Sociology 44:56–
             59.

Cyert, R. M., and J. G. March
   1963   A Behavioral Theory of the Firm. Englewood Cliffs, N.J.: Prentice-Hall.

Dahrendorf, R.
   1959   Class and Class Conflict in Industrial Society. Stanford, Calif.: Stanford Uni-
             versity Press.

Dantzig, G., and L. Saaty
   1973   Compact City. San Francisco: W. H. Freeman.

Davis, K.
   1972   World Urbanization 1950–1970, Volume II: Analysis of Trends, Relation-
             ships and Development. Berkeley, Calif.: Institute of International Studies.

Davis, K., and H. Golden
   1954   "Urbanization and the development of pre-industrial areas." Economic De-
             velopment and Cultural Change 3:16–30.

DeJong, G.
   1977   "Residential preferences and migration." Demography 14:169–178.

Deutsch, M., and M. Collins
1951   Interracial Housing: A Psychological Evaluation of a Social Experiment. Minneapolis: University of Minnesota Press.

Dobriner, W.
1963   Class in Suburbia. Englewood Cliffs, N.J.: Prentice-Hall.

Domencich, J. A., and D. McFadden
1975   Urban Travel Demand: A Behavioral Analysis. Amsterdam: North Holland.

Downs, R. M.
1970   "The cognitive structure of an urban shopping center." Environment and Behavior 2:13–39.

Downs, R. M., and D. Stea
1973   Image and Environment. Chicago: Aldine.
1977   Maps in Minds. New York: Harper & Row.

Dubos, R.
1965   Man Adapting. New Haven: Yale University Press.

Duncan, O. D.
1961   "From ecosystem to social system." Sociological Inquiry 31:140–149.

Duncan, O. D., and B. Duncan
1955   "Residential distribution and occupational stratification." American Journal of Sociology 60:493–503.
1957   The Negro Population of Chicago. Chicago: University of Chicago Press.

Duncan, O.D., D. Featherman, and B. Duncan
1972   Socioeconomic Background and Achievement. New York: Seminar Press.

Duncan, O. D., and S. Lieberson
1959   "Ethnic segregation and assimilation." American Journal of Sociology 64:364–374.

Dunham, H. W.
1947   "Current status of ecological research in mental disorder." Social Forces 25:321–326.

Durkheim, E.
1947   The Division of Labor in Society. Tr. G. Simpson. Glencoe, Ill.: Free Press. Originally published in 1893.
1951   Suicide. Tr. J. Spaulding and G. Simpson. New York: Free Press. Originally published in 1897.

Ekman, G., and O. Bratfisch
1965   "Subjective distance and emotional involvement: a psychological mechanism." Acta Psychologica 24:446–453.

Eliot-Hurst, M. E.
1975   I Came to the City: Essays and Comments on the Urban Scene. Boston: Houghton-Mifflin.

Erikson, E.
1974   Childhood and Society. New York: Norton.

Esser, A. H.
  1971a   International Symposium on the Use of Space by Man. New York: Plenum.
  1971b   "Social pollution." Sociology of Education 35:10–18.

Everitt, J., and M. Cadwallader
  1972   "The home area concept in urban analysis." In W. J. Mitchell (ed.), Envi-
           ronmental Design: Research and Practice. Los Angeles: University of Cali-
           fornia/EDRA 3.

Ewing, G.
  1976   "Environmental and spatial preferences of interstate migrants in the United
           States." Pp. 249–300 in R. Golledge and G. Rushton, Spatial Choice and Spa-
           tial Behavior. Columbus: Ohio State University Press.

Faris, R. E. L., and H. W. Dunham
  1939   Mental Disorders in Urban Areas. Chicago: University of Chicago Press.

Farley, R., H. Schuman, S. Bianchi, D. Colasanto, and S. Hatchett
  1976   "'Chocolate city, Vanilla suburbs': will the trend toward racially separate
           communities continue?" Paper presented at the annual meetings of the Pop-
           ulation Association of America.

Feldman, A., and C. Tilly
  1960   "The interaction of social and physical space." American Sociological Re-
           view 25:877–884.

Festinger, L.
  1957   The Theory of Cognitive Dissonance. New York: Harper & Row.

Festinger, L., S. Schacter, and K. Back
  1950   Social Pressures in Informal Groups: A Study of Human Factors in Housing.
           Stanford, Calif.: Stanford University Press.

Firey, W.
  1945   "Sentiment and symbolism as ecological variables." American Sociological
           Review 10:140–148.

Fischer, C.
  1971   "A research note on urbanism and tolerance." American Journal of Sociolo-
           gy 76:847–856.
  1973   "On urban alienation and anomie." American Sociological Review 38:311–
           326.
  1975   "Toward a subcultural theory of urbanism." American Journal of Sociology
           80:1319–1341.
  1976   The Urban Experience. New York: Harcourt Brace Jovanovich.

Fischer, C., and R. M. Jackson
  1976   "Suburbs, networks and attitudes." Pp. 279–308 in B. Schwartz (ed.), The
           Changing Face of the Suburbs. Chicago: University of Chicago Press.

Fischer, C., R. Jackson, C. A. Stueve, K. Gerson, L. Jones, and M. Baldasare
  1978   Networks and Places: Social Relations in the Urban Setting. New York: Free
           Press.

Fishbein, M.
  1967   Readings in Attitude Theory and Measurement. New York: Wiley.

Fishman, J.
   1961   "Some social and psychological determinants of intergroup relations in changing neighborhoods." Social Forces 40:42–51.

Foote, N., J. Abu-Lughod, M. Foley, and L. Winni
   1960   Housing Choices and Housing Constraints. New York: McGraw-Hill.

Ford, R.
   1950   "Population succession in Chicago." American Journal of Sociology 56:151–160.

Ford, W. S.
   1973   "Another look at the contact hypothesis." American Journal of Sociology 6:1426–1447.

Form, W.
   1954   "The place of social structure in the determination of land use: some implications for a theory of urban ecology." Social Forces 32:317–323.

Fraser Hart, J.
   1960   "The changing distribution of the American Negro." Annals of the Association of American Geographers 50:242–266.

Freedman, J.
   1975   Crowding and Human Behavior. San Francisco: W. H. Freeman.

Freedman, Y.
   1975   Toward a Scientific Architecture. Cambridge, Mass.: M.I.T. Press.

Fremon, C.
   1970   Central City and Suburban Employment Growth: 1965–1967. Washington, D.C.: Urban Institute.

Fried, M., and P. Gleicher
   1961   "Some sources of residential satisfaction." Journal of the American Institute of Planners 27:305–315.

Friedmann, J.
   1973   "The urban field as human habitat." In G. P. Snow (ed.), The Place of Planning. Auburn, Ala.: Auburn University Press.

Fuguitt, G., and J. Zuiches
   1972   "Residential preferences and population/distribution." Demography 12:491–504.

Fustel de Coulanges, N. D.
   1956   The Ancient City. New York: Doubleday. Originally published in 1864.

Galle, O., W. Gove, and J. McPherson
   1972   "Population density and social pathology: what are the relations for man?" Science 176:23–30.

Gallion, A. B., and Eisner, S.
   1963   The Urban Pattern. New York: Van Nostrand.

Gans, H.
   1961   "The balanced community: homogeneity or heterogeneity in residential areas." Journal of the American Institute of Planners 27:176–184.

1962a   The Urban Villagers. New York: Free Press.
1962b   "Urbanism and suburbanism as ways of life." Pp. 625–648 in A. M. Rose (ed.), Human Behavior and Social Processes. Boston: Houghton Mifflin.
1965   "The failure of urban renewal: a critique and some proposals." Commentary 39:29–37.
1967   The Levittowners. New York: Pantheon.
1978   "Toward a human architecture." Journal of Architectural Education 21:26–31.

Gazzaniga, M. S.
1972   "One brain—two minds?" American Scientist 60:311–317.

Geddes, P.
1968   Cities in Evolution. New York: H. Fertig. Originally published in 1915.

Gelfand, J.
1966   "The credit elasticity of lower-middle income housing demand." Land Economics, November, pp. 464–472.

Geruson, R., and D. McGrath
1977   Cities and Modernization. New York: Praeger.

Gillis, R.
1973   "Population density and social pathology." Social Forces 53:306–314.

Ginsberg, R. B.
1971   "Two papers on the use and interpretation of probabilistic models : with applications to the analysis of migration. " Working Paper No. 73. London: Centre for Environmental Studies.

Gist, N., and S. Fava
1974   Urban Society. New York: Crowell.

Glazer, N., and D. P. Moynihan
1970   Beyond the Melting Pot. Cambridge, Mass.: M.I.T. Press.

Goffman, E.
1959   The Presentation of Self in Everyday Life. New York: Doubleday-Anchor.

Goldscheider, C.
1971   Population, Modernization, and Social Structure. Boston: Little, Brown.

Golledge, R.
1967   "Conceptualizing the market decision process." Journal of Regional Science 7:239–258.
1969   "The geographical relevance of some learning theories." In K. Cox and R. Golledge (eds.), Behavioral Problems in Geography. Evanston, Ill.: Northwestern University Studies in Geography.
1978   "Representing, interpreting, and using cognized environments," Papers, Regional Science Association 41:169–203.

Golledge, R., and J. Rayner
1975   Cognitive Configurations of a City, Vol. 1. Columbus: Ohio State University Research Foundation.
1977   On Determining Cognitive Configurations of a City, Vol. 2. Columbus: Ohio State University Press.

Golledge, R., and G. Rushton
    1976   Spatial Choice and Spatial Behavior. Columbus: Ohio State University Press.

Goodchild, B.
    1974   "Class differences in environmental perception." Urban Studies 11:157–169.

Goode, W.
    1972   Explorations in Social Theory. New York: Oxford University Press.

Goodman, N., and G. Marx
    1978   Society Today. New York: CRM/Random House.

Gordon, M.
    1961   Assimilation in American Life: The Role of Race, Religion and National Origin. New York: Oxford University Press.

Gottman, J.
    1961   Megalopolis, the Urbanized Northeastern Region of the United States. Cambridge, Mass.: M.I.T. Press.

Gould, P.
    1965   On Mental Maps. Ann Arbor: Michigan Inter-University Community of Mathematical Geographers.
    1973   "Geographic exposition, information and location." Pp. 25–40 in Geographical Perspectives and Urban Problems: A Symposium. Washington, D.C.: National Academy of Sciences.

Gould, P., and R. White
    1974   Mental Maps. Baltimore: Penguin.

Granovetter, M.
    1973   "The strength of weak ties." American Journal of Sociology 78:1360–1380.

Gras, N. S. B.
    1922   An Introduction to Economic History. New York: Harper & Row.

Gray Eaton, G.
    1976   "The social order of Japanese macaques." Scientific American 235:96–107.

Greeley, A.
    1971   Why Can't They Be Like Us? New York: Dutton.

Greenbie, B.
    1976   Design for Diversity. New York: Elsevier.

Greenfield, R.
    1961   "Factors associated with attitudes toward desegregation in a Florida residential suburb." Social Forces 40:31–42.

Greer, S.
    1956   "Urbanism reconsidered: a comparative study of local areas in a metropolis." American Sociological Review 21:19–25.
    1960   "The social structure and political process of suburbia." American Sociological Review 25:514–526.
    1962a   The Emerging City. New York: Free Press.
    1962b   Governing the Metropolis. New York: Wiley.

Greer, S., and E. Kube

1972   "Urbanism and social structure: a Los Angeles study." Pp. 34–54 in S. Greer (ed.), The Urbane View. New York: Oxford University Press.

Greer, S., and P. Orleans
1962   "The mass and parapolitical structure." American Sociological Review 27:643–649.

Gruenberg, E.
1954   "Community conditions and psychoses of the elderly." American Journal of Psychiatry 110:880–903.

Guest, A.
1973   "Urban growth and population densities." Demography 10:53–70.
1977   "Residential segregation in urban areas." Pp. 264–276 in K. Schwirian (ed.), Contemporary Topics in Urban Sociology. Morristown, N.J.: General Learning.

Haggerty, L.
1971   "Another look at the Burgess hypothesis: time as an important variable." American Journal of Sociology 76:1084–1093.

Haggett, P.
1965   Locational Analysis in Human Geography. London: Edward Arnold.

Haig, M.
1926   "Toward an understanding of the metropolis." Quarterly Journal of Economics 40:179–208, 402–434.

Hall, E.
1966   The Hidden Dimension. Garden City, N.Y.: Doubleday.

Hall, P.
1966   The World Cities. New York: McGraw-Hill.
1975   Urban and Regional Planning. London: David and Charles.

Hanson, P. O., D. F. Marble, and F. Pitts
1972   "Individual movement and communication fields." Regional Science Perspectives 2:80–94.

Harris, C., and E. Ullman
1945   "The nature of cities." Annals of the American Academy of Political and Social Sciences 242:7–17.

Harrison, B.
1974   Urban Economic Development: Suburbanization, Minority Opportunity, and the Condition of the Central City. Washington: Urban Institute.

Hart, C., and A. Pilling
1966   The Tiwi of North Australia. New York: Holt, Rinehart and Winston.

Hart, R. A., and G. T. Moore
1973   "The development of spatial cognition: a review." Pp. 246–288 in R. Downs and D. Stea (eds.), Image and Environment. Chicago: Aldine.

Hartman, C.
1964   "The housing of relocated families." Journal of the American Institute of Planners 30:266–286.
1975   Housing and Social Policy. Englewood Cliffs, N.J.: Prentice-Hall.

Harvey, D.
 1970   "Social processes and spatial form." Proceedings of the Regional Science As-
         sociation 25:47–69.
 1972a   The City and the Space-Economy of Urbanism. Resource Paper No. 18, Com-
         mission on College Geography. Washington, D.C.: Association of American
         Geographers.
 1972b   "Social justice and spatial systems." Antipode Monographs in Social Geogra-
         phy 1.
 1973   Social Justice and the City. London: Arnold.
 1974   "Class monopoly rent, finance capital, and the urban revolution." Regional
         Studies 8:239–255.

Hatch, J.
 1966   "Collective territories in Galapagos mockingbirds with notes on other be-
         havior." Wilson Bulletin 78:198–207.

Hauser, P.
 1963   The Population Dilemma. Englewood Cliffs, N.J.: Prentice-Hall.

Hawkes, J.
 1974   Atlas of Ancient Archaeology. New York: McGraw-Hill.

Hawley, A.
 1944   "Dispersion versus segregation: apropos of a solution of race problems." Pa-
         pers of the Michigan Academy of Science Arts and Letters, 30
 1950   Human Ecology: A Theory of Community Structure. New York: Ronald
         Press.
 1956   "Metropolitan population and municipal government expenditures in cen-
         tral cities." Pp. 773–782 in P. Hatt and A. Reiss (eds.), Cities and Society.
         Glencoe, Ill.: Free Press.
 1971   Urban Society. New York: Ronald Press

Hawley, A., and O. D. Duncan
 1957   "Social area analysis, a critical appraisal." Land Economics 33:337–345.

Heberle, R.
 1960   "The normative elements in neighborhood relations." Pacific Sociological
         Review 3:3–11.

Heider, F.
 1958   The Psychology of Interpersonal Relations. New York: Wiley.

Heider, K.
 1972   The Dugum Dani. Chicago: Aldine.

Hensley, M. M., and J. B. Cope
 1951   "Further data on removal and repopulation of breeding birds in a spruce fir
         community." Auk 68:483–493.

Hinde, R. A.
 1970   Animal Behavior: A Synthesis of Ethology and Comparative Psychology.
         New York: McGraw-Hill.

Homans, G.
 1950   The Human Group. New York: Free Press.

Hoover, E., and R. Vernon
1959   Anatomy of a Metropolis. Cambridge, Mass.: Harvard University Press.

Horton, E., and D. Reynolds
1971   "Effects of urban spatial structure on individual behavior." Economic Geography 47:36–48.

House, J. D.
1977   Contemporary Entrepreneurs: The Sociology of Residential Real Estate Agents. London: Greenwood Press.

Howard, E.
1920   Territory in Bird Life. New York: Dutton.

Howard, E.
1965   Garden Cities of Tomorrow. Cambridge, Mass.: M.I.T. Press. Originally published in 1902.

Hoyt, H.
1939   The Structure and Growth of Residential Neighborhoods in the United States. Washington, D.C.: Federal Housing Administration.
1964   "Recent distortions of the classical models of urban structure." Land Economics 40:199–212.

Huff, D. L.
1963   "A probabilistic analysis of shopping center trade areas." Land Economics 53:81–90.

Hunter, F.
1953   Community Power Structure. Chapel Hill, N.C.: University of North Carolina Press.

Huntington, E.
1915   Civilization and Climate. New Haven: Yale University Press.

Hurd, R.
1903   Principles of City Land Values. New York: Record and Guide.

Isard, W.
1956   Location and Space Economy. Cambridge, Mass.: M.I.T. Press.

Ittelson, W., H. Proshansky, L. Rivlin, and G. Winkel
1974   An Introduction to Environmental Psychology. New York: Holt, Rinehart and Winston.

Jacobs, J.
1961   The Death and Life of Great American Cities. New York: Random House.
1969   Economy of Cities. New York: Random House.

Jakle, J. A., S. Brunn, and C. C. Roseman
1976   Human Spatial Behavior: A Social Geography. North Scituate, Mass.: Duxbury.

Jeffrey, C. R.
1971   Crime Prevention Through Environmental Design. Beverly Hills: Sage.

Johnston, R. J.
  1968   "Social status and residential desirability: a pilot study of residential loca-
          tions in Christchurch New Zealand." Mimeographed paper, Department of
          Geography, University of Canterbury, New Zealand.
  1970   Urban Residential Patterns. London: Bell.
  1971   "Mental maps of the city: suburban preference patterns." Environment and
          Planning 3:63–72
  1972   "Activity spaces and residential preferences: some tests of the hypothesis of
          sectoral mental maps." Economic Geography 48:199–211.

Jonassen, C.
  1949   "Cultural variables in the ecology of an ethnic group." American Sociologi-
          cal Review 14:32–41.

Jones, F. L.
  1967   "Ethnic assimilation and concentration: an Australian case study." Social
          Forces 45:412–423.

Jones, W. T.
  1952   A History of Western Philosophy. New York: Harcourt, Brace and World.

Kain, J.
  1968   "The distribution and movement of jobs and industry." Pp 1–43 in J. Q. Wil-
          son (ed.), The Metropolitan Enigma. Cambridge, Mass.: Harvard University
          Press.

Kantrowitz, N.
  1969   "Ethnic and racial segregation in the New York metropolitan area." Ameri-
          can Journal of Sociology 74:685–695.

Kasarda, J.
  1972   "The impact of suburban growth on central city service functions." Ameri-
          can Journal of Sociology 77:1111–1124.

Keller, S.
  1968   The Urban Neighborhood: A Sociological Perspective. New York: Random
          House.

Kemeny, J.
  1959   A Philosopher Looks at Science. Princeton, N.J.: Van Nostrand.

Kennedy, R. J.
  1943   "Premarital propinquity and ethnic endogamy." American Journal of Soci-
          ology 48:580–584.

Kerr, M.
  1958   The People of Ship Street. New York: Humanities Press.

Kessen, W., M. Haith, and P. Salapatek
  1970   "Human infancy: a bibliography and guide." Pp. 287–445 in P. H. Mussen
          (ed.), Carmichael's Manual of Child Psychology. New York: Wiley.

Keyfitz, Nathan
  1967   "Political-economic aspects of urbanization in South and Southeast Asia."
          Pp. 265–310 in P. Hauser and L. Schnore (ed.), The Study of Urbanization.
          New York: Wiley.

Khodzhaev, D. G., and B. S. Khorev
 1973   "The concept of a unified settlement system and the planned control of growth of towns in the U.S.S.R." Geographia Polonica 27:43–51.

King L., and R. Golledge
 1978   Cities, Space, and Behavior: The Elements of Urban Geography. Englewood Cliffs, N.J.: Prentice-Hall.

Kleck, R., P. L. Buck, W. L. Goller, R. S. London, J. R. Pfeiffer, and D. P. Vukcevic
 1968   "Effect of stigmatizing conditions on the use of personal space." Psychological Reports 23:111–118.

Klopfer, P. H.
 1969   Habitats and Territories: A Study of the Use of Space by Animals. New York: Basic Books.

Koffka, K.
 1935   Principles of Gestalt Psychology. New York: Harcourt Brace.

Kohler, H.
 1973   Economics and Urban Problems. Lexington, Mass.: Heath.

Kohler, W.
 1929   Gestalt Psychology. New York: Liveright.

Koller, M. R.
 1948   "Residential propinquity of white mates at marriage in relation to age and occupation of males, Columbus, Ohio, 1938 and 1946." American Sociological Review 613–616.

Kramer, J. (ed.)
 1972   North American Suburbs. Berkeley: Glendessary.

Kuhn, T. S.
 1962   The Structure of Scientific Revolutions. Chicago: University of Chicago Press.

Kuper, L. (ed.)
 1953   Living in Towns. London: Cresset.

La Greca, A., and K. Schwirian
 1974   "Social class and race as factors of residential density." Paper presented at the annual meeting of the Southern Sociological Association.

La Rue, G.
 1978   "An application of the constant utility model of human spatial interaction to the problem of predicting retail drugstore patronage." Master's thesis, Department of Geography, State University of New York at Albany.

Lack, D.
 1966   Population Studies in Birds. New York: Oxford University Press.

Ladd, F. C.
 1967   "A note on the world across the street." Harvard Graduate School of Education Association Bulletin 12:47–48.
 1970   "Black youths view their environment: neighborhood maps." Environment and Behavior 2:64–79.

Lakshmanan, T. R., and W. G. Hansen
  1965   "A retail market potential model." Journal of the American Institute of
          Planners 31:134–143.

Lang, J. C., C. Burnette, W. Moleski, and D. Vachon (eds.)
  1974   Designing for Human Behavior. Stroudsburg, Pa.: Dowden, Hutchinson and
          Ross.

Lansing, J., C. W. Clifton, and J. Morgan
  1969   New Homes and Poor People. Ann Arbor: Survey Research Center, Univer-
          sity of Michigan.

Lansing, J., E. Muller, and N. Barth
  1964   Residential Location and Urban Mobility. Ann Arbor: Survey Research Cen-
          ter, Institute for Social Research, University of Michigan.

Laurenti, L.
  1960   Property Values and Race. Los Angeles: University of California Press.

Lawton, M., and L. Nahemow
  1973   "Ecology and the aging process." In C. Eisdorfer and M. Lawton (eds.), The
          Psychology of Adult Development and Aging. Washington D.C.: American
          Psychological Association.

Le Corbusier
  1929   City of Tomorrow. London: Architectural Press. Originally published in
          1922.
  1933   Radiant City. Boulogne: Editions de L'Architecture d'Aujourd'hui.

Lee, E.
  1966   "A theory of migration." Demography 3:47–57.

Lee, T.
  1970   "Perceived distance as a function of direction in the city." Environment and
          Behavior 2:40–51.

Lenski, G.
  1966   Power and Privilege: A Theory of Social Stratification. New York: McGraw-
          Hill.

Leslie, G., and A. Richardson
  1961   "Life cycle, career pattern, and the decision to move." American Sociologi-
          cal Review 26:894–902.

Lessard, Suzannah
  1978   "The towers of light." The New Yorker, July 10, pp. 32–58.

Leven, C., J. Little, H. Nourse, and R. Read
  1976   Neighborhood Change: Lessons in the Dynamics of Urban Decay. New
          York: Praeger.

Lewin, K.
  1951   "Field theory and learning." Pp. 60–86 in D. Cartwright (ed.), Field Theory
          in Social Science. New York: Harper & Row.

Lewis, O.
  1952   "Urbanization without breakdown." Scientific Monthly 75:31–41.

Lewis, W.
    1969   Urban Growth and Suburbanization of Employment: Some New Data.
            Washington, D.C.: Brookings Institute.

Lieberson, S.
    1961   "The import of residential segregation on ethnic assimilation." Social Forces
            40:52–57.
    1962   "Suburbs and ethnic residential patterns." American Journal of Sociology
            64:673–681.

Linder, D.
    1974   "Personal space." University Programs Modular Studies. Morristown, N.J.:
            General Learning.

Lofland, Lyn
    1973   A World of Strangers. New York: Basic Books.

Long, N.
    1956   "The local community as an ecology of games." American Journal of Sociol-
            ogy 79:620–638.

Lorenz, K.
    1966   On Aggression. New York: Harcourt, Brace and World.
    1971   Studies in Animal and Human Behavior, Vol 2. Cambridge, Mass.: Harvard
            University Press.

Lott, D. and R. Sommer
    1967   "Seating arrangements and status." Journal of Personality and Social Psy-
            chology 7:90–95.

Louviere, J.
    1976   "Information processing theory and functional form in spatial behavior."
            Pp. 211–248 in R. G. Golledge and G. Rushton (eds.), Spatial Choice and Spa-
            tial Behavior. Columbus: Ohio State University Press.

Lowrey, R. A.
    1970   "Distance concepts of urban residents." Environment and Behavior 2:52–73.

Lynch, K.
    1960   The Image of the City. Cambridge, Mass.: M.I.T. Press.

MacLean, P. D.
    1978   A Triune Concept of Brain and Behavior. Toronto: University of Toronto
            Press.

McGinnis, R.
    1968   "A stochastic model of social mobility." American Sociological Review
            33:712–721.

McKenzie, R. D.
    1968   "The ecological approach to the study of the human community." Pp. 3–18
            in A. Hawley (ed.), Roderick D. McKenzie on Human Ecology. Chicago:
            University of Chicago Press.

Malthus, T.
    1926   First Essay on Population. London: Royal Economic Society. Originally pub-
            lished in 1798.

Marx, K.
  1951   The Eighteenth Brumaire of Louis Bonaparte. Tr. D. DeLeon. New York:
          New York Labor News.

Marx, K., and F. Engels
  1969   The Communist Manifesto. New York: Washington Square. Originally pub-
          lished in 1848.

Maslow, A.
  1954   Motivation and Personality. New York: Harper & Row.

Maslow, A., and L. Mintz
  1956   "Effects of esthetic surroundings: 1. Initial short-term effects of three esthet-
          ic conditions upon perceiving 'energy' and well-being in faces." Journal of
          Psychology 41:247–254.

Mayer, K., and W. Buckley
  1970   Class and Society. New York: Random House.

Mehrabian, A.
  1969a   "Some referrents and measures of nonverbal behavior." Behavior Research
          Methods and Instrumentation 1:203–207.
  1969b   "Significance of posture and position in the communication of attitude and
          status relationships." Psychological Bulletin 71:359–372.
  1972   Nonverbal Communication. Chicago: Aldine-Atherton.

Mehta, S. K.
  1969   "Patterns of residence in Poona (India) by income, education and occupa-
          tion (1937–65)." American Journal of Sociology 73:496–508.

Mercer, J., and J. Hultquist
  1976   "National progress toward housing and urban renewal goals." Pp. 101–162
          in J. S. Adams (ed.), Urban Policymaking and Metropolitan Dynamics: A
          Comparative Geographical Analysis. Cambridge, Mass.: Ballinger.

Merton, R. K.
  1948   "The social psychology of housing." Pp. 163–217 in W. Dennis (ed.), Current
          Trends in Social Psychology. Pittsburgh: University of Pittsburgh Press.
  1957   Social Theory and Social Structure. New York: Free Press.

Meyer, J. R., J. F. Kain, and M. Wohl
  1965   The Urban Transportation Problem. Cambridge, Mass.: Harvard University
          Press.

Michelson, W.
  1976   Man and His Urban Environment. Reading, Mass.: Addison Wesley.
  1977   Environmental Choice, Human Behavior, and Residential Satisfaction. New
          York: Oxford University Press.

Milgram, S.
  1972   "The experience of living in cities." Science 167:1461–1468.

Mills, E. S., and M. R. Lav
  1964   "A model of market areas with free entry." Journal of Political Economy
          72:278–288.

Miner, H.
1968   "Community-society continua." International Encyclopedia of the Social Sciences 3:175.

Mitchell, R.
1971   "Some social implications of high-density housing." American Sociological Review 36:18–29.

Molotch, H.
1972   Managed Integration: Dilemmas of Doing Good in the City. Berkeley: University of California Press.

Moore, E.
1969   "The structure of intra-urban movement rates: an ecological model." Urban Studies 6:17–33.
1971   "Comments on the use of ecological models in the study of residential mobility in the city." Economic Geography 47:73–85.
1972   Residential Mobility in the City. Commission on College Geography Resource Paper No. 13. Washington, D.C.: Association of American Geographers.

Moore, E., and L. Brown
1970   "Urban acquaintance fields: an evaluation of a spatial model." Environment and Planning 2:443–454.

Morrill, R. L.
1965   "The Negro ghetto: problems and alternatives." Geographical Review 55:339–361.

Morrill, R., and R. Earickson
1969   "Locational efficiency of Chicago hospitals: an experimental model." Health Services Research 4:128–141.

Morris, A. E. J.
1972   History of Urban Form: Prehistory to the Renaissance. New York: Wiley.

Morris, D.
1968   The Naked Ape. New York: McGraw-Hill.

Mowrer, E. W.
1942   Disorganization, Personal and Social. Philadelphia: Lippincott.

Moynihan, D. P.
1968   "Poverty in cities." Pp. 367–385 in J. W. Wilson (ed.), The Metropolitan Enigma. Cambridge, Mass.: Harvard University Press.

Mumford, L.
1961   The City in History: Its Origins, Transformations, and Its Prospects. New York: Harcourt, Brace and World.

Muth, R.
1969   Cities and Housing: The Spatial Pattern of Urban Residential Land Use. Chicago: University of Chicago Press.
1975   Urban Economic Problems. New York: Harper & Row.

Natoli, S.
   1971   "Zoning and the development of urban landuse patterns." Economic Geography 47:171–184.

National Advisory Commission on Civil Disorders
   1969   Report of the National Advisory Commission on Civil Disorders. Washington, D.C.: U.S. Government Printing Office.

National Commission on Urban Problems
   1969   Building the American City. Washington, D.C.: U.S. Government Printing Office.

National Resources Committee
   1937   Our Cities: Their Role in the National Economy. Washington, D.C.: U.S. Government Printing Office.

Newling, B.
   1966   "Urban growth and spatial structure: mathematical models and empirical evidence." Geographical Review 56:213–225.
   1969   "The spatial variation of urban population densities." Geographical Review 59:242–252.

Newman, D. K.
   1967   "The Decentralization of Jobs." Monthly Labor Review, May, pp. 7–13.

Newman, O.
   1973   "Defensible space: crime prevention through urban design." Ekistics 36:325–332.

Nice, M. M.
   1941   "The role of territory in bird life." American Midland Naturalist 26:441–487.

Niedercorn, J., and E. Hearle
   1964   "Recent land-use trends in forty-eight large American cities." Land Economics 40:105–109.

Noll, R.
   1970   "Metropolitan employment and population distributions and the conditions of the urban poor." Pp. 481–514 in J. P. Crecine (ed.), Financing the Metropolis. Beverly Hills, Calif.: Sage.

Novak, M.
   1971   The Rise of the Unmeltable Ethnic. New York: Macmillan.

Ogburn, W., and O. Duncan
   1964   "City size as a sociological variable." Pp. 58–76 in E. W. Burgess and D. J. Bogue (eds.), Urban Sociology. Chicago: University of Chicago Press.

Olsson, G.
   1965   Distance and Human Interaction: A Review and Bibliography. Philadelphia: Regional Science Research Institute, Bibliography Series No. 7.

Orleans, P. and M. Orleans
   1976   Urban Life: Diversity and Inequality. Dubuque, Iowa: Brown.

Orwell, G.
  1968   "The Lion and the Unicorn" (1941). In S. Orwell and I. Angus (eds.), The
          Collected Essays, Journalism and Letters of George Orwell. New York: Har-
          court, Brace and World.

Osofsky, G.
  1966   Harlem: The Making of the Ghetto. New York: Harper & Row.

Ottensman, J.
  1975   The Changing Spatial Structure of American Cities. Lexington, Mass.: Lex-
          ington.

Owen, R.
  1927   A New View of Society. New York: Dutton. Originally published in 1813.

Palmore, E.
  1966   "Integration and property values in Washington, D.C." Phylon 27:15–19.

Papageorgiou, G. J.
  1976   Mathematical Landuse Theory. Lexington, Mass.: Lexington.

Park, R.
  1936   "Human Ecology." The American Journal of Sociology 42:1–15.
  1952   Human Communities. New York: Free Press.

Park, R., E. W. Burgess, and R. D. McKenzie
  1925   The City. Chicago: University of Chicago Press.

Partridge, E.
  1958   Origins: A Short Etymological Dictionary of Modern English. London: Rout-
          ledge, Kegan, and Paul.

Peach, C. (ed.)
  1975   Urban Social Segregation. New York: Longman.

Perevedentsev, V.
  1972   Comments reported in Current Digest of the Soviet Press 21, 9:104–107.

Perry, C.
  1929   The Neighborhood Unit, Vol. 7. Neighborhood and Community Planning,
          Regional Survey of New York and its Environs. New York: Regional Plan
          Association.

Peterson, G.
  1967   "A model of preference." Journal of Regional Science 7:19–32.

Pettengill, R., and J. Uppal
  1974   Can Cities Survive? The Fiscal Plight of American Cities. New York: St. Mar-
          tin's.

Piaget, J., and B. Inhelder
  1967   The Child's Conception of Space. New York: Norton.

Pirenne, H.
  1925   Medieval Cities. Princeton, N.J.: Princeton University Press.

Polanyi, K.
  1957   Trade and Market in Early Empires. New York: Free Press.

Porteous, J. D.
1970   "The nature of the company towns." Transactions of the Institute of British Geographers 51:127–142.
1971   "Design with people: the quality of the urban environment." Environment and Behavior 3:155–178.
1977   Environment and Behavior: Planning and Everyday Life. Reading, Mass.: Addison Wesley.

Pred, A.
1966   Urban Growth and the Circulation of Information. Cambridge, Mass.: Harvard University Press.

Price, H. H.
1969   Thinking and Experience. London: Hutchinson.

Rainwater, L.
1966   "Fear and the house as haven in the lower class." Journal of the American Institute of Planners 32:23–31.
1970   Behind Ghetto Walls: Black Families in a Federal Slum. Chicago: Aldine.

Rapoport, A.
1969   House Form and Culture. Englewood Cliffs, N.J.: Prentice-Hall.

Ratcliff
1949   Urban Land Economics. New York: McGraw-Hill.

Ratzel, F.
1896   History of Mankind. London: MacMillan.

Redding, M.
1970   "The quality of residential environments." Ph.D. dissertation, Civil Engineering, Northwestern University.

Redfield, R.
1947   "The folk society." The American Journal of Sociology 41:293–308.

Rees, P.
1968   The Factorial Ecology of Metropolitan Chicago. Master's thesis, University of Chicago.

Reilly, W. K.
1976   "Conservation, community, and personal responsibility." Vital Speeches of the Day (January 15), pp. 202–210.

Reiss, A.
1955   "An analysis of urban phenomena." Pp. 41–54 in R. M. Fisher (ed.), The Metropolis in Modern Life. New York: Doubleday.
1959   "Rural-urban and status differences in interpersonal contacts." American Journal of Sociology 65:182–195.

Reith Committee
1946   Final Report of the New Towns Committee, Cmnd. 6876. London: H.M.S.O.

Riesman, D.
1957   "The suburban dislocation." Annals of the American Academy of Political and Social Science 314:123–146.

Riew, J.
1970   "Metropolitan disparities and fiscal federalism." Pp. 137–162 in J. Crecine (ed.), Financing the Metropolis. Beverly Hills, Calif.: Sage.

Rivers, C.
1972   "The specialness of growing up in Washington, D.C." The New York Times Magazine, May 7, p. 34.

Rivizzigno, V.
1976   Cognitive Representations of an Urban Area. Ph.D. dissertation, Department of Geography, Ohio State University Press.

Robinson, W. S.
1950   "Ecological correlations and the behavior of individuals." American Sociological Review 3:351–357.

Rodwin, L.
1970   Nations and Cities. New York: Houghton-Mifflin.

Rose, H. M.
1969   Social Processes in the City: Race and Urban Residential Choice. Washington, D.C.: Association of American Geographers Resource Paper 6.

Rosenfeld, H. M.
1965   "Effect of an approval-seeking induction on interpersonal proximity." Psychological Reports 17:120–122.

Rosow, I.
1961   "The social effects of the physical environment." Journal of the American Institute of Planners 27:321–332.

Rossi, P.
1955   Why Families Move. Glencoe, Ill. Free Press.

Rushton, G.
1969   "Analysis of spatial behavior by revealed space preference." Annals of the Association of American Geographers 59:391–400.
1976   "Decomposition of space preference functions." Pp. 119–134 in R. G. Golledge and G. Rushton (eds.), Spatial Choice and Spatial Behavior. Columbus: Ohio State University Press.

Sargent, C. S.
1976   "Land speculation and urban morphology." In J. S. Adams (ed.), Urban Policymaking and Metropolitan Dynamics. Cambridge, Mass.: Ballinger.

Schaffer, F.
1972   The New Town Story. London: Paladin.

Schnore, L.
1965   "On the spatial structure of cities in the Americas." Pp. 347–398 in P. Hauser and L. Schnore (ed.), The Study of Urbanization. New York: Wiley.
1965   The Urban Scene. New York: Free Press.
1972   Class and Race in Cities and Suburbs. New York: Markham.

Schroeder, C. W.
        "Mental disorders in cities." American Journal of Sociology 48:40–47.

Schwirian, K. (ed.)
    1977   Contemporary Topics in Urban Sociology. Morristown, N.J.: General Learn-
            ing.
    1979   "Review of contemporary urban ecology by B. J. L. Berry and J. Kasarda."
            Geographical Analysis 11:212–215.

Schwirian, K., and R. Smith
    1974   "Primacy, modernization, and urban structure: the ecology of Puerto Rican
            cities." Pp. 324–337 in K. Schwirian (ed.), Comparative Urban Structure:
            Studies in the Ecology of Cities. Lexington, Mass.: Heath.

Segall, M., D. Campbell, and M. Herskovits
    1966   The Influence of Culture on Visual Perception. Indianapolis: Bobbs-Merrill.

Shaw, C., and H. McKay
    1942   Juvenile Delinquency and Urban Areas. Chicago: University of Chicago
            Press.

Shevky, E., and W. Bell
    1955   Social Area Analysis: Theory, Illustrative Applications and Computation
            Procedures. Stanford, Calif.: Stanford University Press.

Shevky, E., and M. Williams
    1949   The Social Areas of Los Angeles, Analysis and Typology. Berkeley: Univer-
            sity of California Press.

Shibutani, T., and K. M. Kwan
    1965   Ethnic Stratification. New York: Macmillan.

Siegel, S.
    1957   "Level of aspiration and decision-making." Psychological Review 64:253–
            262.

Simmel, G.
    1969   "The metropolis and mental life." Pp. 635–646 in R. Sennet (ed.), Classic Es-
            says on the Culture of Cities. New York: Appleton-Century-Crofts. Original-
            ly published in 1905.

Simon, H.
    1957   Models of Man. New York: Wiley.

Sjoberg, G.
    1960   The Preindustrial City: Past and Present. Glencoe, Ill.: Free Press.
    1965   "Theory and research in urban sociology." Pp. 157–190 in P. Hauser and L.
            Schnore (eds.), The Study of Urbanization. New York: Wiley.

Smith, A.
    1937   The Wealth of Nations. New York: Modern Library. Originally published in
            1776.

Smith, D.
    1971   "Household space and family organization." Pacific Sociological Review
            14:53–78.

Smith, H.
    1976   The Russians. New York: Ballantine.

Smith, R., and R. Weller
   1977   "Growth and structure of the metropolitan community." Pp. 77–149 in K.
           Schwirian (ed.), Contemporary Issues in Urban Sociology. Morristown, N.J.:
           General Learning.

Soffen, E.
   1963   The Miami Metropolitan Experiment. Bloomington: Indiana University
           Press.

Soleri, P.
   1969   Arcology, The City in the Image of Man. Cambridge, Mass.: M.I.T. Press.

Sommer, R.
   1969   Personal Space: The Behavioral Basis of Design. Englewood Cliffs, N.J.:
           Prentice-Hall.

Speare, A.
   1974   "Residential satisfaction as an intervening variable in residential mobility."
           Demography 11:173–188.

Speer, A.
   1970   Inside the Third Reich: Memoirs. New York: Macmillan.

Stanley, T. J., and M. A. Sewall
   1976   "Image inputs to a probabilistic model predicting retail potential." Journal
           of Marketing 40:48–53.

Steinzor, B.
   1950   "The spatial factor in face to face discussion groups." Journal of Abnormal
           and Social Psychology 45:552–555.

Stevens, S. S.
   1958   "Measurement and man." Science 127:383–389.

Stevens, S. S., and E. H. Galanter
   1957   "Ratio scales and category scales for a dozen perceptual continua." Journal
           of Experimental Psychology 54:377–409.

Stokols, D.
   1972   "A social-psychological model of human crowding phenomena." Journal of
           American Institute of Planners 38:72–82.

Stopher, P. R., and A. H. Meyburg
   1976   Behavioral Travel Demand Models. Lexington, Mass.: Lexington.

Strauss, A.
   1961   Images of the American City. Glencoe, Ill.: Free Press.

Strodtbeck, F., and L. N. Hook
   1961   "The social dimensions of a twelve-man jury table." Sociometry 24:397–415.

Struyk, R.
   1976   Urban Homeownership. Lexington, Mass.: Lexington.

Sutherland, E. H., and D. Cressy
   1960   Principles of Criminology. Philadelphia: Lippincott.

Suttles, G.
   1968   The Social Order of the Slum: Ethnicity and Territory in the Inner City. Chicago: University of Chicago Press.
   1972   The Social Construction of Communities. Chicago: University of Chicago Press.

Sweetser, D.
   1974   "Factorial ecology: Helsinki 1960." Pp. 371–384 in K. P. Schwirian (ed.), Comparative Urban Structure. Lexington, Mass.: Heath.

Tabb, W.
   1970   The Political Economy of the Black Ghetto. New York: Norton.

Taeuber, K., and A. Taeuber
   1972   Negroes in Cities. New York: Atheneum.

Taylor, A.
   1972   "Integrative principles in human society." Pp. 211–290 in H. Margenau (ed.), Integrative Principles of Modern Thought. New York: Gordon and Breach.

Thomas, D. S.
   1938   Research Memorandum on Migration Differentials. New York: Social Science Research Council.

Thomlinson, R.
   1969   Urban Structure. New York: Random House.
   1976   Population Dynamics. New York: Random House.

Thompson, D. L.
   1965   "New concept: subjective distance." Journal of Retailing 39:1–6.

Thrasher, F.
   1927   The Gang. Chicago: University of Chicago Press.

Tilly, C.
   1961   "Occupational rank and grade of residence in a metropolis." American Journal of Sociology 67:323–330.

Timms, D. W. G.
   1971   The Urban Mosaic. New York: Cambridge University Press.

Tinbergen, N.
   1951   The Study of Instinct. London: Oxford University Press.

Tobler, W.
   1976   "The geometry of mental maps." Pp. 69–82 in R. G. Golledge and G. Rushton (eds.), Spatial Choice and Spatial Behavior. Columbus: Ohio State University Press.

Toffler, A.
   1970   Future Shock. New York: Random House.

Tolman, E.
   1948   "Cognitive maps in rats and men." Psychological Review 55:189–208.

Tönnies, F.
1957   Community and Society. Ed. and tr. Charles A. Loomis. East Lansing: Michigan State University Press. Originally published in 1887.

Tuan, Y-F.
1974   Topophilia. Englewood Cliffs, N.J.: Prentice-Hall.

Turnbull, C.
1961   The Forest People. New York: Simon and Schuster.

Turner, M. B.
1967   Psychology and the Philosophy of Science. New York: Appleton.

Udry, J.
1964   "Increasing scale and spatial differentiation: new tests of two theories from Shevky and Bell." Social Forces 42:403–413.

U. S. Bureau of Census
1973   Statistical Abstract of the United States. Washington, D.C.: Department of Commerce.

Uyeki, E.
1964   "Residential distribution and stratification." American Journal of Sociology 69:490–498.

Van Arsdol, M., S. Camilleri, and C. Schmid
1958   "The generality of urban social area indexes." American Sociological Review 23:277–284.

Van den Berghe, P.
1967   Race and Racism: A Comparative Perspective. New York: Wiley.

Van Liere, K.
1977   "Ecological succession and community development: an examination and critique." Paper presented at the annual meeting of the American Sociological Association, Chicago, Illinois.

Van Valey, T., W. Roof, and J. Wilcox
1977   "Trends in residential segregation." American Journal of Sociology 82:826–844.

Vanneman, R.
1977   "The occupational composition of American classes." American Journal of Sociology 82:783–807.

Veblen, T.
1899   The Theory of the Leisure Class. New York: Macmillan.

Volkart, E. H.
1951   Social Behavior and Personality. New York: Social Science Research Council.

Von Thünen, J. H.
1826   Der Isolierte Staat in Beziehung auf Landwirtschaft und Nationokonomie. Hamburg: Perthes.

Ward, D.
1971   Cities and Immigrants: A Geography of Change in Nineteenth Century America. New York: Oxford University Press.

Warner, S. B.
1962   Streetcar Suburbs: The Process of Growth in Boston. Cambridge: Harvard University Press.

Webber, M.
1964   "The urban place and the nonplace urban realm." Pp. 79–153 in M. Webber et al. (eds.), Explorations into Urban Structure. Philadelphia: University of Pennsylvania Press.
1970   "Order in diversity: community without propinquity." Pp. 791–810 in R. Gutman and D. Popenoe (eds.), Neighborhood, City, and Metropolis. New York: Random House.

Webber, M., and C. Webber
1964   "Culture, territoriality, and the elastic mile." Papers of the Regional Science Association 13:59–70.

Weber, A.
1958   The Growth of Cities in the Nineteenth Century. New York: Free Press. Originally published in 1899.

Weber, M.
1946   From Max Weber. Eds. and trs. H. Gerth and C. W. Mills. New York: Oxford University Press.
1958   The City. Ed. and tr. D. Martindale. New York: Free Press. Originally published in 1921.

Weicher, J.
1972   "The effect of metropolitan political fragmentation on central city budgets." Pp. 177–204 in D. Sweet (ed.), Models of Urban Structure. Lexington, Mass.: Heath.

Weiser, D.
1977   Three Models of Metropolitan Deconcentration. Master's thesis, State University of New York at Albany.

Wellman, B.
1976   Urban Connections. Research Paper No. 84. Toronto: University of Toronto, Center for Urban and Community Studies.
1979   "East Yonkers and the community question." American Journal of Sociology 84:1201–1231.

Westin, A. F.
1967   Privacy and Freedom. New York: Atheneum.

Wheeler, L.
1967   Behavioral Research for Architectural Planning and Design. Terre Haute, Ind.: Ewing Miller.

White, H.
1971   "Multipliers, vacancy chains, and filtering in housing." Journal of the American Institute of Planners 37:88–94.

White, L.
  1949   The Science of Culture: A Study of Man and Civilization. New York: Farrar,
          Strauss.

White, R.
  1967   Space Preference and Migration. Unpublished Master's thesis, Pennsylvania
          State University.

The White House
  1978   A Status Report on the President's Urban Policy. Washington, D.C.

Whorf, B. L.
  1956   Language, Thought, and Reality. Cambridge, Mass.: M.I.T. Press.

Whyte, W. F.
  1943   Street Corner Society. Chicago: University of Chicago Press.

Whyte, W. H.
  1956   The Organization Man. Garden City, N.Y.: Doubleday.
  1962   "The anti-city." In E. Green et al. (eds.), Man and the Modern City. Pitts-
          burgh: University of Pittsburgh Press.

Williams, R. L.
  1979   "Our older cities are showing their age but also signs of fight." Smithsonian
          9:66–74.

Wilner, D., R. Walkley, and S. Cook
  1955   Human Relations in Interracial Housing—A Study of the Contact Hypoth-
          esis. Minneapolis: University of Minnesota Press.

Wilson, A. G.
  1970   Entropy in Urban and Regional Modelling. London: Pion.

Wilson, E. O.
  1975   Sociobiology: The New Synthesis. Cambridge, Mass.: Harvard University
          Press.

Wingo, L.
  1961   Transportation and Urban Land. Baltimore: Johns Hopkins University Press.

Winsborough, H.
  1965   "The social consequences of high population density." Law and Contempo-
          rary Problems 30:120–126.

Wirth, Louis
  1938   "Urbanism as a way of life." The American Journal of Sociology 44:1–24.

Wolpert, J.
  1965   "Behavioral aspects of the decision to migrate." Papers and Proceedings of
          the Regional Science Association 15:59–69.
  1973   "Community discretion over neighborhood change." Pp. 41–54 in Geo-
          graphical Perspectives and Urban Problems: A Symposium. Washington,
          D.C.: National Academy of Sciences.

Wolpert, J., A. Mumphrey, and J. Seley
  1971   Metropolitan Neighborhoods: Participation and Conflict Over Change.
          Washington, D.C.: Association of American Geographers.

Wrigley, E. A.
  1969   Population and History. New York: McGraw-Hill.

Wright, F. L.
  1945   When Democracy Builds. Chicago: University of Chicago Press.
  1958   The Living City. New York: Horizon Press.

Wycherly, R. E.
  1972   How the Greeks Built Cities. London: MacMillan.

Wynne-Edwards, V. C.
  1971   "Space use and the social community in animals and men." In A. H. Esser
          (ed.), Behavior and Environment. New York: Plenum.

Yancey, W.
  1971   "Architecture, interaction and social control." Environment and Behavior
          3:3–21.

Yeates, M.
  1972   "The congruence between housing space, social space and community space
          and some experiments concerning its implications." Environment and Plan-
          ning 4:395–414.

Yeates, M., and B. Garner
  1976   The North American City. New York: Harper & Row.

Yuill, R. S.
  1967   "Spatial behavior of retail customers: some empirical measurements." Geo-
          grafiska Annaler 49:105–116.

Zangwill, I.
  1909   The Melting Pot. New York: Jewish Publication Society of America.

Zeisel, J.
  1975   Sociology and Architectural Design. New York: Sage.

Zimmern, A.
  1931   The Greek Commonwealth. New York: Modern Library.

Zipf, G. K.
  1949   Human Behavior and the Principles of Least Effort. New York: Hafner.

Zorbaugh, H.
  1926   "The natural areas of the city." Publications of the American Sociological
          Society 20:188–197.

Index

349